THE LOST JEWS OF CORNWALL

To the memory of Alex Jacob and Bernard Susser

THE LOST JEWS OF CORNWALL

From the Middle Ages to the Nineteenth Century

EDITED BY KEITH PEARCE
AND HELEN FRY
CONSULTANT: GODFREY SIMMONS

With very best wishes
to Cyril Fox,

[signature]

Keith Pearce

9/1/2000

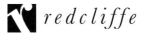 *redcliffe*

First published in 2000 by Redcliffe Press Ltd
81g, Pembroke Road, Bristol BS8 3EA

© The contributors and editors

ISBN 1 900178 27 3

British Cataloguing-in-Publication Data.
A catalogue record for this book is available
from the British Library.

Typeset by Mayhew Typesetting, Rhayader, Powys
Printed in Great Britain by WBC Print, Bridgend, Mid Glamorgan

CONTENTS

Acknowledgements   vi
The Editors   viii
Introduction   *Helen Fry*   ix

1 The Jews of Cornwall in Local Tradition: *Venetia Newall*   13
2 The Jews and Mining: 18
    1. Mediaeval Jewry and Cornish Tin: *David Giddings*   18
    2. The Jews' Houses and Cornish Place-Names: *Keith Pearce*   34
3 The Jews of Falmouth – 1740–1860: *Alex M. Jacob*   49
4 The Jews of Penzance – 1720–1913   69
    1. Penzance: the Decline and Fall of an Anglo-Jewish
    Community: *Cecil Roth*   69
    2. The Penzance Community Records: *Godfrey Simmons and*
    Keith Pearce   86
5 The Jewish Cemeteries: *Godfrey Simmons and Keith Pearce*   100
    Surveys by *Nicholas de Lange and Jennifer Speake*
    Translations by *Herman Zeffertt*
    Additional notes by *Eric Dawkins*
6 The Rabbis: *Godfrey Simmons and Keith Pearce*   158
7 The People: *Godfrey Simmons and Keith Pearce*   196
    1. Introduction, marriage and conversion, trades and
    occupations   196
    2. Falmouth   205
    3. Penzance   222
    4. Truro and towns of minor settlement   257
    5. Freemasonry   269
    6. The Josephs of Cornwall   272
8 Records of my Family – 1887–5647: *Israel Solomon*   279
9 The Disappearing Heritage: the Synagogues and their ritual
    Artefacts: *Evelyn Friedlander and Helen Fry*   292
10 Conclusion   306

    Appendices 1–3 *Godfrey Simmons*   307
    Appendix 4 *Bernard Susser*   316
    Appendix 5   319
    Bibliography *Helen Fry*   322
    Glossary   327
    List of Illustrations   328
    Index *Keith Pearce*   330

ACKNOWLEDGEMENTS

Godfrey Simmons' generosity in making available extensive material from his research archive and his advisory role throughout this project have been invaluable in the compilation of this text.

The editors wish to thank the Hidden Legacy Foundation and also John Simmons for their support, without which the publication of this book would not have been possible. John Simmons's academic contribution and proof-reading of the final text have also been much appreciated.

The editors would like to give special thanks to those who hold copyright to various articles, research and archival material for permission to reproduce them in this book, and for their generosity in doing so without charge. The editors hold copyright over the editorial notes attached to the chapters.

Other copyright holders are: Venetia Newall and the Jewish Historical Society of England (JHSE), Chapter 1; David Giddings and Keith Pearce, Chapter 2; the legal executors of the estate of the late Alex Jacob and the JHSE, Chapter 3; *The Jewish Chronicle*, and the legal executors of the Roth Estate, Chapter 4; Nicholas de Lange, Jennifer Speake, Herman Zeffertt and the editors, Chapter 5; Godfrey Simmons and Keith Pearce, Chapters 6 and 7; Evelyn Friedlander and Helen Fry, Chapter 9; the legal executors of the estate of the late Rabbi Bernard Susser; Bernard Simmons and the archive and papers of Godfrey Simmons; D.B. and R.M. Barton.

Special thanks also to the following:

Eric Dawkins, H.C. Faulkner, and Tony Pawlyn, trustee of the Falmouth Maritime Museum, Nicholas de Lange, Reader in Jewish Studies at the University of Cambridge, and Jennifer Speake, who have all made a substantial contribution in making available extensive material from their research.

To Sandra Doney for proof-reading and helping to compile the text, Natasha Lawrenson-Reid and Mandy Pearce for helping to compile the index, Bill Smith for designing the maps, over which he holds sole copyright, Anthony P. Joseph for advice on various aspects of genealogy and to Herman Zeffertt for the translation of the cemetery headstones and other Hebrew texts.

Our thanks also to: John Adler, Richard Fass, managing director, Meir Persoff and David Sonin of *The Jewish Chronicle*, and to Joyce Channon, Richard Vanhinsbergh, managing director, and Alison

Weeks of *The Cornishman*; Christine North, county archivist, David Thomas, archivist, County Record Office, Truro; Angela Broome, librarian, and Leslie Douch, Courtney Library; Tamsin Daniel, curator, Caroline Dudley, director, and Roger Penhallurick, senior curator of the City Museum, The Royal Institution of Cornwall, Truro; Peter Gilson and The Historical Research Unit, Royal Cornwall Polytechnic, Falmouth; Philip Payton of the Institute of Cornish Studies, Truro; Allen Buckley, mining historian; Jonathan Holmes and Nick Sharp of the Penlee House Museum and Art Gallery, Penzance; the staff of the Morrab Library, Penzance, the Penzance Reference Library, and Terry Knight of the Cornish Studies Library, Redruth; Steve Ottery, curator, Isles of Scilly Museum; Neville Nagler, Sandra Clark and Michael Harris of the Board of Deputies of British Jews; Joanne Liddle and Simon Reeves of Allied Domecq; Josephine Parker, archivist, Waltham Forest Archives; John Lee and Diane Pryce of the Office for National Statistics, Southport; Esra Kahn, head librarian, Jews' College, London; Jonathan Magonet, principal of Leo Baeck College, London; Jennifer Marin of the Jewish Museum, London; The Jewish Memorial Council; Charles Tucker, record-keeper, the London Beth Din; Malcolm C. Davis, assistant librarian, the Brotherton Library, University of Leeds (Roth Collection); C.M. Woolgar, archivist & head of special collections, Hartley Library, the University of Southampton; Geoff Pick, the London Metropolitan Archives; the staff of the Bodleian Library, Oxford; the Jewish Historical Society of England; Margaret Shepherd, director, Jonathan Gorsky and Jane Clements of The Council of Christians and Jews. A.J. Brown and J.M. Wraight, Admiralty librarian, Ministry of Defence, Whitehall, London; Wendy Tomlin, librarian, Britannia Royal Naval College, Dartmouth; Alan Giddings, The National Maritime Museum Library, Greenwich; The Royal Naval Museum, Portsmouth; Michael Duffy, The Centre for Maritime Studies, and Stuart McWilliam, history librarian, The University of Exeter; The British Newspaper Library, London; E.A. Churchill, genealogy officer, The Society of Genealogists; Richard Cooper, the Jewish Genealogical Society, and the Edgar Astaire and Sons Charitable Trust.

Many individuals, in this country and from abroad, have given information or provided assistance to the editors, and we would like to thank: Eric Ackstine, Roger Ainsworth, Lena and Mikha Ashkenazi, Ralph Barnes, Rachel Berg, David and Victor Bishop, John Bodilly, Brian Bramson, Elizabeth Brock, Lali Broido, Gordon Brown, John Burn, Harry Carter, Anne Chappell, Rita Collier, Tamsin Daniel, Eric Dawkins, Alfred Dunitz, Colin and Dee Eimer,

Eileen Essam, Leslie and Naomi Falkson, Cyril and Judith Fisher, Esther Fishman, Evelyn Friedlander, Michael Gandy, Frank Gent, David Giddings, Jean and Tony Gillman, R. John Hall, Brian Hammonde, David Hampshire, John Harris, Sheila Huftel, Saul Issroff, David Jacobs, Henrietta Jacobs, David James, Ron James, Michael Jolles, Judith Joseph, Sharman Kadish, Sonia Kemelmager, David Lang, Norman Levine, Philip Levy, Mira Little, Bernard Maker, Neil Marcuson, Stephen Massil, the late Monty Miller, Betty Naggar, Eileen Nethercott, Anthony Penhaul, the late Peter Pool, Tracy Poulton, Gail and Stuart Raine, Pat Robson, Graham Rogers, Joseph Roth, Edgar Samuel, David Samuelson, Sidney Schultz, Ivan Segal, Lily Segal, Jack Schofield, Arnold Schwartzman, Michael Shapiro, Bernard Simmons, Mrs. B. Susser, Kenneth Teacher, Peter Towey, Syma Weinberg, Malcolm Weisman, Michael Wohl, and Hanna Yaffe.

Chief academic consultant:
Godfrey Simmons has been researching the history of the Cornish Jewish communities for many years. After a career in business he lived in Penzance where he was the custodian of the Penzance Jewish cemetery. He is a great-grandson of Cornwall's longest serving rabbi, Barnett Asher Simmons.

The editors:
Keith Pearce was born in Cornwall and studied at Emmanuel College, Cambridge and Exeter College, Oxford. He has spent most of his career as a lecturer in further and adult education, and recently retired from Penwith College, Penzance where he was a lecturer in law and politics. He is now the custodian of the Penzance Jewish cemetery, and has been researching the history of the Cornish Jewish communities with Godfrey Simmons since the early 1980s.

Helen Fry is an honorary research fellow in the Department of Hebrew and Jewish Studies at University College, London, having obtained her Ph.D. at the University of Exeter in 1996. She has compiled and edited *Christian-Jewish Dialogue: A Reader*. She is a research consultant for The Hidden Legacy Foundation, in particular relating to south-west Jewry.

INTRODUCTION

Helen Fry

F ew people realise that Cornwall once had a thriving Jewish community that made a valuable contribution to the wider Cornish life. Such a rich heritage often passes one by, but even so there are still traces of that often-forgotten life. This book brings together diverse and disparate material in an attempt to reconstruct the life and times of Jews living in eighteenth- and nineteenth-century Cornwall. A picture emerges of Jewish life in Falmouth and Penzance, the main centres of Cornish Jewry, as well as the smaller Jewish settlements in places such as Truro, Redruth and Camborne.

The editors here reprint three previously published classic texts in the field: those of Cecil Roth, Alex Jacob and Venetia Newall. Chapters 2, 6, 7 and 9 contain newly commissioned work for the book. Most of the other material marks the culmination and continuation of 60 years of research by Godfrey Simmons whose family links and own life in Penzance first sparked his search to piece together not only his own family history but also that of the wider Jewish community in Cornwall. Through painstaking research in many public records in Cornwall and London, writing to descendants, and drawing on the personal archives of scholars and historians, he has enabled a full picture of Cornish Jewish life to be reconstructed. A full and coherent picture can be drawn from quite diverse and disparate material. The articles in chapters 1, 3, 4 and 8 have been reprinted with very minor modifications and with the integrity of their original texts preserved, together with their original footnotes. The editors would encourage readers not to overlook these footnotes. In addition, editorial notes at the end of the chapters are of special significance in that they revise and up-date the material in the light of recent research.

In chapter 2, David Giddings has provided a careful but sceptical overview of the evidence for a mediaeval Jewish community in Cornwall. He looks at a number of classical sources and argues that any conclusive evidence for such a community eludes us. He points out that often the arguments in favour of an early Jewish settlement are based on prior unsubstantiated research – hence perpetuating the myth that Jews were involved in early tin production. He does, however, find evidence to suggest that Jews were involved in the tin mines after the sixteenth century. In the second part of this chapter, Keith Pearce looks at the origins of some Jewish-sounding names in Cornwall, including the origin of the name *Marazion*. He argues that certain place-names, assumed to be based on Hebrew origins, and the archaeological evidence for *Jews Houses*, do not have their origins in an early Jewish influence on the Cornish language.

Chapter 3 reproduces the classic paper by Alex Jacob on the Jews of Falmouth. Editorial notes provide an update on recent research which has superseded some of Jacob's original findings. This chapter is followed by the reprinting of Cecil Roth's article on the Jews of Penzance which appeared in *The Jewish Chronicle* in 1933. Again, the editors have added notes to update the reader on new research. A section by Godfrey Simmons and Keith Pearce analyses the Penzance conveyances and minute books and provides much previously unpublished documentary material, illuminating the congregation's religious and organisational life.

Chapter 5 publishes for the first time a comprehensive list of the headstones and their inscriptions in the Falmouth and Penzance Jewish cemeteries. This work builds on the surveys of earlier researchers especially Nicholas de Lange and Jennifer Speake and includes a recently commissioned translation of all the legible Hebrew inscriptions. Each cemetery section opens with an historical overview of how and when the land was purchased. The chapter concludes with new research and material about the former Truro Jewish cemetery, now no longer visible and hence with no known recorded inscriptions; even so, some county records have enabled Godfrey Simmons and Keith Pearce to piece together some details of its existence.

This book would not be complete without a mention of the rabbis who served the communities. Chapter 6 provides as full a picture as can reasonably be reconstructed of the lives and families of the Cornish rabbis. In the case of Penzance, some of the material has been extracted from the minute books which do provide some scant references to their rabbis – often recording the tensions and disagreements between them and the congregation. It has been possible from a range of reliable sources to construct a reasonably accurate list of the rabbis who served Falmouth and Penzance during the eighteenth and nineteenth centuries.

Chapter 7 brings together a wide range of quite disparate material about the lives and occupations of Cornish Jews. Using trade directories, marriage registers, census returns, and merchant & shipping records it has been possible to record here the vast majority of known Cornish Jews of the eighteenth and nineteenth centuries. Some actively served in the life of the synagogue as well as contributing much to the wider community. Chapter 8 reprints a privately published record of Israel Solomon from the 1880s. *Records of My Family* is a particularly important text as it provides a view not only of his own family life but also of many of the other characters who were part of the Jewish community during the end of the eighteenth and throughout the nineteenth century.

Chapter 9 focuses on the disappearing heritage which fast eludes us. Fortunately it has been possible to reconstruct some of that heritage from literary and documentary sources, but even so many religious artefacts have already disappeared. This chapter reconstructs, insofar as is possible, the history of the two synagogues and their ritual objects. For Penzance we have some idea of the interior of the synagogue from a newspaper description and two photographs taken in the 1980s when some of the synagogue interior was still intact. However, the ritual objects and textiles from Penzance have not been traced: that part of the heritage has completely disappeared. For Falmouth, no interior photographs or sketches have come to light to provide posterity with an idea of its original design; however, some ritual objects have survived and photographs have been included in that chapter.

In bringing this material together, the editors have made a conscious decision not to include detailed genealogies because the interconnectedness and inter-marriage of Cornish Jewish families is very complex. To do justice to genealogical research would require the work of an expert genealogist in a separate complementary publication. Readers are referred to the work of Anthony P. Joseph in the bibliography.

The editors wish this book to be not only a contribution to Anglo-Jewish history but also to Cornish studies. It is hoped that its publication will result in new material being forthcoming to enable the publication of a second edition.

ESTABLISHED A.D. 1822.

Shops, Show-rooms, and Warehouses:

19, KING ST., TRURO.

Experienced Workmen sent to any part of the Country.

T. SOLOMON,
PLUMBER, GLAZIER & CHURCH WINDOW MAKER.
T. SOLOMON,
CARVER, GILDER AND PICTURE-FRAME MAKER.
T. SOLOMON,
PAINTER, GRAINER AND DECORATOR.
T. SOLOMON,
PAPER-HANGER AND BELL-HANGER.
T. SOLOMON,
ARTISTS' COLOURMAN.
T. SOLOMON,
OIL, COLOUR, AND GLASS MERCHANT.
T. SOLOMON,
WHOLESALE & RETAIL DEALER IN WALL PAPERS.
T. SOLOMON,
GENERAL CONTRACTOR.

From *Kelly's Directory*, 1873. [courtesy: The Morrab Library, Penzance]

S. JACOB,
JEWELLER, &c.,

HAVING just finished Taking Stock, and being desirous of reducing the same, will Offer at wholesale prices, Gold Pins, Studs, Sleeve Links, Alberts, Pencil Cases, Ladies' and Gentlemen's Finger Rings, Seals, Keys, Masonic Jewels, Brooches, Earrings, Lockets, Necklets, Chains, Charms. Hooks, Swivels, Split Rings, Thimbles, Crosses, Watches, Ornaments in Glass and Bronze, Clocks, Time-pieces, Plated and Silver Spoons, Forks, Tea Scoops, Snuff Boxes, Cruet Tops, Pickle Prongs, Butter Knives, Cream and Sauce Ladles, Vinaigrettes, Scent Bottles, Aneroids, Spy Glasses, Serpentine, Cruets, Cake Baskets, Violin Material, Musical Boxes, Concertinas, Accordeons, and a variety of other articles.

Several DIAMOND RINGS, great bargains.

From the *Falmouth Packet*, May 29th, 1875. [courtesy: The Cornish Studies Library, Redruth]

The Jews of Cornwall in Local Tradition

Venetia Newall

In his paper 'Jew's Houses' the late Cecil Roth observes that numerous ancient sites and buildings in England have nomenclature which brings them into hypothetical association with the Jews. He includes in his list the town of Market Jew in Cornwall, noting that "only a single Cornish Jew is on record throughout the entire Middle Ages."[1]

There is a belief, with no apparent substance, that in the decades before Edward I expelled the English Jewry (1290) the Cornish tin industry was "in the hands of the Jews and not doing well."[2] When the local language became gradually disused, down to its extinction in the eighteenth century, a large number of unintelligible place-names were left and many curious fantasies consequently arose. From place-names like Marazion and Market Jew it was assumed that Jews had emigrated to Cornwall in large numbers after the fall of Jerusalem, and that they were in some cases forced to work in the tin mines. Incorrect etymologies were taken for granted and it was the eminent philologist Max Müller who finally showed the foolishness of these notions in a paper entitled 'Are there Jews in Cornwall?' published in 1867.[3]

A brief account of the last two Earls of Cornwall with more than a titular interest in their domain may help to explain the odd frequency of Jews in Cornish folklore. The Norman Earldom of Cornwall had been established just after the Norman conquest of England in a grant to Robert, Count of Mortain, King William's half-brother. In 1216 Henry III came to the throne, and nine years later he in turn gave the county and tin mines of Cornwall to his brother Richard, then aged only 16. Two years later Richard was created Earl, he and his son

---

[1] Cecil Roth, 'Jews' Houses,' *Antiquity*, Vol XXV (June 1951), 66.
[2] Robert Hunt, *Popular Romances of the West of England* (London, 1871), pp. 341, 346.
[3] Peter Berresford Ellis, *The Cornish Language and its Literature* (London, 1974), pp. 140–141.

Edmund (Earl from 1272 to 1299) being the last holders of the title to live in the county.

Richard, in fact, turned his energies to Cornish affairs in about 1265, seven years before his death. An ambitious politician, he had in 1257 succeeded in becoming King of the Romans, an ultimately sterile honour for which, however, he obtained recognition in considerable parts of Germany. Although disappointed abroad, he was both wealthy and influential at home and by 1265 had been closely associated for at least fifteen years with Abraham of Berkhamsted. Abraham, one of the richest members of his community, had apparently unscrupulously profited from the misfortunes of his fellow-Jews. After an eventful career, he was granted to Richard in 1255 and empowered to lend money. That Richard was comparatively well disposed for the period towards the oppressed English Jews, but also fully prepared to exploit them, is clear from various accounts.[4]

The year 1255 saw not only Abraham of Berkhamsted in particular but also the whole of English Jewry under Richard's aegis, by way of mortgage against the King's debts – a pledge in human form. Nor was this the last time the English monarchy mortgaged its Jews to Cornwall. Richard again received them in pledge about a year before his death, and the process was repeated under Earl Edmund.[5]

A belief exists that, once the Jews were at his mercy, Richard put them to work in the Cornish tin mines. No evidence supports this improbable tale, though it would accord better with the position of hazard and penury in which most of English Jewry existed at the time than other quite contrary accounts. Hunt, for example, retailed as 'historical fact' that the tin mines were then being farmed out to the Jews.[6] In fact, Jewish merchants seem to have had little to do with the tin trade. Among others, they are mentioned as buying tin in Prague three centuries earlier, but there is no hint that their activity exceeded that of other purchasers and it need not, incidentally, have been British tin.[7]

Almost contemporaneously with Earl Richard's birth, (Edit 1) the first initiatives towards the Hanseatic League took place in Lübeck and Hamburg and, quite contrary to popular tradition about the Jews, it was the Hansa which, in Henry III's time, came to dominate commerce in

---

[4] Cecil Roth, *A History of the Jews in England* (Oxford, 1964), pp. 46–48, 56; H.G. Richardson, *The English Jewry under Angevin Kings* (London, 1960), pp. 16–17; Albert M. Hyamson, *A History of the Jews in England* (London, 1928), pp. 63–6.

[5] Roth, *History*, p. 67.

[6] Hunt, op. cit., p. 346.

[7] John Hatcher, *English Tin Production and Trade before 1550* (Oxford, 1973), p. 17.

tin. By the time Richard actively bent himself towards his Earldom, the two German towns had an agent at Falmouth.

As John Hatcher explains, during the thirteenth century an economic and social system based on pre-industrial capitalism became dominant in the Cornish tin industry, and even non-working shareholders existed. Oddly enough, the so-called Stannery privileges, originally evidently a kind of immunity of which titular remnants still survive, may well have contributed to this. At any rate, the same system was to dominate tin production through the ensuing centuries, economic precocity which is the more striking the earlier the period under review. That its initiation coincided exactly with a period when English Jewry was linked to the Cornish Earldom, an era which culminated in the Jews' notorious expulsion from the country, (Edit 2) may help to account for their peculiar place in local tradition. It is worth speculating, therefore, whether the equivocal attitude of Cornish folklore towards the Jews stems from their having been made whipping-boys (as has so often happened since) for the perennial anti-cosmopolitanism of the exploited. The general attitude towards Jewry in thirteenth-century England is well illustrated by a caricature of 1233. Drawn in the margin of a public document, it has a negative frame as the earliest such caricature to survive. In it, Isaac of Norwich, a slightly older contemporary of Abraham of Berkhamsted, is shown together with his wife and some of his household. Though evidently, from surviving information, a notable philanthropist, vicious horned demons are preparing to drag him and his companions down to hell.[8]

Deane and Shaw, in their book on Cornwall which I edited, point out that mining communities throughout the world have evolved special fairy stories. In Cornwall, the 'knockers' or 'nuggies' were imagined as living in the mine shafts, beneath the ground. A. K. Hamilton Jenkin, a Cornish writer, described them as 'withered, dried-up creatures,' no bigger, apparently, than a young baby. They had big, ugly heads, with faces like old men, and their limbs were disproportionate and clumsy. One opinion has them descending from a forgotten tribe which inhabited Cornwall before the Celts, but the more usual explanation, which is unpleasantly antisemitic, makes them the ghosts of Jews who incited the crucifixion of Jesus. A series of inconsistent beliefs accompany this notion. They were said never to work on major Christian festivals – Christmas Day, Easter Day, and All Saints' Day – as well as the Jewish Sabbath. For fear of offending

---

[8] Alfred Rubens, *A History of Jewish Costume* (London, 1973), p. 94; Venetia Newall, *The Encyclopedia of Witchcraft and Magic* (London, 1974), p. 107; Hyamson, op. cit., 54; Roth, *History*, 41, 95 n.1.

them, the tin miners themselves tended not to work on these days. A knockers' mass was celebrated, according to these beliefs, on Christmas Eve in the deeper levels of the mines. Miners have reported listening to them singing Christmas carols on this occasion, with an organ accompaniment.[9]

The knocker legends apart, quite a number of other terms exist, apparently linking Jews to the tin-mines. A particular type of disused smelting works is a Jew's house, and the bits of tin found in disused workings generally are Jew's bowels. Larger blocks are Jew's tin, while tin mixed up with mine refuse is Jew's leavings. Old mine-workings are Jew's works or Jew's whidn, and earlier were known as Jew's offcasts, a term later applied to the refuse beside them. A scattering of other expressions, while they have no connection with mining, are recorded in the immediate vicinity of Cornwall, if not in the county itself. These include a Jew's eye for something of great value, and 'to Jew' as an offensive verb to describe cheating. Both of these were once widespread terms, not exclusive to south-west England. Jew's ear for a type of red fungus also occurs in Cornwall, but is not peculiar to that area.[10]

Figures of speech which appear to be specifically Cornish are naturally the most interesting. Besides those connected with tin-mining, seemingly unique to Cornwall except for some usage among Devon miners on the other side of the River Tamar, there are two more. Jew's fish was a name for halibut, supposedly because it was among Jewry's favourite delicacies, and a type of beetle was termed 'Jew' on the grounds that it exudes a pinkish froth. There is probably a link here with the infamous blood libel, since there was a practice of holding it in the hand and calling out: 'Jew, Jew, spit blood.'[11]

A number of antiquarian accounts exist of how Jews, as well as Phoenicians, are supposed to have traded with Cornwall in ancient times.[12] More interestingly is the curious notion that Joseph of Arimathea came specifically to Marazion to purchase tin, and that it subsequently became a Jewish settlement.[13] In popular etymology the

[9] Tony Deane and Tony Shaw, *The Folklore of Cornwall*, Introduction by V. Newall (London, 1975), p. 69; A.K. Hamilton Jenkin, *The Cornish Miner* (London, 1927), pp. 294–295.

[10] Mrs. Bray, *The Borders of the Tamar and the Tavy* (London, 1838), Vol. III, p. 255; Hamilton Jenkin, op. cit., 29, 68–69, 72; Hunt, op. cit., 343; Joseph Wright, ed., *The English Dialect Dictionary* (London, 1902), Vol. III, p. 361; *Compact Edition of the Oxford Dictionary* (Oxford, 1971), Vol. I, pp. 1507–1508.

[11] Wright, op. cit., p. 361.

[12] John Bannister, 'Jews in Cornwall,' *Journal of the Royal Institution of Cornwall* (1867), No. VIII, 17.

[13] Deane and Shaw, op. cit., 63.

name means Market Zion, and it is further said that, in earlier times, the place was known as Market Jew or Jew's Town. Marazion actually derives from two Cornish words, *marchas*, which is indeed 'market,' and *bichan* meaning 'small.' Market Jew itself did exist, but appears to have been a separate place just outside Marghasbighan, the contemporary fourteenth-century spelling for Marazion, and it was then known as Marghasdiow. '-diow' is probably from the Cornish word *dyow* ('south'); equally it might hark back to *Yow*, Cornish for Thursday, supposing that the market was once held on that day. *Yow* is sometimes corrupted to Jew, though in the toponomical context here, this last word seems to have appeared late.[14]

Another Cornish expression, Market Jew Crow, was the local term for a hooded crow, given this name because the species frequented that particular neighbourhood.[15] The bird not only has a poor local reputation – St. Neot had to impound the whole species every Sunday, because people were absent from church scaring them off the crops – but its appearance is unattractive, so that any racialist undertones may seem unhappy. But this is not necessarily so. There is a widespread belief, based apparently in popular tradition, that King Arthur's soul inhabits a Cornish chough, and this, too, is a type of crow, though, sadly, it is now on the road to extinction. The important point is that King Arthur is the national hero of the Cornish myth.

Editorial notes

Edit 1. In 1209.
Edit 2. In 1290.

---

[14] Friedrich Max Müller, 'Are there Jews in Cornwall?', *Chips from a German Workshop* (London, 1867), pp. 305–311; Eilert Ekwall, *The Concise Oxford Dictionary of English Place-names* (Oxford, 1960), p. 314; Bannister, op. cit., 10–19; Berresford Ellis, op. cit., 140–141.

[15] Charles Swainson, *The Folklore and Provincial Names of British Birds* (London, 1885), pp. 74, 86.

The Jews and Mining

David Giddings and Keith Pearce

1: Mediaeval Jewry and Cornish Tin

David Giddings

Herodotus, writing in the fifth century BCE, was uncertain about the reality of the Cassiterides, or Tin Islands, but he knew that amber and tin came to Greece from the ends of the earth.[1] In his time the Carthaginians may have been the Greeks' immediate suppliers; however, this Semitic people guarded its commercial secrets so that the precise origins and trade routes of their tin remain unknown. Nor do we know whether the Carthaginians or their cousins, the Phoenicians, tapped the trade at its putative Cornish source. In the well-known account of Pytheas of Massilia, the fourth century BCE navigator, whose extraordinary voyage to Norway is probably preserved by Diodorus Siculus, we are told that the inhabitants of Belerion (Land's End) are: "very fond of strangers, and, from their intercourse with foreign merchants are civilised in their manner of life. . . . Here then the merchants buy the tin from the natives and carry it over to Gaul, and after travelling over land for about thirty days they finally bring their loads on horses to the mouth of the river Rhone."[2] Unfortunately, nowhere do we learn the identity of these merchants.

Since the sixteenth century CE the notion that Cornwall's first Semitic visitors were the Phoenicians has gained a convinced following by reason of frequent repetition. The mythopoeic moment can be traced to 1590 when John Twyne's book, *De Rebus Albionicis*, was printed by his son, Thomas. In it the Phoenicians joined the crush of Trojans, Druids and lost tribes of Israel who were already jostling to fill the void before the beginning of recorded history following the Roman conquest. Subsequently it has been claimed that the joint voyage of Solomon and Hiram, King of Tyre, to Tarshish (?Spain) in the tenth

---

[1] *Herodotus: The Histories* (London: Penguin, 1972), Book 3, 115, p. 250.
[2] Cited by J. Hatcher (1973, p. 12).

century BCE may have taken them further to Cornwall.[3] Not only Bible reading but also philological temptation has encouraged an enduring belief in early Semitic connections with Cornwall. From the seventeenth century CE it was believed that *Berat-Anach* or *Bartanac*, 'country of tin' in the Phoenician language, was the origin of the name Britain.[4] William Borlase, the great Cornish antiquary, derived 'tin' from the Phoenician for mud or slime,[5] although just over one hundred years later, while allowing the Phoenicians their place, Richard Edmonds was of the opinion that Britain took its name from *Bretin* which, he says, is the Cornish for tin mount, i.e. St Michael's Mount.[6]

Toponymy has also been employed to suggest Cornish-Jewish links from early times. Marazion, supposedly 'bitterness of Zion', has done great service in this respect.[7] Cairo, evocative of Levantine traders, actually derives from *kerrow* or forts in Cornish; Menheniot has been ascribed a Hebrew origin, *min oniyot*, meaning 'from ships', but is readily construed in Cornish as *ma* (plain) with a personal name.[8] Approximation of the common pronunciation of Mousehole as *Muzzle* to the Hebrew *mazel*, or 'luck' in English, has also excited comment,[9] although both topography, in the form of a cave in the cliff, and the earliest recorded written form, *Pertusum muris*, 1242,[10] suggest a more prosaic derivation. Ostensibly more helpful in establishing a Jewish connection is the place name Landjew in the Parish of Withiel and a nearby *Jews' House* smelting hearth. At, or before, the date of Diodorus' account of tin-smelting in Belerion the casting of white tin into astragali (roughly H shaped blocks) shows that the furnaces were tapped to permit the metal to be run off into moulds. This improvement in smelting technology has been attributed to the Jews,[11] and continued to be used into the mediaeval period. *Jews' Houses* are widely distributed throughout the metalliferous districts of Cornwall; in Penwith at the county's westernmost extremity, a total of five, either extant or documented, are known.[12]

---

[3] Hyamson (1908, p. 1).

[4] Samuel Bochart, *Geographica Sacra, 1640*: cited by R.D. Penhallurick in *Tin in Antiquity* (London: Institute of Metals, 1986), p. 125.

[5] Borlase (1758, reprinted 1970, p. 164).

[6] Edmonds (1862, p. 8). For a traditional account of the Phoenicians and British tin, see R. Hunt (1884, chapter 1). R.D. Penhallurick, op. cit., presents a well reasoned dissenting view on any such connection.

[7] See part 2 of this chapter by Keith Pearce which explains this in further depth.

[8] Padel (1988, p. 119).

[9] Susser (1993, p. 2).

[10] Padel, op. cit., p. 125.

[11] For a description of a Jew's House, see G.R. Lewis (1908, reprinted 1965, p. 16).

[12] Russell (1971, p. 64).

Nevertheless care is needed with the nomenclature because of the virtual extinction of Cornish as a mother tongue; its place names have become the archaeology of human speech and difficult to interpret outside the language and culture of those who speak or spoke it because of anglicising influences. 'Landjew' probably transliterates Cornish *lyn du* which means 'black pool'. Similarly, other suggestive sounding place names become commonplace topographical features, for example: *Baldhu*, black mine, and *Cardew*, black fort.[13] A seventeenth century CE account of tin working may give some cause for doubt about Jews' Houses as evidence for a Jewish presence in Cornwall. Thomas Fuller describes the later tin 'blowing-house' as being periodically burned down in order to save tin particles driven by the bellows blast into the thatch of the roof.[14] On the reasonable assumption that the rough granite walls would have been reused, we may infer the origin of the term Jews' House. It lay in the Cornish *chy du*, 'black house', a name which was perhaps extended generically to all smelting hearths including earlier examples which had fallen into disuse.

Even personal names of a resounding biblical character and the occasional Hannibal have been adduced as evidence of early Semitic connections, as also have the use of saffron in cooking and physical appearance but these are more likely to be wishful thinking than sound surmise.

Christian era folklore would have us believe that Cornwall received various Jewish visitors, even Jesus himself. Joseph of Arimathea, a wealthy Essene Jew and a merchant, came to Cornwall, it is said, with Jesus in his boyhood. Stories abound of their travels from Looe in the east to Ding Dong mine in the far west; at St Just in Roseland, a stone upon which Joseph stepped on landing used to be pointed out to visitors. Tinners used to sing:

> Joseph was a tin man
> And the miners loved him well.[15]

Legend further has it that St Paul came to Britain as a missionary to found the British Church, a journey which, if its historicity could be proven, might presuppose a Jewish community given his zeal to convert Jews. However, his execution, traditionally dated to 66 CE, would have precluded exertions among any Jews in Cornwall who may have been working tin as Roman slaves as a consequence of their revolt in Palestine four years later when, according to St Jerome, "an

[13] Padel (1985, p. 244, 250 & 276).
[14] *History of the Worthies of England* (1811, p. 195).
[15] Deane & Shaw (1975, p. 63).

incredible number of Jews were sold like horses and dispersed over the face of the whole earth."[16]

In his contemporary account of the Jewish Wars, Flavius Josephus relates that in the aftermath of the fall of Jerusalem in 70 CE: "as for the rest of the multitude, that were about seventeen years old, he [Fronto] put them into bonds and sent them to the Egyptian mines." Titus, commander of the Jerusalem campaign, sent many captives to the provinces to suffer sentence ad gladium or ad bestias, "but those under seventeen years of age were sold for slaves."[17] It is at least possible that some of these Jews were employed in tin extraction in the recently pacified lowland zone of Britannia. On the slender archaeological evidence of coins minted in Judaea and found in England there were some links between Britain and Palestine in the first and second centuries CE.[18] Another of the early church fathers, St. John Chrysostom, tells of how the fourth-century CE emperor Constantine created a new diaspora of enslaved Jews, sending them into "all the territories of his empire."[19] Very likely the Romans were interested in Cornish tin, as discoveries of ingots, ornaments, coin caches and milestones attest, yet whether they employed slave labour or had any direct supervision of the works, which had been conducted by the native population for more than two thousand years, it is impossible to say.

During the fourth century CE we have references to a Solomon, Duke of Cornwall, who was so named even before his conversion to Christianity.[20] His father, Geraint, was a Christian and, while the name may be evidence of Jewish influence from earlier times, there must be a possibility that it stems from the work of Christian missionaries, Jewish converts or otherwise. As the Dark Age Saxon conquest extended inexorably westward, Celtic Christianity in Cornwall pursued its own forms and observances, apparently retaining a regard for biblical names. Evidence from the Bodmin Manumissions shows that between 940 CE and 1040, of 122 liberated slaves 98 were Cornishmen with names such as Noah, Isaac and Jesu. Firm conclusions from such evidence are difficult to make.

Discoveries of bracelets and other ornaments in old workings suggest that the Saxons,[21] who completed their conquest of Cornwall

---

[16] Quoted by J. Bannister (1867, p. 329. n.14).

[17] Josephus, *History of the Jewish Wars* (trans. Whiston, London, 1811) vol IV, book VI, chapter IX.2. p. 267.

[18] Roth (1964, p. 1).

[19] Quoted by Bannister, op. cit., p. 329.

[20] Susser (1993, p. 4).

[21] Lewis, op. cit., p. 33.

under Athelstan during the first half of the tenth century CE, continued to exploit tin. Folklore is, by its fanciful nature, not susceptible to accurate dating but subscribers to the view that folklore is a damaged version of history might locate tales of Jews' workings in the Saxon period, although descriptions of discoveries of crude wooden and horn implements by Carew in his survey of Cornwall[22] and others could apply to almost any time until the recent past. Polwhele[23] cites Norden's *Topographical and Historical Description of Cornwall* (1728) on tools found in "old-forsaken workes which to this day retayn the name Attall Sarazin: the Jews cast-off workes, in their Hebrew speache." To John Norden the language may have resembled Hebrew but it was, in fact, Cornish and as another antiquary, Thomas Tonkin, pointed out meant "leavings of the Saracins and from thence infers, that the Saxons did not work the mines, but employed the Saracens for that purpose."[24] Among the thickets of language and ethnicity Polwhele,[25] sounding a wise note of caution, quotes from 'Pearce's Preface' which, referring to Attall Sarazin as *Jews' Feast*, continues: "but whether they [the Jews] had liberty to work and search for tin does not appear because they had their dwellings chiefly in great towns and cities."

Such stories, with their outlandish conflation of Saxons, Jews and Saracens among a devout, mostly illiterate and uneducated people, speak of the otherness of times remote and unrecorded but also of a familiarity with poverty which could be ascribed to the exploitation of Cornwall's natural wealth by outsiders. Through the perceived alienness of the Jews in almost every respect they, particularly, were qualified to be objects of speculation and suspicion. This is shown in the folk-tales of the *knockers* who were said to inhabit the subterranean levels of tin mines in the spirit form of Jews who had incited the crucifixion of Jesus and needed to be propitiated by tinners.[26] Charles Henderson,[27] on the other hand, plausibly proposes that *knocker* derives from *Nicor*, a Saxon water sprite, but folklore tells us what people were capable of believing, wished to believe and did believe rather than what is true.

Under the Norman kings the Jews take on a concrete historical existence in England although at what precise point it is uncertain. Since the early eleventh century CE there had been a Jewish settlement

---

[22] Carew (1602, reprinted 1953, p. 89).
[23] Polwhele (1808, p. 8).
[24] Cited by C.S. Gilbert (1817, p. 208).
[25] op. cit., p. 8.
[26] Deane and Shaw, op. cit., p. 69.
[27] Henderson (1935, p. 202).

in Rouen and John Stow,[28] probably following the mediaeval chronicler, William of Malmesbury, declares: "King William brought the Jewes from Rhoane to inhabit here." There is, however, no authentic reference to a Jewish presence during William's reign, so perhaps the incentive to settle away from Normandy was provided by the massacre of Rouen's Jews by knights crusader in 1096 CE. Under William Rufus (1087–1100 CE) and his successor, Henry I (1100–1135 CE), Jews were offered royal protection and communities began to develop but there is no evidence to confirm settlement in Cornwall nor involvement in tin extraction until the end of Richard I's reign (1189–1199 CE) and perhaps not even then. Nevertheless, records show that by 1188 CE there were enough Jews in Exeter to form a distinctive community[29] at a time when the Dartmoor area of Devon was a major tin producer within the stannaries (those districts of Devon and Cornwall where John's Charter of 1201 CE recognised the special rights and immunities of tinners).

Although secure proof of Jewish participation from an early date in Cornish, or for that matter Devonian, tin production is lacking, some insight into either possibility or probability can be gained by examining the role of the Jews under the Norman and Angevin monarchs. Societies which function beyond the level of a subsistence economy require both coinage and credit. Norman England, which had undergone the systematic infeudation of society, had little of either but the king preferred to have his vassals pay their dues not in kind but in coin; in this way he could readily meet his military necessities in Normandy, Ireland, France or Palestine; he could acquire luxuries and have great buildings constructed. In their turn, on the strength of their own accumulation, the barons could reliably meet their obligations to their lord and satisfy their own acquisitiveness. Should there be a shortage of coin for immediate expenditure, credit, secured against future revenue, would meet the need.

As yet there was no middle class in England but the Jews took on some of its attributes. Debarred from most other activities wherever they settled, the Jews had been obliged to become merchants and financiers. Their success in these spheres, though tax records show that there were many poor Jews in England, was assisted by the Church which imposed stringent laws against usury, a term which included not only money-lending but also commercial speculation. Thus the way was left open to the Jews who were, of course, not constrained by canon law. They brought capital; facilitated government by

---

28 Stow (1631), fol. 103, 2, 8.
29 Susser, op. cit., p. 5.

advancing funds; contributed to some of the great abbatial and cathedral building of the age; and financed military expeditions such as Richard Strongbow's against Ireland in 1170 CE. They were also a source of income through amercements and regular forms of feudal exaction for their lord the king. They were the king's Jews and the relationship was mutually advantageous until Angevin rapacity removed its simple arithmetical foundations. Finally the Jews themselves were removed in 1290 CE.

Requirements for capital certainly existed in the stannaries, although the shallow working of stream (i.e. alluvial) tin deposits in open-cast fashion, in 'coffins' (trenches) or by costeaning (the sinking of pits up to about twelve feet deep linked by horizontal drifts) meant that fixed capital was relatively modest. Wooden shovels, possibly iron-shod, and picks were the basic tools;[30] elaborate deep rock mining which necessitated blasting and steam pumping came much later. However, if the profitability of the stannaries was to be realised for tinners, landholders and (through taxation and pre-emption) the king, finance was needed because of the hazards and delays which characterised the work. Shoding, the search for tin stones, was a lengthy, labour-intensive process involving extensive excavation and large-scale diversion of water courses. A group of tinners or a landlord, stirred by the promise of mineral wealth, might be compelled to wait a considerable period before white tin began to flow into ingot moulds. Such a delay could oblige borrowing against the future to meet present needs or attracting non-working shareholders.

It is difficult to believe that Jewish capital did not find its way into the stannaries; yet the evidence for it is elusive, as it is for any direct participation in the work or actual settlement in Cornwall up to the moment of the Expulsion. To complicate the matter further, it was the case by 1290 that other sources of capital had become available. Whether these displaced Jewish finance or were the original source is uncertain. At the close of the twelfth century CE, in the reign of Richard I, we seem to come close to evidence of a Jewish connection with the stannaries through the *Liber Rubeus* (The Red Book) of the Exchequer which contains the Capitula concerning the smelting, assay and taxation of tin in Cornwall. Bannister unequivocally asserts, "That during, and before the reign of Richard, Jews had to do with the tin trade of Cornwall is evident from the Capitula, or Ordinances, respecting tin and the stannaries, made by William de Wrotham, Chief Warden [of the Stannaries] and others, 1197–8."[31] Part of it reads:

---

[30] G.R. Lewis (1906, p. 546).

[31] Op. cit., p. 326.

Also neither man nor woman, Christian nor Jew, shall presume to buy or sell any tin of the first smelting, nor to give or remove any of the first smelting from the Stannary, or out of the place appointed for weighing and stamping, until it shall be weighed and stamped in the presence of the keepers and clerks of the weight and stamp of the farm.

Also neither man nor woman, Christian nor Jew, shall presume, in the Stannaries or out of the Stannaries, to have in his or her possession any tin of the first smelting beyond a fortnight, unless it be weighed and stamped by the keepers and clerk of the weight and farm stamp.

Also neither man nor woman, Christian nor Jew, in market-towns and boroughs, on sea or on land, shall presume to keep beyond thirteen weeks tin of the first smelting weighed and stamped, unless it be put into the second smelting and the mark discharged.

Also neither man nor woman, Christian nor Jew, shall presume in any manner to remove tin, either by sea or by land, out of the counties of Devon and Cornwall, unless he or she first have a licence of the Chief-Warden of the Stannaries.

A motive for creating a more efficient stannary bureaucracy is not far to seek. Richard, a lavish and extrovert monarch, incurred huge expenses during the Third Crusade; his ransom from Emperor Henry VI is said to have cost the country a quarter of its income. His outlay on Château Gaillard was great and his defeat of the French at Gisors in 1198 also consumed the royal substance. Furthermore, he spent a fortune on arranging the election of his nephew, Otto, to the dignity of the King of the Romans. Since he died in pursuit of an alleged treasure trove at Chaluz it is reasonable to assume that the king would wish for his treasure in tin to fructify. Nevertheless, it would be unwise to assume from the Capitula alone that Jews had played, or were to play, a part in the drive to improve the king's income from the stannaries. If the phrases: ". . . neither man nor woman, Christian nor Jew," were a legal coverall meaning "nobody whosoever" or "neither Christian nor non-Christian", it would be difficult to draw firm conclusions from the *Liber Rubeus*. Even if there was an intention to regulate specifically Jewish participation in the mediaeval tin trade, de Wrotham's ordinances do not presuppose a settled Jewish community; he may have been concerned with individual itinerant Jews or their agents. Certainly claims of the Jews' direct activity in tin-working under the Angevins are persistent. It is true that *Camden's Britannia* (1586)[32] is emphatic that in

---

[32] Camden (1695 ed, p. 19). See also an abstract from *Camden's Britannia* with editorial addenda, editor and date uncertain but probably eighteenth century CE, pp. 10–11, in the Cornish Studies Library, Redruth.

John's reign (1199–1216 CE) the mines were farmed for one hundred marks; a later editor adds that the Jews themselves were the farmers but it is not clear on what evidence this claim is based. In his *Natural History of Cornwall* (1758) Borlase, describing small blocks of white tin found in old workings, writes that they are "probably as old as the time when the Jews had engrossed the tin manufacture in the time of King John."[33] Polwhele's *History* (1808) follows suit,[34] as does Gilbert's *Survey* (1817).[35] William Hals, in his *Compleat History of Cornwall* (1703),[36] declares that in the Angevin period Jews were employed in the mines as slaves while Carew's *Survey of Cornwall* (1602) also refers to the consequences of the Expulsion which "left the mines unwrought."[37] All or some of these propositions could be true but they are unlikely to be so as will later appear. If positive evidence of Jewish enslavement is lacking there are also difficulties arising from statements about the farm of stannary revenues.

During a reign when Jewry was tallaged severely as never before it is extremely unlikely that John would have permitted Jews to enjoy his revenues from tin at a price of only one hundred marks for the farm. Production in Cornwall did decline from eight hundred thousand pound weight in 1200 CE to six hundred thousand in 1209 but then it rose to a record one million two hundred thousand pound weight of tin (c.600 long tons) in 1214.[38] In such circumstances a payment of one hundred marks (£66. 13s. 4d) would have exposed contractors to the needy John's savagery, but of this we have no record. John's Stannary Charter of 1201 may have served to revive confidence among the tinners to an extent which explains the rise in output in Cornwall; on the other hand the incentive could have come, if the antiquaries are to be believed, from tinners being squeezed by the Jews who, in turn were being pressed by the King. Bannister[39] seems to argue for both possibilities when he quotes from John's Charter which, among other concessions, granted that the tinners should be, "liberi et quieti de placitis *nativorum*." By the use of italics his implication is that despite allowing tinners immunity from lawsuits brought by those belonging to a place

---

[33] Borlase (1970, op. cit., pp. 163–184).

[34] Polwhele, op. cit., pp. 7–8.

[35] C.S. Gilbert, op. cit., p. 208.

[36] Hals – entry for St Ewe in Gilbert (1838, vol. 1, p. 414).

[37] Carew, op. cit., p. 99. Bannister (1867, p. 327) and his antagonist, Professor Max Müller, appear to have misread Carew; "the cut throate and abominable dealing" of "the merchants of London" in relation to tinners is clearly a contemporary Elizabethan reference to Gentiles and not a mediaeval one to Jews.

[38] G.R. Lewis (1906, p. 540).

[39] Op. cit., p. 327.

The Lanlivery-Bodwen figurine. [courtesy: The Royal Institution of Cornwall, Truro]

(*nativi*) the Charter did not permit immunity from legal proceedings initiated by others, that is to say, Jews. In the context of the document, however, it is beyond doubt that the King is referring to the perennial problem of local landowners seeking to restrain the widespread and disruptive activities of the tinners. In such a context Jews were neither likely to be landowners in Cornwall nor to be exempted from recognising tinners' immunities if they were. As a final point on this vexed matter it may be significant that for the period from de Wrotham's reforms until 1220 the farm of tin revenues fell into abeyance and tinners paid dues directly to royal treasurers.[40] In this way John's Jewish tax farmers may be laid to the rest which Jewish mine-slaves richly deserve.

While it is apparent that there is a paucity of straightforward evidence connecting mediaeval Anglo-Jewry and Cornish tin there does exist a fascinating, enigmatic artefact which is as difficult to explain as it is to ignore. In 1853 a hollow tin alloy figurine was discovered three metres below ground surface on Bodwen Moor in the parish of Lanlivery and, curiously enough, near a *Jews' House*. Fourteen point two centimetres high and four point four kilos in weight, the piece portrays a bearded man sitting on a high-backed chair; until it was lost in a fire during the late nineteenth century CE there was a crown on the head. Scattered over the cloak or gown of the figure are four incised Hebrew letters: *Nun, Resh, Shin* and *Mem*. Unfortunately no certain archaeological context for the 'tin king' exists but it has been tentatively dated as early as the thirteenth century CE which would place it in the reign of John or possibly the earldom of Richard (1227–1272 CE), younger brother of Henry III (1216–1272 CE). Though hardly flattering, the representation has been claimed to be that of Richard, King of the Romans and Earl of Cornwall. It has also been proposed that the object was made by a Cornish tinner and given as a pledge to a Jew, that it was used in pseudo-Cabbalistic rites or even that it served as a mediaeval chess piece.[41]

---

[40] G.R. Lewis (1908, pp. 134–136).

[41] Susser, op. cit., p. 24. In a personal communication, Nicholas de Lange (Reader in Hebrew and Jewish Studies at the University of Cambridge) makes a number of very cautious suggestions about the figurine. He distinguishes three Hebrew characters: *nun, resh* and *shin*. These could form the initials, but without the characteristic 'son of', which would designate a Jew. They might be some kind of code or, with numerical values attaching to Hebrew letters, a chronogram. In the latter case the total yielded would be 550; as a year this sum would represent the year 1789–90 in Christian reckoning, although de Lange is at pains to point out that these particular characters would not normally be employed in such a calculation. He concludes on the subject of the significance of the letters that perhaps the most

During the regency years of Henry III's reign and the ascendancy of William the Marshal and Hubert de Burgh, English Jewry recovered from the depredations of John, being once again offered the protection of the Crown. Henry, who assumed power in 1232, was a lavish patron of the arts with a passion for building. At home he faced civil war with the barons but he was also concerned to pursue an elaborate foreign policy to outflank the Capetians by recovering the lost dominions in France and the Hohenstaufen by promoting the candidacy of his brother, Richard, for the Holy Roman Empire. Given a combination of high ambition and financial ineptitude on the King's part it was not long before the Jews were once again suffering repeated tallages.

Both Richard and his son, Edmund, were resident Earls of Cornwall and were indeed the last to be so, but their presence was rare. As far as can be known, Richard spent three or four brief periods of months rather than years in the county.[42] Advanced by Henry to the lands and revenues of the earldom in 1225 CE then to the title two years later, Richard was evidently an able man and a more competent financial administrator than his older brother. Twice in his life, in 1255 CE and around 1270 CE, Richard was granted the Jews of England as a pledge against loans he had made to the king. His concerns for his revenues from the stannaries and his moderation in dealings with the Jews[43] suggest a degree of humanity tempered by an awareness of economic self-interest. It may be that the mortgaging of English Jewry to Earl Richard is the origin of the later belief that enslaved Jews were compelled to work in the tin mines. Jews were, after all, *servi camerae regis*, but *servi* in the feudal context is better translated as 'vassals' of the royal chamber rather than slaves. They would have been of greater profit to Richard in the role of financiers whose bonds would provide a sound basis for amercement.

Already in 1237 CE Jews had been mulcted of three thousand marks so that Richard could go on crusade to the Holy Land, but twenty years

---

attractive solution is a haphazard choice made for exotic effect. As to the nature of the letters, de Lange tentatively proposes that the formality of the incised characters with their serifs is unlike the more typical cursive style of Jews versed in Hebrew script from an early age. Although a Jewish hand cannot be ruled out it is conceivable that Christian masons, who presumably carved Hebrew tombstones in Cornwall in the late eighteenth and nineteenth centuries CE, would be familiar with formal and ornamental Hebrew lettering and might have had hand in that appearing on the tin king. Needless to say the date of the lettering has no bearing on the date of the object.

[42] Denholm-Young (1947, pp. 38, 39, 40, 72–3).
[43] Roth, op. cit., p. 57.

later his election as King of the Romans, followed by years of sterile efforts among the German states to give meaning to this title, also necessitated large sums of money. Unfortunately evidence for a close association between Jewry and Cornish tin is not sufficient to claim that it was through their efforts in the county that Richard was able to further his imperial ambition. By the thirteenth century CE there were sources of credit other than the Jews, for instance the first initiatives towards the Hanseatic League took place in Lübeck and Hamburg early in the century. ". . . Quite contrary to popular tradition about the Jews, it was the Hansa which, in Henry III's time, came to dominate commerce in tin. By the time Richard actively bent himself towards his Earldom the two German towns had an agent in Falmouth."[44] On the other hand this is not necessarily to say that the Hansa's mercantile interest in tin extended to the extraction process. Quickening of commerce had brought a diminishing of conscience on the point of usury so, with resort to convenient, obscuring fictions, wealthy Christians became moneylenders and suffered no qualms over dealing in Jewish bonds.[45] Around 1235 CE the Cahorsin merchants appeared in England from Italy as moneylenders in all but name and were followed by Florentines, Venetians and Genoans.

Questions as to the financial operations of the Jews in Cornwall are made more difficult by the fact that, up to the time of the Expulsion in 1290 CE there was no *archa* in the county. These triple-locked chests, containing copies of all Jewish financial transactions and administered by both Jewish and Christian chirographers, had been instituted shortly after the anti-semitic outrages of 1190 CE primarily to protect the Crown's pecuniary interest. *Archae* do not presuppose a large community; indeed there is an instance of one being set up for a single Jew,[46] so their non-existence in Cornwall casts into doubt any notions of a permanent Jewish presence there in the thirteenth century CE. An archa was established in Exeter early in the century but even here the Jewish community was neither large nor conspicuously wealthy, facts which may have limited their role in tin across the river Tamar. In 1221 CE seventeen Jewish centres paid a total fine of £564 towards a dowry for Henry III's sister, Joan. Exeter's share in this amounted to £8 5s. 8d and was met by six people. Two years later fifteen Exonian Jews contributed £78 10s. 6d to a tallage on English Jewry totalling £1,680. These were the prosperous years of England's Jews, but under Henry III's personal rule they were brought low by his repeated

---

[44] V. Newall in Deane and Shaw, op. cit., p. 20.
[45] H.G. Richardson (1960, chapters 3 & 4).
[46] Susser, op. cit., p. 7.

demands. By 1276 there seem to have been only two Jews actively engaged in money-lending in Exeter; numbers rose again but by 1290 the community was reduced to a solitary Jewess, Comitissa.[47]

Despite question-marks over a settled community in Cornwall and the activities of Jews in neighbouring Devon in connection with advancing funds against Cornish tin, a Jewish financial presence cannot be discounted. In discussing "a few prominent consortia" of Jews dealing with the Treasury in the twelfth century, Roth[48] mentions Isaac fil' Rabbi of London and Aaron of Lincoln: "Between the two of them English Jewry was organised to a certain extent into a great co-operative banking association spread throughout the country." Evidently this level of financial organisation in respect of advances to the Crown could have been translated into the stannaries and have worked at a remove with little in the way of a Jewish presence in the far south-west. Aaron's example provides some insight into what might have happened. When he died in 1186 CE his property escheated to the Crown and his loans of £20,000 were so extensive and complicated that it took a specially created Exchequer department nearly five years to sort them out. "He [had] advanced money to private individuals on corn, armour, estates, and houses, acquiring thus important interests in twenty-five counties (especially in the east and the south-east of England), in at least seventeen of which he maintained his agents." While there is no record of the existence of a Jewish community in Rutland, Aaron's agents had evidently been at work there since we have a full account of eleven bonds from that county and ample evidence from elsewhere that Aaron counted Jews among his clients (probably for re-lending) as well as Christians.[49]

In the next century Aaron of York occupied a similar position as the greatest financier among Anglo-Jewry with some twenty co-religionists serving as his local agents.[50] Another powerful figure in Henry III's reign was the dubious character, Abraham of Berkhamsted, with debtors in half the counties of England, who, charged with profaning an image of the Virgin and the murder of his wife, was saved by the intervention of Richard of Cornwall. If the *archae* accounts were preserved in full we might know the details about any outlays by Jews in Cornwall, but when there was unrest, during the Barons' Wars of Henry III's reign, for instance, the chests were sought out so that records of indebtedness could be destroyed. Complementary evidence

---

[47] Susser, op. cit., pp. 7–9.
[48] Roth (1964, pp. 14–15).
[49] Richardson (1960, pp. 68–69).
[50] Roth, op. cit., p. 49.

on the administrative side is also lacking: "This confused history of grants, resumptions and re-grants from 1231 to 1300, taken in connection with the passing of Cornwall into the hands of Richard Plantagenet and his son Edmund, helps to explain why no entries for the Cornish stannaries appear in the Pipe Rolls for the above mentioned period, and why in consequence, the fiscal history at this point remains obscure."[51]

After the *Statutum de Judeismo*, banning loans at interest, was promulgated at Winchester in 1275 Anglo-Jewry was brought to ruin by further tallages. There were also accusations and 293 hangings for coin clipping, a hardening of Papal attitudes and the revival of ritual murder allegations, all of which served further to undermine the very existence of Jews in England. Preparatory to one of these late tallages a writ was issued in 1283 CE to twenty sheriffs with Jews under their jurisdiction to inspect the chests of the chirographers of the Jews whose transactions would have had a life extending well past the date of the *Statutum*. Interestingly, the sheriff of Cornwall received a writ and it is a pertinent question why he did if there were no Jews in his county.[52] If they were in Cornwall, however, it was not for much longer. On 18th July 1290, Edward I, by an act in Council, took the final step of expelling the Jews on pain of death.

Hints of an elusive, unverifiable Jewish presence, perhaps in the form of Christian converts, remained. In the *White Book of Cornwall*, the Council Book of the Duchy, during the time of Edward, the Black Prince, we read of John Jeu's suit to end his wardship exercised by the royal Duke so as to inherit his father's, Sir Roger Jeu's, Cornish estate.[53] A little later in 1358, "Abraham, a tinner, complains of imprisonment by the Sheriff for working to the nuisance of the haven of Fowey. He states that he employs three hundred men in the stream works of Brodhok, Tremorwode, Greystone, and Dosmery. The prince issues his mandate to W. de Spridlington, one of his auditors, to enquire into the facts." Although the name is highly suggestive it is impossible to be certain that Abraham the tinner was not a Christian; there is the example of Abraham of Felmingham, who received a land grant from Henry II, and his son Isaac who, from other references and contrary to appearances, were not Jews.[54] Similarly the *Jeu* surname

---

[51] Lewis (1908, p. 136).

[52] *Transactions of the Jewish Historical Society of England, IV*, 1899, cited by Susser (1993, p. 24).

[53] Cf. Onions' *Oxford Dictionary of English Etymology* which gives twelfth-century CE variants of Jew as *Giw, Gyu, Iu, Iuw, Ieu*. In another source from Edward III's reign the name is rendered *le Jeu*, cited by Lysons (1814, p. 646).

[54] Roth, op. cit., n. p. 15.

may have been a variant spelling of *lew*, which is *yew* in Cornish, and a name mentioned in that form by Carew in a list of those who had married into the Arundell family.[55]

Figures for post-Expulsion tin production have been used in order to suggest a causal relationship between the events of 1290 and a declining output,[56] but this argument can only be adduced by selective presentation of statistics. Between 1291 and 1296 it is true that production was more than halved in the Devon stannary. While there are no year-on-year figures available for Cornish output until 1301, when, in round figures, five hundred and sixty thousand weight were produced in contrast with Devon's fifty three, thereafter Cornwall shows annual increase until the era of the Black Death, 1348–1351. Although there are gaps in Devon's statistics it is abundantly clear that not only was the eastern stannary in relative decline against the west's performance but that it was also in absolute decline, a process which had probably begun in the thirteenth century CE but was marked in the fourteenth and owed more to geological circumstances than the absence of Jewish capital.[57]

Eventually, after an interval of nearly three hundred years, we do encounter a Jew of some solidity in the historical record of Cornwall and its metals. A German-Jewish mining engineer, Joachim Ganz, or Gaunze, was invited by the Company for the Mines Royal to advise on copper extraction. He went to Keswick to inspect copper mines and produced a report on the treatment of copper ores, then he is said to have spent three years in Cornwall from 1586 to 1589 CE, until he was expelled after drawing too much unfavourable attention to his religious beliefs.[58] Between the Expulsion of 1290 and these events not even a tenuous connection linked the Jews with Cornwall through the mediaeval and early modern periods. Even before 1290 any association seems to have been highly uncertain, probably impermanent and only insecurely recorded. Philology, folklore, tradition, historical documentation – none of these provides a satisfactory footing to establish firmly the activities of Jews in Cornwall. All this, as subsequent chapters will testify, would change with the Resettlement under Cromwell during the Interregnum and especially in the eighteenth century CE when Cornwall experienced a great age of tin production.

---

[55] Carew, op. cit., 1602 ed. fol. 145.
[56] Susser, op. cit., p. 5.
[57] Figures from G.R. Lewis, op. cit., App. J, p. 252.
[58] Susser, op. cit., p. 25.

2: The "Jews Houses" and Cornish Place-Names

Keith Pearce

In his paper "Jews' Houses"[59], Cecil Roth refers to the Jews' Tower in Winchester, Jews' Mount in Oxford and Villejuif near Paris as well as many other examples as putative ancient Jewish landmarks.[60] He maintains that no conclusive evidence exists of an early and contemporaneous Jewish presence in most of these places and that the origins of these topographical features, and in some cases large structures, were unknown. They were ascribed to the Jews for aetiological reasons to confer some ancient mythical origin upon unusual constructions where the identity of the makers remained a mystery and their exact historical context in the distant past had been lost to memory.

Roth points out that the twelfth-century Arab geographer, Edrisi, called the city of Tarragona in Spain, "a city of Jews"[61] and comments thus: ". . . as far as we know the Jewish settlement there was never of exceptional importance nor large enough in proportion to the total population at any given time to justify this description." Further, Benjamin of Tudela, a younger contemporary of Edrisi, visited Tarragona and did not refer to Jews at all but said that Tarragona "was built by the giant Greeks", which Roth takes to refer to the massive fortification walls which so distinguish the city.

> . . . Edrisi's phrase 'a city of the Jews' is the equivalent of Benjamin's 'built by the giant Greeks', both expressions . . . loosely corresponding to the term 'Cyclopaean' . . . to describe massive structures of great or even mysterious antiquity.[62]

He points out that the *size* of the structures is not the key to the ascriptive process, however, and concludes:

---

[59] "Jews' Houses" in *Antiquity*, vol. 25, June 1951, pp. 66–68. It should be noted that the title of this paper could be misleading in this context in that it does not concentrate on the Cornish *Jews' (smelting) Houses* as such. However, various sites and buildings in this country and elsewhere (all of which Roth refers to as houses) have been linked, hypothetically, with Jews.

[60] For a complete list of Roth's extensive examples, see the note at the end of this chapter. I am grateful to John Simmons for providing some sources for this chapter.

[61] Roth's reference: Edrisi's *Geography*, II, 235.

[62] Roth's reference: *Itinerary*, ed. Adler, p. 2.

. . . in the Greek islands, the term *Hebraeokastron* was 'applied in contempt by Greek peasants to *any* ancient building whatsoever erected by strangers':[63] this may now be amended to 'any ancient building of unknown origin' . . .[64]

Susser quotes the first part of the passage above but then omits its crucial conclusion.[65] Thus, without addressing Roth's contention that any building could be so ascribed, Susser declines to apply this same explanation to the *Jews' smelting-Houses* precisely because they *were* small (3ft high) rather than large structures. Even so, this could involve a misapplication of the term *Jews House* to the smelting-*furnace* or *oven*, which would have been about 3ft. high instead of its application to the entire structure of the original building, the smelting-*house*, in which it was situated. Moreover, the proliferation of these buildings, their mysterious origin and unusual structure would have impressed the onlookers as much as their size and could lead to a similar attributive process, especially at a time when the smelting-houses were the only striking constructions to be seen.

The scale of these houses, none of which survived intact into the early nineteenth century, has also been underestimated. In the Annual Report to the Royal Institution of Cornwall,[66] a record from Francis Rodd describes the finding of a stone smelting-ladle in the 1830s near Trebartha, underneath the ruins of an old building (formerly a cottage), known locally as the *Jews House*.[67] The ruin contained two "troughs", the larger being some 4ft in length, over 2½ ft wide and almost 1½ ft high, and the smaller about a third of these measurements. Both were in quadrangular or oblong shape, presumably to accommodate the moulds. The original mason who built the cottage on the site of the smelting confirmed that the space on which the troughs lay was ". . . like the floor of a house . . ." and that there were blocks of granite which ". . . once formed the end walls of this *Jews House* . . . he estimated the weight of . . . two blocks . . . at from 10 to 15 cwt." Clearly these dimensions imply an original construction of significant proportions. Even if the granite-block walls and the solidity of their foundations and their construction served, to some extent, to

---

[63] Roth's references: Murray's *Handbook for travellers in Greece*, 1854; W. Ettinghausen (Eytan) in the *Jewish Quarterly Review*, N.S. XXXVI, 1946, 419–21.

[64] Roth, ibid, p. 67.

[65] Susser (1993, p. 266).

[66] RIC: 1850. p.58.

[67] For convenience, this term will be given as "*Jews House*" without the use of the conventional apostrophe (*Jew's or Jews'*) to indicate both the singular and plural forms.

contain the fierce heat from the furnace, they also suggest, together with the extent of the floor area, a height significantly in excess of 3ft. A building of some height and proportion would also be necessary for practical reasons to disperse the transmitted heat and so allow safe access to and around the smelting-furnace.

To such sites as these, and in the absence of any firm evidence or memory of their genesis, the Cornish people eventually ascribed mythological titles and origins, amongst which, but not exclusively, was the use of the term *Jews Houses*. This particular title, however, is a comparatively late usage and, crucially, is in English, a language which did not displace Cornish as the spoken tongue until the eighteenth century. Long before that, both in the Celtic and mediaeval world, language and legend evolved to weave a very different story around these artefacts.

When the much later term *Jews Houses* did emerge and find currency, it proved deeply persistent and gave rise to legendary traditions which became entrenched as historical fact; namely that the Jews had come to Cornwall in Old Testament times and that later they had been brought over by the Romans in large numbers as slaves, either after the Fall of Jerusalem (70 CE) or the Bar Kochba rising (135 CE). It was said that they were forced to work in the mines, introducing a new and unusual method of smelting, eventually acquiring a monopoly over this aspect of tin-production and the construction of the smelting-houses. In reality, little if any evidence for this exists and far too much has subsequently been read into the term *Jews House* and its derivative connotations. The term *Jews House* may conjure and convey ready images of material resemblance, but it bears no meaning which follows as a matter of logical necessity. It is a term of considerable ambiguity allowing a range of equally hypothetical and plausible meanings, none of which is rationally preferable and none of which is verifiable.

Conservative exegesis has viewed it as causative and historic: that Jews built, or owned and ran the smelting-houses at some time, monopolising the tin-trade. The term *Jews House*, however, could equally refer to an idiosyncratic method of oven-smelting which had come to be used by the isolated Cornish miners themselves and the oddity of which, in time, came to be associated with foreign, Jewish origins. This is a form of causative speculation, not of causative verification. The term *Jew*, moreover, in a non-pluralistic society and age could refer to anyone who was not a Christian, operating as an exclusive term rather than a generic-specific category.[68] In this sense,

---

[68] cf. the terms *heathen, stranger* or *Gentile* in the Bible to denote anyone, without differentiation, who is not a *Jew*.

the *Jews Houses* have become an uncharacteristic and mysterious oddity, an ancient importation of the foreign.

It has been mentioned in part one of this chapter by David Giddings that the extract from the Charter of William of Wrotham (c 1197–8), the *Liber Rubeus* of the Treasury,[69] which is often used to argue that Jews can be identified as the architects of the smelting-houses and as practitioners in the Stannaries, is in fact open to an entirely different interpretation. The expression "neither man or woman, Christian or Jew . . ." may be a stereotyped legal term which meant 'everybody'. If this was so then no inference can be drawn from the *Liber Rubeus* about medieval Jewish tin-trading.[70] In this sense the term *Jew* can be seen to function as a comprehensive formula, as an inclusive rather than an exclusive term.

Jews Houses can also be understood from the perspective of pre-judice and superstition. It could operate as an anti-semitic reference, or to the vulgarity of the product, or the crude and irregular con-struction of the smelting-houses. The unusually fierce, white heat could evoke notions derived from Christian preaching and embedded in Christian consciousness of the recalcitrant Jews burning in Hell. The eerie subterranean noises deep within the mines (at times indi-cative of imminent disaster) assume the identity of the goblin-type Jewish spirits, called the *Knockers* of Cornish mining legend – mis-chievous or malevolent counterparts to the Cornish Pixies. In this way, the confusion between mythology and archaeology can be established and reinforced.

Whatever the administrative system which operated over the Cornish tin-mines in the thirteenth century, it is not axiomatic that if Jews were involved (in numbers impossible to determine) that they would ever have been *present* in Cornwall. When Richard, Earl of Cornwall "privatised" metal production to various entrepreneurs as his business managers, including some Jews such as Abraham of Berkhamsted, he appears to have established centres to which the Cornish miners had to bring the ore for smelting and stamping and to pay taxes to the king on the products. Thus Edgar Samuel has said:

> Anyone could mine tin, but all smelting had to be done in designated smelteries, where it was weighed and stamped by the officers of the Stannary, once charges for the smelting had been paid. Only stamped tin could be legally sold. This is typical of medieval estate management. All corn had to be ground in the

---

[69] From the *Capitula de Stannatoribus*, 9 Ric. I.
[70] Susser, op. cit., p. 22.

landlord's mill. All cloth had to be fulled in the landlord's fulling mills. In each case, the owner of the estate charged accordingly. . . . (The) Jews . . . were engaged in collecting the revenue from the smelteries, first for the king, and then later in the thirteenth century for the Earl of Cornwall. When Richard of Almain, brother to Henry III was Earl of Cornwall, his Jew, Abraham of Berkhamsted was one of his business managers.[71]

Not only is this an excellent account of the feudal-based system, but it affords a basis for an interpretation quite distinct from that which has often been applied to the *Jews Houses*. Neither the officers who regulated the smelting-centres *in situ* nor those who physically collected the revenue (if distinct from the former), nor those who operated the smelting-process at the smelteries were necessarily Jews. The king, or the Earl of Cornwall, owned the smelteries which became known as *Jews Houses* because a *Jew* or *Jews*, such as Abraham of Berkhamsted, laid claim (through his agents) to the smelteries and their revenues on behalf of the Earl of Cornwall. Abraham would have been based at Exeter where there was a Jewish community in the thirteenth century and from where the whole enterprise was regulated. Such Jews as Abraham ran the smelting-houses in an administrative sense on behalf of their owner, although Abraham's own agents regulated them in practice, in stamping the produce and collecting the revenues. In turn, the Cornish miners would have operated the smelting-process itself. This does not mean that there were Jews operating the smelting-houses or indeed that there were any Jews in Cornwall at the time,[72] but that these smelteries were the *Jews Houses*, *de facto*, and it is in this sense that they could have been viewed by the Cornish miners. There is, however, no direct evidence that they were given the name of Jews Houses by the miners at that time. There are linguistic reasons why this is unlikely to have been the case when Cornish, and not English, was the *lingua franca* of Cornwall. The expression *Jews Houses* is likely, therefore, to have been a later, retrospective English appellation at a time when there was an increasing historical awareness of how the feudal system had operated.

In any event, little evidence exists of any significant or sizeable Jewish presence in Cornwall at any time before the eighteenth century. Susser cites only isolated examples of individuals, not all of whom are certain to have been Jews:[73] He mentions Abraham the Tinner, a mine-owner around 1342 who was the employer of several

---

[71] Extract from a letter to Keith Pearce, January 24th 1999.
[72] Letter from Stephen Massil to Evelyn Friedlander, 4th October 1998.
[73] Susser, op. cit., pp. 5, 25 & 273.

hundred men in Devon.[74] There was Aaron of Cornwall in 1244; however, he does not appear in Cornwall but in Uxbridge where he was arrested. "Joachim of Gaunze . . . a Jewish-German mining engineer . . ." who is said by Susser to have spent three years in Cornwall from 1586–1589 supplying copper-ore to Wales, although Israel Abrahams,[75] who wrote of Gaunse's (or Ganz's) career in some detail gives the only reference to Cornwall, saying only that the engineer was "probably" there (at some unspecified time).[76]

Max Müller refers to only three known Jews in the third year of the reign of King John in 1202:[77] Simon de Dena; Deudone, the son of Samuel; and an Aaron, all "*praedictus Judeus*", and comments: "Their transactions are purely financial and do not lead us to suppose that the Jews . . . condescended in the time of King John, or at any other time, to the drudgery of working in the mines." In no way, therefore, can such occasional references as these suggest a substantial Jewish presence in Cornwall and the question as to the presence of a population of Jews in the Stannaries is most certainly unproven,[78] even though the involvement of a few Jews in their administration is entirely credible.

A distinctive language and hagiography have also played their part in Cornwall's past and it is these, rather than any Jewish presence, which can help unravel some of the threads which make up the veil of obscurity and misunderstanding surrounding some of the present-day Cornish place-names which have come to be linked with Jews. In a paper written in 1933 and reprinted in the journal of the RIC in 1973, R. Morton Nance surveys a wide range of evidence that Cornish may have survived beyond the eighteenth century and even into the nineteenth.[79] He concludes that some usage, limited topographically and linguistically, may have been possible but in the form of memorised verses and phrases or dialect terminology. Some people may have been able to lapse into brief, occasional usage but no firm evidence exists of a fluent Cornish speaker after the death of its last exponent in the late

---

[74] He may not have been Jewish. He is also mentioned as having been arrested at Fowey in Cornwall.

[75] Israel Abrahams, "Joachim Gaunse – A Mining Incident in the Reign of Queen Elizabeth" in *Transactions of the Jewish Historical Society*, IV, pp. 83–97. Susser, op.cit., p. 273.

[76] *Abrahams*, op. cit., p. 89.

[77] *Chips from a German Workshop*, London 1867. From the 1870 edition, 3, XIV, pp. 298–329: "Are there Jews in Cornwall?". This ref. p. 329 from the *Rotulus Cancellarii vel Antigraphum Magni Rotuli Pipae de tertio anno Regni Regis Johannis*, Public records 1863, p. 96.

[78] G.R. Lewis and G. Randall (1908, p. 212n).

[79] R. Morton Nance (1973, pp. 76–82).

eighteenth century, Dolly Pentreath of Paul near Penzance, whose great age of 102 cannot be taken as accurate and whose precise birth-date is uncertain. William Bodener of Mousehole (who died in 1789) was able to converse with Dolly for hours, but as Nance points out, no one else understood and the conversation may have been possible by the avoidance of problematical areas rather than propelled by complete facility on Bodener's part. Cornish was primarily a spoken language before its extinction in the eighteenth century and the majority of those who had spoken it would have been illiterate. Pronunciation would have varied considerably from place to place and possibly from person to person in the same locality. Müller argues that as the Cornish language began to die and was "losing its consciousness and vitality" and English began to replace it, in about the time of the Reformation, a "metamorphic process" would have taken place:[80] Cornish words were no longer understood and became slightly changed. These verbal relics created puzzlement and confusion and so it became both necessary and desirable to give them an intelligible meaning. The search for a meaning could be satisfied most easily by drawing upon English, near-sounding equivalents (a kind of phonetic transfer, or fusion), or by allocating a reference from legend, history or religion for the same reason. Müller says, "This new meaning is mostly a mistaken one, yet is not only readily accepted, but the word in its new dress and with its new character is frequently made to support facts or fictions which could be supported by no other evidence."[81]

This process, according to Müller, is accelerated wherever two languages come into contact and where one supersedes the other. Cornish, while still spoken, became disturbed and invaded from time to time by Latin, Saxon and Norman: the Celtic language adopted words from them and they from it. This is the "metamorphic process" which continued with English.[82] Names were transformed, legends were born, and these in turn came to acquire the status of generally accepted facts. From such a long process the names of *Marazion* and *Market Jew* eventually came into existence, their aetiology forgotten and their significance mistaken. The old name for Falmouth, for example, was *Penny-Come-Quick* from the Cornish *Pen y cwm qwic*,[83] *Bryn whella* (highest hill) became *Brown Willy*, and *Cwm ty goed* (Valley-house-wood) became *Come-to Good*.[84]

---

[80] Müller, op. cit.
[81] Müller, op. cit., p. 300.
[82] Müller, op. cit., p. 301.
[83] Head of the Creek Valley.
[84] Müller, op. cit., p. 304.

The two place-names which have given rise to the persistent notion that Jews were resident in Cornwall in ancient times are *Marazion*, the little town opposite St. Michael's Mount just outside Penzance, and the latter's main street *Market Jew*. *Marazion* sounds very similar to two Hebrew words: *Marah*, (bitterness, grief) and *Zion* (of Zion). This has encouraged considerable speculation that Jewish coins found in Cornwall from the period of the first Jewish revolt against the Romans (66–70 CE), which ended with the destruction of the Temple on Mount Zion, are evidence of the dispersal of thousands of Jewish prisoners as slaves all over the Roman world. Many of these are said to have ended up in Cornwall working in the tin-mines. These exiled Jewish slaves and their descendants, it is claimed, called the settlement *Marazion* – 'Bitter Zion'.

Little of this is verifiable, of course, and such notions have clearly been influenced by the Biblical accounts of the Exile of the Hebrews from the ancient Kingdoms of Israel and Judah to Assyria and Babylon in the period circa 731–536 BCE, reflected also in Psalm 137. Moreover, there are a number of obvious weaknesses in the theory. The finding of Jewish coins would be intriguing, and although such fragmentary material might point to the presence of some Jews attached to a contingent of the Roman army as conscripts or slaves, it cannot be used to postulate the presence of a population of Jews, let alone many thousands . . . "working in the tin-mines". Nor is it likely that a settlement named *Marazion* in Roman times would have been variously re-named, with unrelated titles, in thirteenth and fourteenth century Cornish (as below), only to revert to the Hebrew name (with its persecutory overtones) in the seventeenth or eighteenth centuries when by the 1720s Jews came to live in Cornwall in conditions of freedom and peace. Moreover, if this term did indeed reflect the grief of dispersed Jewish slaves, as suggested, and Jewish captives of the Roman legions displaced to Britain really originated the name *Marazion* in Cornwall, such captives consigned to other outposts would have been likely to have given other such places around the Roman Empire the same, or a similar name. The evidence for this simply does not exist.[85] As Müller points out,[86] *Mara* could be ascribed just as arbitrarily to a corruption of the Latin *Amara*, "bitter" (which would undermine the "Jewish argument"). He says:

> It cannot be too often repeated that inquiries into the origin of local names are, in the first place historical, and only in the

---

[85] Stephen Massil ibid; 14th September 1998.
[86] Müller, op.cit., pp. 305–306.

second place, philological. To attempt an explanation of any name, without having first traced it back to the earliest form in which we can find it, is to set at defiance the plainest rules of the science of language as well as the science of history.

It was the common practice in the Cornish language to write and pronounce the names of places in various ways thus increasing the ignorance of their original meanings still further. What came to be Marazion had been known variously over time as: *Merkiu*,[87] *Marcaiew*,[88] *Markesin*, *Markine*, and *Marasdethyon*,[89] *Markysyoo*, *Marchew*, *Margew*, *Marchasyowe*, and *Markysyow*.[90] In a charter of 1257, Richard Earl of Cornwall calls it *Marchadyon*, possibly the oldest known version. In 1261 this has become *Markesiou* and *Markesion* and in 1309, *Marchasyon*. In 1595, a charter of Queen Elizabeth calls it *Marghasiewe*. Other varieties proliferated such as *Marghasion* and *Maryazion*.[91]

What these examples clearly show is the variety of spelling and pronunciation. The varieties and inconsistencies of spoken Cornish would have shaped the written words. Consonants could be soft or hard, vowels, dental or nasal. An *s* could become a *z*, a *iewe* become a *dyewe* or *jewe*. Vowels could be retained (*Marachasyowe*) or partially dropped with an extra ending consonant (*Markesin*) and the central sounds, possibly omitted altogether. Such features have survived today in spoken Cornish dialect where place-names such as Saint Ives may become *Snives* or Redruth, *Druth*.

As Newall points out, *Marc(g)has* was Cornish for market.[92] Ancient Marazion originally consisted of at least two (possibly three) settlements, the smaller inland known as *Marchas-bic(z)han* (small market) and the larger, by the sea facing the Island, or Mount, as *Marchas-di(y)ew*. This may mean *Thursday market* as the Cornish for Thursday was *deyow*.[93] It may have been known at times as *Marchas-yow* (southerly market) or *Marchas-ion* (St.) (John's Market), although Müller suggests that the *ion*, *yon*, or *in* endings may indicate a diminutive termination (little market) also commonly found in Welsh.

---

[87] Camden (c. 1586).
[88] Carew (c. 1602).
[89] Leland (c. 1538).
[90] William of Worcester (c. 1478).
[91] Müller op.cit., pp. 306–7. See also Henry Hawkins, "The Jews in Cornwall", op. cit., pp. 125–128.
[92] cf. Latin, *mercatus*; Breton, *marchad*; and French, *marche*.
[93] The monks on the Mount held a Thursday market, by permission of Robert, Earl of Cornwall.

Some form of *diew* can also suggest "second",[94] or the "other market". Müller says that no one who spoke Cornish would have taken *Marchas-diew* for *Jew* because the Cornish for *Jew* was *(Y)Edhow*, and "Jew's Market or Market Jew" would have been *Marchas-Yedhewon*. But to the Saxon (English) ear, *Marchas-diew* could become *Market Jew*, and *Marchas-bic(z)han* (where the *ch* or *bic* sounds may have been corrupted by omission, contraction, and the hardening into *z*) become, by the same metamorphic process, Marazion which clearly is some kind of name for "market". The town of Penzance (in Cornish called *Pen sans*, "Holy Headland"), or at least its main street, was also known as *Marchas-diew* (because it led directly to what later came to be known as Marazion) and eventually as *Market Jew*.

Müller dates the emergence of *Market-Jew* to the period from 1634 when it is mentioned in a State Paper, dated 3rd October 1634.[95] In another State Paper dated 7th February 1634–5, the cargo of a wrecked Spanish galleon off "Gwavas Lake" in Mount's Bay was threatened by an unlawful gathering of inhabitants from "Mousehole and *Marka-jew*". In 1720, *Merkju* is mentioned as a little market-town which had taken its name from the market on Thursdays (*Magna Britannia et Hibernia*) and in 1728, *Marca-iewe* is explained in the same way (Norden's *Specul. Britanniae*).[96] Gibson's 1772 edition of *Camden's Britannia* gives *Market-Jew*. Gough's of 1789 states that "*Merkiu* signifies the *Market of Jupiter*, from the market being held on a Thursday, the day sacred to Jupiter." The 1769 edition of Carew's *Survey of Cornwall* has: "Over against the Mount fronteth a towne of petty fortune, pertinently named *Marcaiew*, or *Marhas diow*, in English 'the Thursdaies market'".

The possibilities for such subtle changes and associations may also have been influenced by external factors and by corruption within Cornish itself. Sea-faring contacts with France may have played a part in this process. Nance writes:

> In the sixth century Breton and Cornish were one language, but in the interim Breton had aquired many French, and Cornish almost as many English words; besides which the Cornish intonation, and sounds of consonants as well as vowels, had developed on lines of their own, making them as unlike those of other Celtic languages, as they were unlike the oldest forms of Cornish.[97]

---

[94] cf. French *deux*.
[95] All references from Müller, op. cit., pp. 310–311.
[96] As Norden had been born in 1548, his late sixteenth-century work, published in 1728, might suggest an even earlier usage.
[97] Nance, op. cit., p. 78.

Eventually such processes as these may have allowed *Marchas-diew* to be overlaid with the French *Marché de Jeudi*, both meaning "Thursday market" and "*jeudi*" itself could easily have assisted the process towards *Market Jew*. Moreover, the Cornish for Jew (*Yedhow*) came to be corrupted to *Ezow* so that *Mar(ch)as-bic(z)an* could have been confused with *Mar(ch)as-ezuon*, and the "little" market could, in this way, have acquired an aural connection with Jews or Zion for both Cornish and English speakers. The castle on St. Michael's Mount in the bay would have reinforced this association by re-calling to Cornish Christians familar with the Old Testament, the Temple on Mount Zion in Jerusalem. The eventual establishment in the eighteenth and nineteenth centuries of a Jewish community and Jewish shops in Penzance (especially along its main street) likewise strengthened the name Market Jew.[98]

Although the smelting-centres, or *Jews Houses*, are most likely to have been so-called for the reasons above, a similar process less readily traceable through its main phases, may have occurred here. In Cornish these houses were known as *Chiwidden*, from the Cornish *ty* or *chy* (house), no doubt shortened in pronunciation (as today) to *chi* or *chew*, and the old Cornish *gwyn* (white) which became corrupted to *gwydn*. The original name clearly reflected the distinctive colour and intense heat of the smelting furnaces, but the capacity for the Cornish *chew* to be confused with the later *Jew* is self-evident. Sacred legend also attached to the *Chiwidden* in the form of St. Chiwidden, the companion of St. Piran, the Cornish Miner-Saint whose name occurs (as Perran) in such places as Perranporth, Perranuthno and Perranaworthall.

> The legend relates that St. Piran, when still in Cornwall, employed a heavy black stone as part of his fire-place. The fire was more intense than usual, and a stream of beautiful white metal flowed out of the fire. Great was the joy of the saint, and he communicated his discover to St. Chiwidden, . . . who soon devised a process for producing this metal in large quantities. The two saints called the Cornishmen together . . . they taught them how to dig the ore from the earth, and how, by the agency of fire, to obtain the metal.[99]

---

[98] The proliferation of Jewish forenames such as Eleazar, Isaac, Esther, Benjamin, Joseph, and Samuel amongst the Cornish population proves nothing, of course, when the adoption of Biblical (Old Testament) names by Christians would have been very fashionable and even desirable. Common Jewish surnames such as Jacobs, Joseph and even Moses are to be found amongst Jews and Gentiles in Cornwall at this time.

[99] Müller, op. cit., pp. 318.

The *Chiwidden* were also known by the Cornish *tshey* or *dzhey*, a later form of *ty*, or house. Variations in pronunciation, similar to those seen in the case of *Mar(ch)as-diew*, from which the "Saxon mouth and . . . Saxon ear might have elicited a sound . . . like the English *Jew*", could easily have turned *dzhey* or *dzeyew* into *Jew* so that *Jew* and *house* become phonetically indistinguishable.[100] In contrast to the *white* of the heat in the smelting-furnaces, the smelting houses would have become *blackened* and it is likely that *chy du* (black house), as an alternative name for the smelting houses, also played its part in the transition from *du* to *Jew*.

The pronunciation of the word *ty*, or *chy(ew)*, may likewise have influenced the name for *Market Jew Street*. Between what is today the Greenmarket, the imposing Lloyds Bank building with its dome and the statue of Sir Humphry Davy facing down the main street, there was the site of the town's ancient market. The Lloyds building is known today as Market House and the town's market required then, as now, a "House" where financial and commercial transactions could take place. The combination and phonetic conflation of *Marchas* and *dzey(ew)* would also produce *Market Jew*.

And so the term *Jews Houses* and the ostensible Jewish place-names had no necessary original connection with Jews. They are entirely explicable in terms of their derivation from the Cornish language and its legendary products. The much later need to ascribe meaning to a forgotten and foreign language from which people had become excluded and estranged also played a creative and imaginative part in this process. This, in turn, gave birth to the Jewish connections and legends which have become attached to them. As Müller writes: "these names had given rise to the assumed presence of Jews in Cornwall, and not that the presence of Jews in Cornwall had given rise to these names."[101] Even if some Jews lived and settled in Cornwall in mediaeval times, their numbers and activities are unknown, and their contribution, if any, to topography and nomenclature was incidental and peripheral to the seminal forces at work in the history, indigenous culture and language of the Cornish people.

In view of the extravagant and unsubstantiated claims, based on little or no evidence at all, that there was a sizeable Jewish population in Cornwall in ancient times and a later monopoly over the con-struction and control of the tin-mining industry in mediaeval times, by a comparable *resident* population of Jews, it is all the more surprising that today few people, even in Cornwall itself, are aware that

---

[100] Müller, op. cit., pp. 311–312, 318–320.
[101] Müller, op. cit., p. 328.

significant Jewish communities became established and settled there in the eighteenth and nineteenth centuries. Moreover, these communities survived for almost two centuries, and their history and the Jews who lived in them can be traced and identified from accessible documentary sources. The exteriors of the former synagogues, and their sacred burial grounds at Falmouth and Penzance can still be seen. Hopefully, the chapters which follow will shift the perspective away from the dubious to the credible and demonstrable, and towards a little-known aspect of modern Anglo-Jewish and Cornish history.

Roth's List of Ancient Sites and Buildings with Jewish Nomenclature

For Roth's sources, see the original article.

Identifiable Sites

The Jewry Hall, Leicester
Market Jew, Cornwall
Jews' Mount, Oxford
The Jews' Hall, Winchelsea
The Jew Gate, Newcastle (Silver Street)
The Jews' Meadow, Horsham
The Jew's House, Lincoln
The Jewry, Martley, Worcs

Unidentifiable Sites[102]

The Jews Way, Bury St. Edmunds
The Jews' Houses, Southampton
The Jews' Tower, Winchester
Jews' Tin, and Jews' Houses, Cornwall

Continental Sites

Roth: "In France, there are many place-names embodying the word "Juif", or something like it."

---

[102] Roth refers to these as ". . . no longer identifiable on the ground but known from historical records." His "identifiable" is taken to refer to the original construction in its entirety, and so does not exclude previous or subsequent archaeological work at the sites, and his "known from" is understood here as "referred to".

Villejuif, near Paris
Baigneux-les-Juifs, Cote d'Or
La Roche aux Juifs, Orleans

Roth: "Similarly there are in Germany many place-names like Judenberg or Judendorf etc. . . ."[103]

Zydaczow (Poland)

Greece

Hebraeokastron (Jews' Castle), the island of Kythnos, Thermia in the Cyclades
Evraeonisi (Jews' Island), in the Saronic Gulf
Ovriokastro (Ebraeokastro, Jews' Town), near Marathon (the ancient Rhamnus)

Jews and the Cornish Emblem

A curious and little known legend has been woven around the Cornish emblem (fifteen gold balls in the shape of an inverted triangular shield) linking its origin to Jewish pawnbrokers.[104] On the south wall of Westminster Abbey can be seen the coat of arms of Richard, Count of Poitou (second son of King John), who was created Earl of Cornwall in 1225. It consists of a silver shield and a red lion with a gold crown. The shield's black border is dotted with twenty-two bezants, or gold balls. It has been supposed that these may represent gold peas (French *poix*) as a "punning allusion" to *Poitou*, but that during or after Richard's earldom, the shield began to acquire usage as Cornwall's emblem. The theory would presuppose that a considerably modified version of the shield was eventually adopted, with Richard's lion and crown excised, and with only fifteen balls (perhaps for reasons of spatial economy) being re-located to the shield's centre.

Whilst this aetiology is in itself uncertain, and there will be other theories as to the origin of the Cornish emblem, there is an even more

---

[103] It should be noted that Roth does not exclude the possibility that Jews may have formed communities in *some* of these places in Germany.

[104] An outline of this theory appeared as a brief article, "Duchy's Fifteen Bezants", as part of the Peterborough column in the *Daily Telegraph and Morning Post* on October 7th 1937.

colourful explanation attached to it. This theory is based upon a tradition that in Plantagenet times the Jewish pawnbrokers of Cornwall were the most prosperous merchants in England, and that when King John wished to mortgage his crown to finance a war in France, five Jewish pawnbrokers agreed amongst themselves to form a consortium so that they could jointly take over the king's debts. The story supposes that the fifteen inverted gold balls represent the combined symbols (of three inverted balls) of these five pawnbrokers, who were based in five Cornish towns, spread across the county. They were said to have been Ben Levy of Truro, Ben Ezra of Penzance, Moses of Mevagissey,[105] and two others whose names and location are lost (as illegible). Purportedly, their motto "One and All" (which has since become the motto of Cornwall) signified that no business or financial transaction could be conducted without a quorum of all five pawnbrokers. Accordingly, each pawnbroker's symbol (three inverted balls) was incorporated into the fifteen balls of their emblem and, presumably in time, its familiar appearance across the county led to its adoption as Cornwall's emblem of solidarity. Needless to say, this theory, based upon the dubious premise that wealthy money-lenders will necessarily be Jews, remains unsubstantiated but it may well be a hybrid reflection combining the Jewish co-operative banking system which Roth refers to as a national phenomenon, and a curious reversal of the tradition of the mortgaging of the Jews to Earl Richard (in 1255 and 1270).

The oral traditions of history, legend and folklore, elaborated over many centuries, have in this way become entrenched into a powerful symbiosis, negligent in its attention to verification from substantial and credible documentary sources, but nonetheless repeated uncritically by respected authorities and others, as if they were unquestionable fact. Indeed the traditions themselves have been shaped not only by a history of poverty, but also an age-old prejudice and latent anti-semitism with its perception of the Jew as eager predator and willing accomplice in exploitation. Thus, Coulthard,[106] with reference to Richard: "We gather that this Earl was most kindly disposed towards the Jewish race; which assertion lends colour to the statement of Carew that the tin trade of Cornwall in ancient times was *largely in the hands of Jews, who grievously exploited the Cornish Tinners.*"

It is hoped that the critical survey in this chapter contributes to some extent towards a re-assessment of these traditional assumptions.

---

[105] These names were apparently found in British Museum manuscripts.

[106] Coulthard (1913) p. 42: (present author's italics). Cf. Ch. 1, p. 14.

The Jews of Falmouth – 1740–1860[1]

Alex M. Jacob

[original styling and punctuation retained]

About 1740, there began one of those phases of immigration from the Continent which, since the seventeenth-century Re-admission, have been a recurrent feature of Anglo-Jewry and within a short period two sharply contrasted groups had become noticeable in the Community. Under the later Stuarts the newly-won right of entry had attracted bankers, brokers and foreign merchants from Holland and (to a less extent) from the great trading centres of Northern Germany, whilst from the West Indies there was a steady, if smaller, influx of planters and traders who wished to spend their retirement in England and its more temperate climate. At that period retail trade in the City of London was permitted only to members of the jealously restricted Merchants Guilds, but these earlier settlers were not affected since their main interests were finance and foreign trade. For these activities London was the obvious centre and as late as the year of George I's death no Community existed outside the capital. By the end of the century, however, Jews were to be found in all the major towns of England and in most cases ministers had been appointed and synagogues built.

These provincial settlements were formed almost entirely by Jews belonging to a social and economic level very different from those of their co-religionists in London. By 1750 there was a regular flow of immigrants from Alsace and the German Rhineland, where those who had not left their homes too young to have a trade had been artisans or small shopkeepers. To them London presented few opportunities, owing to the restrictions on retail trade, their lack of capital and the difficulty of obtaining employment caused by sabbath observance. In a short time a "Jewish Problem" had arisen and vagrancy and crime spread to an extent that alarmed Londoners, both Gentile and Jew alike.

---

[1] Paper read before the Jewish Historical Society of England on 7th March 1949.

That this problem was solved was due to the fact that the Ghetto system never applied in England and Jews enjoyed complete freedom of movement. To overcome the difficulties of earning a livelihood in London many immigrants took to the road as peddlers of second-hand clothing, jewellry, trinkets and such other small articles as could conveniently be carried in a pack – a life to which the many immigrants from Alsace were accustomed since in their homeland they had been forbidden to live in towns. These earliest peddlers would choose a market town as their centre, working the surrounding countryside, and in due course many settled in these centres, notably as silversmiths. The first towns to attract Jews in this manner were the seaports of the South and West coasts of which Falmouth was one of the earliest.

At the present time, Falmouth is regarded as an agreeable resort. In the eighteenth century, however, it was a flourishing port of some consequence in the country's economic life. Since 1688 it had been a packet station for mail to the West Indies, Portugal and the Cape and these connections stimulated trading with those regions. Being the most westerly port of the south coast of England, Falmouth – which is one of the finest natural harbours in the world, being capable of accommodating some 200 sailing vessels   would receive calls from ships awaiting instructions from owners as to the disposal of cargoes, or requiring provisions, water or the execution of minor repairs, whilst, when gales were blowing, its sheltered position was of great value to shipping. At this period too, Falmouth was the centre of a district where copper, tin, and lead were still being mined and its market served as the shopping and meeting place of miners and their families.

The first Jew to settle in Falmouth was one Alexander Moses[2] who, with his wife, Phoebe, set up there as a silversmith about 1740. Though both he and his wife were in all probability immigrants, his first years in this country may well have been spent in London where a niece lived. But that he was long settled in Cornwall is proved by his having been generally known as Zender Falmouth, Zender being a common diminutive among Jews for Alexander and the use of the home-town's name[3] being a widely-spread practice in the Jewish community at a time when surnames were still something of a novelty.

---

[2] Alexander Moses died 17th April 1791; his wife 15th September 1804. Both are buried at Falmouth. His will, dated 13th April 1791, was proved 21st November 1793 and was preserved at the District Probate Registry at Exeter until destruction of all records at that Registry by enemy action during the Second World War. See Edit 1.

[3] cf. two ancestors of the present writer, Moses Lazarus of Rochford (c. 1740–1814) known as Moshe Rochford and Simon Hyam of Ipswich (c. 1740–1824) known as Simcha Ipswich. Both are mentioned in C. Roth: *The Rise of Provincial Jewry* (London 1950), pp. 19 and 72.

During his earliest years at Falmouth, Zender no doubt relied upon the communities at Plymouth or at Exeter[4] for communal worship and the provision of *kosher* meat; (Edit 2) his main contacts with other Jews were, however, with those peddlers[5] or chapmen who were becoming a feature of the English countryside[6] and of whom a picture has been given by Israel Solomon, who was born in 1803 at Falmouth, where both his grand-fathers had settled after some years of peddling in the district. In the reminiscences,[7] written by him in his old age, he related how, until about 1830, there were inns on all the main roads, where Jews could put up, the landlord keeping a cupboard which contained cooking utensils used only by them so as to comply with the dietary laws. This cupboard was kept locked

> And when a Jew used the utensils, he saw to the cleaning of them and before putting them away . . . wrote with chalk in the bottom of the utensil his name, [the] day of the [Jewish] month and year together with the portion of the Law read on the Sabbath of that week – all in Hebrew. . . . Some of the hotels were in the centre of populated districts, and the peddlers . . . would congregate of a Friday evening at these hotels and stay over Sabbath. . . . They generally formed a club and one of their number, licensed by the rabbi to slaughter animals, was paid by the club for one day's loss of profit . . . to get to the hotel on Friday early enough to kill animal or poultry [or to] purchase fish . . . and cook or super-intend it [so] that it should be quite kosher. (Edit 3)

Such visitors to Falmouth kept Zender in touch with his co-religionists and made possible the necessary quorum for services. But as he saw his six children growing up, he must have felt the need of giving them better opportunities of associating with their fellow-Jews and of making more formal arrangements for communal life. With a number of these peddlers therefore, Zender entered into a compact whereby he paid for their peddlers' licences and advanced, on credit, a stock of small cutlery, buckles, jewelry and watches which they hawked around the country. They, for their parts, undertook to return to Falmouth every Friday in time to act as one of the *Minyan*; on Sunday they settled their accounts and received fresh stock before

---

[4] Both founded c. 1740.

[5] Editorial comment: Jacob uses this alternative spelling: elsewhere the word occurs in its more common form of pedlar.

[6] Item 1580 of the *Lady Ludlow Collection of English Porcelain* at Luton Hoo (Beds.) is a figure in Derby China c. 1760 of a "Jew Pedlar and his Wife."

[7] Israel Solomon: *Records of My Family*, printed for private circulation, New York, 1887.

resuming their travels of the following week. Zender also insisted on their renouncing their foreign names in favour of forms which, whilst still Jewish, were more English. At a time when use of synagogal names was still more prevalent than that of surnames, which were subject to wide variations, this caused little difficulty. Thus included among Zender's proteges was Israel Solomon, who had been born in Ehrenbreitstein, where his family name had been Behrends; whilst another protégé who had started life as Bernard (or Issachar) Beer appears variously as Bernard or Barnet and his surname as Joel, Jewell or Levy.[8]

The experiences[9] during his first years in England of this Barnet Levy, as he seems most usually to have been called, are typical of many of those who ultimately made their homes in Falmouth. Coming to London from his native Alsace about the middle of the eighteenth century, he was looking for a friend from his native town when he met a young Jewish girl – Esther Elias by name – whom he promptly resolved to make his wife. In London, however, it was impossible for him to earn a living from his trade – that of a soap-boiler – so he reluctantly took to peddling, his travels bringing him to Falmouth where Zender befriended him. After some years in the district as a peddler, he had saved enough to set up shop at Falmouth, whereupon he travelled back to London to ask for Esther's hand. When her father asked for references, Barnet Levy gave him the name of Zender who, by a coincidence, was the uncle of Esther's mother; the marriage was approved and shortly after the newly married couple set out for Cornwall. In later years their grandson described the journey of over 300 miles. Both the mail coach and the post-chaise, were too expensive and "the next great travelling conveyance" he explained "was Russel's wagon, an immense vehicle covered by canvas, with six heavy horses, a driver and a heavily-armed guard . . . [The journey from London to Falmouth took three to four days] . . . In front . . . space was kept for passengers and their seats were straw and hay . . . Such a

---

[8] When administration of his estate (he having died intestate on 15th May 1791) was granted to his son, he was described as Barnett Levy. After this son's death in the following year, administration was granted to his three daughters and two others, when he was described as Barnet Levy (like the will of Zender Falmouth, these documents were destroyed by enemy bombing at Exeter during the 1939/45 War). See editorial note 1.

[9] *Records of My Family*. The story was also told in a slightly different version by Major William Schonfield in a paper given before the J.H.S.E. on 20th December 1938, entitled "The Josephs of Cornwall." Major Schonfield was married to Florence, daughter of Lionel Joseph and great-great-grand-daughter of Barnet Levy, whose daughter Judith married Lyon Joseph.

conveyance did not suit Esther, so she rode behind her husband on a horse-pack all the way."

By 1766, Zender had attracted a number of Jews to Falmouth and in that year he acquired a building on the sea-front for use as a synagogue.[10] He also engaged a minister, whose duties, apart from officiating at services, must also have included those of *shochet*, *mohel* and religious instructor to the rapidly increasing number of children in the youthful community.[11] For these services the salary as late as 1860 was 25/- weekly, which no doubt explains why one holder of the office[12] later supplemented it by book-binding. Amongst the first duties falling to the minister must have been to officiate at the *Bar-mitzvah* of Zender's younger son and at the wedding of his eldest daughter.[13] And in the years that followed, the *Chuppah* seems to have been in constant use, so that the inter-relationship of the various members of the congregation soon became very involved. (Edit 5) At a later stage, marriage between first cousins was to become very common, but in these early days there was little likelihood of its happening, since those settling in Falmouth were not related to each other. But from the beginning there were many instances of several members of one family all marrying into the same other family. Thus the brothers Henry and Isaac Joseph married, the one a daughter and the other a grand-daughter of Zender, the one sister-in-law thus being the other's niece – and to add to the confusion both bore the name Judith; whilst the two step-brothers and the step-sister of Henry and Isaac Joseph married the two daughters and the son of that Barnet Levy who has already been mentioned and who had himself married a

---

[10] Situated in Hamblyn's Court, later called Dunstan's Court, ultimately the site of the gas-works.

[11] Ministers at Falmouth include: – (a) "Rabbi Saavill" (Samuel ben Samuel ha-Levi), died 22nd March 1814; (b) Moses (the Precentor) ben Hayim, died 24th October 1832 (see Edit 4); (c) Joseph Benedict Rintel (born 1810) son of Benedict Jacob Rintel, at Falmouth, c. 1832–1849; (d) Rev. N. Lipman, subsequently Chief Shochet in London. Between 1821 and 1829, Barnet Asher Simmons, Minister at Penzance from 1811 to 1853, circumcised seven children of members of the Falmouth Community. Simmons married Flora Jacob (1790–1874) grand-daughter of Zender Falmouth. Their daughter Fanny married J.B. Rintel. Lay Presidents of the Congregation were: (i) Alexander Moses (Zender Falmouth) died 1791. (ii) Moses Jacob, son-in-law of last, 1733–25th April 1807. (iii) Lyon Joseph, retired to Bath c. 1815, died 1825. (iv) Jacob Jacob, son of (ii) 10th March 1774–3rd Feb. 1853. (v) Moses Moss Jacob Jacob, son of last, 10th Nov. 1812–14th March 1860.

[12] J.B. Lintel.

[13] Zender's younger son was Moses Moses. His eldest daughter, Sarah (1748–15th January 1831) married Moses Jacob. Their eldest child was born in 1767.

great-niece of Zender.[14] Barnet Levy's youngest daughter, Sheba, married her maternal uncle, Elias Elias, who was something of an eccentric and who, having failed in business in London — because, his nephew related, his education gave him a foolish pride which disinclined him to follow his father's trade as a tailor — settled about 1815 in Falmouth, where his family supported him.[15] There he became a conspicuous figure not only on account of his political views but also because of his attire. For he continued to wear the French pre-revolutionary style of clothing — a full cloth coat and wide waist-coat, velvet knee breeches buckled at the side, worsted stockings and shoes adorned with white metal buckles. Around his throat and covering half his chin was a broad white neck-tie, whilst his hair, which was slightly powdered and secured by a large black ribbon below the neck, was covered by a high-crowned hat which took the place of the three-cornered head-gear which was then the normal wear. Thus attired, he would inveigh against Lord Castlereagh whom he accused of framing the "Cato Street Conspiracy" of 1820 in order to discredit his opponents.

As the number of married men increased, so the community changed its character. It had started as a centre for peddlers, but, with marriage, they naturally wished for a more settled life and for homes for their families. Several opened shops in Falmouth; others settled in neighbouring towns and villages and about this period Jewish families were to be found at Redruth, Truro, Penryn, Camborne and St. Austell. In these towns they lived over their shops carrying on business during the week — and in many cases the womenfolk seem to have contributed to the family income by millinery or dress-making;[16] (Edit 6) for Sabbath and the Festivals they would return to Falmouth. Thus by the year of Zender's death — 1791 — some ten or twelve families had settled in the district, including those of his four daughters, all of whom had married local Jews, and his son.[17]

---

[14] Henry Joseph married Judith daughter of Zender Moses. She married secondly, Eliezer Lawrence. Isaac Joseph married Judith daughter of Moses and Sarah Jacob. Abraham, Lyon and Rachel Joseph married, respectively, Hannah, Judith, and Joseph, children of Barnet Levy and his wife, Esther (see Elias).

[15] *Records of My Family* and *The Josephs of Cornwall*.

[16] Kitty (née Jacob) wife of Simon Solomon was described as a milliner in the *Guide to Falmouth* of 1825. Israel Solomon states that his aunts, the daughters of Barnet Levy, were similarly trained.

[17] Sarah, wife of Moses Jacob of Redruth; Rose, wife of Samuel Simons of Truro; Hannah, wife of Israel Levi of Truro; Judith, wife of Henry Joseph of St. Austell; Philip (? married Betsy Jacobs). Moses, the younger son, is said to have married a non-Jewess and to have settled in Le Havre.

Some ten years before Zender's death, the need for a cemetery had arisen and Lord de Dunstanville, a local landowner, had presented a plot of ground on the Falmouth-Penryn road jointly to the Jewish and Congregational communities. A hedge separates the two grounds and the Jewish section continued to be used until 1913, stones marking the graves of forty-five members of the Congregation.[18] (Edit 7)

On Zender's death it might have been expected that he would have been succeeded as President of the Congregation by his son, Philip, who carried on his father's business until his own death forty years later.[19] That he did not assume the Presidency was probably due to the forceful personality of his sister, Sarah, whose husband, Moses Jacob, a dealer in clocks and watches at Redruth some ten miles from Falmouth, now became warden. Sarah, who became the mother of twelve children, all but two of whom married, was noted for her strict orthodoxy[20] – indeed she carried out more duties than were strictly demanded of her, since she is said to have laid *tephillin* and to have presided at services as warden if her husband chanced to be absent. On Mondays and Thursdays, as well as twice yearly to commemorate the ascent and descent of Mount Sinai by Moses she regularly fasted for half a day. Physically at least, her husband was of smaller stature, since he is said to have been a very short man who travelled extensively through the country-side on a very tall horse, no doubt visiting the larger country houses to attend to their clocks. As orthodox as his wife, he never omitted mid-day prayers and to that end, he trained his horse to stand still whilst he recited the *Amidah* and to take the appropriate three steps backwards at its conclusion – at which point the over-zealous mount is said on one occasion to have thrown its rider into a ditch!

Shortly after Moses Jacob's death, the Congregation built a new and larger synagogue on a site leased from the Lord of the Manor, which was opened in time for the High Holydays of 1808 (Edit 8) –

---

[18] Though the earliest decipherable stone is dated 1790, the first burial was probably that of Esther, wife of Barnet Levy, who died c.1780.

[19] Philip Moses died 19th November 1831. (See pp. 59, 71 and 99 postscript.)

[20] This account of Moses and Sarah Jacob was given by their great-grandson, Samuel Jacob (1837–1912) in letters to *The Jewish Chronicle* and *The Jewish World* of 15th May, 1903. The twelve children of Moses and Sarah Jacob were:- (i) Betsy, died unmarried; (ii) Judith married Isaac Joseph; (iii) Rose, married Alexander; (iv) Kitty married Simon Solomon; (v) Jacob married his first cousin, Sarah Kate, daughter of Samuel Simons and his wife Rose, daughter of Zender of Falmouth; (vi) Hannah married S. Ezekiel (of Exeter); (vii) Samuel married his first cousin, Sarah, daughter of Israel Levi and his wife Hannah daughter of Zender Falmouth; (viii) Rebecca married Lemon Woolf of Penzance; (ix) Esther married Henry Harris of Truro; (x) Amelia died unmarried; (xi) Levy married S. Mordecai; (xii) Flora married Barnet Asher Simmons, Minister at Penzance.

possibly in emulation of the Penzance Community whose new place of worship had been completed in the previous year.[21] This building, which still stands on Parham Hill overlooking the town, was later described by a Directory to Falmouth as "an excellent and convenient building for the performance of their ancient worship, as detailed in the Old Testament."[22] In the Congregation's possession were five scrolls with two sets of silver bells and pointers; a curtain for the Ark; and Notice Boards recording donations of ten guineas and more, together with two wooden panels, one displaying the Commandments and the other the Prayer for the Royal Family.[23] Prominent amongst the building's decorations were four or five elaborate and massive candelabra.[24]

Social historians have frequently pointed out that, by comparison with more recent conflicts, the impact of the Napoleonic wars on English life was but slight. The case of a town such as Falmouth, with its sea-going activities, was, however, rather different; and its Jewish Community had before it a constant reminder in the career of Lyon Joseph who presided over it from 1807 until 1815. Joseph was the son (by his second marriage) of Joseph Joseph[25] who came to London from Mühlhausen (Alsace) about the middle of the eighteenth century. The father seems to have died whilst his family was still youthful and his eldest two sons took to the road as peddlers, at one time making their centre in Canterbury. After some time, however, they moved further afield and at Falmouth received the patronage of Zender. They now persuaded their step-brother, Lyon, with his brother and sister, to join them in Cornwall where Lyon began his career as a peddler in the established pattern. His ambitions, however, seem to have been higher than those of his fellows, for, not content with having saved enough to open a shop, he later bought a ship which at first brought considerable profits from his early recognition of the benefits to be gained from the Allies' control of the Spanish and Portuguese ports.[26] After the

---

[21] C. Roth "Penzance: The Decline and Fall of an Anglo-Jewish Community." *Jewish Chronicle Supplement*, May 1933.

[22] *Falmouth and Penryn Directory and Guide*, 1864.

[23] An account of the Synagogue was given in a letter dated 3rd June, 1914 (of which the present writer possesses a copy) written by Lawrence Jacob (1843–1923) to Charles H.L. Emanuel as Secretary to the Board of Deputies.

[24] These candelabra are mentioned in the 64th Annual Report (1913–1916 session) of the Board of Deputies.

[25] The career of Lyon Joseph is described in *The Josephs of Cornwall*.

[26] Joseph's brother-in-law, Solomon Solomon, whose wife was a sister of Joseph's wife, also had interests in Portugal where he died whilst visiting Lisbon in 1819 (*Records of My Family*, p. 10). Solomon's name appears in the list of Navy Agents for 1816 (*Transactions*, J.H.S.E, Vol. XIII, p. 186).

evacuation of the Peninsula, however, he was unwise enough to continue these operations, which resulted in the seizure of a cargo as contraband involving him in a loss said to have amounted to £20,000. Despite this experience he continued shipping – in the main to Gibraltar and Malta, one of his vessels being aptly named "Perseverance"; but misfortune – or, more probably, lack of judgement – dogged him and there were tales of absconding ships' captains and dishonest agents, ship-wrecks and salvaged goods later found to have been damaged by salt water. . . . Another of Lyon Joseph's activities consisted in the collection of gold on behalf of the Government for the commissariat and payment of troops. It was whilst acting as an agent for this branch of Joseph's activities that a Polish Jew, Isaiah Falk Vallentine, was murdered at Fowey by an innkeeper of the name of Wyatt, who, after suffocating his victim, stripped him of £260 and threw the body into the sea – a crime for which he was sentenced to death at the Launceston Assizes in 1812.[27] At an early age Joseph retired to Bath, worn out by the strain of his adventures; he died at the age of 51 and was buried at Plymouth where one of his sons had settled.

There were other links with the wars. In the nearby town of Penzance lived Lemon Hart, purveyor of rum to the Royal Navy, who was connected by marriage with a number of the Falmouth Jews.[28] There too lived Barnet Asher Simmons, (Edit 9) who, after spending his early life at sea, losing a finger in action – it is said at Trafalgar – acted as Chazan and Mohel at Penzance from 1811 until 1857. By his marriage to Flora Jacob, a grand-daughter of Zender, he became well-known in Falmouth where he officiated during a ministerial vacancy.[29] His brother-in-law, Simon Solomon, a painter, married to Flora Jacob's sister, Kitty, was much in demand on occasions of national rejoicing, when he contributed to Falmouth's celebrations illuminated transparencies on patriotic themes, whilst his other works included a series of panels depicting fish and a painting of Joseph and his brethren.[30]

There was now growing up a generation that had been born in Falmouth and this led to a closer association with the life of the port. As in most sea-towns, Jews are to be found acting as ship's chandlers,

---

[27] J. Picciotto: *Sketches of Anglo-Jewish History*, (London 1875) p. 287; *Records of My Family*. (Editorial note: see the Falmouth section of chapter 7.)

[28] Lemon Hart's maternal aunt was Bella, wife of Israel Solomon. A first cousin, Lemon Woolf married Rebecca Jacob, grand-daughter of Zender and another first cousin married a son of Samuel and Rose Simons, grandson of Zender. The sister of Lemon Hart's wife married Joseph Joseph, son of Isaac and Judith Jacob and great-grandson of Zender.

[29] Probably after the death of "Rabbi Saavill" in 1814.

[30] *Records of My Family*.

sailors' outfitters and navy agents; whilst for the benefit of ships' crews returning from abroad they made arrangements to exchange foreign coins. In many cases these crews would arrive at Falmouth as their first port of call after long periods at sea or in foreign parts and would have many months' accumulated wages unspent in their pockets; to exchange their foreign currency and to tempt the sailors with trinkets, the local Jews owned small boats known as "Tailors' Cutters" in which they would meet incoming shipping; the craft owned by the Jacob family was given the appropriate name of "The Synagogue."[31] This association with the sea led to the local legend that to carry a piece of the *Afikoman* in the pocket of the *Arbang Konfas* was a protection against drowning; it also caused visitors to the town to suggest that the synagogue's position had been chosen so as to enable worshippers there to observe the entry of any ships into the harbour. In another respect, Falmouth's position as a sea-port had its effects on the local Community which received visits from travellers setting off on foreign journeys, those whose names appeared on the list of the Synagogue's benefactors including Sir Moses Montefiore – who may well have embarked there on one of his voyages on behalf of foreign co-religionists – and David Abarbanel Lindo, the communal worker and father of a numerous family prominent in the Jewish Community.

The Jews of Falmouth played their part in local affairs. As in other parts of the country, one of the first institutions to welcome them on equal terms with non-Jews was Freemasonry (Edit 10) – and, as Mr. Roth has pointed out[32] at least two Falmouth Jews were active in that Society during the 1780s. Of these one was Wolf Benjamin[33] whose daughter was married at Leatherseller's Hall, London, in 1783 to Lyon Levy, on which occasion *The London Magazine* noted that "the young couple's united age amounted to 35."[34] In 1809, Levy's suicide by throwing himself off the Monument was to gain such notoriety that reference to it was made in the "Ingoldsby Legends" which first appeared in print twenty-eight years later.[35] Local Jews also seem to have joined debating

---

[31] *Cornish Echo*, 26th September 1930: Interview with K. Wills.

[32] *The Rise of Provincial Jewry*, p. 62.

[33] Wolf Benjamin, died 12th January 1790 and his wife Gitle, died 25th August 1794, are both buried in Falmouth. (Editorial note: in his 1939 survey of the Falmouth cemetery headstones, Alex Jacob gives Woolf Benjamin's date of death as 25th October 1790 for the Hebrew date 17 Heshvan 5551).

[34] *The London Magazine*, 1783, p. 86. Quoted in *Anglo-Jewish Notabilities* (J.H.S.E. London 1949), p. 229.

[35] Ingoldsby Legends – Misadventures at Margate, verse 6 ". . . it is my fixed intent to jump as Master Levy did, from off the Monument." The "Legends" first appeared in *Blackwood's Magazine* in 1837.

and similar societies, whilst in a demonstration at the time of the agitation for the Reform Bill, the Mayor walked in procession between a Roman Catholic Priest and the then Jewish Minister, Joseph Rintel. But though they constituted a small minority, separated by large distances from any Community other than the equally small one at Penzance and though they played their part on equal terms with their neighbours, both economically and socially, the Jews of Falmouth remained loyal to their faith. In a period approaching a century and a half only two mixed marriages have been noted;[36] and although two Missionary Societies had offices in the town,[37] their only known success was the baptism of an eight-year-old lad in 1791.[38] These insignificant exceptions apart, observance of the precepts of traditional Judaism, and in particular of sabbaths and festivals, seems to have been rigorous and to have gained respect in a district where the "Nonconformist Conscience" is still an important force. (Edit 11) It is recorded of Jacob Jacob, who presided over the Community for some thirty-five years during the first half of the nineteenth century, that in his young days when carrying on a tailoring business in the town of Camborne, his neighbours would refrain from approaching him on business matters on a Saturday night until three stars, marking the conclusion of the Sabbath were clearly visible in the sky. In his old age, when he had retired to a house near the Main Street in Falmouth – which, ironically became the local headquarters of the Y.M.C.A. after his death – Jacob Jacob spent much of his time composing Biblical texts with a view to refuting conversionist claims; two small note-books on these themes, in his hand-writing, survive. His son, Moses Jacob, who presided over the Congregation from 1853 until 1860, used to pay an annual visit to London, where he never failed to call on the Chief Rabbi – at whose election in 1844 Falmouth had been represented on the Committee of Delegates[39] – when Dr. Adler would welcome him as representing one of the few Congregations which never had disputes to bring before him. (Edit 12)

---

[36] Moses Moses, son of Zender Falmouth, is said to have married out of the faith. An aunt of Israel Solomon married a soldier and eloped to India, whence she eventually returned to Falmouth a childless widow (*Records of My Family*).

[37] *The London Society for Promoting Christianity among the Jews* and *The British Society for Promoting Christianity among the Jews* are both mentioned as having offices at Falmouth in the Guide of the town of 1864.

[38] Susan E. Gay and Mrs. Howard Fox: *The Register of Baptisms, Marriages and Burials of the parish of Falmouth, 1663–1812. Part I. Marriages, Baptisms* (Devon and Cornwall Record Society. Exeter 1914), Op. 464 – William Cohen, born June 1783, son of Moses and Betsy Cohen was baptised at Falmouth on 8th April 1791. In the baptismal records, he is described as "formerly a Jew."

[39] C. Roth – *History of the Great Synagogue* (London 1950), p. 266.

Falmouth High Street c.1904, where many Jewish shops were once located.

Falmouth Church Street c.1910. The Greyhound Inn, left, run by Mary Ann
Vos, wife of Nathan Vos, two of the last Jewish residents. [both pictures
courtesy: Historical Research Unit, Royal Polytechnic of Cornwall, Falmouth]

Towards the middle of the nineteenth century, Falmouth's importance began to dwindle. (Edit 13) As early as 1836 the port had sent a
delegation, headed by its Mayor, to London in consequence of a
rumour that the Post Office was to withdraw its packet service, and in
1850 this withdrawal took place; in 1857 a telegraph service was
installed so that it was no longer necessary for shipping to wait in the
harbour for instructions (whose receipt might take a week or more)
from London. Falmouth was rapidly becoming less isolated. Until
1863, the quickest route to London and other parts of the country had
been by boat to Plymouth, whence the railways ran; in that year,
however, a railway was built from Truro and the improved commu-
nications resulted in a fairly rapid exodus of the local Jews who moved
to Bristol, Birmingham, Plymouth and London; whilst some went
further afield as did Alexander Jacob,[40] (Edit 14) who went as a prospector, accompanied by three Cornish tin-miners, to British Columbia
at the time of the gold rush in 1859, and the brothers Lionel and
Josephus Joseph who inherited something of the venturesome spirit of
their grand-father, Lyon Joseph; for, after trying their luck in California
and Hawaii, they bought a number of building sites on Vancouver
Island from the Hudson Bay Company which subsequently became
known as the "Joseph Brothers' Estate."[41] Departures such as these
brought a swift decline to the always small community at Falmouth.
When *The Jewish Chronicle*, in the first year of its existence, surveyed
provincial Jewry, the Falmouth Community was still, in 1842, a
flourishing one of some fourteen families – which, bearing in mind the
size of the Victorian household, must have represented at least seventy
or eighty individuals; (Edit 15) within thirty-five years, this number had
shrunk to three families,[42] services were no longer regularly held, the
Community had ceased to enjoy the presence of a minister and from
1864 onwards, (Edit 16) it was necessary to have recourse to Penzance –
itself by now a dwindling Community – for supplies of Kosher meat.[43]

Apart from a burial in 1913,[44] the end came in 1880 with the
departure for London of Samuel Jacob, whose family had been

---

[40] Alexander Jacob (born 8th November 1841 at Falmouth) returned to England c.
1861. After a short period in Birmingham, he settled in London, where he died
3rd May 1903.

[41] *The Josephs of Cornwall.*

[42] *The Jewish Chronicle*, 18th March 1842, refers to 14 families; on 23rd July 1847 to 9
heads of households and 50 individuals. The Jewish Directory for 1875 gives the
membership as three families.

[43] C. Roth: *Penzance: The Decline and Fall of an Anglo-Jewish Community.*

[44] Nathan Vos buried 9th November 1913. An account of the funeral appeared in
The Jewish Chronicle, 14th November 1913.

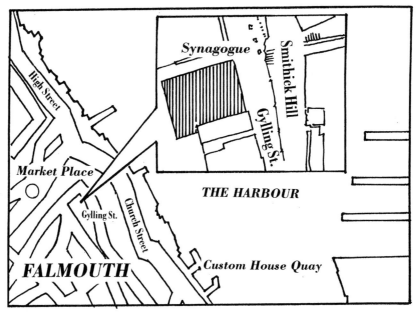

Falmouth: showing the site of the Synagogue,

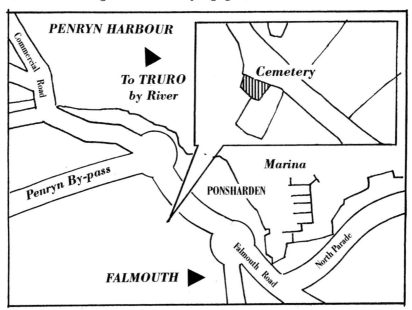

Penryn: showing the site of the Jewish cemetery

Maps by Bill Smith

the mainstay of the Congregation during four generations. The Synagogue was sold, and in 1939 was in use as an auctioneer's store; even the Cemetery came into the market – an event that caused comment in the Jewish Press[45] – and was purchased by Alfred de Pass who had made his home in the town. Of the Synagogue's appurtenances, the *Sepharim* were distributed to Hampstead Synagogue and the Convict Synagogue at Parkhurst (Isle of Wight), whilst the Board bearing the Commandments, formerly fixed outside the Synagogue, is now in the possession of the Jewish Museum, Woburn House,[46] where also are exhibited, on loan from Hampstead Synagogue, a pair of silver bells from a Sepher.

Of the existence of a Jewish Community in Falmouth the only traces that remain are an auctioneer's store, no longer recognisable as having once housed the Synagogue, and a plot of ground on the outskirts of the town marking the resting place of its members. Yet for over a century the Jews of Falmouth played their part in the progress of the town and the sentiments of their fellows were summarized by the Editor of a "Panorama of Falmouth" when he wrote in 1825 that "their numbers are considerable and respectable; and a great deal of commercial business has been conducted by them for a series of years in this town."

NOTE – In the preparation of this paper I am much indebted to Mr. Wilfred S. Samuel for information and suggestions, as well as for help in other ways.

Editorial Notes

Edit 1. The reconstruction of the history of the Jewish community in Falmouth is bedevilled by the wholesale absence of vital records for the town which were held at the District Probate Office in Exeter, destroyed by enemy action during the last war. Crucially this included the original will of Alexander Moses (also known within the Jewish community as Henry Moses and Alexander Zander). A copy of the will has in fact survived and reads:

> Consistory Court, Exeter.
> Alexander Moses of Falmouth, dealer in silverware, being weak in body. To each of my several children hereinafter named, that is to say, Sarah Jacob, wife of Moses Jacob of Redruth, Moses Moses, Rose Simons, wife of Samuel Simons of Truro, Hannah

---

[45] *The Jewish Chronicle*, 5th November 1913.
[46] *The Jewish Chronicle*, 19th July 1935.

Levi, wife of Israel Levi of Truro, and Judith Joseph, wife of Henry Joseph of St Austle, the sum of 5s. Residue of messauges, land, goods, stock in trade, money, etc. to my beloved wife, Phebe Moses and my son Philip Moses and the survivor of them equally between them; but in case my wife shall marry again, then and in such case and not otherwise, all such her part and share of my messauges etc. so bequeathed as aforesaid shall become the sole property of the said Philip Moses, and my wife shall be utterly excluded from all the advantages etc. which she may have by virtue of said bequest.

I appoint my said wife Phebe Moses and my said son Philip Moses Joint executors.

Dated 13 April 1791.
Wits. Barto. Incledon. Richd. Bryn

> Alex Moses
> Seal

21st November 1793 this will was proved and admin. was commuted to Phebe Moses and Philip Moses, executrix and executor in the will named, sworn by commission, no inventory. 18 Nov. 1793 before R.H. Hit(c)hens, Commissioner . . . directed to Richd. Hawkin Hitchens, Philip Webber the younger and Robert Dillon, Clerks."

The will of Barnet Levy has also survived in copy, and reads:

Consistory Court, Exeter.
Admon. of Barnet Levy late of Falmouth granted 24 June 1791 to Levy Levy the son and one of the next of kin of the said decd. Bond of Levy Levy of Falmouth, watchmaker, Philip Moses of same, silversmith, and George Walters of Bredock, husbandman, in £200, dated 24 June 1791. Condit. that said Levy Levy being admitted admr. of Barnet Levy, his father, shall make an invent. etc. signat. of Levy Levy.
Affidavit by Levy Levy that he is son and one of next of kin of Barnet, 24 June 1791.

Consistory Court. Exeter.
Admon. of Barnet Levy of Falmouth.

Whereas Barnet Levy late of Falmouth co. Cornwall, shopkeeper decd. died intestate and admon. of his goods was committed to Levy Levy his son and whereas said Levy Levy did for some time intermeddle in the effects of his father and he is since dead, intestate, leaving some part thereof unadmd., the Vicar General now empowers certain clerks to take oaths of Betsy Levy, Hannah Levy and Judith Levy, spinsters, the three daughters and next of kin of sd. Barnet Levy decd. 27 July 1792. They were sworn 14 Aug. 1792.

Bond of Betsy, Hannah & Judith Levy, of Falmouth, spinsters, Samuel Russell of same, taylor, and Francis Symons of same, mercer, in £100. 14 Aug. 1792. (See Editorial postscript p. 68.)

Edit 2. Contrary to earlier assumptions that Jewish life in Devon and Cornwall began in the 1740s, it is now reasonably certain that Jews settled in Penzance as early as the 1720s. This makes the Cornish communities earlier than those in Exeter or Plymouth, which did not have any sizeable Jewish communal life until the mid-eighteenth century.[47] There is also some reason to believe that Jews were trading in or via Falmouth earlier than the 1740s, even though there may not have been any organised communal life there. Susser (1993, pp. 29–30) refers to the pamphlet published in 1685 by Samuel Hayne, a former customs officer, who detailed illegal trading discovered in 1680 between Barbadian Jews and Amsterdam – with well-connected London Jewish merchants acting as intermediaries. The use of English ships, docking at Falmouth, helped to avoid duty on Dutch goods, and suggests that Dutch-Jewish traders had a representative of their own in Falmouth. There were allegations that Jews tried to bribe Hayne, and also bribed the jury at the trial of two London Jews, Gomasero and Losado, but the case went against Hayne and he was removed from office. What became apparent was that Sir Peter Killigrew, a local landowner with considerable influence and contacts in royal and government circles, and a Falmouth merchant, Brian Rogers, were implicated in the activities and that the self-interest of local residents made them sympathetic to the Jewish traders. There is, however, no direct evidence that Jews were resident in Falmouth at this time.

Edit 3. Roth gives a more substantial quotation from this. Susser (1993, p. 30) refers to the presence of what may have been (two) pedlars, given charity by the Borough of St. Ives in 1703. Over a century later, travelling Jews (some scrupulous in their dietary observance) appear in sympathetic newspaper reports in the *West Briton*:

Shrove Tuesday in Penzance

At a petty sessions, held at Penzance, on Monday last, before the borough justices, James Corin, jun, was convicted of a most atrocious assault upon a poor German Jew. . . . It appears that the gentlemen of the mob, at Penzance, fancy they have a pre-scriptive right, on Shrove-Tuesday, to blacken the faces of persons they meet with burnt cork, and to commit other freaks equally indicative of civilisation and good manners; and accordingly, as the Jew was entering the town on that day, with his little

---

[47] cf. Susser (1993, pp. 30–31). An account of the Hayne case can also be found in an article by Edgar Samuel, "The First Fifty Years", in Lipman (1961, pp. 27–44).

travelling box on his back, he was met by Corin, who seized him, and endeavoured to disfigure his countenance in the most approved fashion of the place. 8 March 1839.

– Life in Cornwall in the Mid and Late Nineteenth Century, edited by R.M. Barton (D. Bradford Barton Ltd, Truro, vol 1971, p. 57)

A Travelling Jew

On Monday last an inquest was held at the Union House, St Austell, on the body of Barnard Youngman, a travelling Jew, aged 51 years. It appeared in evidence that he was liberated from Bodmin gaol on Friday last, and that he was seen at various places on the road betwixt that place and St Austell; and all agreed to the weak state he appeared to be in. At one place, a woman made some tea for him, but he refused to take it. He was found lying against the hedge, on Sunday morning, early, about a mile from the town, and was conveyed in a cart to the Union House, where medical aid was procured; but he expired in less than an hour after he was brought in. Verdict, died from cold and exhaustion. 18 July 1845.

– Life in Cornwall in the Mid and Late Nineteenth Century, edited by R.M. Barton (D. Bradford Barton Ltd, Truro, vol 1971, p. 121)

A Travelling Jew and his Box

It is generally thought a thing almost impossible for a Jew to part with his box; but on Wednesday last the town of St. Austell was greatly disturbed by that very occurrence. The Jew, in going from a jeweller's to his lodgings, finding his box heavy, placed it on a waggon that was passing, which carried it so far, and then took it off the waggon into a shop, saying 'Let me leave this box, please, until I call for it.' He then went to his lodgings, and when he was about to leave, at ten p.m., he went for his box where he usually left it, namely the bedroom – but lo! the box was not there. He swore he had put it there, and told the landlord he should expect him to replace it, to the value of 80 pounds. The box was accidentally discovered the next day, at twelve o'clock, in a butcher's shop, but in the meantime all the policemen in the town were in requisition; three or four houses were searched, and the characters of several honest men questioned by the Jew. 20 January 1865".

– Life in Cornwall in the Mid and Late Nineteenth Century, edited by R.M. Barton (D. Bradford Barton Ltd, Truro, vol 1972, p. 125)

The tolerance of, concern for, and equanimity towards Jews is obvious from these extracts.

Edit 4. The date of Moses ben Hayim's death is given as 22 Elul 5590 (14th September 1830) and not 1832 as it appears on his headstone in the Falmouth Jewish cemetery: row 4:3.

Edit 5. The complexity of the Falmouth genealogies is explained in detail by Anthony P. Joseph in his paper, "Jewry of the South-West and some of its Australian Connections" in *TJHSE*, vol 24, 1970–73, pp. 24–37. This important article also contains comprehensive genealogies. By the same author see also, "Genealogy and Jewish History" in *TJHSE*, vol 34, 1994–6, pp. 111–123.

Edit 6. Zender established a remarkable degree of cohesion and inter-dependence, not only amongst the resident Jews of Falmouth, but also between them and their "satellite" members. It would seem that in business and commerce they came to see themselves as not primarily in competition with one another, but as some form of extended economic "co-operative". Falmouth, with a population of less than half that of Penzance, was hardly a self-sustaining economic environment, despite the opportunities provided by the harbour-trade and the packet boats, and so diversification and expansion were essential and was directed mainly at the expanding industrial mining towns inland. Falmouth's economic outposts were established at such places as Redruth, Camborne, Truro, and St. Austell through marriage, as Jacob observes. However, it is not likely that many of these outlying Jews would return to Falmouth every Sabbath in view of the considerable distances involved, although attendance there at the major festivals would have been feasible.

Edit 7. See Chapter 5, pp. 101–103.

Edit 8. The 1861 census for Falmouth gives the synagogue building as "Synagogue House", with several families (a total of 21 people) living there. One of these is that of Joseph Lawrence. (Information provided from the archive of H.C. Faulkner, ref. the history of Falmouth. cf. letter from H.C. Faulkner to Keith Pearce, dated 17th January 1999). The term "Synagogue House" may apply to the synagogue and the cottages that were attached to it at the time, which would be consistent with the number of people recorded in the census as living there. These cottages were still in existence in 1949 and a photograph of them was taken by Alex Jacob in that year. They are also shown on old Ordnance Survey maps prior to 1949, but they have since been demolished, the former synagogue now being detached. Joseph Lawrence may have been a member of the family of the Moses Lazarus Lawrence who traded as a money broker in Church Street, Falmouth around 1823 (*Pigot's Trade Directory*).

Edit 9. See chapter 6 where B.A. Simmons' career is dealt with in detail, together with the "Trafalgar-finger myth". His widespread activities as a mohel (ritual circumciser) are also recorded.

Edit 10. Freemasonry welcomed Jews and assisted in their integration into British society at a time when they were excluded by legal and trade disabilities. Jews who held key positions in their own congregations were often in the same lodges as influential landowners and businessmen. Lemon Hart and the Branwells, who helped the Penzance Jews with the building of their two synagogues, shared a lodge. Lord de Dunstanville (Sir Frances Bassett of Tehidy), who gave the land for the Falmouth cemetery, was also a freemason.

Edit 11. The influence that Methodism, and other non-conformist denominations, may have had in encouraging a culture of tolerance and acceptance towards Jews and Judaism in Cornwall, and also in South Wales, has been under-emphasised. Both were perceived as religions either of the dispossessed or the refugee, and the Old Testament was cherished and read avidly by non-conformist Christians, amongst whom the adoption of Hebrew (Biblical) names was popular. At Tredavoe, a hamlet near Newlyn, outside Penzance, there is an old non-conformist chapel with a Hebrew inscription above the door. Contrary to speculation, there is no evidence that this was ever a Jewish place of worship, and local (unpublished) research by Elizabeth Brock has shown that it is only recorded as a Christian chapel and a schoolroom, with separate entrances for girls and boys.

Edit 12. Although Dr. Adler may not have had disputes brought to him from Penzance, that community, as its minute books show, was certainly a fractious one, and the same Chief Rabbi is mentioned in the books in 1853 and 1859. It is possible that his comments in relation to Falmouth reflected his awareness of the contrast with Penzance.

Edit 13. See chapter 7, pp. 218–221 for a fuller account of the decline of the Falmouth community.

Edit 14. An account of migration and emigration from the Cornish communities can be found in A.P. Joseph (1970–73) and also in Susser (1993, pp. 26–67).

Edit 15. Jacob's figure may be an over-estimate in that Susser (1993, p. 41) gives the number of individuals in Falmouth in 1845 as 50.

Edit 16. Jacob refers earlier to Rabbi Nathan Lipman, but may not have been aware that he was, in fact, appointed as late as 1871.

Editorial postscript: It is not certain that Russell and Symons (who lived with the three Levy sisters) were Jewish: p. 65. (Copies of these wills from Godfrey Simmons' archive.)

The Jews of Penzance 1720–1913

1: Penzance: The Decline and Fall of an Anglo-Jewish Community[1]

Cecil Roth

[original styling retained]

T he greatest shortcoming of Anglo-Jewish historiography at the present time is obvious, but perhaps inevitable. It concerns itself preponderantly – indeed, almost exclusively – with the community of the capital. This is the case particularly with regard to the post-resettlement period, from the middle of the seventeenth century onwards. The praiseworthy attempts which are being made to trace the origins and vicissitudes of some of the more important provincial centres of to-day are not enough to supply this glaring deficiency. For it is insufficiently realised, even by the professional student, that the distribution of Anglo-Jewry, previous to the accession of Queen Victoria, was radically different to that at the present time. A wedding is recorded at Rochford, in Essex, in 1791, and another (with full panoply of a band of music and upwards of 200 guests) at Godmanchester, in Huntingdonshire, in 1810. It is hardly likely that a full quorum for prayers was to be found permanently in either of these places. Properly organised communities existed, however, even earlier than this in several unexpected country centres and small seaport towns. Most of these utterly decayed in the course of the nineteenth century, and, in many cases, no more than the bare recollection now survives. It is hard to believe that synagogues once functioned – and not so very long ago – in places like Boston, Bedford, Ipswich, and Falmouth. Of the King's Lynn community nothing is now left excepting a decayed burial ground and some records in the custody of the United Synagogue. The once thriving *Kahal Kadosh* of Canterbury (certainly founded not later than 1760, and perhaps some time earlier) came to an end in our own day.

---

[1] This first appeared as two articles in the *Jewish Chronicle* in 1933 (May & June Supplements).

The history of the majority of these defunct Jewries will probably never be written, from sheer dearth of material. The position from this point of view of Penzance, the most remote of all, is more fortunate. Its records, from the beginning of the nineteenth century down to the period of final decay, are still extant, (Edit 1) and (thanks to the courtesy and generosity of Mr. George L. Joseph, of Birmingham, a member of one of the last surviving families) have now been entrusted to the present writer. In attempting to reconstruct from these registers the story of Penzance Jewry he feels that he is throwing light, not on that community alone, but on the group which it represents, and on the formative period of provincial Anglo-Jewish life as a whole.

As to the date of the earliest settlement of the Jews in Penzance, it is difficult to speak with certainty. Jews were to be found in Plymouth in the first half of the eighteenth century, and it is highly probable that they settled in the more remote seaport not long after. (Edit 2) (This, at least, is the testimony of that zealous, though apostate, historian, Moses Margoliouth) In any case there is ample evidence that they were there before the century had closed.[2] As to its composition it is not difficult to conjecture. We must imagine one or two shopkeepers, or perhaps ship chandlers, who formed the aristocracy, and a larger number of itinerant pedlars, ranging the countryside during the week but returning to their homes for the Sabbath, who were the proletariat. Such, in fact, was the origin of all, or almost all, of the provincial Anglo-Jewish communities, and of not a few of the Anglo-Jewish aristocracy, of to-day. Entries in the *Gentleman's Magazine* and *The Newgate Calendar* prove that the profession was not always a safe one, more than one of these wandering Jews being waylaid and murdered in some desolate spot. The record of another Cornish Jew, from the neighbouring harbour town of Falmouth, gives a good general idea of life in these remote centres at the period:[3]

---

[2] On the occasion of the death of one of the communal magnates, in 1848, it was stated that he had been a great support to it for nearly half a century. Jacob James Hart, later Consul-General at Dresden was apparently born at Penzance in 1784. Among the founders of the community we may perhaps reckon his father, Jacobs.

[3] Israel Solomon, *Records of My Family*, New York, 1887 (privately printed). With regard to the community of Falmouth, here in question, the following tentative notes may be found useful:

> According to Margoliouth's *History of the Jews of Great Britain*, III, 138–9, the community was formed about 1740, and organised by a certain Moses Alexander, acquiring a synagogue "beautifully situated on Parram Hill." The *Falmouth and Penryn Directory and Guide* of 1864 informs us that the synagogue was established in 1766, and the present structure erected in 1806 in Smithick Hill, "being an excellent and convenient building for the performance of their ancient religious worship." Prior to this there was a small synagogue situated in a courtilage named

Bernard Beer . . . a soap boiler, wished to obtain employment at the London manufacturers, but the Shabas prevented his obtaining any employment unless he sacrificed his religious scruples, which he could not do, and he was obliged, against his wishes, to become a peddler of small wares for a sustenance. He struggled on until he arrived at Falmouth; there he was hospitably received by Zender Falmouth, whose real name was Henry Moses, but in those days any Jew settling down within a town and having a certain respectability amongst Jews had the name of the town attached to his first name. Zender kept a stock of buckles, small cutlery, jewellery and watches to supply the hawkers, and gave credit to young men on certain conditions, and, where it was necessary, advanced money to obtain the hawker's licence. The conditions were to return every Friday early enough to form one of the *Minyan*, and on Sunday morning square up the accounts by paying over what money he had and receive fresh goods on credit. But when the hawker's licence was procured Zender insisted that his name should be quite a Jewish name, and, instead of the name Bernard Beer, his name was inscribed Barnet Levy, and his family ever after became Levy instead of Beer . . .

In that time, down to 1830, inns where Jewish travellers rested were to be found in all the roads and towns of England. . . . The landlord then, especially to gain their custom, kept a cupboard or closet containing cooking utensils entirely for their use, so that they might eat *kosher*. The landlord kept the cupboard locked and guarded the key on his own person, and when a Jew used the utensils he saw to the cleaning of them, and before putting them away he wrote with chalk within the bottom of the utensil his name, day of the month and year, with the portion from the law read on the Sabbath of that week – all in Hebrew. Some of these hotels were in the centre of populated districts, and the pedlars

---

Hamblyn's Court (subsequently Dunstan's Court) on the site of the present gasworks. A burial ground, adjacent to the Congregational ground, midway between Falmouth and Penzance, was presented to the community by Lord Dunstanville. In 1851 the community numbered about twenty families, who were occupied as merchants or shopkeepers, and were "remarkable for their sympathy with their poorer brethren." The mainstay in the first half of the nineteenth century was Samuel Jacob, a son-in-law of Zender Falmouth, (see postscript p. 99) who figures so prominently in Israel Solomon's *Reminiscences*. On his death, in 1852, his son took over his position, being succeeded in turn by one of his sons. After 1880 the community fell into complete decadence. The synagogue – the outside of which still bears a Hebrew inscription – is now [i.e in 1933] used as a carpenter's shop. A Scroll of the Law, together with an antique pair of silver bells [at present on exhibition at the Jewish Museum], was transferred to the Hampstead Synagogue, London, and other of the appurtenances to the convict prison at Parkhurst, Isle of Wight. An early member of the Falmouth community appears to have been Isaac Polack, of the adjacent township of Penryn, letters of administration over whose property were granted to his daughter in 1794.

going the rounds of the district would congregate on a Friday evening at these hotels and stay over Saturday, and on Sunday they trudged again on their laborious rounds. They generally formed a club, and one of the number, who was licensed by the rabbi to slaughter animals, was paid by the club for one day's loss of profit from his business to get to the hotel on Friday early enough to kill animal or poultry, purchase fish, etc., and either cook or superintend it that it should be quite *kosher* by the time the brotherhood came there and ushered in the Sabbath, gladly singing hymns, and after a copious but frugal repast some Hebrew literature or tales of the past and present were related by one or the other . . .

Before the first decade of the nineteenth century had closed, the community of Penzance had increased sufficiently to set about the construction of a synagogue building (hitherto, presumably, they had worshipped in a private house, or in temporary accommodation). (Edit 3) The edifice, situated in New Street, was "very handsome," and a credit to all concerned, according to Margoliouth's testimony. To signalise the event they purchased an account book at the cost of two shillings and sixpence, and from this date – 1807 – the records commence. The ground rental of the synagogue appears to have been six guineas, while the amount outstanding for the construction of the new edifice (obviously plain and austere to a degree) was some £120. The community owned also a burial ground, the rent of which was one guinea per annum (afterwards increased – no doubt in consequence of extensions – to three guineas). (Edit 4) The synagogal furniture does not seem to have been very copious, for the congregation as such owned only one scroll of the law, with its appurtenances, and a curtain for the Ark. The congregational library consisted apparently of a copy of the *Midrash Rabbah*. This attenuated supply could, however, be supplemented, when occasion arose, from private sources. (Edit 5)

The enterprise of the community in erecting its synagogue is all the more striking in view of the fact that it comprised at this period no more than six householders, though there must be added to this number in all probability a few poor pedlars and others. The communal Maecenas was Asher Laemle ben Eleazar, known as Lemon Hart, a distiller, subsequently to become one of the largest spirits merchants in the country, who for many years held the contract for supplying the British Navy with rum, that all-important accessory of Nelson's victories.[4] His

---

[4] Lemon Hart's products are still marketed under his name. The firm, established in 1804, was absorbed by Dingwall, Portal & Co (now Portal, Dingwall & Norris) in 1878. [NB – see the editors' note 6 at the end of this chapter].

family had already been established at Penzance for some time; (Edit 6) his father, Lazarus Hart, who had died in 1803 at the age of 64, and his grandfather, "Rabbi" Abraham Hart, who had passed away in 1784,[5] and had enjoyed some reputation as a scholar, both having apparently been local residents. Lemon Hart was now perpetual *Parnass* (Warden). He had contributed £20 to the building fund, and his annual subscription was set down at 10 guineas. Next to him in prominence was his brother-in-law, Hayim b. Benjamin, known as Hyman Woolf, the perpetual treasurer. The other members were the latter's son Lemon Woolf, Elias Magnus, Henry Ralph, (Edit 7) and L. Jacobs. In addition, the *Parnass* of the Bristol community and Jacob Emden, of the same place, had given financial assistance in the work of the construction.

The opening of the new Synagogue was signalised by the drawing up of a code of regulations. Considering the prevailing monetary straits it is not surprising that these were largely concerned with financial matters. It was enacted that any person called to the Reading of the Law on Sabbaths or Festivals should offer at least sixpence to the building fund and as much more to the congregation (on other occasions, another penny offering would be deemed sufficient). Every Sabbath morning in the summer, service was to begin at 8 o'clock, and in winter at 8.30. If any member failed to attend service, or arrived late without proper excuse, he was to pay threepence. On the occasion of a marriage or circumcision, or of the prayers on the anniversary of the death of a parent (*Jahrzeit*), all members must help to make up the necessary quorum of ten, under penalty of a fine of half a guinea. (Edit 8)

The early members originated exclusively, or almost exclusively, from Poland. (Edit 9) The Polish rite of prayers, we are informed, had been in use in the congregation "from its earliest days." It is, indeed, doubtful whether more than one or two were of native birth. All could sign their names in Hebrew; one or two could not, apparently, write English. Some of the surnames appear to have been assumed at very short notice. Solomon Johnson, a new member in 1825, signs himself "Johson"; the brothers Davidson, at the same period, were unable to get nearer than "Dawidson"; while another prominent member wavers between Henry David, Henry Levin and Henry Lavin. The regulations of 1807 were composed as a matter of course in Yiddish. Subsequently the accounts were kept in the vernacular, interspersed with one or two Hebrew words – which, as time went on, came to be

---

[5] I am indebted for this information, as for other points embodied in this paper, to Sir Thomas Colyer Fergusson. It is my pleasant duty to express my thanks also to Mr. Wilfred Samuel for many fruitful suggestions.

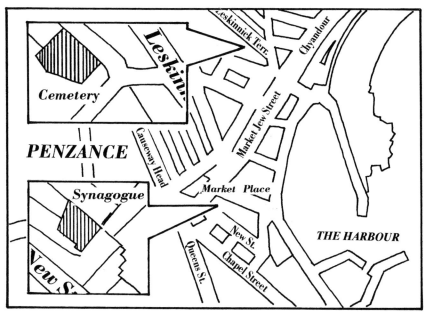

Penzance: the sites of the Synagogue and the Jewish cemetery.

Map by Bill Smith

phenomenally mis-spelled. Formal contracts or similar arrangements continued to be drawn up in Hebrew or in Yiddish. (Edit 10)

The congregational staff was necessarily economical to a degree. Though at one prosperous interlude we read of a Beadle, at a salary of a few pence weekly, it was generally a one-man position, and the one man had perforce to see to many matters.[6] The main requirement was a reader and *shochet*; but activities extended, in fact, far beyond this. An agreement of 1817 lays down the functions of the communal factotum (the *Rav*, or *Rebbe*, as they called him) in detail. He was to slaughter animals for food whenever any of his employers should require it; to porge the meat (attending at the market twice weekly for a couple of hours for this purpose, as we learn from another record); to instruct the children belonging to the congregation in Hebrew and cognate subjects; to supervise the cleaning of the Synagogue; to conduct Divine service; to read the Law; to prepare the Scrolls for the next day, on the eve of Sabbaths and Festivals; to bind the Palm Branches on the Feast of Tabernacles; and to procure the willow twigs on *Hosanna Rabba*. In addition, according to the original regulations, he was to collect week by week all offerings made by members. He had to recite the *Megilla* on Purim, and to supervise the preparation of the flour on Passover. Finally, every Sabbath he was to conduct a lesson for adults in the forenoon. In return for all this, he enjoyed the princely salary of some £40, or a little less, per annum.

It is not surprising, under such circumstances, that there was a constant *va et vient* of incumbents, few of whom seem to have exceeded, or even completed, the term of two years for which they were engaged. We read in rapid succession of R. Moses and R. Feivel and R. Selig and R. Aaron and R. Moses Levi and R. Hirsch and Hart Symons and Abraham Joseph. One or two (like the last named, a German by birth) settled down in Penzance and became members of the Community, after their period of office was ended. The most scholarly of all (to judge from the elegant Hebrew contract which he drew up, in 1817) was Moses, son of Rabbi Judah Leib, *Dayyan* of Frankfort-on-Main. The R. Feivel mentioned above is perhaps to be identified with Philip Samuel, son of the Secretary of the Warsaw Community, who set up in business at Vilna as a silk merchant and inexpressibly scandalised his contemporaries by refusing to take a *minyan* with him when he went to Danzig on business. He was a well-known figure in Moscow, at a time

---

[6] Editorial note: The minute books and accounts confirm Roth's point in that (apart from the isolated example of the beadle) there were no salaries drawn or paid to any member of the congregation except the incumbent rabbi in relation to his various duties, or to meet routine bills and re-imburse occasional expenses.

when a house in which a Jew had set foot would be scrubbed out with holy water. Ruined through the cracking of the ice while he was crossing a frozen river with his property, he made his way to England, where Solomon Hirschell, then Chief Rabbi, secured him his appointment at Penzance. Here he dabbled in business, being employed by Lyon Joseph, of Falmouth, to purchase gold for Government use, and then settled at Saint Austell as jeweller with a fellow countryman. Ultimately, he went to Lisbon, being one of the creators of the Jewish Community of that city and the first English Jew to enter into touch with the romantic remnant of the Marranos.[7] Hardly less extraordinary was a certain Italian Jew – Elhanan Joseph Mortara (apparently a son of Hayim Solomon Levi Mortara, Rabbi of Verona) – who officiated at Penzance in 1813–1814. What strange vicissitude, what curious eddy, can have thrown him up in this remote backwater, in such incongruous surroundings? It is a problem the solution of which we are never likely to know. (Edit 12)

One is apt to regard the period under consideration as a halcyon age, when life was easy and everything was cheap. This was not so in all respects. It was before the days of railways, and conveyance proved extraordinarily expensive for a Community so distant as Penzance. Even correspondence was a costly item. When a new *shochet* was engaged, his journey from London by stage wagon took upwards of a week, and his expenses might be as much as £6 – something like one-sixth of his annual salary. The citron for Tabernacles cost one guinea, but its transmission, by express, came to 8s 7d, with a shilling more for postage. Similarly, the carriage on a new slaughterer's knife, costing only 13s, totalled no less than 7s 9d.

Needless to say, the Community, though small, was punctilious in its attachment to tradition. Hyman Woolf had a *Mikva* in his private house, the use of which he allowed to the congregation in return for a consideration of two guineas yearly (subsequently, it seems, increased to twice that amount). We have seen how the members retained the ancestral devotion to study, arranging a weekly lesson each Sabbath for the adults, as well as elementary instruction for the children. There were special arrangements for the traditional watch night of "learning" on the eve of Pentecost and of *Hosanna Rabba*. The communal factotum received a special fee for his exertions on these occasions, and provision was made out of the congregation funds for spirits and refreshments to enliven the proceedings.

The problem of the poor is always with Jewry, and, notwithstanding the distance, persons in need of assistance managed to penetrate even to

---

[7] Israel Solomon, op. cit.

Penzance. Charitable donations appear to have taken up quite a considerable proportion of the slender budget of the Community. According to the original regulations of 1807, the Treasurer was empowered to disburse amounts not exceeding half a crown on deserving cases, without consulting the Warden. The members of the Community took it in turn to give a meal to itinerant mendicants – as well as, on occasion, to the Rabbi. On October 1st, 1809, the five householders solemnly bound themselves in writing to allow the sum of seven shillings each week out of their private pockets to a certain old man, R. Leb Hanau, on condition that he should be "at Penzance every Night if Possible to prevent any Accident happening to him from travelling to distant Places." Like most infirm paupers, R. Leb showed considerable power of resistance, for he survived until 1817, when his burial cost the Community £2 13s. 5d. (Edit 13) In 1821 we find a reference to the expenditure entailed in the release of one Godfrey from prison.

The congregation was, then, something more than an institution for the purpose of maintaining a Synagogue. It had a corporate life of its own. New members had to submit themselves to election and to pay a fee on entry. In addition to this there was, of course, the annual subscription, the amount of which would not be considered negligible even to-day. A vote took place on every fresh name; and sometimes (as we shall see) there were expulsions, as well as admittances. A tell-tale motion was passed in 1826 to the effect that "any Member that shall devulge (sic) or disclose any of the proceedings this day or in the future, shall be fined 10s.6d."

Penzance naturally served as the centre for the religious life of isolated Jews living in the neighbourhood, for there was no other Community nearer than Falmouth, the condition of which was no doubt very similar in every respect. There were Jews at Truro at this period. On one occasion, indeed, during an interregnum in the office of Shochet, a certain R. Liepman was imported thence to serve the congregation temporarily; (Edit 14) while Mr. Hymans and Mr. Simmons, of the same place, together with the brothers Levy, contributed to the congregational funds over a considerable period. The first-named, with E. Cohen, of Redruth, was subsequently admitted full membership. Other scattered individuals who attached themselves to the Community included Isaac Joseph, of Redruth; Jacob Jacobs, of Camborne; Samuel Jacobs of Hayle; and F. Michael of Swansea.[8] An even more isolated

---

[8] Editorial note: This would have been F. Michael, a relative of Lemon Hart's first wife Letitia (or Letty) Michael of Swansea. F. Michael is mentioned in the Penzance minute books as contributing to the cost of rebuilding the synagogue in 1808. Letitia is mentioned in a letter from Geoffrey H. White to Cecil Roth, dated 25th February 1955, now in the Roth Collection, Leeds. Courtesy of Evelyn Friedlander's research.

subscriber was Samuel Jacobs, of Scilly. In 1815 a donation of £10 was received from Mr. Joseph Barrow, of Jamaica.

The composition of the Community was meanwhile changing. In 1811, Mr. Lemon Hart removed to London, whence he continued in his laudable occupation of supplying the British blue-jackets with rum. The blow to the Community was tempered by the fact that, in lieu of his annual contribution of twenty guineas, he agreed to make himself responsible for the payment of the rent of the Synagogue and burial ground. At the same time, he left for the use of the Synagogue (not as a gift) certain objects of his which had been deposited in it, including a Scroll of the Law with silver pointer, a *Megilla* and a *Shophar*. (The year previous, he had made over to it another Scroll which had belonged to the late Lazarus Solomon, his father-in-law, together with a pointer, six candlesticks, two chandeliers, and a curtain.) In return for this, the congregation bound itself to mention the names of his father and grandfather in its periodical Commemoration Services. Lemon Hart's position as Life Warden was henceforth to be occupied by Hyman Woolf, while Elias Magnus became *Gabbai*. This loss was compensated, numerically at least, by the admission of a number of new members – three in 1813, one in 1817, one in 1820, two in 1825, two in 1828, and so on. This was without counting a sprinkling who hired seats without assuming full membership. On the other hand, Elias Magnus "withdrew" from the congregation in 1819, without any cause, and leaving his accounts unpaid, to the great disgust of his fellow members, who solemnly decided that he should "no longer be considered to have any right or title to this Congregation whatsoever." Similar treatment was meted out in 1821 to Aaron Selig (probably the former Shochet), who not only resigned from the congregation without paying his dues, but even "attempted to make great disturbance amongst them." He seems to have been reinstated, but embroiled himself again with his fellow congregants four years later, and once more in 1829. Notwithstanding disturbances of this sort, the Community prospered. In 1811 it had been able to have the burial ground surrounded by a wall.[9] (Edit 15) In 1828 it could afford the extravagance of purchasing from Mr. Ansell, of London, a new Scroll of the Law, at the cost of £12, bringing the number in its possession up to at least three. In 1808 not half a dozen names had figured in the congregational accounts. Twenty years later,

---

[9] The burial ground was in existence at least from 1803, when Lemon Hart's first wife was buried there. Mr. Charles H. Benn, the librarian of the Penzance Public Library writes to me: "The cemetery is small and situated in a thickly populated part of Penzance. It contains about fifty graves. The oldest tombstone that I could read was of the year 5599 A.D. 1839. There are some older stones, but I could not decipher them."

the number had doubled. At the beginning of the period the annual balance sheet oscillated between £30 and £35; at the end it stood at £52.

The most distinguished person whose name is associated with the Penzance Community in this generation is in all probability Solomon (in Hebrew, Isaac) Ezekiel. He was a son of Ezekiel Abraham Ezekiel (1757–1806), the artist, who engraved various portraits by Opie, Reynolds and others, and was also known as a miniature painter and scientific optician. The latter was a native of Exeter, where he was born in 1757 and died in 1806. His son, Solomon Ezekiel (born at Newton Abbot on 7th June 1781), transferred himself to Penzance. In 1817 we find him admitted as a member of the Community on paying (in two instalments!) entrance money to the amount of one guinea, his membership fee being fixed at five guineas each year. After a year or two his name disappears from the books – perhaps by reason of temporary absence from the town. But, though in very humble circumstances (he was a plumber by profession), the place which he subsequently occupied in the Community was unique. In 1820, when the sentimental conversionist movement was at its height, the Society for the Promotion of Christianity amongst the Jews proposed to establish a branch in Penzance. Ezekiel took up the cudgels on behalf of his people, writing a trenchant letter to Sir Rose Price, Bart., a local squire, who had approached Lemon Woolf on the subject. Whether this was responsible or not, the fact remains that the Baronet withdrew his support, and the proposal was abandoned. This episode was possibly the reason for the establishment of *The Penzance Hebrew Society for Promoting the Diffusion of Religious Knowledge*. Before this body, Solomon Ezekiel delivered two series of lectures, on the life of Abraham and Isaac, which were subsequently published (Penzance and London, 1844–7). He lived for a quarter of a century after this, dying in March, 1867, at the age of eighty-six. (Edit 16) Another local defender of Judaism was H. Simmonds, who in 1824 had published at Penzance *A Letter to G.V. le Grice concerning some words used in his Sermon about the Jews.*

An enigmatic character makes his appearance in the records in 1825. On August 26th of that year a certain Dr. John Messina wrote to "Mr. L. Woolf and the Instituted Members of the Penzance Synagogue" in the following terms: – "Gentlemen, – I beg your acceptance of a Cocked Hat, Gown, and Cuffs (?) as a Donation, and if you permit them to be worn at all times of Public Devotion you will oblige the donor." Nothing in all this, or in the name, indicates that the latter was a Jew. But, a little over a week later, we find the person in question admitted as a full member of the congregation, on the payment of one guinea entrance money and a seat rental of four guineas

79

per annum. In the course of the next year his voluntary offerings amounted to £1. 7s. Not that he allowed religion to interfere with business, since he charged the congregation when he attended upon the so-called *"Rebbe"* during an illness. After little more than a year, however, on November 30th, 1826, Dr John Messina left the town and his name disappears from the books. An Italian Jew? A belated Marrano? A Proselyte? It is now too late to say. But a Dr Messina, formerly physician to the Emperor Napoleon I, makes his appearance in Portsmouth almost immediately afterwards, and it is hardly to be doubted that he is identical with the person here in question.

The earliest minute and account book, from which the foregoing information has in the main been derived, closes with the end of the third decade of the nineteenth century. Thereafter there is a blank for fourteen years. The record is resumed in 1843 in the first of a couple of minute books which chronicle the subsequent history of the community till its final decay. The gap is short. The atmosphere is by now, however, entirely different. In the brief interval the community has become Anglicised. The minutes are kept regularly and in English as pure as the writer could achieve. Penzance is no longer isolated. The era of railways has begun. Penny postage is already introduced. The community has a banking account. We read before long of bye-laws, and the Board of Deputies, and Jewish emancipation, and the Chief Rabbi, and advertisements, and *The Jewish Chronicle*.

In its general condition, the community seems to have been in 1843 in very much the same condition as we left it in 1829. There are now about ten full resident members. Lemon Woolf, son of Hyman Woolf, is still President. Abraham Joseph is succeeded in the records by Henry Joseph, presumably his son, now secretary and treasurer. New names are those of Hyman Lazarus, Alexander Levin, Samuel Harris, Moses Hart Harris, Samuel Oppenheim and Moses Woolf – presumably the President's brother. The names of one or two other residents who were not full members of the community also figure from time to time. In addition, there are still some outlying members, such as H. Harris, of Truro (a native, as it happens, of Penzance), who was elected to honorary membership in one of the earliest minutes recorded in the volume: Harris Bernstein, of Dowlais (South Wales), and – Friedman, of Aberdare (1869). In 1856 Solomon Teacher, long a member of the congregation, and Joseph Barnet – both of St Ives – were buried locally. (Edit 17) During the temporary indisposition of the Minister-*Shochet* in 1846, and again in 1848, Joseph Rintel, of Falmouth, lent his services in a voluntary capacity – *vice versa*, in 1864, meat was supplied from Penzance to Samuel Jacob, of Falmouth, one of the last surviving Jews of that place. From the financial point of view, the community is in a comparatively flourishing condition. In the first year its accounts show a credit balance of upwards of £15. An outstanding token of prosperity is found in 1845, when the burial ground, hitherto held on lease, was purchased for £50. It is refreshing to note that a certain Dr. Barham, of Exeter, ceded to the congregation without charge his rights in a contiguous strip which they required.

Congregational meetings at this period are held quarterly, with special meetings interspersed at liberal intervals. Presence is still enforced by fine, in cases where no reasonable ground for absence can be shown. Notwithstanding the inevitable paucity of attendance, the proceedings are not always humdrum, for we read on one occasion, in 1846, that the meeting had to be adjourned because of the unruliness of Mr. Oppenheim. (Edit 18) Members of certain of the families formerly associated with Penzance still retain their sentimental attachment to the congregation. There was a touching proof of this fact a little later in the same year, when permission was given for the body of Mr. Jacob James Hart, late Her Britannic Majesty's Consul-General for the Kingdom of Saxony, to be interred in the "House of Life".[10] (Edit 19) Local Jewry contributed generously within its means to all Jewish causes – for example, in 1848 for the distressed Jews of Tiberias; in 1852 for the Smyrna Schools; in 1854 for the poor of Jerusalem (there being on this occasion nineteen contributors, including women); in 1861 for Syria; in 1869 for Russia and Poland; in 1874 for the Bengal Famine Relief Fund; and in 1875 (on which occasion a few Gentile fellow-townsmen were glad to associate themselves with the subscription) to the Sir Moses Montefiore Testimonial Fund. The most pressing public question in those days was, of course, Jewish Parliamentary Emancipation – a matter in which a local non-Jew, Mr. Colenso, who secured numerous signatures for a petition, interested himself wholeheartedly. A series of resolutions passed at a public meeting of the congregation, held on January 23rd, 1848, gives an idea of how this problem reacted upon an outlying Jewish community:

> At a public meeting of the congregation held this day, January 23rd, 5608, for the purpose of petitioning Parliament for the Removal of the Jewish Disabilities, Mr. H. Levin in the Chair, the following Resolutions were unanimously agreed to:-

---

[10] A good deal of information regarding this worthy, is to be found in Israel Solomon's *Reminiscences*. He was a nephew of Lemon Hart, whose surname he adopted instead of that of Jacobs, which he had previously borne, and whom he assisted in business. In consequence of supplying the clubs with wine, he became friendly with Lord Palmerston, his appointment in the Consular service being due to this fact.

1st. – Proposed by Mr. H. Joseph, and seconded by Mr. B. A. Simmons, that Petitions be presented to both Houses of Parliament in favour of the measure for the Removal of Jewish Disabilities, and signed by the Wardens of the Congregation on their behalf.

2nd. – Proposed by Mr. M.B. Simmons, and seconded by Mr. B. Selig, that the Petition to the House of Lords be sent to the Secretary of the Board of Deputies of British Jews for their disposal and the Petition to the House of Commons to E.W.W. Pendarves, Esq., M.P., to be presented by him.

3rd. – Proposed by Mr. B. Selig, and seconded by Mr. M. Woolf, that a Memorial be drawn up and forwarded to the Member of Parliament presenting the Petition, soliciting his support and interest.

4th. – Proposed by Mr. M.B. Simmons, and seconded by Mr. H. Joseph, that in consequence of Mr. Harris, of Truro, having forwarded to his son in this Town Petitions for the Removal of the Jewish Disabilities to be signed by the Christians which precluded the possibility of this Congregation getting up one, a letter be written to him requesting the favour of his allowing the said Petition (now in the hands of his son) to remain with the Congregation for presentation.

5th. – Proposed by Mr. S. Ezekiel, and seconded by Mr. I. Oppenheim, that the thanks of this Meeting is due to our Christian Brethren of Penzance in having so readily and nobly supported the Petitions for the Removal of the Jewish Disabilities, being the last vestige of Religious Intolerance now remaining on the Statute Book of this free and enlightened nation.

Proposed by Mr. B.A. Simmons, and seconded by Mr. S. Ezekiel a vote of thanks to the Chairman for his able conduct in the Chair, after which the meeting terminated.

The congregation is under the ultimate spiritual direction of the Chief Rabbi, in London. Towards the Chief Rabbi's stipend an annual contribution of £5 was made. No doubt, by virtue of this, the Penzance community took part in the election which followed the death of Rabbi Solomon Hirschell, resulting in the appointment of Dr. N.M. Adler. The new Chief Rabbi's authority was effective even in this remote spot. He was referred to when there was any question of appointing or dismissing a minister, and when, in 1847, he issued his *Laws and Regulations for All the Hebrew Synagogues of the British Empire*, the new code was immediately taken into consideration. Even earlier, one reforming member had proposed the discontinuance of the sale of synagogal honours, for the sake of decorum. The pecuniary yoke of the Rabbinate appears, however, to have become irksome, for in 1848, from motives of economy, the contribution to the Chief Rabbi's Fund was discontinued.

For the same reason, probably, the invitation to send a representative to the Board of Deputies of British Jews, received in 1853, was rejected, though a little later in the same year a Mr. Samuel Solomon, of Poland Street, London, was elected by the congregation to that honour. He does not appear to have served for long, if at all, and another application was received, and refused, in 1882. Small though the community was, we find a Benevolent Society in connection with it, as well as the Society for Promoting the Diffusion of Religious Knowledge. The general condition and organisation are reflected in a set of bye-laws under ninety-five heads, and filling the whole of a separate register, drawn up and approved in 1844. (Edit 20)

The majority of the congregational business naturally revolved, as always, about the person of the Minister. Over a long period of years, this was a certain B.A. Simmons, whose career appears to have been a chequered one.[11] (Edit 21) In 1846 and 1848 he was incapacitated from work by sickness. A little later the financial condition of the Community was so parlous that his wages were reduced. His temper now grew worse, and one day, in 1852, he publicly insulted a *senior* member. In consequence he had to resign, a letter being written to the Chief Rabbi to explain the circumstances. However, he did not leave the town; and, when a vacancy was declared, he applied for the post again. Strangely enough, he was re-elected, on condition that he behaved himself in future and "did away with his vow" rashly made when he resigned. Controversy still continued to such an extent that his dismissal was again discussed shortly after. He anticipated this by a second resignation. In the following year, 1854, he was replaced by a certain Mr. Solomon Cohen, at a salary of 14s. weekly. In 1857 he was re-engaged. Two years later, however, we find him registered as an ordinary member, and his former post occupied by a certain Hyman Greenburgh; a very good

---

[11] B.A. (Barnett) Simmons, or Abraham Issachar b. Asher, was sent down from London as *shochet* in 1811, with a recommendation from the "High Priest" (!) Solomon Hirschell. He had been engaged by the late Warden, Lemon Hart, who ventured to hope that the community would "behave to him properly, for you may rest assured those articles are very scarce in this Market." He seems to have continued in office intermittently for upwards of forty years. He was a man of some learning and possibly identical with the H. Simmons mentioned above, author of *A Letter to G.V. le Grice*. [Editorial note: H. Simmons was not related to B.A. Simmons]. A large quantity of his papers (upon which these details are based) are in the possession of his descendant, Mr. J.S.C. Simmons of Birmingham, who kindly communicated them to me after the first part of this article was published. These include: (i) a register of circumcisions performed in Penzance, Truro, and Falmouth, 1821–1847; (ii) Order of Service on the Rededication of the Penzance Synagogue on Friday, 12th Shebat, 1823; (iii) Sermon preached on death of George IV, in 1830.

type, apparently, voluntarily assuming the functions of Secretary and delivering a discourse in the Synagogue on the Sabbath preceding the Passover of 1859. His tenure of office was made memorable by the fact that a clerical hat was presented for his use to make the services more dignified. He was succeeded in turn by A. Lüpschütz (1861) and – Spero (1863). One Friday the latter went off to Plymouth without giving notice – conduct, as his employers informed him, "not becoming a Revd." In consequence, he was severely reprimanded and his salary reduced. Nevertheless, he appears to have retained his patience and his office for a long period. The next incumbent of the office of whom we have any particulars is Mr. Isaac Bischofswerder. The latter was the father of a numerous family – a fortunate circumstance which gave the Community a new lease of life. (Edit 22)

For it was by now obvious that Penzance Jewry was far advanced in decay. As early as in 1848 the complaint had been made that the "congregation had sustained the loss of several members." The balance in the hand of the Treasurer at the end of every year was reduced to derisory sums, not exceeding a few shillings at the best, though there was a welcome legacy of £50 in 1869 under the will of a Mr. Gorfunkle, of Liverpool, and another in 1864 from Mrs. George Goodman, of New Bridge, Wales. Periodically the scale of contributions had to be increased in order to meet expenditure; and from 1855 the collection was made (as at the very beginning) in weekly instalments. The death of a member, or his removal to another town, was a real disaster. In 1848 the number of signatories to the minutes had been ten. In the following year it was reduced to seven. By 1854 the effective membership was only five. Henceforth quarterly meetings were considered superfluous, and it was decided that a half-yearly meeting would be sufficient. The business transacted became more and more formal, consisting in little more than approving the accounts.

In 1850, the President of the Community, M.H. Harris, had left Penzance. Henry Joseph was elected in his place; and, in the succeeding period, he and Henry Levin alternated in the presidency, excepting for brief periods when the office was filled by B.A. Selig and I. Oppenheim. There was a premonition of the end in 1865, when it was found necessary to hire a person to come from Plymouth to make *Minyan* over the Holydays. However, the advent of Mr. Bischofswerder as Minister, with his brood of sons, saved the situation. He remained in office for a long period, towards the close of which his own children appear to have begun to make a position for themselves in the town and in the Community.

In 1881, David Bischofswerder was elected a member and in successive years a couple of his brothers entered into enjoyment of the same honour. In 1886, the brothers Bischofswerder comprised two out of a total membership of five, the others being I. Oppenheim, I. Levin, and B.H. Joseph, who, incidentally, was now resident at Birmingham. In the following year David Bischofswerder was elected President. A little later a meeting was held, at which only one person attended in addition to himself and his two brothers. At this period their father resigned his position by reason of ill-health. He was succeeded in turn by I. Rubinstein, formerly of Northampton and subsequently of Cardiff (1886), and Michael Lancrour (1887). (Edit 23)

By this time it must have been plain that the existence of the congregation was nearing its close. (Edit 24) In 1890 it was decided that, if no *Minyan* should have presented itself in Synagogue on Sabbath morning by 9.40, the service was to be continued without any reading from the Scroll. This was a clear portent. For the next couple of years the business meetings of the congregation (now annual) continued to take place regularly. On March 7th, 1892, three of the Bischofswerder family came together with I. Oppenheim and B.H. Joseph (on a visit to his sisters in Penzance) to contract formal business. There was a deficit of upwards of £6 on the year's budget. Possibly in that year the dwindling congregation suffered some further loss by death, and it did not seem worth while to summon another meeting. In any case, this is the last minute on record, though there was a final burst of gaiety four months later, when the last local Jewish wedding took place.[12] (Edit 25)

In the course of the next few years the last of the congregation died or else transferred themselves elsewhere. The services of the Minister were discontinued. (Edit 26) No one now remained excepting Mr. Morris Bischofswerder, a son of the former officiant. On the High Festivals he would open the Synagogue and recite his prayers in melancholy solitude. At last, in 1913, he too left the town. The Synagogue, constructed in a burst of eager enthusiasm just over a century before, was sold and became a Plymouth Brethren Meeting House. The fittings were removed and scattered. (Edit 27) All that is left to-day is the burial ground at the back of Leskinnick Terrace (the last interment in which took place in 1911), (Edit 28) with its array of tombstones, inscribed in strange Oriental characters. The Holy Congregation of Penzance had been long a-dying, but its decay is now complete.

---

[12] According to the marriage register, extending from June 6th, 1838, in the custody of the Board of Deputies of British Jews, which at present has charge also of the burial ground. An "Omer" Calendar, presented to the Penzance Congregation by the first Lord Swaythling, was recently deposited in the Western Synagogue, Hull.

2: The Penzance Community Records

Godfrey Simmons and Keith Pearce

The Records of the Penzance congregation consist of:

i   Early records: the 1768 conveyance document for the first synagogue, which was lost after 1983; and the cemetery lease.

ii The Tikkunim, or regulations (1808) in Yiddish. (Hebrew plural, *Takkanot*).

iii 1808–29: minutes and bi-annual accounts in Yiddish and English, including the 1808 synagogue conveyance and the various cemetery leases (up to 1844).

iv 1829–43: no records, except for one item of accounts in March 1830.

v   1843–1892: minute books in English and a separate register of revised regulations (1844).

The Tikkunim (1808), summarised on the next page, show a community anxious to order itself along strict lines. Its isolation may have intensified and influenced this concern, and in 1844 a total of 95 revised regulations were drawn up for the benefit of only 11 full members. Susser (1993, p. 169) gives the date incorrectly as 1884. However, he usefully contrasts the number of Penzance regulations with those smaller regulations which governed the larger communities of Plymouth and Exeter. Plymouth had 64 regulations from 1779, and Exeter had 48 in 1823, although both were eventually revised. This over-bureaucratic ethos may well have contributed to the tensions and fractiousness which came to characterise the congregation's meetings, as reflected in the minute books. Penzance followed other congregations at that time in its oligarchic structure which distinguished between *Baalei Batim* (full members who had *Hezkat HaKehillah*: full and permanent rights and privileges), *Toshavim* (seatholders with a one year rental: of which Penzance had none), and *Orchim* (strangers or guests, even though they may have been residents of the town), 1845.

This clearly suggests that the congregation was effectively run and owned by an exclusive, and presumably, relatively affluent elite. It was the only community at that time to be without seatholders (Falmouth had three, Exeter had eight, and Plymouth had 33).

The Penzance Tikkunim: A Summary Translation from the Yiddish

The scroll of the Law and the holy objects belong to the Holy Congregation of Penzance.

Obligation on those called up to the reading of the Law to make a donation to the synagogue.

Obligation of every householder to attend synagogue at stated times.

Rabbi's obligation to collect donations, and when they are to be collected.

Obligation of congregation to make donation at the time of Yahrzeit (anniversary of a death), and to come to prayers or to pay a fine of half a guinea.

Whole congregation obliged to attend for personal celebrations (weddings, circumcision, bar Mitzvah) or pay a fine of half a guinea.

Rabbi obliged to study before noon each day with the Gabbai (treasurer).

Rabbi is entitled receive half a crown as part of his salary: before reading Megillah (the Scroll of Esther read at the Feast of Purim, but also a portion of the Mishnah, or Oral Tradition, which relates to holy objects), and at Passover, and after a woman gives birth.

The Hatan Torah (the last man called to read the Torah, or law, at the end of the annual cycle of reading) and the Hatan Bereishith (the first man called to begin the reading of the first section of the new cycle) must donate (at Simchas Torah, the festival of "Rejoicing in the Law") 2 shillings to charity and half crown to the Rabbi.

On the eve of Shavuot (the festival of Weeks) and Hoshana Raba (during the festival of Tabernacles) congregants must come to study.

The Parnas (president of the synagogue: Hayim Benjamin Woolf, president for life) authorises donations for charity.

The congregation is obliged to give guests or visitors who come to it, food and drink, and named householders must give the guest 2 shillings if he comes on a Friday (the eve of Sabbath: to make up minyan).

(Some of these rules may have been added after 1808, because Hayyim (Hyman) Woolf did not, according to Roth, become president until Lemon Hart's departure for London in 1811.)

The names of householders each of which is obliged to make an annual payment:

President: Asher Laemle ben Eliezer (Lemon Hart)	20 pounds
Treasurer: Hayim ben Benjamin (Hyman Woolf)	10 pounds
Moses Hayim ben Abraham (Hyman Levin)	10 pounds
Elimeleh ben Joseph (Henry Joseph)	4 pounds and 10 pence
Asher Laemle ben Hayim (Lemon Woolf)	4 pounds and 10 pence
the unmarried Asher	
Laemle ben Solomon Aharon ha-Levi	1 guinea

Asher ben Eliezer promised to pay 20 pounds every year for the needs of the congregation.

Hayim ben Benjamin, also, 7 pounds . . . and other names.

All householders took upon themselves to promise to give . . . (amounts unclear) to charity and to the repair of the cemetery.

Hayim ben Benjamin has allowed his Mikveh for the use of the congregation for 2 pounds every year. He agrees to give the key over to the women, on the day of their immersion, and that he will keep it at all times in good order. He also agreed to keep the copper to heat water for the women who need it.

The Parnas is obliged every year to send (to London, or to Israel) for an Ethrog (citrus fruit used at the festival of Tabernacles) for the congregation. When it is more than 1 guinea it must be paid for from the charity fund, but up to 1 guinea, every member of the congregation must pay from his pocket proportionately.

The regulations are signed by	Hayim ben Benjamin Wolf (Hyman Woolf)
	Elimeleh ben Joseph (Henry Joseph)
	Asher Laemle ben Hayim (Lemon Woolf)

The Conveyances and the Minute Books

The editors have been fortunate to have gained access to most of the congregation's original conveyances of property and its minute books. These documents allow a glimpse into the community's affairs and concerns from the early 1800s, until its last days in 1892.

Unfortunately the oldest conveyance, dated 1768, relating to a plot of land in New Street, was in existence until 1983, but cannot be located and appears to have been lost. The original had not been copied. A Penzance accountant, however, who had sight of the document recalled, in a conversation with Godfrey Simmons some years ago, that the lease was from a member of the Branwell family, possibly Branwell Sutherland, who was a butcher by trade. The plot was referred to in the document as ". . . adjoining a killing place. . .," presumably where Branwell slaughtered. The date of 1768 for the building of the first synagogue is confirmed by *Saundry's Almanac*,[13] which was published annually by the stationer Saundry of Chapel Street, Penzance in the years prior to 1939.[14]

By the beginning of the 1800s the congregation must have found the original building too small for their requirements and resolved to build another synagogue on the same site. On 11th December 1807 they signed a lease for twenty-one years from Christmas Day of that year.[15] The parties concerned were Joseph Branwell, who made over ". . . a Meeting House or Synagogue, lately erected in New Street, Penzance where there was a slaughterhouse used by Branwell" to ". . . Lemon Hart, Hyman Woolf, Henry Ralph, Elias Magnus and Lemon Woolf (all of Penzance)." The annual rent of six guineas was payable quarterly from Christmas of that year.

In 1818 Barbara Eva, wife of William Eva, had inherited a dwelling-house in New Street together with an adjoining property, from her aunt

---

[13] *Saundry's Almanacs* for 1933 (p. 35) and 1936 (p. 33) mention: "1768: Old Jews' Synagogue built". The synagogue is also mentioned in Thomas, *History of Mounts Bay* (1820, p. 47): "the Jews have a synagogue which was built in 1807; but prior to this, they had one that was erected in 1768." The editors have seen two editions of this work: the 2nd edition of 1820, titled *The History of Mount's Bay*, and the 3rd of 1831, titled *Ancient & Modern History of Mount's Bay*. Both were printed as "Thomas' History . . . etc. . . . Printed & sold by J. Thomas of Penzance. *The Bibliotheca Cornubiensis* (Boase & Courtney, Vol ii, 1878, p. 173) in the RIC, Truro suggests that the book was not written by Thomas, but is reported to have been compiled by a William Colenso, who was apprenticed to J. Thomas. *The Universal British Directory for Devon and Cornwall* for 1799 in its section for Penzance also mentions that: ". . . the Jews have a synagogue" (i.e. referring to the earlier one of 1768).

[14] Apart from the synagogues at Penzance and Falmouth, the Editors have been unable, despite extensive searches and enquiries, to trace and identify any specific documentary evidence of a synagogue in any other part of Cornwall, especially in the area between Truro, Falmouth and Penzance, where most Jews lived at this time. cf. letters from: David Thomas, Archivist, the County Record Office, Truro, February 1999; Leslie Douch, the Courtney Library, RIC, Truro, March 1999; Allen Buckley, March 1999.

[15] The information here concerning the various conveyances has been extracted from Godfrey Simmons' archive. Joseph Branwell (b. 1748) was most likely the butcher involved in these negotiations. In 1805 he had been a co-owner, with Lemon Hart and four others, of the ship *Speculation*: see chapter 7. He was married to Temperance Matthews who owned the property adjoining the synagogue. There was a younger Joseph Branwell (1789–1857) who was only 18 in 1807 and so, legally a minor. He is not known to have been a butcher, but (later) a schoolmaster and then a banker. cf. Pool (1990, p. 5).

Temperance Branwell, who is also referred to in the records of the Corporation of Penzance. The Corporation had borrowed the sum of £200 from her. On 27th December 1837 a release (conveyance) was signed between William Eva of Gwinear, a wheelwright, and his wife Barbara to ". . . Lemon Woolf, merchant, Aaron Selig, jeweller, Henry Levin, jeweller, Moses Woolf, brewer, and Benjamin Selig, watchmaker, all of Penzance." The consideration was the sum of £160 for the sale of a dwelling-house and the adjoining house, "formerly two messuages". The latter was then added to the existing synagogue and the lease records that (the enlarged building) ". . . is now used as a Synagogue." The congregation set up a building fund for this purpose in 1836.[16]

There are no further property documents relating to the synagogue in the records until 24th September 1880, when "Henry Joseph of Penzance, jeweller, and Israel Levin, also of Penzance, wholesale jeweller," conveyed the freehold of the synagogue to "Barnett Henry Joseph of Birmingham, wholesale jeweller, and Israel Oppenheim of Penzance, merchant," for a peppercorn ten shillings.

On 11th October 1901 another conveyance was executed between members of the congregation, but the end came in 1906 when, on 31st May, Thomas Lean of Marazion bought the premises at auction for £172 on behalf of the Plymouth Brethren. The building was formally conveyed to him on 23rd June 1906 by Barnett H. Joseph, Israel Oppenheim and Morris Bischofswerder.[17] It was then used by the Brethren as a meeting-house for prayer. The building was eventually purchased by Devenish Brewery and incorporated into the adjoining public house, the Star Hotel. Today, nothing remains of the synagogue's interior to identify its former use, the upper part (formerly the women's gallery) is now an enclosed children's playroom and the lower body of the building has become the pub's chilled beer cellar. In view of Lemon Hart's involvement in the rum trade, and Lemon and Moses Woolf's with the wine and distillery business, this is perhaps a better and more fitting use for the building than has befallen other disused places of worship.

---

[16] J.S. Courtney (1845, p. 44) gives a list of seven religious buildings, including the synagogue, and dismisses them collectively as functional but lacking in any architectural merit. He says that he will give further details of the various buildings in an appendix, but, curiously, did not do so. He had previously referred to the synagogue's existence in a contribution to the *7th Annual Report to the Royal Polytechnic of Cornwall* (1839, p. 22). Sadly, in neither of these sources did he see fit to include a description of the exterior or interior of the synagogue which, of course, he may not have entered. Likewise no description is to be found in Saundry's *Almanacs*, Thomas' *History*, or the *Universal Directory*.

[17] Saundry's *Almanacs*, ibid, p. 40 and 38 respectively: "July 1906: Jews' synagogue sold."

Various leases and conveyances relating to the purchase and development of the cemetery are also to be found in the congregation's records and are examined in chapter 5. There are no known minutes or similar documents relating to the period between 1768 and 1808; but from 1st November 1807 Lemon Hart, the president and treasurer of the synagogue, kept a six-monthly income and expenditure account. Records in this form were maintained until 31st May 1829, after which there is a complete gap in the records until 12th March 1843, when the surviving minutes began, and from this point they were kept on either a quarterly or half-yearly basis until 1892, by which time the congregation was in terminal decline.

The earliest accounts are probably the most interesting. Apart from recording the comings and goings of various rabbis, they also detail the costs of building the 1808 synagogue. They are headed: "Mr. Lemon Hart, President and Treasurer of the Hebrew Synagogue" and they demonstrate the importance of the connection with the Branwell family. One of the earliest entries records ". . . cash received of Mr. Joseph Branwell towards the building of the synagogue, 20 pounds". This was an advance that was partially offset by a payment to Branwell of ". . . 4 pounds, 14 shillings and 6 pence . . . for. . . 3/4 year rent due 25th December last." Among other items noted was a payment of three shillings for three loads of hay, which was laid under the floor as an insulator and was still in place when the building was stripped in 1983. Other payments include: five pounds, three shillings and six pence to Bolitho & Co. for lime; a progress payment made to Jno. Wallis, a builder; 15 pounds was advanced to the Rabbi for his wages; on 11th April 1808, 11 pounds was paid to bring another incumbent from London, and on the 21st September the sum of 19 pounds 10 shillings was paid to him for his half-year's salary.

The congregation's income came from members' subscriptions, donations from visiting strangers and offerings from members and regular attenders. This pattern was to continue throughout the life of the congregation and was just sufficient to keep heads above water, and even at this early stage allowed scope for charitable purposes. An early note made on 1st October 1809 committed Lemon Hart, Henry Ralph, Elias Magnus and Lemon Woolf to contribute a total of seven shillings a week towards the keep "of an infirm old man", subject to his being in Penzance every night, if possible, "to prevent any accident happening from travelling to distant places."

Outgoings were mainly restricted to payments to Branwell for the synagogue ground-rent and rent for the burial ground.[18] Travelling

18 See chapter 5 for further details.

expenses were also paid to newly-engaged rabbis, most of whom seem to have enjoyed only a short term of office, and so this particular form of expenditure was a frequent occurrence. Maintenance of the congregation's property was also necessary, and in 1815, one pound, 14 shillings and four pence was paid to "Harvey the carpenter . . . for a new door to the burial ground." He also received three pounds and seven shillings for work done in the synagogue.

From 1816 the accounts were presented by Lemon Woolf on behalf of his father, Hyman Woolf, who may have been incapacitated by illness. An intriguing and mysterious entry without explanation occurred in 1821, when a sum of 14 shillings was paid out ". . . in achieving Godfrey from prison", presumably either bail or the payment of a court-imposed fine. During this period new names appear in the minutes from time to time, but most of them disappear after a year or two, possibly because they failed to find the opportunities they sought in Penzance.

The fact that there is no trace of minutes between 1829 and 1843 has been mentioned. Either they were lost or they were not kept. This situation came to be regarded as unsatisfactory, possibly resulting in some deterioration of the congregation's affairs and arrangements, because one of the first decisions noted in the new 1843 minute book was that "a select committee" of five members should be charged with the task of "forming a code of Rules for the better government of the Congregation." The results of their deliberations cover many pages and attempt to regulate every eventuality the congregation might encounter. By this time reference is made to "Vestry Meetings", and the new rules, after some changes, were finally approved and signed by twelve members at a general meeting held later that same year.

This new minute book begun in 1843 and continued until 1857, together with accounts, mostly undetailed, were presented and approved; but most of the entries consisted of copies of letters written by and to the congregation. The rabbi, Barnett Asher Simmons, was the subject of a number of complaints about the way in which he carried out his duties, including alleged neglect in not "porging" (the removal of veins and other forbidden, "unclean" portions from meat) correctly. References were made to threats of resignation, dismissal and re-engagement. Some representation must have been made to the Chief Rabbi, by, or about Simmons, because he went to London to be examined regarding his skills as shochet (ritual slaughterer), and the subsequent letter to the congregation from the Chief Rabbi was supportive of him. Despite such differences, B.A. Simmons remained in Penzance, available to serve the congregation for more than forty years, which in itself helps to explain the number of times he was mentioned in the minutes. He eventually achieved the distinction of becoming Cornwall's longest-serving rabbi.[19]

The burial ground and its wall had been the subject of a number of reports going back to the early days of the century, and on 6th July 1845 it was agreed that a letter should be sent to Dr. Barham of Exeter thanking him for the gift of a strip of land adjoining the cemetery which he had presented to the congregation.[20]

In 1848 a meeting was convened "for the purpose of petitioning Parliament for the removal of Jewish disabilities." Two petitions were made, one to the House of Lords and the other to the Commons. The first was sent "to the Secretary of the Board of Deputies of British Jews for their disposal" and the second to E.W.W. Pendarves MP. Another resolution passed by the members at the same meeting was: "that the thanks of this meeting is due to our Christian Brethren of Penzance, in having so readily and nobly supported the petition for the Removal of the Jewish disabilities, being the last Vestige of Religious Intolerance now remaining on the Statute Book of this free and enlightened Nation."

Meetings began to be held on a six-monthly basis; and from 1853 until 1857 the only entries were to cash drawn for expenses. However, an inventory of congregational property (which appears to have been drawn up much later in 1883 when, perhaps, the already dwindling community was evaluating its assets against the likelihood of closure), appears in the minutes at this point. The finances of the congregation, always finely balanced, were strengthened by a legacy of £50, sufficient for them to have gas lighting installed. Subscriptions from new members with addresses in South Wales, all relatives of present and past Penzance residents, must have helped still further.

Charitable donations were not confined to co-religionists. On 23rd May 1874 a collection raised a total of four pounds, 11 shillings and six pence, which was eventually split "between our Brethren co-religionists in Jerusalem now suffering a severe distress", and "sub-scriptions towards the famine now raging so severely in the Presidence of Bengal in India." Non-Jewish friends of the congregation also contributed to the Sir Moses Montefiore Testimonial Fund in 1875: these included "Alderman Coulson, Councillor Mapwell, a Mr. Cornish and a Mr. Mounder".

Dates of the arrival and departure of ministers are no longer recorded, but one of the last to be noted was that of "Mr. Spero" who

---

[19] See chapter 6 for a more detailed study of his life.

[20] This Dr. Barham was obviously a broadminded individual in his empathy towards the Jews. He was also much concerned with social matters and had completed a survey on the living conditions of the poor of Exeter.

went to Plymouth without permission. He was reprimanded and had his salary reduced on 1st October 1865. On 9th April 1866 he resigned. Soon after, a Mr. Rittenberg was appointed, although on 14th April 1867, whether for disciplinary reasons or because of financial restrictions, a special annual allowance of £1.10s was discontinued. The first reference to Revd. Isaac Bischofswerder was made in April 1874, although he had conducted a marriage in Penzance as early as 9th June 1869. In 1875 the congregation agreed to his request for a salary increase from 47 pounds and 12 shillings to 52 pounds per annum. Although he continued to live in Penzance for the rest of his life, he did not serve the congregation without a break. In 1887 a Revd. Rubinstein was given a written testimonial when he left Penzance to minister in Cardiff.

Despite the shaky finances, another minister, Michael Leinkram was engaged. However, on 25th September 1887, a bill of 38 pounds 15 shillings from "Mr. Wallis . . . for work to the architect's specification" must have caused concern to the remaining congregants, especially as the cost of Leinkram's engagement made another hole in the finances, as the travelling expenses of the newly-married rabbi and his wife from London drained away further funds. A further item of expense was noted on 3rd September 1888 when the half-yearly meeting of members voted "that a sum of two guineas should be given to the Rabbi on account of his wife's forthcoming accouchment." The last minutes dated 27th March 1892 record a meeting at the Hollies, Alverton, Penzance, the home of Mr. David Bischofswerder, one of Isaac Bischofswerder's sons, when five members were present. By that time, the Bischofswerder family made up most of the numbers and the Penzance Jewish Congregation then passes into history.

Editorial Notes to Part 1

Edit 1. The records referred to by Roth are analysed on pp. 86–94 under the heading "The Penzance Community Records".

Edit 2. Jews are likely to have settled in Penzance earlier than Roth assumed: by the 1720s, families from the Rhineland area of Germany and also from Holland settled in Penzance. Whether they arrived directly by sea-passage to the town or travelled down from London or the south coast is unclear. The Hart family represent the earliest known settlers. For a further study of the Harts, see chapter 7. Recent research has shown that in his ledger, William Borlase referred to the purchase of silverware from Lemon Hart's grandfather, Abraham Hart, in 1756. It would be safe to assume therefore that the Harts were well-established in the town by then, along with other Jewish families. Susser, in 1993, did not have access to the recent research on the Borlase ledger and so his statement that ". . . there is no evidence of any Jew there [in Penzance] before 1781 when the name of Lemon Hart appears on a clockface . . ." (p. 32) is mistaken. Presumably he also intended this to relate to potential evidence of early, primary residence because he does not acknowledge that a Solomon Solomon was apprenticed in 1769 to a Gentile, John Sampson of Penzance, a watchmaker (p.94), but assumes that this Solomon came from Falmouth (p.293). There is no headstone bearing that name in the Falmouth cemetery, only an Israel Solomon (row 2:1) and a Simon Solomon (row 3:3; died 1825). However it is possible that this apprentice was a Penzance resident in 1769, Solomon Zalman, who died in 1823 and is buried in the Penzance cemetery (row 5:4).

Edit 3. Roth was, apparently, not aware that there had been a Jewish presence in Penzance since circa 1720s (the earliest burial in the Jewish cemetery being in 1741) and that an earlier synagogue had been built on the New Street site in 1768.

Edit 4. See chapter 5, pp. 130–133.

Edit 5. See chapter 9, pp. 300–301.

Edit 6. The Lemon Hart firm was subsequently taken over by United Distillers. The Lemon Hart ® label is now a registered trade mark of Allied Domecq plc.

Edit 7. Henry Ralph was licensed as a Navy Agent in Penzance in 1809 and remained in town until 1811. He had moved to Plymouth Dock (Devonport) by 1814, where he is said to have become a leading member of the "Dock Minyan" of Jews who traded there and who met together for their own worship: cf. Green (1989), p. 147. Ralph's name and signature appear frequently in the minutes and accounts in the early 1800s. It is probable that he was related to Abraham Ralph of Barnstaple (d. 1805). Around 1800, three Devon Jews named Betsy Ralph, Miriam Ralph and Catherine Ralph (daughters of Abraham Ralph) married the three Jackson brothers, sons of Isaac Jacobs of Totnes and Betsy Jacobs (née Levy, from Barnstaple). cf. Roth, *Rise of Provincial Jewry*, p. 22. Another relative of Henry Ralph was Rosie Ralph of Devon who married into the Hyam (Halford) family. This information was taken from a letter from Wilfred Samuel to Cecil Roth, dated 3rd January 1933, in the Roth Collection, Leeds; and courtesy of Evelyn Friedlander's research. Before Henry Ralph left Penzance he donated a number of ritual items to the synagogue, including two curtains for the Ark (one for general use and a white one for use on the High Holy Days), and one white cover for use on the reading desk, also for use on the High Holy Days (cf. early minutes, 19th October 1810).

Edit 8. See part 2 of this chapter for more details of the *Tikkunim*.

Edit 9. This is not correct. They were primarily from the Rhineland area and Alsace as well as Holland. Like Plymouth, they used the German rather than the Polish or Russian rite, although some Eastern European influence may have been present (Susser, 1993, pp. 32–4). The names of those who came to be buried in the Jewish cemetery show Germanic origin (Selig, Woolf, Hart). Solomon Teacher whose descendants still hold that the family may have originated in Spain, before migrating to Germany, gave "Bavaria" as his place of origin in the 1851 census (see Susser, 1995, p. 23).

Edit 10. For example: the *Tikkunim* and sections of the minute books.

Edit 11. In such a small community as Penzance it is not surprising that Jews from disparate backgrounds, central and eastern European, Ashkenazi and Sephardi should come together, if only temporarily. The Dr. Messina referred to by Roth (see later) may have been Italian. In the early 1820s, a new Scroll of the Law was installed in the Penzance synagogue and customary donations were received, including one from a "Mocato". In European cities it is common for there to be established Ashkenazi and Sephardi congregations with their separate synagogues. Paris is the best example of this today, but it is to be found elsewhere, and London and Lisbon, with predominant Ashkenazi and Sephardi populations respectively, both have synagogues for the other tradition. The Philip Samuel from Warsaw referred to by Roth may have helped in founding the Ashkenazi community in Lisbon. Michael Leinkram was also from Warsaw, and Isaac Aryeh Rubinstein was Russian (see chapter 6 and Susser, 1993, pp. 42, 44 and 156). For general patterns of immigration in the south-west see Susser (1993, pp. 26–67).

Edit 13. His grave will be one of those unmarked in Row 3 of the cemetery.

Edit 14. Roth's reference to R. Liepman is surprising in that it is doubtful if the Truro Jewish community was ever large enough to summon or sustain a minyan. It is not known to have had a synagogue or a rabbi. It would seem unlikely therefore that it could have afforded to employ a *shochet*, especially as kosher meat could be obtained from Falmouth, only a short river-journey away. If a member of the Truro community was skilled as a *shochet* then he could have been given the courtesy title *Rav*. R. Liepman may only have been a temporary resident of Truro in that his name does not appear in trade directories for that period. Roth does not give a source for this information, and although an H. Lipman is noted in a solitary accounts-note of the Penzance congregation on 1st March 1830 this is in relation to the receipt of a donation (of ten shillings and nine pence), and not to the payment of wages. The Penzance minutes of 1808–1829 have no mention of Liepman or the employment of a *shochet* from Truro.

Edit 15. This is misleading: in 1810 a new lease on the cemetery was agreed (see the introduction to the Penzance cemetery in chapter 5). A note in the synagogue records of 14th April 1811 states that a sum of just 35 pounds had been set aside towards the eventual building of a wall. Building may have started in 1822, but the entire ground was not enclosed until after the purchase of the freehold in 1844. The cemetery was first acquired around the early 1740s. The earliest headstone is dated 1741.

Edit 16. Solomon Ezekiel lived for a time in Falmouth before moving to Penzance. The *Bibliotheca Cornubiensis* B.C. Vol. I (1874) p. 145 (RIC Truro) records his writings as:

> "Remarks on the Censures of the authorized version of the Holy Scriptures", included in a pamphlet by the Rev. Hart Symons (pub. 1822).
> *The Life of Abraham: a series of three lectures on the Lives of the Patriarchs* (pub. 1844).
> *The Life of Isaac*: three further lectures (pub. 1845).
> *The Hebrew Festivals* (pub. 1847).
> "A Letter to Sir Rose Price on the Christianizing of the Jews" (31st January 1820; reprinted on the occasion of his death in the *Cornish Telegraph*, 13th March 1867. He had died four days earlier on 9th March).
> *A Lecture on the Passions and Feelings of Mankind* (undated).

He is buried in the Penzance cemetery (Row 2:3). His headstone does not give the year of his birth or his age at the time of his death. Roth gives 1781 for the former and 86 years for the latter. Susser, however, (op. cit., pp.129, 208 & 346) gives his dates as 1786–1867, and his place of birth as Exeter rather than Newton Abbot (as per Roth and the *Bibliotheca Cornubiensis*).

Edit 17. Solomon Teacher may once have lived in St.Ives, as Roth suggests. In the 1851 census he is recorded as living with his wife and daughter at 35 Leskinnick Terrace in Penzance (Susser, 1995). In view of the frequency of his attendance at congregational meetings it is unlikely that he lived outside the town. He died in 1856 and is buried in the cemetery in Row 7:1. His headstone, like those of Joseph Barnet and Catherine Levy, is not the original. See also p. 247.

For more details about Rabbi Joseph Rintel, see chapter 6, pp. 162–7.

Edit 18. The Oppenheims became successful business people in the town, operating a general purpose household and clothes store in large premises occupying a prominent position at the top of the main street. Their success can be seen in that in the first issue of the *Cornishman* newspaper on Thursday 18th July 1878, they were able to occupy two identical columns of advertisements, one on the front cover and the other on the inside page. See p. 242.

Edit 19. His beautiful headstone (and unique raised, coffin-shaped, horizontal surround) is to be found in the cemetery in Row 4:3.

Edit 20. See part II of this chapter.

Edit 21. See chapter 6, pp. 170–181, and also Susser's various references in his index.

Edit 22. See chapter 6 for further details about the Rabbi Bischofswerder and his family. The "advanced . . . decay" mentioned by Roth in his next section had been brought about by a long-term process of migration from Penzance. Several of Rabbi Barnett Asher Simmons' children emigrated; and others moved away, including a daughter to South Wales. Benjamin Aaron Selig, who was a watchmaker (whose parents Aaron and Hannah, died in 1841 and 1847, and are buried alongside one another in the Penzance cemetery, Row 1:10 and 11), left for Australia in 1854. He had been the *Parnas* of the small Penzance congregation in 1852, and he eventually settled in Wellington, New Zealand as that community's rabbi. The marriage registers for Penzance from 1838-1892 show four marriages contracted with people from Falmouth, one from Plymouth, two from Newcastle and five from Wales. Only five of the 17 marriages recorded were between local couples. This, as well as the desire to better economic opportunities, and the commercial or social advantages in moving to centres with a larger Jewish population, all took their toll. (See Susser, 1993, p. 65 and also chapter 7, pp. 251–255).

Edit 23. His name was Leinkram. Roth and Susser give this name incorrectly: Roth uses "Lancrour" and Susser uses "Lankion" (Susser, 1993, p. 156).

Edit 24. The bar-mitzvah of Harry, a grandson of Isaac Bischofswerder, in the synagogue was described in more detail in the *Cornishman* newspaper, August 1889. This article is also referred to in chapters 6 and 9, and the editors are grateful to Elizabeth Brock for drawing their attention to this article from her research.

Edit 25. This was the wedding of Marcus Bischofswerder to Emma Boramlagh Hawke, a Gentile, on 12th June 1892. Rabbi Isaac Bischofswerder was recorded as "Retired Rabbi". Rabbi Michael Leinkram officiated at the service held in a private house at 22 Rosevean Road, not at the synagogue. The last three Jewish marriages in Penzance (between 1876 and 1892) were of Bischofswerders.

Edit 26. This may have been effectively the case since 1890, and Isaac Bischofswerder lived until 1899. Also Rabbi Michael Leinkram may have remained in, or returned to, Penzance after 1887; at least two of his children were born in the town in 1892 and 1894.

Edit 27. The synagogue was not sold in 1913 as Roth has implied and as subsequently assumed. It was sold seven years earlier in 1906. Despite the fact that some fixtures remained in the building, there is no direct evidence that the Plymouth Brethren permitted, or that the few Jews remaining, like Morris Bischofswerder, felt it appropriate to continue to use the building for Jewish worship. This was more likely to have taken place in a modified form in a private house. The 1911 burial, mentioned in edit 28 below, would not have necessitated the use of a synagogue.

Edit 28. This was the burial of Julia, wife of Morris Bischofswerder, who died on 20th April 1911 (Pz. 7:6). The only subsequent burial was that of Adolf Salzman (Pz. 8:4) who died on 22nd February 1964.

Editorial Postscript: Roth (p. 71 footnote 3, cont'd) is incorrect in identifying a "*Samuel* Jacob, a son-in-law of Zender Falmouth" as the Falmouth congregation's leader in the first half of the nineteenth century. Alex Jacob (pp. 55 and 59) gives the correct position. After Alexander Moses in 1791, the wardenship did not pass to Alexander's son Philip, but to his son-in-law Moses Jacob (1733–1807), married to Sarah Moses, who herself took an active part in congregational affairs. Lyon Joseph was Parnas from 1807–1815, but subsequently the position passed through the Jacob family (apparently exclusively): Moses Jacob's son, Jacob (John) Jacob (from c.1816–52), then his son Moses ("Moss") Jacob Jacob (from 1853 to 1860), and subsequently his son Samuel Jacob (b. 1837), who remained until 1879, when he closed the synagogue and left for London, in 1880. (Ref. pp. 103, 109, 111–113, 123, 127, 220, 276, 295 and 302.)

The Jewish Cemeteries

Godfrey Simmons and Keith Pearce

Based upon a survey (1975) by Nicholas de Lange and Jennifer Speake

Hebrew Transcriptions by Nicholas de Lange and Jennifer Speake

Translations by Herman Zeffertt

T he Jewish burial grounds at Falmouth and Penzance are visible, extant legacies of the eighteenth- and nineteenth-century Jewish communities in Cornwall. The synagogue buildings can still be viewed from the outside, but are no longer in use as synagogues. They are both now in private ownership. The cemeteries, however, are still under Jewish supervision with the Board of Deputies of British Jews as the trustees. They represent a vital link with the past. They remain sacred Jewish sites even today after more than a century of disuse and can still be visited by appointment with the custodians. Time has taken its inevitable toll despite ongoing, if irregular, maintenance over the years. The Falmouth ground, especially, has suffered considerable decay whilst the Penzance cemetery is almost perfectly preserved.

Much of the credit for the survival of these grounds must go to the inconspicuous but devoted work of individuals who, over the years, have taken a personal interest in their protection and upkeep. Special mention should be made of the work of Alfred Dunitz, a Justice of the Peace and member of the Board of Deputies of British Jews in London, who, year after year, has travelled many miles to supervise and check on the security and maintenance of the cemeteries. He has initiated schemes for their necessary maintenance through the Probation and Community Services. This has been essential to their preservation. Penzance has been fortunate in having Godfrey Simmons as the custodian for over twenty years; his great-grandfather, Barnett Asher Simmons, was the longest-serving rabbi in Cornwall. Godfrey Simmons ensured that the Penzance cemetery's high surrounding wall (so important for its protection) was rebuilt when it required attention in the early 1990s. The Falmouth and Penzance cemeteries now have non-Jews acting as the custodians for the Board of Deputies.

Fortunately, the cemeteries have been surveyed and their tombstones recorded on several occasions over the course of the last century. These surveys have been combined to form the basis of this chapter. Without them, much of the inscription material would be lost to us today as, inevitably, some of the stones have disappeared or been weathered by time and are no longer legible. This is particularly true of the Falmouth cemetery. Barnet Lyon Joseph (1801–1880) compiled a list of head-stones for Falmouth in the last century and this was eventually published in the *Jewish Chronicle* on 22nd July 1910. It was reprinted privately with some corrections and further details by Anthony P. Joseph in 1954. Alex Jacob also carried out a complete survey in 1939. He converted the Hebrew dates on the headstones into the secular equivalent and so his dates have been adopted in this chapter. This earlier work has proved invaluable for Falmouth, and without it, the complete record in this book would not have been possible.

In 1975, Nicholas de Lange and Jennifer Speake carried out a wide-ranging general survey of Jewish cemeteries across the United Kingdom, with particular attention to Gloucester, Cheltenham, Canterbury, and the two Cornish burial grounds. This 1975 survey, which was part of a wider survey of older Jewish burial grounds in the British Isles supported jointly by the Jewish Historical Society of England and Anglo-Jewish Archives, included the recording of the complete Hebrew headstone transcriptions for Falmouth and Penzance. In 1988, this part of the survey was updated by Godfrey Simmons, Keith Pearce, Rachel Berg, Tracy Poulton and Mira Little, to take into account the correct re-allocation of misplaced headstones and to draw up plans of both sites. The survey also made cross-reference to some of the family connections between the two cemeteries and their communities. The recent translation of the Hebrew inscriptions on the headstones by Herman Zeffertt now brings this collective enterprise to its completion and records for posterity all of those known to have been laid to rest in these cemeteries.

The Jewish Cemetery, Falmouth

Introductory notes by Eric Dawkins and Keith Pearce

The Falmouth cemetery lies outside Falmouth itself at Ponsharden, near Penryn, on a steep incline beside a busy main road. It adjoins a now derelict Christian (Congregational) cemetery. It can be entered from houses nearby and the Jewish cemetery is now only partially walled. Over the years, it has seen some considerable decay. Some of the headstones have inevitably disappeared or been weathered by the damp climate or pollution. However, the most serious threat to its preservation are the mature, proliferate, overgrown trees which surround the cemetery. Their extensive root-systems have surfaced over the years, effectively destroying the Christian ground next to it and dislodging many of the headstones in the Jewish cemetery. Fortunately it has been surveyed several times over the years and comparison of these records has allowed a list of those buried there to be completed, even though some headstones have not survived.

The cemetery was founded in the latter part of the eighteenth century when the need for a burial ground became pressing. We know that the first Jewish settlers came to Falmouth around the 1720s, encouraged to settle there by the leading figure of Alexander Moses (known as Zender Falmouth). The community soon became well-established and therefore had a need for its own burial ground. An application was made to the Bassett Estate of Tehidy, near Redruth, (later under Sir Francis Bassett, to become Lord de Dunstanville, 1757–1835) which owned land in the Penryn area. The Bassett Memorandum and Proposal Book contains an entry dated 8th June 1759 under *Penwerris* 1: "Moses, a Jew of Penryn, applies for leave to enclose a burying place for the Jews, 50ft. square, out of the green plot at Penwerris now in Dr. Turner's pos(ses)sion . . . to have an absolute term of 99 years."[1] The Jew was presumably Alexander Moses of the Falmouth congregation. There is no recorded answer to the proposal. The calendar of Bassett leases does not show that one was executed on this occasion and so the matter must have lapsed. It is not known how many years passed before a plot at Ponsharden was granted by the Bassett estate,[2] but eventually Lord de Dunstanville presented a plot of land jointly to the Jewish and Congregational

---

[1] See TM, CRO, Truro, ref: AD 894/7/5, Manor No. in Rent-Book: 1754. The editors are grateful to Allen Buckley, and also to David Thomas, Archivist, County Record Office (Truro) for this information, March 1999. David Thomas' letter of 19th March 1999 points out that many of the Bassett leases were destroyed. As a result, they may have been issued but are not recorded in the calendar.

[2] In the 1975 survey, de Lange and Speake note that Roth appears to date the gift after 1808, but that Jacob's date is c.1780 and the latter accords better with the actual headstones. Neither the Bassett proposal book nor the boxes of unlisted Bassett leases (Penwerris Barton), both held at CRO Truro, give the opening date of the Jewish burial ground. Lands in the Penryn/Budock area, formerly belonging to R. Scott Bickford, passed into Bassett ownership in the 1770s (Bassett volume of destroyed leases, ref. B37, NO. 1536, p. 115, Manor of Penwerris), but we cannot be certain if the burial ground comprised any part of these lands. The Jewish burial ground is shown on Richard Thomas' 1814 Survey of Penwerris at CRO Truro, ref. AD894/7/35. Letter from David Thomas, Archivist, April 1999.

communities. Amongst the earliest burials was that of Esther, wife of Barnet Levy in 1780, although the earliest decipherable stone is that of Isaac ben Benjamin in 1790. Over a period of 140 years, some 50 burials have taken place in the cemetery.[3] B.L. Joseph surveyed the cemetery in about 1870 and read the oldest surviving headstones (1:1 and 1:2) as dating to 5534 (1774). Jacob (1939) and de Lange/Speake (1975) read them correctly as 1794 for 1:1 and 1790 for 1:2. Susser's date in fact refers to 1:2 as 1791 and this would be correct if Heshvan 5551 were to be reckoned to the New rather than the previous Jewish or seasonal year. Susser is undoubtedly correct in saying that the cemetery, like any other, would have been used before the date of the oldest surviving tombstones. There are about 20 unidentified graves in the Falmouth cemetery and nine in Penzance, and although it may not be the case that all of these are earlier than the earliest dated stones (1791 for Falmouth; and 1741 for Penzance) it is reasonable to suppose that some of them are.

The decline of the community in the late nineteenth century, and the subsequent closure of the synagogue in 1880, led to the disuse of the Falmouth cemetery.[4] Samuel Jacob had kept the synagogue open for services up until 1879, but in 1880 he left with his family for London after carrying out repairs to the building. Communal life ceased and the synagogue building fell into deplorable disrepair. There may have been vague hopes that the community might revive, and the Lawrence family may have lived in it, or in an adjoining cottage (now demolished), as caretakers of what came to be known as "Synagogue House". In 1892, the Chief Rabbi ordered the trustees to sell it and to use the proceeds to help maintain the cemetery which had itself begun to fall into neglect. In 1889, a solicitor, Lewis Emanuel of Finsbury Circus, London launched a Restoration Fund Appeal for the Jewish cemetery.[5] It was

---

[3] Susser (1993, p. 129) notes that "at Falmouth, only a fireplace against a wall indicates where the chapel stood." Upon further research, there is no documentary evidence or visible trace in the cemetery grounds to support this. An original, redundant entrance with an arch lies along one side, now largely submerged and overgrown. This could have given the appearance of an alcove. It is most likely that it was this feature which Susser took to be the remnant of a fireplace and so drew the conclusion that it had been contained within a chapel. No other similar feature can be seen on the site (The Falmouth synagogue, however, once had a fireplace and oven). Likewise, the perfectly preserved walls of the Penzance cemetery show no sign of a fireplace or chapel, although the original similar entrance and archway still remains. cf. Letter from Eric Dawkins to Keith Pearce, 21st December 1998.

[4] Although, the last burial actually took place in 1913.

[5] Lewis Emanuel was probably the A.L. Emanuel, one of the trustees of the synagogue. Much of the information which follows is from Eric Dawkins research and from information kindly supplied by the Board of Deputies of British Jews from their records.

estimated that six guineas was required for reclamation and repair, and two guineas annually for maintenance. Mrs. Charles and Mrs. George Goodman each donated one guinea, as did Alex Laurance and Samuel Jacob, Ray (Hyman) Joseph, and Walter Symons. These sums, totalling about 800 pounds in today's currency, may have led to an immediate improvement, but the Falmouth Town Clerk wrote to Lewis Emanuel in 1896 implying that it was unlikely that anyone could be found ". . . who would undertake to see to the disused Jewish cemetery being kept in order . . .", although he offered the possibility that a (presumed) publican, "Mr. Nathan, of Marine Hotel, Quay Hill" might be worth contacting.

In October 1913, a wealthy entrepreneur, Alfred Aaron de Pass, from a Sephardic background, and with family connections in South Africa, purchased the freehold of the cemetery, undertook its maintenance, and granted permission for what came to be the last Jewish burial there, the first for 55 years (since that of Moses ben Jacob in 1860), that of Nathan Vos, who had run a public house in the town. The occasion became the little cemetery's "swansong" and was by all accounts ". . . a deeply impressive service . . ." as reported in *The Jewish Chronicle* on 14th November 1913:

> Those present were: The Rev. D. Jacobs (Minister), The Rev. I. Slavinsky (Reader), Mr Joseph L. Jacobs of Plymouth, Mr. Max von Bosch (Nephew), Mr. A. Costa and Mr. E. Franks. The chief mourner was Mr. J.B. Vos (son), whilst amongst the many others present were Mr. C.S. Goldman M.P., The Mayor of Falmouth (Alderman A.W. Chard, J.P.) and many Freemasons, for Mr. Vos was a Brother of the "Love and Honour" Lodge, Falmouth.

When Alex Jacob made a visit to Falmouth in 1939,[6] he carried out a survey of the headstones in the cemetery. In his papers, he noted that he had obtained the key from a Mr. Vos of Falmouth. It would seem therefore that the remaining Vos family held this key on behalf of de Pass. They may also have arranged the cemetery's maintenance, although de Pass's subsequent bequest for this purpose may suggest that the key was entrusted to Mr. Vos primarily out of respect for his need to have access to the family grave.

While de Pass remained in the country, his efforts to maintain the cemetery no doubt continued, but in 1939 he travelled to South Africa at the age of 78. The outbreak of the war prevented his return. In 1947, his son, Daniel de Pass, wrote to the Board of Deputies of British Jews in London, asking them to take over the burial ground.

---

[6] This is the same Alex Jacob who was the author of chapter 3.

He also gave one hundred pounds towards clearing the weeds and undergrowth, and so it is unclear if Alfred de Pass had maintained contributions during his absence, or if such contributions had been inadequate.

The Board did not resume formal responsibility for the ground until August 1962, perhaps being reluctant to take on the liability of such a far-flung plot. Attempts were made to persuade the Plymouth community to take it over as they had used it for burials in the past, but to no avail. In the meantime, de Pass died in Cape Town on 17th December 1952, leaving a legacy of two hundred pounds for the cemetery. On 24th December, the *Cape Times* published an obituary notice referring to him as ". . . a connoisseur, collector and patron of the arts. Of a Sephardic family, his grandfather, Elias, arrived in South Africa in 1846."[7]

For some time it is likely that the cemetery was maintained irregularly, if at all. In 1973, the general manager of Dales Garage, adjacent to the cemetery, who had worked in Stamford Hill, London, and who had developed an interest in Jewish custom and tradition, influenced by his many Jewish customers there, wrote to the Board to offer to restore and maintain the cemetery grounds, to be the voluntary custodian and keyholder, and to show visitors around. This he did at his own expense until his retirement, after which the renamed Vospers Garage continued to act as keyholder.

Tombstone Transcriptions

All headstones transcribed below are known to have been in place at the time of one or more of the surveys. The headstones which currently exist in the cemetery date from 1790 to 1868, and one stone from 1913. The transcriptions have been set out first with the full name of the person buried there to identify the grave, followed by a translation of the Hebrew inscription where known or legible. The translation from the original Hebrew inscription has been indicated for the reader by the use of *Heb.* On some of the headstones there is English as well as Hebrew. The English inscription has been indicated

---

[7] De Pass, in fact, left the most important and sizeable collection of art ever to be given to the county. It is housed in the Royal Institution of Cornwall in Truro and its museum, including a number of sacred religious texts. It is not clear if any of the religious texts came from the Falmouth synagogue. An article on Alfred de Pass by Norman Nail can be found in the *Journal of the Royal Institution of Cornwall* (New Series II), 1993, vol 1, pt. 3, pp. 277–289.

The Jewish cemetery, Falmouth. [courtesy: David Sonin, the *Jewish Chronicle*]

Alexander Moses – Fal 1:3.

Barnet Levy – Fal 1:4. [both pictures courtesy: Rachel Berg]

by being prefaced with *Eng.* The editors have added some biographical information where possible. Familial information and marriage connections have been included to allow individuals to be cross-referenced within each list, as well as between the Falmouth and Penzance lists. It is hoped that this will give the material as a whole, a degree of coherence. A full plan of the cemetery showing the location of headstones has been included at the end of the chapter.

ROW 1 *(starting in the Upper Corner)*

1. GITELEH BENJAMIN (Mrs Woolly Benjamin: Deborah Giteleh, wife of Isaac Menasseh)

   Died 6 Ellul 5554 (25 August 1794)

   Heb. Here lies the modest woman Deborah Gitteleh, wife of Isaac. The deceased was close to the Lord. She died on 6th and was buried on 7th Ellul, 5554. May her soul be bound up in the bond of eternal life.

2. WOLF BENJAMIN (Woolly Benjamin: Isaac, son of Benjamin)

   Died 17 Cheshvan 5551 (25 October 1790)

   Heb. Here lies an upright generous man who went in the path of the good. All his deeds were for the sake of heaven. Isaac the son of Benjamin. He died on Monday, 17th Marcheshvan and was buried on Tuesday, 5551. May his soul be bound up in the bond of eternal life.

   A son, renamed Benson, lived in Bristol and a daughter lived in Haydon Square, London. This daughter married a Lyon Levy who committed suicide by throwing himself off the Monument circa 1809. This dramatic incident is mentioned in the Ingoldsby Legends.

3. ALEXANDER MOSES ("Zender Falmouth")

   Died 24th Nisan 5551 (28 April 1791)

   Heb. May his soul be bound up in the bond of eternal life. Here dwells and takes delight a faithful man, a leader and guide; a shield to his generation with his body, his blood and his flesh. His house was open and his table laid for all. He stood righteously until the Lord, in whom he trusted, gathered him. Alexander the son of Moses. Died on the 24th and was buried on the 25th Nisan 5551.

Alexander Moses was married to Phoebe (2:3). There were two sons: (i) Philip (known as "Phill") Moses (2:2) who married Betsy Jacobs (3:9); (ii) Moses Moses who went to live in Le Havre and who may have become estranged from his family for marrying a non-Jewess. The daughters were: (i) Rosa (4:2), the wife of Samuel Simons (4:4); (ii) Hannah (Pz. 5:I) wife of Israel Levy (3:11); (iii) Judith (4:5), wife of (first) Henry Joseph (2:4) and then Lazarus Lawrence (4:6); (iv) and Sarah (4:1), wife of Moses Jacob (2:9).

Zender Falmouth was the founder of the Falmouth Jewish community and he presided over it as a strict, controlling "Godfather" figure. He instigated a system of "synagogal identity" whereby newly arrived members, often with Anglicized, or German or (to the local inhabitants) difficult foreign names, would assume traditional Hebrew names by which they were known within the congregation, if not outside it. Zender also gave patronage and work to those willing to undertake that they would be in the town to take part in the Sabbath and Festival services, and to make up the required minyan of ten adult males to celebrate the full service. Zender may also have devised an economic system which substituted co-operation rather than competition between fellow-Jews, and also by placing members of his family and of the congregation in "satellite" communities, he linked the commercial prospects of the Falmouth Jewish community with that of other towns.

4. BARNET LEVY (Behr, son of Joel)

Died 11 Iyar 5551 (15 May 1791)

Heb. Here lies Behr the son of Joel. He died on the 11th and was buried on the 12th Iyar 5551. May his soul be bound up in the bond of eternal life.

Barnet Levy, also known as Bernard Beer or Jewell, was an immigrant from Alsace. He was by trade a soap-boiler but became a pedlar and prospered through Zender Falmouth's patronage. He married Esther Elias (1:11) from London, whose family were originally from Germany. Their sons were Levy Levy (1:6); Joel Levy who married Rachel Joseph; and Abraham Levy who married Zipporah Benjamin of Plymouth. Their daughters were

Judith Levy (not 3:7 or 4:5) who married Lyon Joseph; Hendele (Hannah) Levy (Pz. 1:2) the wife of Abraham Joseph (3:5); Elizabeth (Betsy) Levy (not 3:9 or 5:1). She married Solomon Solomon (son of 2:1 and 3:2). She died in Bristol; her husband died in Lisbon. They were the parents of the Israel Solomon who emigrated to New York (author of chapter 8). Sally Levy; and Shevya Levy (Pz. 6:4) who married her uncle Hart Elias (3:8). Chapters 3 and 8 contain information on Barnet Levy and some of the above.

5. JOSEPH JOSEPH

This headstone has no dates.

This is the infant son of Lyon Joseph of Falmouth and Judith Levy (above).

6. LEVY LEVY (Levi, son of Issachar)

Died 1 Kislev 5552 (27 November 1791)

Heb. Here lies Levi the son of Issachar. Died New Moon Kislev and was buried on the 2nd Kislev 5552. May his soul be bound up in the bond of eternal life.

The eldest son of Barnet Levy (1:4).

7. ALEXANDER (son of Zvi)

Died 5 Ab 5564 (1804)

Heb. Here lies Alexander the son of Zvi. He died on Friday, Sabbath eve and was laid to rest on Sunday 7th Av 5564. May his soul be bound up in the bond of eternal life.

8. MOSES (son of Israel Segal)

Died 5559 (1798–9)

Heb. Here lies the unmarried male, Moses the son of Israel Segal. 5559. May his soul be bound up in the bond of eternal life.

The son of Israel Solomon (2:1).

9. JACOB (son of Reuven)

Died 5561 (1800–1)

10. LEAH (daughter of Israel)

Died 15 Tevet 5602 (1842)

Heb. Here lies the single woman Leah, the daughter of Israel Aaron Segal. She died on Tuesday, 15th Tevet and was buried the next day Wednesday, in the year 5602. may her soul be bound up in the bond of eternal life.

The daughter of Israel Aaron Segal (Israel Solomon, 2:1).

Note: This stone may have been displaced to 4:8 at some time.

11. ESTHER ELIAS

She died circa. 1780. She was the wife of Barnet Levy (1:4) and may have been the first to be buried in the Falmouth cemetery.

ROW 2

1. ISRAEL SOLOMON (Israel Aaron Levi, son of Isaac Segal)

Died 23 Sivan 5562 (23 June 1802), aged about 78.

Heb. Here lies an upright and perfect man. All his deeds he performed with propriety. "As strong as a lion, fleet as a deer and swift as an eagle" (Mishnah, Ethics of the Fathers 5:23). Israel Aaron Ha-Levi, the son of Isaac Segal. He died on Wednesday and was buried on Thursday, 24th Sivan 5562. May his soul be bound up in the bond of eternal life.

Israel Solomon was from Ehrenbreitstein, opposite Koblenz on the Rhine. His family name in Germany was Behrends. He was married to Bella Woolf (3:2) from Holland. Their daughters were Judith (4:7) who married Samuel Harris (3:12); Leah who was unmarried (2:1/4:8); and a daughter who eloped to India. Their sons were Solomon who married Betsy Levy (see 1:4); and Simon (3:3) who married Kitty Jacob (5:4). Israel Solomon and Bella Woolf were the paternal grandparents of the Israel Solomon who emigrated to New York (see 1:4).

2. PHILL MOSES (Uri Shraga, son of Alexander)

Died 14 Kislev 5592 (19 November 1831)

Heb. Here lies Uri Shraga, the son of the Manyah (? the teacher) Alexander – may his memory be for a blessing. Died on the 14th Kislev 5592. May his soul be bound up in the bond of eternal life.

111

The son of Alexander Moses (1:3) and Phoebe (2:3). He was married to Betsy Jacob (3:9).

3. PHOEBE MOSES (Feigele, daughter of Moses)

Died Yom Kippur 5565 (15 September 1804)

Heb. Here lies a woman of worth (Proverbs 31:10), Feigele, the daughter of Moses, the wife of Alexander. She died at the dawn of the Day of Atonement and was buried Sunday at the termination of the Day of Atonement, 5565. May her soul be bound up in the bond of eternal life.

The wife of Alexander Moses (1:3).

4. HENRY JOSEPH (Zvi, son of Joseph)

Died 3rd Adar 5563 (1803)

Heb. Here lies Zvi the son of Joseph. He died in the night (Tuesday), the 3rd and was buried on the 4th Adar 5563. May his soul be bound up in the bond of eternal life.

This is the Henry Joseph, of St Austell, not the Henry Joseph of Penzance (Pz. 6:5). He was the first husband of Judith Moses (4:5) who was the daughter of Alexander Moses (1:3). They had three children: Alexander, Philip and Joseph who all died in infancy (see 2:6, 2:7 and 2:8).

5. MOSES ISAAC JOSEPH (Isaac, son of Joseph)

No dates on the headstone.

This is the brother of Henry Joseph (2:4). He married Judith Jacob (3:7) who was a daughter of Moses Jacob (2:9). They had six children: Henry, unmarried, who died in Brazil; Rose who emigrated to Australia; Phoebe (3:6) who married Isaac Davidson (not the Isaac of p. 213, b. 1830); Joseph who married Fanny Solomon; Solomon who died unmarried in London; and Bella who married Rabbi Meyer Stadhagen of Plymouth.

6. ALEXANDER JOSEPH

No dates on the headstone.

He was the infant son of Henry Joseph (2:4) and Judith Joseph (née Moses, later Lawrence, of 4:5).

7 and 8 UNMARKED

These two graves are unmarked but they are likely to be the other two infant sons of Henry Joseph, Philip and Joseph.

See 6:1 and 6:2.

9. MOSES JACOB of Redruth

Died the first of the middle Days of Passover 5567 (25 April 1807)

Heb. Here lies an upright man. All his deeds he performed with propriety. He fed and supported the numerous members of his household with honour and not in need. Moses the son of Jacob of Redruth. He died on Sabbath, the first of the intermediate days of Passover and was buried on the second of the intermediate days of Passover 5567. May his soul be bound up in the bond of eternal life.

This Moses Jacob should not be confused with 4:10 or 5:5.

Moses Jacob married Sarah Moses (4:1), a daughter of Alexander Moses (1:3). They had 12 children: Betsy (not 3:9 or 5:1) who died unmarried (see the note to Pz. 3:1); Judith (3:7) who married Isaac Joseph (2:5); Rose who married Alexander; Killa or Kitty (5:4) who married Simon Solomon (3:3); Jacob Jacob (5:3) who married Sarah Simons (5:2); Henne or Hannah (Pz. 3:2) who married Solomon Ezekiel (Pz. 2:3); Samuel Jacob (Pz. 2:1) who married Sarah Levi (Pz. 1:9); Rebecca who married Lemon Woolf (Pz. 1:1); Esther who married Henry Harris (see 3:12); Mirele or Amelia (Pz. 3:1) who was unmarried; Levi who married S. Mordecai; and Flora (who is buried at Merthyr Tydfil) and who married Rabbi Barnett Asher Simmons (Pz. 1:8). Four other children died young. There are further details of Moses Jacob in chapters 3 and 7.

10. UNKNOWN

11. "Rabbi SAAVIL" (Samuel, son of Samuel Levi)

Died 1 Nisan 5574 (22 March 1814) aged 73

Heb. Here lies a generous man, going in righteousness. His actions were perfect in faith. He ate from the labour of his hands and stood in his righteousness until he was gathered to his rest on high. Samuel the son of Samuel Ha-Levi. He died on Tuesday, New

Moon Nisan and was buried on Wednesday, 5574. May his soul be bound up in the bond of eternal life.

12. GERSHAN ELIAS (Gershom, son of Elijah)

Died 17th Adar 5628 (11 March 1868), aged 84

Heb. Here lies a man who walked in uprightness. All his deeds were perfect in faith, and gave to the needy with joy according to his ability until he was gathered on high to his rest. Gershan the son of Elijah, died on Wednesday, 17th Adar and was buried the next day, Thursday, 18th Adar, 5628. May his soul be bound up in the bond of eternal life.

Eng. In memory of Gershan Elias who died 11th March 5628, 1868, aged 84.

It is possible that this stone has been displaced in view of the surrounding stones being much earlier.

A relative of Esther Elias (1:11) and Barnet Levy (1:4) and also of Shevya Levy (Pz 6:4) and Hart Elias (3:8).

ROW 3

1. A. H. H.

Died 5607 (1846/7)

There is no inscription. It is a small tombstone partly hidden by a hedge. Thought to be the infant son of Morris and Rebecca Harris.

2. BELLA WOOLF (Beila, daughter of Benjamin)

Died 2 Adar 5576 (1816)

Heb. Here lies Beila, the daughter of Benjamin – may his memory be for a blessing, the wife of Israel Segal. She died at dawn on the Sabbath and was buried on Sunday, 3rd Adar 5576. May her soul be bound up in the bond of eternal life.

She was born in Holland and was the wife of Israel Solomon (2:1). See chapter 8.

3. SIMON (Segal) SOLOMON (Abraham Simeon, son of Israel Aaron Levi)

Died 4 Tevet 5586 (14 December 1825)

Heb. Here lies buried a man who was upright in generosity. He walked in the path of the good. All his actions he performed with propriety. His soul cleaved to the Lord with uprightness. He did not turn aside from all the commandments of the Lord. Abraham Simeon, the son of Israel Aaron Ha-Levi. He died on the 4th and was buried on the 5th of Tevet 5586. May his soul be bound up in the bond of eternal life. Amen.

He was a son of Israel Solomon (2:1) and Bella Woolf (3:2). He married Kitty Jacob (2:9 and 5:4) the daughter of Moses Jacob. He was a painter and had a brother and sister who were also painters. See chapter 8.

4.   ISHAYA (son of Moses)

Died 1 Nisan 5587 (30 March 1827) aged 17½ years

Heb. Your God chose you to take delight in your soul, for day and night you meditated on your Torah, and you went in an upright way all the days of your life. You listened to the voice of your teachers, and in the resurrection you will be restored to life. Isaiah the son of Moses – may God preserve and protect him. Aged seventeen and half when he died on Thursday, New Moon Nisan and was buried on Sabbath eve, 2nd Nisan 5587. May his soul be bound up in the bond of eternal life. Amen.

5.   ABRAHAM (son of Joseph)

Died 6 Tishri 5589 (27 September 1828) aged 60

Heb. Here lies a man who was upright in generosity, who went in the way of the good. He gave charity generously to the needy. He was a tree of life to those who strengthen the hands of the learned. Righteous and upright. All his deeds he did with propriety. His soul cleaved to the Lord with uprightness. His body sleeps in the earth and his spirit was summoned to the Garden of Eden. All his deeds were for the sake of heaven. He himself clove to the living God. Abraham the son of Joseph. 60 years of age when he died on Sabbath night, and he was buried on Sunday, 8th Tishri 5589. May his soul be bound up in the bond of eternal life.

This is the son of Joseph Joseph of Alsace by his second marriage. Abraham was the husband of Hannah Levy (Pz 1:2) who was the daughter of Barnet Levy (1:4). Their son Henry Joseph is buried in the Penzance cemetery (6:5).

6. PHOEBE JOSEPH (Feigele, daughter of Joseph)

Died 25 Shevat 5590 (21 February 1830), aged 24

Heb. Here lies Feigele the daughter of Joseph. The wife of Isaac the son of Moses. She was 24 when she died, 25th Shevat 5590. May her soul be bound up in the bond of eternal life.

She was the daughter of Isaac Joseph (2:5) and Judith Jacob (3:7). She was the first wife of Isaac Davidson (not the Isaac of p. 213).

7. JUDITH JACOB (daughter of Moses)

Died 26 Kislev 5610 (8 December 1849)

Heb. The woman who fears the Lord, she shall be praised (Proverbs 31:30). She stretched out her hand to the poor; she put forth her hand to the needy (Proverbs 31:20). Judith the daughter of Moses, wife of Moses Isaac. She died on Sabbath, 26th Kislev and was buried the next day, Sunday 5610. May her soul be bound up in the bond of eternal life.

Judith Rebecca Joseph was a daughter of Moses Jacob (2:9) and Sarah Moses (4:1). She married Moses Isaac Joseph (2:5).

8. HART ELIAS (Jacob Elijah, son of Naphtali)

Died Kislev 5596 (1835)

Heb. Here lies Jacob Elijah the son of Naphtali. He died and was buried in the month of Kislev 5596. May his soul be bound up in the bond of eternal life.

He married his niece Shevya Levy (see 1:4 and Pz 6:4, also chapter 8).

9. BETSY JACOB

Died 29 March 1838 (5600)

This was the wife of Philip Moses (see 1:3 and 2:2). She is not to be confused with the unmarried daughter of Moses Jacob (2:9) or Betsy Jacob of 5:1, also unmarried.

10. PHOEBE SIMONS (Feigele, daughter of Isaac the son of Samuel)

Died the first day of Pesach 5584 (14 April 1824).

Heb. Here lies the girl Feigele the daughter of Isaac the son of Samuel. She died the first day of Passover and was buried on the second, 5584. May her soul be bound up in the bond of eternal life. Amen.

This was the infant granddaughter of Rosa Moses (4:2) and Samuel Simons (4:4). Phoebe was the daughter of their son Isaac.

11. ISRAEL LEVY (Israel, son of Ezekiel Aryeh)

Died second day of Shauvot 5584 (1824)

Heb. Here lies a generous man. He went uprightly. His deeds were perfect in faith. He ate from the labour of his hands. He stood in his perfection until he was gathered. Israel the son of Ezekiel Arieh. He died on the second day of the Feast of Weeks and was buried on the next day (Isru Hag) 5584. May his soul be bound up in the bond of eternal life. Amen.

Israel Levy of Truro was married to Hannah Moses (Pz 5:1), the daughter of Alexander Moses (1:3). Their children were Henry, Sarah (Pz 1:9) who married Samuel Jacob (Pz 2:1), Judith, and Elizabeth (Pz 1:6) who married Samuel Oppenheim (Pz 1:7).

12. SAMUEL HARRIS (Samuel, son of Naphtali)

Died 29 Tammuz 5584 (24 July 1824)

Heb. Here lies an upright man in generosity. He walked in the way of the good. His soul cleaved to the Lord in uprightness. Strong as a lion and fleet as a deer, swift as an eagle (Mishnah, Ethics of the Fathers 5:23). He did not turn aside from any commandments of the Lord included in the ten commandments. Samuel the son of Naphtali. Died and was buried on 29th Tammuz, in the year 5584. May his soul be bound up in the bond of eternal life. Amen.

Samuel Harris was the husband of Judith Solomon (4:7) the daughter of Israel Solomon (2:1) and Bella Woolf (3:2). His family was German in origin, although he came from London. He was the father of Henry Harris of Truro, who married Esther Jacob (2:9) a daughter of Moses Jacob.

Hart Elias – Fal 3:8.

Lewis Falkson – Fal 4:9. [both
pictures courtesy: Rachel Berg]

13. ESTHER FALKSON (Esther, daughter of Samuel)

Died 25 July 1863 (5623)

Heb. Here lies the woman Esther the daughter of Samuel. The wife of Judah the son of Joshua. She died on Sabbath Eve, the eve of Tisha (9th) b' Av, and was buried on Sunday 10th Av 5623. May her soul be bound up in the bond of eternal life.

Eng. In memory of Esther Falkson, who departed this life July 25th 5623, 1863.

Esther was the wife of Lewis Falkson (4:9).

ROW 4

1. SARAH (Moses) JACOB

Died 1 Shevat 5591 (15 January 1831) aged 83 years.

Heb. Here lies the woman Sarah, the wife of Moses the son of Jacob – may his memory be for a blessing. She stored up the fear of the Lord. Charity and peace were the fruits of her deeds. Fullness of days were her years, for children and the children of children received kisses from her mouth (Song of Songs 1:2). She went to her everlasting rest to see the delight of the Lord on New Moon, Shevat 5591. May her soul be bound up in the bond of eternal life.

Sarah Moses was born in 1748 and her age was 83 years at the time of her death in 1831. The Hebrew inscription shows a dot above the letter yod, and it was recorded (de Lange and Speake) as such, giving an age of 93 years.

Sarah Jacob was a daughter of Alexander Moses (1:3) and the wife of Moses Jacob (2:9).

2. ROSA (Moses) SIMONS (Rosa, daughter of Alexander)

Died 15 Tevet 5598 (1838) in her 82nd year.

Heb. Here lies the woman Rosa the daughter of Alexander, the wife of Samuel. She died on Sabbath eve 15th Tevet and was buried on Sunday 17th Tevet 5598. May her soul be bound up in the bond of eternal life.

Rosa Simons was a daughter of Alexander Moses (1:3), the wife of Samuel Simons (4:4). She was the mother-in-law of Jacob Jacob (5:3) and sister to Sarah (4:1). Rosa and Samuel had two children: Isaac and Kitty (5:2).

3. Rev. MOSES HYMAN ("Rabbi Mowsha: Moses, son of Hayyim)

Died 22 Ellul 5590 (14 September 1830)

Heb. Here lies a perfect man; he went in the path of the good; righteous and upright, he performed his deeds with propriety. Moses the son of Hayyim, cantor – may his memory be for a blessing. From here Falmouth. He died on Friday 22nd Ellul 5590. May his soul be bound up in the bond of eternal life.

See chapter 6 for possible confusion over the secular date of his death, for details of the length of his ministry, and for his daughter's conversion to Christianity: pp. 161–162.

4. SAMUEL SIMONS of Truro (Samuel, son of Simeon)

Died 29 Cheshvan 5593 (24 October 1832) aged 92 years

Heb. Here lies Samuel the son of Simon. He died on Tuesday, the eve of the New Moon of Cheshvan, and was buried on Wednesday, New Moon of Cheshvan 5593. May his soul be bound up in the bond of eternal life.

Samuel Simons was married to Rosa (4:2).

5. JUDITH MOSES (Yetele, daughter of Alexander)

Died 6th Kislev 5604 (29 November 1843)

Heb. Here lies a woman of worth (Proverbs 31:10); the king's daughter is all glorious within (Psalms 45:14); her name is known in the gates for her hand she always stretched out to the poor. Yetele the daughter of Alexander. She died on Wednesday, 6th Kislev and was buried on Thursday 7th Kislev 5604. May her soul be bound up in the bond of eternal life.

Eng. Judith Lawrance. Died 29th November, 5604.

Judith was a daughter of Alexander Moses (1:3). She married Henry Joseph of St Austell (2:4), who died in 1803. Their three infant sons died (see 2:6 to 2:8). She later married Lazarus Lawrence (4:6). There were no children of Judith Joseph's second marriage to Lazarus Lawrence (4:5 and 4:6).

6. LAZARUS LAWRENCE (Eliezer, son of Jacob)

Died 12 Ab 5601 (30 July 1841)

Heb. Here lies a generous man who went with perfection. All his deeds were perfect in faith. He gave amply to the hungry far and near. He was free with his wealth; his business dealings were with faith. At all times he was one of those who paid attention to the cry of the poor and needy. His name was known with love. Eliezer the son of Jacob who went to his eternal rest on Friday, Sabbath eve, 12th Av, and was buried on Sunday, 14th Av 5601. May you rest and bear your lot until the end of days. May your soul be bound up in the bond of eternal life.

Eng. Lazarus Lawrance, 5601.

There was a Lawrence family which lived in the disused Falmouth synagogue as its caretakers. It was known at that time as "Synagogue House". This family may have been related to Lazarus Lawrence.

7. JUDITH SOLOMON (Yetele, daughter of Israel Aaron Segal)

Died Adar 5599 (5 March 1839) aged 75

Heb. Here lies a woman of worth, pious and upright. She did the righteousness of the Lord. The wise woman, her spirit went on high. All her days she proceeded on the right path. She observed the commandment of the Lord. Yetele the daughter of Israel Aaron Segal. She died on Tuesday, 19th Adar and was buried on Thursday 21st Adar 5599. May her soul be bound up in the bond of eternal life.

Eng. Mrs Judith Harris, 5th March 5599. Aged 75.

The daughter of Israel Solomon (2:1) and the wife of Samuel Harris (3:12).

8. LEAH (daughter of Israel Solomon; as 1:2)

The unmarried sister of Judith (4:7).

9. LEWIS FALKSON (Judah, son of Joshua)

Died 19 Cheshvan 5613 (1 November 1852) aged 65 years

Heb. Here lies a man upright in generosity, who went in the way of the good. He was strong as a lion in carrying out the will of his

Father in heaven; and his spirit ascended to heaven amongst the beloved and delightful. Judah the son of Joshua. He died and was buried on Monday, 19th Cheshvan 5613. May his soul be bound up in the bond of eternal life.

Eng. Lewis Falkson, died 1852, aged 65 years.

Lewis was the husband of Esther (3:13).

10. MOSES SAMUEL JACOB ("Mosam": Moses, son of Samuel of Penzance)

Died Falmouth 17 Ellul 5618 (27 August 1858) aged 43

Heb. Here lies Moses the son of Samuel from Penzance. He died the eve of Sabbath, 17th Ellul and was buried on the 19th Ellul 5618. May his soul be bound up in the bond of eternal life.

Eng. Moses Samuel Jacob, son of S. & S. Jacob of Penzance; died at Falmouth. August 27th 5618/1858, aged 43. The stone was erected to his memory by his cousin Moss. J. Jacob.

Moses Samuel Jacob was the unmarried son of Samuel Jacob (Pz 2:1) and Sarah Levy Pz 1:9), the daughter of Israel Levy of Truro (3:11). "Mosam" was therefore a grandson of Moses Jacob of Redruth (2:9) and Sarah Moses (4:1), the daughter of Alexander Moses (1:3). He was a prominent Freemason and was elevated to the Provincial Grand Lodge Honours at a very early age.

ROW 5

1. BETSY JACOB (Beila, daughter of Jacob of Falmouth)

Died 5598 (29 March 1838) aged 16 years

Heb. Here lies the unmarried woman, Beila the daughter of Jacob from Falmouth. She died on the eve of Sabbath, 4th Nisan and was buried on Sunday, 7th Nisan 5598. May her soul be bound up in the bond of eternal life.

Eng. To the memory of Betsy, third daughter of J & K Jacob, Falmouth, who departed this life 29th March 5598. Aged 16 years. A dutiful child, an affectionate sister, beloved and esteemed by all of her acquaintances.

Betsy Jacob was the third daughter of Jacob Jacob (5:3) and Sarah Kate Jacob (5:2). She is not to be confused with the unmarried daughter of Moses Jacob (2:9) or the Betsy Jacob of 3:9.

2. SARAH KATE SIMONS ("Kitty" Jacob: Sarah Killa, daughter of Samuel)

Died 12th Kislev 5607 (1 December 1846), aged 69 years

Heb. Here lies a pious and upright woman. Here deeds were pleasantness. Her husband's heart had trust in her because she planted a vineyard from the fruits of her hands. Her children rise up and call her happy. For fear of God her soul desired, and her spirit went on high, and her body will sleep in peace. The woman Sarah Killa, the daughter of Samuel. Wife of Jacob the son of Moses, who went to her eternal rest on Tuesday 12th Kislev and was buried on Thursday, 14th Kislev, in the year 5607. May her soul be bound up in the bond of eternal life.

Eng. To the memory of Sarah Kitty, the beloved wife of J. Jacob of Falmouth, who died on 1st December 5607, 1846. Aged 69 years.

She was known as "Kitty" Jacob, but should not be confused with her sister-in-law also "Kitty" Jacob (Segal or Solomon: 5:4). Her sister-in-law was a daughter of Moses Jacob 2:9) and was married to Simon Solomon (3:3). Sarah Kate Simons was the daughter of Samuel Simons (4:4) and Rosa Moses (4:2). She married Jacob Jacob (5:3), her first cousin. They had 10 children. Four died very young or in infancy: Alexander, Simon, Phoebe and Henry. Betsy died aged 16 years (5:1), Esther was unmarried, Amelia (Pz. 6:6 married Henry Joseph (Pz. 6:5), Moses Jacob Jacob (5:5), Isaac who married Sophia Lazarus, and Rebecca who married Morris Hart Harris (son of Henry Harris of Truro).

3. JACOB JACOB of Falmouth (Jacob, son of Moses)

Died 3 February 1853 (5613), aged 79

Heb. Here lies a God-fearing man, who kept his covenant . . . in death and in life. On his death, in his piety he turned towards God (?) . . . he called on his God with all his heart; he drew near to God humbly. Jacob with a good name; as with flute and drum . . . he went and returned from the place (roundabout ?). Whilst still alive he generously opened doors to the wretched and poor. His hands supported the house of his Lord. He magnified it as a Sanctuary. . . . How goodly are thy tents, O Jacob (Num 24:5). Loved ones, children, dear ones sent to the God of Jacob entreating him on behalf of the soul of Jacob, may his memory be for a blessing. By the God of the system he was given and was taken on Thursday, 25th Shevat and returned to dust on Sunday

28th of the same year {5}613. May his soul be bound up in the bond of eternal life.

This inscription was extremely difficult to translate. It consists of many acrostics on the name Jacob and is a kind of mediaeval poem. There are two unusual features of the Hebrew wording. Firstly, the name of God is given in the unusual form *Elokei* on several occasions rather than the usual *Elohei*. The former usage may denote a secular substitute name to avoid the association of *Elohei* with the strictly religious context. This may be linked with the extremely unusual phrase "God of the system". It is possible that this is a reference to freemasonry. Jacob Jacob's father, Moses Jacob, was a Mason (see chapter 7, pp. 263, 270, 271).

Eng. To the memory of Jacob Jacob of Falmouth who died on the 3rd February 5617, 1853, aged 79 years.

Jacob Jacob was a son of Moses Jacob (2:9) and the husband of Sarah Kate Simons (5:2). Her sister, Kitty, is buried next to him (5:4). He was, apparently, a competent amateur painter. His sister, Kitty, also married into an artistic family (5:4 and 3:3). In an article, "A Journey's End" in the *Jewish Chronicle* (March 18th 1960), Florence Abrahams descibed how she had discovered, in an antique shop in Philadelphia, two miniature portraits painted by Jacob Jacob, of himself and his wife Sarah. On the back of one of the miniatures was inscribed "Drawn by me, July 1820, in my 46 year of age. J. Jacob" and on the other, "In her 42 year of age, Mrs. J. Jacob." (Jacob Jacob was born in 1774, and Sarah in 1778). These portraits must have left the possession of the family at some point. They were bought during the War by an American serviceman called Smith who took them back to the USA where he eventually sold them to an antique dealer. Florence traced the great, great grandson, Alex M. Jacob, from whose archives these details have been drawn. She purchased the portraits for him for 35 dollars, bringing them back to London in July 1958. Sadly, they were stolen when Alex Jacob's flat was burgled in the 1980s and have never been recovered.

4. KITTY (Segal) SOLOMON (Killa, daughter of Moses)

Died 19 Iyar 5614 (10 May 1854)

Heb. Here lies a God-fearing woman; she shall be praised; she stretched her hand out to the poor and she put out her hands to the needy (Proverbs 31:20). Killa the daughter of Moses, wife of

Portrait of Sarah Kate Simons of Falmouth. [courtesy: executors of the archive of Alex Jacob, and the *Jewish Chronicle*; photography by E.H. Emanuel]

Portrait of Jacob Jacob of Falmouth, married his first cousin Sarah Kate.
[credits as overleaf]

Abraham Simeon Segal. She died Wednesday, and was buried on Sabbath eve, 21st Iyar, 5614. May her soul be bound up in the bond of eternal life.

She was a daughter of Moses Jacob (2:9) and the wife of Abraham Simeon (Segal) Solomon, or Simon Solomon (3:3), and was also a painter.

5. "MOSS" JACOB JACOB (Moses, son of Jacob of Falmouth)

Died 21st Shevat 5620 (14 February 1860), aged 47

Heb. Here lies a man upright in generosity. He went in the path of the good; as a righteous man he walked in peace and may he repose in his resting place. Moses the son of Jacob, may his memory be for a blessing. Leader and guide of the Holy Congregation of Falmouth. He died on Tuesday 21st Shevat and was buried next day, Wednesday 22nd, 5620. May his soul be bound up in the bond of eternal life.

Moss was a son of Jacob Jacob (5:3) and Sarah Kate Simons (5:2). This was the last Jewish burial in the cemetery of a member of the congregation.

ROW 6

1. PHILIP JOSEPH and JOSEPH JOSEPH (Uri and Joseph, sons of Zvi)

Philip Joseph died 4 Sivan 5550 (18 May 1790) and Joseph Joseph died 14 Ab 5550/4 (January 1790) respectively.

Heb. Here lies Uri the son of Zvi. He died on 4th and was buried on the 5th Sivan.

Heb. Here lies Joseph the son of Zvi. He died on the 14th and was buried on 15th Av.

These were the infant sons of Henry Joseph (2:4) and Judith Moses (4:5).

Note: The early dates on these stones suggest that they have been displaced from 2:7 and 2:8.

2. NATHAN VOS

Died 28 Tishri 5674 (29 October 1913), aged 80.

Heb. Here lies Nathan the son of Meir Vos. He died on Wednesday 28th Tishri. May his soul be bound up in the bond of eternal life.

Eng. In loving memory of my dearly beloved husband, Nathan Vos, born 25th April 1833, who died on 28th Tishri 5674, 29th October 1913, aged 80 years. Gone but not forgotten.

The last Jewish burial in Falmouth. Nathan Vos was a Freemason, and ran a pub in the town.

Plan of Falmouth Jewish Cemetery

Row 1.   1 2 3 4   5*   6   7*   8*   9*   10*   11*

       2.   1*   2*   3   4   5*6*7*8*   9*   10*   11*   12*

       3.   1   2   3   4 5 6*7* 8   9*   10*   11   12   13*

       4.   1 2   3 4   5 6   7   8   9   10

       5.   1 2   3   4   5

       6. 1*   2

This burial ground has been maintained on an irregular basis over the last 130 years or so. Many stones have been displaced or lost. Some may have been buried beneath the grass, and later re-appeared, because surveys have noted stones not included in earlier surveys, and noted the loss of stones once present. Some headstones have been broken and damaged. * The asterisk marks the location of graves either unmarked, without a headstone, or marked with a damaged, displaced, or illegible headstone (1998).

53 graves
33 graves with headstones

The Jewish Cemetery, Penzance

Introductory notes by Godfrey Simmons and Keith Pearce

Hidden in a triangle of back alleys in the heart of Penzance lies the Jewish cemetery. It is situated in an enclosed and secure location devoid of invasive trees and inaccessible to the public. It is perfectly preserved and, unlike the Falmouth burial ground, has not weathered with time. Apart from four unidentifiable stones, the tombstones remain intact and the lettering on them as clear as the day that they were erected.

When Jews first came to Penzance from the Rhineland area of Germany and Holland in about the 1720s, arrangements for worship at this time are unknown, as is the size of the Jewish population.[8] Burial arrangements are also unclear. The Cornish historian and author of the official *History of Penzance*, Peter Pool, assumed in 1974 that there had been an earlier, separate Jewish burial ground in the Rosevean area of the town.[9] By 1994 however, he came to doubt that this was the case and that the Leskinnick cemetery was the only one.[10] Certainly no evidence from old maps or records or leases has so far come to light to substantiate the existence of the "Rosevean cemetery" conclusively, and there are no visual signs today of what could have been a burial ground in the area.

It is likely that a plot of unenclosed land in or on the periphery of virgin fields in the Leskinnick area of the town was acquired by lease for a cemetery just before or around the 1740s. A fragment of an anonymous headstone transcribed from the Hebrew in 1975,[11] but

---

[8] Most likely, worship took place in a private house.

[9] Pool (1974, p. 155). He refers to what appeared to be a burial ground as a field name in a document of 1837.

[10] Letter from Peter Pool to Godfrey Simmons, June 1994. Much of the information in this introduction has been drawn from the original lease documents (some of which are held by the Morrab Library) and also from the Jewish congregation's minute books and accounts. The editors are also grateful to Anne Chappell for making available an original lease (dated 13th August 1835) containing a plan of the cemetery plots, to Harry Carter for information from aspects of his research into the cemetery's history, and especially to the late Peter Pool for advising Godfrey Simmons on the role played by the Barham, Borlase and Rogers families in the various lease negotiations.

[11] This was in the survey carried out by Nicholas de Lange and Jennifer Speake in April 1975.

which has only recently been translated,[12] bears the date 1741. Such an early date clearly confirms Pool's suspicions of 1994 that there had not been an earlier cemetery. It also revises Susser's dating of the earliest headstone as 1791.[13] It is not surprising that this early nascent community was concerned to have its own burial ground even before it was sizeable enough to contemplate the acquisition of its first purpose-built synagogue.[14]

The freehold of the cemetery land was eventually acquired by Canon John Rogers who owned land and estates at Treassowe in Ludgvan, near Penzance, Sithney near Helston, and the Leskinnick and Lescudjack areas of Penzance. The cemetery lay on the boundary which divided the land owned by Canon Rogers and land owned by a Dr. Barham of Exeter (1766–1844). Roth mentions that his son, whose full name was identical to that of his father, Thomas Foster Barham (1794–1869), helped the Jews by ". . . ceding his rights in a contiguous strip which they required . . .", so that the burial ground could be enlarged. The development of the burial ground actually took place in stages.

In 1808 the Jews were paying an annual rent of one guinea for the cemetery. On 31st March 1810, a "three life" lease for 99 years was granted to Lemon Hart by Canon Rogers at a rent of three guineas, which would not begin until Mary Borlase died.[15] Until then they continued to pay one guinea a year to "Mr. Foxhole", who was John Foxell, a non-conformist (congregational) minister in Penzance, Mary Borlase's son-in-law, acting on her behalf. At this stage the "Jews Burying Field" consisted of the wedge-shaped plot (roughly row 3 on the plan) which has the oldest, anonymous graves.

At that time landlords would often grant leases for a period of 99 years, calculated as likely to end on the death of the last of three "lives". The tenant could name each of these "lives", for example, by picking three people known to him personally, such as a member of his family. Walter Borlase probably held a lease from the Rogers family of part of Leskinnick, and nominated his wife Mary as one of the "lives". It was most likely a small section of this leased ground that the Jews obtained from the Borlase's as a sub-lease. The new lease was agreed in 1810 directly with the Rogers family, and in 1811 the Jews agreed to build a new wall around the cemetery ". . . when the

---

[12] Translated in 1998 by Herman Zeffertt. See Row 4:4.

[13] Susser (1993, p. 129).

[14] The first purpose-built synagogue was built in 1768, leased to the congregation under contract by a member of the Branwell family.

[15] In fact in 1822.

present lease or old life drops off . . .", to begin building when Mary died. In the synagogue records there is a note dated 14th April 1811 to the effect that a sum of 35 pounds, ten shillings, and eleven and a half pence had been put aside on deposit at 5% towards this eventual purpose, with any outstanding balance of the cost to be returned for the benefit of the congregation. The negotiations for the various leases between 1811 and 1844 were conducted by Lemon Woolf, and Henry Joseph.

In 1827, the congregation had to pay rental arrears in court for the difference between what they had paid and the new rental dating from Mary Borlase's death. By this time the whole area around the cemetery had become known as the "Jews' Fields", lying on a gentle gradient falling towards the sea. In 1834 a meadow called the Jews Field, together with the (higher) part of "Lower Jews Field" (probably in the area of rows 5 to 8 on the plan) was sold by Canon Rogers to Thomas Barham. On 13th August 1835 Canon Rogers granted a 99-year lease, to begin from 24th June, to Richard Rowe, a mason, to build a house on ". . . part of the Jews Burial Ground" (near row 3). In 1838 and 1841,[16] Rogers agreed to the further development of Leskinnick Terrace (which became known locally as "Jerusalem Row"), and granted building leases for plots in the "Higher Jews Burial Ground Field" (near rows 1 and 2). To prevent the incursion of this building, the Jews bought the freehold of the cemetery for fifty pounds on 29th September 1844 (the whole area within rows 1 to 8 of the present ground).[17] This was negotiated by and granted to Lemon Woolf, "spirit merchant", and to Henry Joseph, "pawnbroker", "wardens of the congregation of the Jews of Penzance" as "The Jews burial ground . . . and adjoining triangular plots". The entire perimeter of the ground was eventually enclosed with the completion of the building of a very substantial high wall. The foresight and wisdom of this can be seen today, in that the buildings have encroached right up to the edge of the cemetery.

These walls were so well constructed that they remained intact until bomb damage during the war (in October 1941) destroyed part of the lower walls near the entrance, and also several headstones. Repairs were carried out, presumably by the Town Council, to the walls, but they also replaced the headstones with several mini-headstones; they are in English script only (those of Solomon Teacher, 7:1; Catherine

---

[16] The cemetery first appeared on a map in 1841; c.f. Pool, op. cit., p. 155. The map clearly shows the burial ground in relation to the adjacent properties, and hangs in the basement of the Morrab Library.

[17] Roth gives the year incorrectly as 1845.

Levy, 7:2; and Joseph Barnet, 8:2). Further weakening to the walls may have resulted, and in the early 1990s several sections of the exterior-facing walls were substantially rebuilt.

There are 49 identified headstones, many of which are in remarkably good condition with beautiful Hebrew inscriptions and five which are decayed and unidentifiable. The last burials of members of the congregation were of Bessie Joseph in 1900, and the family of the last Rabbi, Isaac Bischofswerder, who were interred between 1880 and 1911. The solitary grave of Adolf Salzmann who died in 1964, and who may have been a refugee who settled in Redruth, lies at the entrance in the front row. Despite the absence of a Jewish community in the town for almost a century, this walled Georgian cemetery is one of the finest surviving examples of the Anglo-Jewish heritage.

Tombstone Transcriptions

ROW 1

reading from left to right

1. LEMON WOOLF (Asher, son of Hayyim: son of Hyman Woolf)

   Died 9th Adar II 5608 (February 1848), aged 65 years

   Heb. Here lies a steadfast man, leader and guide who went in the ways of the good, strong like a lion, running like a deer (Mishnah, Ethics of the Fathers 5:24) to the sound of the Torah and prayers, evening and morning. His house was open wide (Ethics of the Fathers 1:5); he gave of his bread to the hungry. His body dwells with the holy ones who are in the earth, and his soul is in the garden of Eden. Our teacher, leader and guide, Asher the son of the leader of the community, Hayyim. Died 9th of Second Adar and was buried on the 10th, 5608. May his soul be bound up in the bond of eternal life.

   Eng. In memory of Lemon Woolf, aged 65 years.

   Lemon Woolf, the son of Hyman (5:5), was married to Rebecca Jacob, a daughter of Moses Jacob of Redruth (Fal. 2:9). He owned a wine and spirit business in Market Jew Street and another in Chapel Street. He may have occupied other premises (possibly in Causewayhead) as a pawnbroker.

The Jewish cemetery, Penzance. [courtesy: Godfrey Simmons]

2. HANNAH LEVY (or Elra Joseph: Hendele, daughter of Issachar Jacob)

    Died 28th Cheshvan 5612 (22nd November 1851), aged 82 years

    Heb. Here lies a woman of worth (Proverbs 31:10), the righteousness of the Lord she did. She perceived that her earnings were good (Proverbs 31:18); she was humble like a bee; her deeds were pleasant; the daughter of the king is all glorious within (Psalms 45:14), she the wise woman whose soul went up to the heights; she went on the straight path all her life; she kept the commandments of the Lord. Hendela the daughter of Issachar Jacob. She died on Saturday night, 28th Cheshvan and was buried on Tuesday, the eve of the New Moon of Kislev 5612. May her soul be bound up in the bond of eternal life.

    The daughter of Barnet Levy of Falmouth (Issachar Jacob; Fal. 1:4). She was the widow of Abraham Joseph of Falmouth (Fal. 3:5). Her son Henry is buried in 6:5.

3. ISRAEL LEVIN (Israel, son of Zvi)

    Died 9th Nisan 5647 (3rd April 1887), aged 58 years

    Heb. To the memory of Israel the son of Zvi. Died 9th Nisan 5647. Israel to the cradle of the Lord. And Israel did valiantly (Numbers 24:18). May his soul be bound up in the bond of eternal life.

    Eng. Sacred to the memory of Israel Levin who died April 3rd 1887, aged 58 years. May eternal happiness be his portion.

    Israel Levin was a contributor to the Penzance Dispensary in 1839, which was the forerunner of the hospital. He continued his father's jewellery business at 102 Market Jew Street. He was the son of Henry (1:5) and Julia Levin (1:4).

4. JULIA LEVIN (Yuta, daughter of Israel)

    Died 12th Tishri 5640 (29th September 1879), aged 87 years

    Heb. Here lies a woman of worth. Her name – Yota the daughter of Israel. She died 12th Tishri 5640. May her soul be bound up in the bond of eternal life.

Eng. Sacred to the memory of Julia, relict of Henry Levin, who departed this life September 29th 1879, 5640, aged 87 years. Faithful to every duty of life, she is gone to receive her reward.

Julia was the widow of Henry Levin.

5. HENRY LEVIN (Zvi, son of Yekutiel)

Died 12th Cheshvan 5638 (19th October 1877), aged 79 years

Heb. Here lies a man who in his active life chose righteousness and uprightness. His soul is bound up in the bond of eternal life. May his rest be with the righteous of the world. Zvi the son of Yekutiel. He was gathered to his people on the eve of Sabbath 12th Cheshvan and was buried on Monday, 15th 5638. 79 years old. May his soul be bound up in the bond of eternal life.

Eng. Sacred to the memory of Henry Levin, who departed this life Friday October 19th 1877, 5638 in the 79th year of his age. Piety, faith and charity marked his pilgrimage on earth; may God in heaven grant him his due reward. His memory will ever be cherished and revered by his children.

The son of Moses Levin of London and Hannah, the daughter of Lyon Joseph. He was the father of Israel Levin (1:3) and husband of Julia (1:4). Their two sons, David and Hyman, are buried in 5:7 and 5:8. Henry Levin was a general dealer and jeweller.

6. ELIZABETH OPPENHEIM (Beila, daughter of Israel)

Died 23rd Tammuz 5639 (14th July 1879), aged 81 years

Heb. Here lies a cherished and important woman, Beila the daughter of Israel. She died on Monday, 23rd Tammuz 5639. She trod in the paths of uprightness all her days. Her soul has gone to God in heaven. May her soul be bound up in the bond of eternal life.

Eng. In affectionate remembrance of Elizabeth relict of the late Samuel Oppenheim who died on Monday July 14th 1879, 5639 in her 81st year. May all happiness be her portion.

Elizabeth Oppenheim was a daughter of Israel Levy (Fal. 3:11) and Hannah Moses (Pz. 5:1). She was the widow of Samuel Oppenheim.

Elizabeth Oppenheim, widow of
Samuel Oppenheim – Pz 1:6.

Samuel Oppenheim – Pz 1:7. [both
pictures courtesy: Gordon Brown]

7. SAMUEL OPPENHEIM (Samuel, son of Nathan)

Died 13th Sivan 5630 (23rd May 1869), aged 69 years

Heb. Here lies an honest and upright man. Samuel the son of
Nathan, of blessed memory. He died on Sunday, 13th Sivan 5630,
aged 69. In his life and in his death he trusted in the loving
kindness of his Father. In the courtyards of his God he will flourish
for ever like a palm-tree (Psalm 92:13). May his soul be bound up
in the bond of eternal life.

Eng. In affectionate remembrance of Samuel Oppenheim who
died on Sunday May 23rd 1869, 5630, aged 69 years. May all
happiness be his portion.

Samuel Oppenheim was a prosperous, bourgeois businessman
who ran a family furniture and general household store on the
Terrace (opposite the present-day Humphry Davy statue). The
business was continued by his son, Israel. His daughters went to
finishing-schools in Germany. He died as the result of a burst
blood vessel whilst in the Royal Baths on Penzance Promenade.

8. BARNETT ASHER SIMMONS (Abraham Issachar, son of Asher)

Died 4 Kislev 5621 (19th November 1860) aged 76 years

Heb. "And Abraham died in good old age" (Gen 25:8). "this pile is
witness and this tombstone is witness" (gen. 31:51). Here lies a
man true in spirit and fearing heaven; pure in heart and clean of
hands. His honour, Rabbi Abraham Issachar the son of Asher of
blessed memory, Cantor and Shochet, and Mohel. Died on
Sunday, 4th Kislev and was buried on Tuesday 6th, 5621.
Abraham returned to his place. There is a good reward for his
deeds [a play on his name – Issachar is split into two words –
"there is" and "reward"]. (The son of) 77 years old. He was
gathered to his people. Happy is he in his rest in the Garden of
Eden ["Happy is he" is a play on his father's name, Asher.
Therefore the complete name is shown by quotations]. May his
soul be bound up in the bond of eternal life.

Eng. B.A. Simmons died 4th Kislev 5621.

Barnett Asher Simmons was the longest serving rabbi in Cornwall
(from 1811 to 1859): see his full biography in chapter 6. He
married Flora Jacob, a daughter of Moses Jacob (Fal. 2:9). They
had 11 children – see the appendices for a full list.

9. SARAH (or Sally) LEVY (Sarah, daughter of Israel)

Died 10th Iyar 5628 (2nd May 1868) aged 84 years

Heb. Here lies a modest woman Sarah the daughter of Israel. 84 years old. She died on Sabbath, 10th Iyar and was buried on the 12th 5628. May her soul be bound up in the bond of eternal life.

She was the daughter of Israel Levy of Truro (Fal. 3:1) and Hannah Moses (5:1). She was the widow of Samuel Jacob (2:1). They had a daughter Betsey, a dressmaker, who was deaf and dumb, a problem which afflicted a number of Moses Jacob's descendants (3:1). This may explain why several of the females remained unmarried.

10. HANNAH SELIG (Hindele, daughter of Hayyim)

Died 17th Tammuz 5607 (1st July 1847) aged 68 years

Heb. Here lies a woman of worth (Proverbs 31:10), she perceived that her earnings were good (proverbs 31:18). Her soul went to on high. She performed the commandments of the Lord. Hindele the daughter of Hayyim, of blessed memory. She died 17th Tammuz and was buried on the 18th 5607. May her soul be bound up in the bond of eternal life.

Eng. Sacred to the memory of Hannah Selig who died July 1st 5607 aged 68.

Hannah was the widow of Aaron Selig (1:11).

11. AARON SELIG (Aaron, son of Phineas)

Died the eve of New Moon Av 5601 (18th July 1841) aged 59 years

Heb. Here lies a man of integrity and generosity, who walked in the path of the good; his soul clove to the Lord, and he caused friends to enter into the covenant and circumcised them. Aaron the son of Pinchas who died on the eve of the New Moon Av and was buried on the New Moon 5601. May his soul be bound up in the bond of eternal life.

Eng. Sacred to the memory of Aaron Selig who died on 18th day of July 5601, aged 59 years. In life beloved, in death deeply regretted.

Hannah Selig – Pz 1:10.

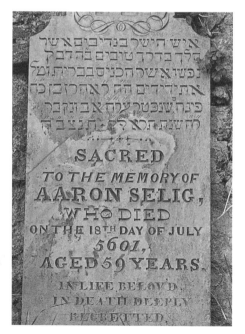

Aaron Selig – Pz 1:11. [both
pictures courtesy: Gordon Brown]

Aaron married Hannah (1:10). Their son, Benjamin, was a watchmaker. After his parents had died, he emigrated to Australia in 1854 with his wife Catherine and their children, Aaron and Lemon. He eventually became minister of the Wellington Congregation in New Zealand.

ROW 2

1. SAMUEL JACOB (Samuel, son of Moses)

   Died 15th Kislev 5621 (30th November 1860) aged 83 years

   Heb. Here lies a perfect and upright man in his deeds, fearing his God, righteous in his faith. Samuel the son of Moses, peace be upon him. 83 years old. He died on the eve of Sabbath 15th Kislev and was buried with a good name on the same day. May his soul be bound up in the bond of eternal life.

   Eng. Samuel Jacob died November 30th 5621, aged 83 years. He who pursues the way of righteousness will repose peaceably in the tomb.

   Samuel was the second son of Moses Jacob of Redruth (Fal. 2:9). He was married to Sarah Levy (1:9).

2. Rev. HYMAN GREENBERG (or Samuel Hillman: son of Simeon Greenberg)

   Died 27th Nisan 5621 (7th April 1861), aged 24 years

   Heb. Here lies the man great in wisdom. His sun speedily set, hastening to evening. His tender shoot soon withered. 24 years old. God will guard him. He died with a good name on Saturday evening and was buried the next day, Sunday 27th Nisan 5621. Our teacher Rabbi Samuel Hillman the son of our honoured Master and Teacher Rabbi Simeon Greenberg. May his soul be bound up in the bond of eternal life.

   Eng. Rev. H. Greenberg died 7th April 5621, aged 24 years.

   A young man, possibly a recent immigrant. He may have been without trade, except some religious (Talmudic) knowledge and was therefore briefly employed by the community between 1859 and his untimely death in 1861.

3. SOLOMON EZEKIEL (Isaac, son of Ezekiel)

Died 2nd Adar II 5627 (9th March 1867)

Heb. Here lies Isaac the son of Ezekiel. Died on Sabbath 2nd Adar II and was buried on the 4th 5627.May his soul be bound up in the bond of eternal life.

Eng. Solomon Ezekiel died March 9th 5627, 1867.

Solomon was from the Ezekiel family of Exeter. He was born in Newton Abbot in 1786. By 1811 he had moved to Falmouth and later to Penzance. He lived in Causewayhead and traded as a plumber and coppersmith. He was married to Hannah Jacob (3:2).

ROW 3

1. AMELIA JACOB (Mirele, daughter of Moses)

Died 22nd Ellul 5624 (23rd September 1864) aged 70

Heb. Here lies the spinster Mirele daughter of Moses. 79 years old. She died on 22nd Ellul 5624 and was buried on the 24th.

Eng. Amelia Jacob died September 23rd 5624, 1864 aged 70 years.

Edit. The English inscription reads aged 70 years at the time of her death, the Hebrew was translated as 79 years.

At least three of Moses Jacob's daughters were deaf mutes. Amelia remained unmarried. Her sister, Betsy, was also a spinster (Fal. 2:9). Their niece, also Betsy or Bessie, is buried in 7:5. Another unmarried niece, Selina, is buried in 4:3. This Amelia's niece, also called Amelia Jacob, is buried in 6:6 and was married to Henry Joseph (6:5).

2. HANNAH JACOB (Henne, daughter of Moses)

Died 29th Ellul 5624 (30th September 1864) aged 89

Heb. Here lies the woman Hannah, the daughter of Moses. 89 years old. She died on Friday, 29th Ellul 5624.

Eng. Hannah the wife of Solomon Ezekiel, died Sept 30th 5624.

Hannah was another of Moses Jacob's daughters. She was the wife of Solomon Ezekiel (2:3). Mirele and Henne were grand-daughters of Zender Falmouth (see also 5:1 below).

ROW 4

1. ABRAHAM JOSEPH (Abraham, son of Zvi)

   Died 26th Sivan 5599 (4th June 1839) aged 5 years

   Heb. Here lies a delightful boy, charming and pleasant. The boy Abraham the son of Zvi who died on 26th Sivan and was buried on Sabbath eve 29th 5599. May his soul be bound up in the bond of eternal life.

   Eng. Abraham Joseph died June 4th 5599.

2. SAMUEL JOSEPH (Samuel, son of Zvi)

   Died 5604 (12th October 1844), aged 5 months

   Heb. Here lies the boy Samuel the son of Zvi. May his soul be bound up in the bond of eternal life.

   Eng. Samuel Joseph, Oct 12th 1844 aged 5 months.

   Abraham and Samuel Joseph may have been grandchildren of Henry Joseph (6:5).

3. SELINA (or Sarah) JOSEPH (Sarah, daughter of Zvi)

   Died 12th Ellul 5632 (15th September 1872), aged 37 years

   Heb. Here lies the spinster, delightful and pleasant in her deeds; she found favour in the eyes of God and man, and in the eyes of all who saw (her). Hayye Sarah daughter of the important, honoured Master and Teacher Zvi, leader of our community. She died on Sunday and was buried on Monday, 13th Ellul 5632. May her soul be bound up in the bond of eternal life.

   Eng. In affectionate memory of Selina Joseph who died on Sunday September 15th 5632, 1872, aged 37 years. The memory of the Just is blessed.

   Selina Joseph was an unmarried daughter of Henry Joseph (6:5) and Amelia Jacob (6:6).

4. JUDAH (Judah, son of Moses)

Died 9 Ellul 5584 (1824)

Heb. Here lies a man upright in his generosity who went in the way of the good; his body will sleep in the ground but his soul was summoned to the Garden of Eden. He devoted himself to the living God. Yehuda the son of Moses who died on Thursday, 9th Ellul and was buried on Sabbath eve, 5584. May his soul be bound up in the bond of eternal life.

4 unidentified headstones

(i) *Heb.* Here lies a woman of worth

(ii) *Heb.* Bu(ried) on Sunday, 25th Shevat 5501 (1741)

This is the earliest dated grave. It places Jewish settlement in Penzance much earlier than had previously been supposed. It may mean that Jews had settled in the town before the establishment of the Falmouth community. The stone virtually rules out the assumption that there had been an earlier Jewish cemetery at Rosevean, north of Leskinnick; but it is not impossible that the headstone was moved from an earlier cemetery.

(iii) *Heb.* A man upright in his generosity who went in the way of the good . . . . son of our honoured Master and Teacher, Rabbi Abraham . . . and was buried on Thursday, 19th Tishri 5583 (1825). May his soul be bound up in the bond of eternal life.

(iv) *Heb.* . . . . the daughter who (was born) 25th Ellul . . . . (year?). She died on . . . . 21 Kislev 5556 . . . (1796) . . . . Sabbath and he was buried . . . . Kislev 5557 . . . (1797). May their soul be bound up in the bond of eternal life.

This stone has at least two inscriptions for a male and female who died within a year of one another; most likely a husband and wife, but it could be a brother and sister.

ROW 5

1. HANNAH MOSES (Henne, daughter of Moses)

Died 2nd day of Pesach 5601 (1841)

Heb. Here lies a pious woman Hannah, the wife of Israel of Truro, who died the 2nd day of Passover 5601. May her soul be bound up in the bond of eternal life.

Hannah was a daughter of "Zender Falmouth" (Fal. 1:3) and the wife of Israel Levy of Truro who died in 1824 and was buried at Falmouth (Fal. 3:11). She may have moved to Penzance to live with a relative, most likely one of her daughters Sarah (1:9), or possibly Mirele (Amelia, 3:1), or Henne (Hannah, 3:2).

2. PESSIA SIMMONS (Pessia, daughter of Abraham)

Died 14 Marcheshvan 5593 (1832)

Heb. Here lies a most beautiful virgin. Our daughters are as polished corner stones (Psalm 144:12) in a grave; your soul is in the Garden of Eden; she died in an epidemic. To be raised to life at the resurrection of the dead. Pessia the daughter of Abraham Issachar. She died and was buried on the Sabbath, 14th Marcheshvan, 5593. May her soul be bound up in the bond of eternal life.

Pessia was a daughter of Rabbi B.A. Simmons (1:8). Like her cousin Ruth (6:7), she became ill with cholera in the great epidemic of 1832 and they both died within 24 hours of one another. Because of emergency regulations, she was buried on the sabbath. Pessia and Ruth are the only known Jewish victims of this epidemic. Strangely, Pessia was not listed by B.A. Simmons in his register of the births of his children (see appendices). She was probably about 8 years old at the time of her death.

3. JACOB JAMES HART (Jacob, son of Solomon Levi)

Died 24th Shevat 5606 (19th February 1846) aged 62

Heb. And the days drew nigh that Jacob must die and he called to his friend (based on Gen 47:29) and said: I will lie with my fathers and you shall bury me in their burying place, give thirty pounds to my sister, (or) for a plot (see p. 287). The grave of Jacob the son of Solomon Ha-Levi, who died Sabbath eve 24th Shevat and was buried on Thursday, the first day of the New Moon of Adar 5606.

Eng. Sacred to the memory of Jacob James Hart, esq. Late her Britannic Majesty's Consul for the Kingdom of Saxony and a native of this town, who departed this life in London on 19th February AM. 5606, aged 62 years.

Jacob James Hart – Pz 5:3. [courtesy: David Sonin, the *Jewish Chronicle*]

Jacob James Hart is mentioned in Israel Solomon's *Records*. He was originally called "Jacobs" and took his surname from his uncle Lemon Hart whilst working in the latter's wine business. He became a friend of the young Lord Palmerston as a result of supplying wine to the London clubs. He appears to have had an irascible temperament. When he eventually fell out with Lemon Hart, Palmerston obtained for Jacob the diplomatic post referred to in the headstone inscription. Although he returned to England, he had become estranged from most of his family and requested that he should be buried in the Penzance cemetery. His beautifully engraved headstone and elaborate raised coffin-shape grave indicate his prosperity. (See pp. 286–7.)

4. SOLOMON ZALMAN (son of Jacob Segal)

Died 10th Iyar 5583 (1823)

Heb. Here lies a man. . . . He died Monday, and was buried . . . 11th Iyar 5583. May his soul be bound up in the bond of eternal life. Solomon Zalman the son of Jacob Segal.

5. HYMAN and EDDLE WOOLF

Eng. In memory of Hyman and Eddle Woolf, parents of Lemon Woolf. Erected by the late Henry Harris of Truro.

No Hebrew Inscription or date.

Hyman Woolf was the second president of the Penzance congregation.

6. EDIL (daughter of Asher)

Died 2nd Sivan 5607 (1847)

Heb. Here lies a young unmarried girl Edil the daughter of Asher the leader and guide of the community, who died 2nd Sivan 5607. May her soul be bound up in the bond of eternal life.

Edil was probably a daughter of Asher ben Hayyim (Lemon Woolf, 1:1).

7. DAVID LEVIN (David, son of Zvi)

Died 10th Marcheshvan 5634 (31st October 1873), aged 40 years

Heb. Here lies a perfect and upright God-fearing man. David the son of Zvi. He was gathered unto his people on the Sabbath eve,

10th Marcheshvan 5634. May his soul be bound up in the bond of eternal life.

Eng. Sacred to the memory of David Levin who died October 31st 1873.

8. HYMAN LEVIN (Hayyim, son of Zvi)

Died (18th June 1844), aged 13 years 3 months

Heb. Here lies. O passer-by look and see! Here lies a delightful young man, on the good path, he walked until he reached 14 years of age. The young man Hayyim the son of Zvi who died on Tuesday the second day of the New Moon Tammuz, and was buried on Wednesday 5604. May his soul be bound up in the bond of eternal life.

Eng. Hyman Levin died June 18th 1844 aged 13 years & 3 months.

Hyman and David were the sons of Henry and Julia Levin (1:5 and 1:4 respectively).

ROW 6

1. SOLOMON LEVY (Phineas, son of Menachem)

Died 4th Ellul 5601 (20th August 1841), aged 56

Heb. Here lies an upright man. He went in the path of the good. A good heart to stengthen the hand of the poor and needy. All his deeds he performed fittingly, and the commandments of the Lord he observed with uprightness. Pinchas the son of Menachem. 56 years old. He died and was buried on 4th Ellul 5601. May his soul be bound up in the bond of eternal life.

Eng. In memory of Solomon Levy, a native of Exeter who died Aug 20th 5601, 1841, aged 56 years. May his soul rest in peace.

Solomon Levy was the son of Menachem Levy of Exeter.

2. ELIEZER (son of Isaac)

Died 14th Sivan 5604 (1844)

Heb. Here lies the young man Eliezer the son of Isaac who died on the Sabbath, 14th Sivan 5604. May his soul be bound up in the bond of eternal life.

3. MILLIE BISCHOFSWERDER (Malka, daughter of David)

    Died 23rd Av 5640 (31st July 1880), aged 11 weeks.

    Heb. Here lies the girl Malka the daughter of David, she died in her illness on the Sabbath day 23rd Av 5640. May her soul be bound up in the bond of eternal life.

    Eng. In memory of Millie, daughter of David & Helena Bischofs-werder who died July 31st 1880, aged 11 weeks.

    Millie was the infant daughter of David and Helena Bischofswer-der, who lost another young child called Sarah (7:4). She was the grand-daughter of one of the last Cornish rabbis, Isaac Bischofs-werder (8:3).

4. SHEVYA LEVY (Shevya, daughter of Issachar Jacob)

    Died 6th Adar 5610 (17th February 1850) aged 84 years

    Heb. Here lies a pious and upright woman, the righteousness of the Lord she did like our mother Sarah; the prayer of the Lord she prayed with devotion; she observed the commandments of the Lord in the house in which she dwelt. Shevya, the daughter of Issachar Jacob who died and was buried on Monday, 6th Adar 5610. May her soul be May her soul be bound up in the bond of eternal life.

    Eng. Mrs. Elias relict of Mr Hart Elias of Falmouth, Feb 17th 1850, aged 84.

    Shevya was the daughter of Barnet Levy of Falmouth (Fal. 1:4). She is mentioned in Israel Solomon's *Records*. She married her uncle Hart Elias in London. Her husband's business failed and they returned to Falmouth where Hart Elias was buried in 1835 (Fal. 3:8). Like Hannah Levy (5:1), she may have moved to Penzance to live with relatives.

5. HENRY JOSEPH (Zvi, son of Abraham)

    Died 28th Kislev 5642 (20th December 1881), aged 75.

    Heb. Here lies an upright man; Zvi the son of Abraham. He was gathered to his people on Tuesday, 28th Kislev 5642, 75 years old. May his soul be bound up in the bond of eternal life.

    Eng. In loving memory of Henry Joseph of this town, born at Falmouth March 18th 1806, died DecR 20th 1881, 5642.

Henry Joseph was born on 18th March 1806 in Falmouth. He was the son of Abraham Joseph (Fal. 3:5) and Hannah Levy (1:2 above). His mother came to live with him after she was widowed. He was married to Amelia Jacob (6:6). He moved to Penzance where he became a prosperous pawnbroker in Queen's Square, living in some style in Market Place. Sarah Simmons, a domestic servant, and Simon Simmons, Henry's shop assistant lived in the house together with Elizabeth Birch, a child's maid, and Nanny Uren, a housemaid. There were nine children: Selina (4:3), Rose, Lionel, Morris, Esther, Jos, Kate, Betsey (7:5) and Julia (7:6). Henry was an influential member of the congregation and was involved in the purchase of the freehold of the cemetery.

6. AMELIA JACOB (Mirele, daughter of Jacob)

Died 3rd Nisan 5651 (11th April 1891) aged 80 years

Heb. Here lies an upright woman, Mirele the daughter of Jacob, the wife of Zvi the son of Abraham. She was gathered to her people on the 3rd Nisan 5651. 80 years old.

Eng. In loving memory of Amelia, wife of Henry Joseph, born at Falmouth March 18th 1811, died April 11th 1891 aged 80 years.

Amelia was the granddaughter of Moses Jacob of Falmouth. Her parents were Jacob Jacob (Fal. 5:3) and Sarah Kate Simons (Fal. 5:2). She was born in Falmouth on 18th March 1811. She married Henry Joseph (6:5 above). The Amelia Jacob of 3:1 was her aunt.

7. RUTH (daughter of Joseph)

Died 13 Marcheshvan 5593 (1832), aged 20

Heb. All who pass by look on me, the praiseworthy spinster Ruth, 20 years old, the daughter of Joseph, son of Rabbi Abraham Isaac, leader and guide in the holy community of Plymouth. Her heart was fearful and perfect; a pure heart to strengthen the hand of the poor and needy to the best of her ability. She died in the epidemic at the time when God punished the inhabitants of the world in his anger. (She died) on the eve of Sabbath, 13th Marcheshvan 5593. May her soul be bound up in the bond of eternal life.

Ruth was the daughter of Abraham Joseph, the president of the Plymouth Hebrew Congregation (not Pz. 4:1 or Fal. 3:5). Ironically, she had been sent by her family to Penzance to stay with her uncle Rabbi B.A. Simmons to escape the cholera outbreak in

Plymouth. She died of cholera in Penzance, along with her cousin Pessia (5:2).

8. ISRAEL (son of Moses)

Heb. Here lies the boy Israel the son of Moses.

No date on the headstone. This was the grave of a child.

ROW 7

1. SOLOMON TEACHER

Eng. Solomon Teacher died 10th March 5616, 1856

Edit. No Hebrew on the headstone, which like those of Catherine Levy (7:2) and Joseph Barnet (8:2) is not the original. The original headstones were destroyed by bomb damage during the Second World War.

Solomon Teacher was married to Maria Selig, the daughter of Hannah and Aaron Selig. See also pp. 97 and 246.

2. CATHERINE LEVY

Eng. Catherine Levy died 14th July 5624, 1864.

3. RACHEL BISCHOFSWERDER (Rachel, daughter of Mann)

Died 4th Adar II 5646 (10th March 1886), aged 55 years

Heb. Here lies the modest and important woman; praised for loving kindness and goodness. Rachel the daughter of Mann the wife of Rabbi Isaac, the Cantor and Shochet who was here twenty years. She was 55 years old. Her pure soul departed from her body on the 4th Adar II, and on the 5th she was led to her burial in the year 5646. May her soul be bound up in the bond of eternal life.

Eng. In loving memory of Rachel the beloved wife of the Rev. Isaac Bischofswerder, who died March 10th 1886 aged 55 years.

She was known by her German forename, Rahle. She was a widow with children when she married Rev. Isaac Bischofswerder.

4. SARAH CICILIA BISCHOFSWERDER (Sarah Zilla, daughter of David)

Died 16th Adar 5651 (26th March 1891), aged 14 months

Heb. Here lies the girl Sarah Tsilla (or Zilla) daughter of David. She died on 16th Adar 5651. May her soul be bound up in the bond of eternal life.

Eng. In memory of Sarah Cicilia beloved daughter of David & Helena Bischofswerder who died March 26th 1891 aged 14 months.

5. BESSIE (or Betsy) JOSEPH (Belia, daughter of Zvi)

Died 2nd Kislev 5661 (21st November 1900)

Heb. Here lies the spinster Beila the daughter of Zvi. She died 2nd Kislev 5661. May her soul be bound up in the bond of eternal life.

Eng. In loving memory of Bessie Joseph born 1st DecR 1848, died 24th NovR 1900, 2nd Kislev 5661. May her soul rest in peace.

Bessie Joseph was born on 1st December 1848. She was an unmarried daughter of Henry Joseph (6:5) and Amelia Jacob (6:6).

6. JULIA BISCHOFSWERDER (Yittel)

Died 8th day of Passover 5671 (20th April 1911)

Heb. May she come to her place in peace. Here lies a dear and important woman Yittell, wife of Moses Bischofswerder. She died on 8th day of Passover 5671. May her soul be bound up in the bond of eternal life.

Eng. In loving memory of Julia, wife of Morris Bischofswerder, born June 1st 1851, died April 20th 1911.

Julia was born on 1st June 1851. She married Morris Bischofswerder. This was the last burial of a member of the original community.

ROW 8

1. JUDAH (son of Naphtali)

Heb. Here lies Judah the son of Napthali.

This (original) headstone may have been displaced before the bomb-damage to surrounding stones of 7:1, 7:2 and 8:2 because this one remains intact. Within recent memory it had been resting against the wall near 6:1 until it was correctly re-positioned (circa 1995).

2. JOSEPH BARNET

    Eng. Joseph Barnet died 7th April 5616 (1856).

    No Hebrew.

3. REV. ISAAC BISCHOFSWERDER

    Died 14th Cheshvan 5660 (18th October 1899), aged 77 years

    Heb. And Isaac entreated the Lord (Gen 25:21). Here lies a perfect and upright man, Isaac the son of Zvi who was Cantor and Shochet here for more than twenty years, and also in the State of Germany he kept guard over holiness for about thirty years. He died on 14th Cheshvan 5640. May his soul be bound up in the bond of eternal life.

    Eng. In affectionate remembrance of our dearly beloved father the Rev. Isaac Bischofswerder who departed this life on the 18th October 1899, aged 77 years. May his dear soul rest in peace.

    See chapter 6 for a fuller profile of his life: pp. 184–189, 193–194.

4. ADOLF SALZMANN

    Died 9th Adar 5724 (22nd February 1964), aged 65 years

    Heb. Here lies. To the memory of Avner the son of Hayyim Israel. He died on 9th Adar 5724. May his soul be bound up in the bond of eternal life.

    Eng. In memory of Adolf Salzmann, died 22 February 1964 aged 65 years.

Plan of Penzance Jewish Cemetery

```
Row 1.  1   2   3   4   5   6   7   8   9   10  11
Row 2.  1   2   3
                                            Am  Au
Row 3.  1   2  Au           Am        Au  Au          Am
Row 4.  1   2   3   4
Row 5.  1   2   3  Au      4(2)        5         6
                                                  7   8
Row 6.  1   2   3   4       ?          5   6   7   8
Row 7.  1   2       3   4   ?              5       6
Row 8.      1       2       3                          4
```

Au = Anon. unmarked grave.
Am = Anon. marked (broken or illegible grave).
? = a flat grave-size space, but no obvious mound as with Au/Am.

58 graves
9 unknown

Note: Rows 3 and 4 probably represent the oldest part of the cemetery, first leased as the "Jews Burying Ground". Rows 1, 2 and 5 may have been added next as the "Higher Burial Ground". Rows 6 to 8 were added last as the "Lower Burial Ground".

The Jewish Cemetery, Truro

The Jewish population of Truro in the eighteenth and nineteenth centuries was very small, unlikely to have comprised more than a few families. The names 'Levy' (or 'Levi') and 'Harris' were the most common. No documentary evidence of the existence of a synagogue there has ever emerged and so it would seem that a private house or other premises may have been used for worship. At one time it was assumed that any burial would have taken place in the Falmouth cemetery. Truro is only about 10 miles up river from Falmouth, and the Falmouth cemetery is only a few hundred yards from the Penryn wharf, and so it would have been relatively easy and cheap to carry coffins from Truro by boat.

In fact a Jewish cemetery or small burial plot did exist in Truro some time around the late eighteenth or early nineteenth century, but it was to all intents and purposes abandoned by the 1840s. When the children of the family of John Levi were all baptised in 1842 (at St. Mary's church, now the cathedral) this may well have effectively marked the end of any noticeable Jewish presence in Truro.

The minute book of what later became the Truro General (Municipal) Cemetery has survived. On 21st February 1840 an initial meeting was called to discuss the proposal that a general, that is non-denominational, cemetery should be established, distinct from those of the Church of England. The issue had been provoked by the case of a non-conformist free-thinker who had been refused burial by a local parson. Present at the meeting was John Levi, who was voted onto a sub-committee, taxed with finding a suitable site for the general cemetery. At a meeting of the provisional committee on 9th March 1840 it was reported that, "Mr. Edwards had applied to the steward of Mrs. Agar respecting what is called the Jews Burying ground, which is not to be obtained."[18]

At one time the very existence of this Jewish burial ground was in doubt because a substantial lower section of a wedge of land at the junction of Trennick Lane and St. Clements Hill was referred to as a "Gue Burying Field" in old survey documents. As *gue* was the Cornish for an enclosure, it was taken that this land was set aside or enclosed for burials. It was thought that the surveyor had written down what he

---

[18] In a collection of unlisted deeds and leases arranged by Parish in the Clifden Collection at Old County Hall, Truro.

had expected to hear, or what he had meant, but nevertheless it was assumed that the Anglicised phonetic similarity to *Jew* had subsequently given rise to the erroneous notion that it was a Jewish burial site. Such misapplication as this could have been common as the largely spoken Cornish language disappeared, leaving sometimes unintelligible words and place names.

The plot in question known as gue appears on some old maps as plot 1082. The Jewish cemetery was, in fact, at the extreme corner of the wedge from plot 1082, in plot 1062, as a waste triangular parcel of land belonging to Sir Samuel Spry, occupied by John Rollins.

The exterior retaining wall at this point shows signs of a bricked-up entrance. The Edmund Turner mortgage document in the Archive Department of Old County Hall in Truro contains this reference:

> . . . three-cornered field and Sopers field, also Jews Burial Ground (Lr), near Trennick Lane in St. Clement . . . and the next of kin of James Trestrail dec.d of meadow in St. Clement (. . . 1812) formerly in possession of William Moore. This ground and the Jews Burial Ground was then one close . . .[19]

The whole of this plot has long since been covered over and built upon, and today no sign exists that it was once the Jewish cemetery. Likewise, no records of names of those buried there have come to light. If such records were kept, they may have been transferred to Falmouth and been lost or perhaps they may have been taken out of the county.

Postscript

What does the future hold for the two Jewish burial grounds? They are far-flung, without any organised Jewish life within the county of Cornwall. Although the Board of Deputies act as trustees, they are reliant upon the goodwill of private individuals to act as caretakers and key-holders, and to oversee voluntary arrangements for maintenance and allow access for visitors. No established fund exists to carry out emergency work if needed. Neither the District or Town Councils, within whose boundaries the cemeteries lie, have any statutory obligation to oversee or maintain them. In the event that the non-Jewish custodians could no longer carry out their work, then no formal structures exist locally to ensure continuity.

---

[19] DD.BRA.1623.

The Penzance cemetery is in excellent condition and is placed in a conservation area, but this confers only limited legal protection. The Falmouth ground has a derelict and vandalised cemetery adjoining it,and the whole area on two sides of the cemetery perimeter has been cleared for commercial development. Its future would seem perilous.

These are very important historical sites as well as sacred burial grounds. They are unique in the county. Without some co-ordinated campaign to save them, and without the will of the councils to preserve them, they may not survive to the end of the next century.

It may be that in time this book will be the only complete and permanent record of their existence.

The Rabbis

Godfrey Simmons and Keith Pearce

A lthough the Jewish communities in Cornwall survived for less than two hundred years, some thirty or more rabbis were associated with the Falmouth and Penzance congregations in the eighteenth and nineteenth centuries. Little is known of the rabbis in the 1700s, but from the early 1800s onwards names appear more frequently. It is not possible to identify the names of all the rabbis who served the Cornish Jewish congregations because records are minimal, particularly for Falmouth. Details of the Penzance rabbis have survived in some detail and in various forms in the minute books and legal documents. For both communities cemetery headstones, census returns and newspaper reports are helpful. From these sources over thirty names have been identified: twenty-two for Penzance and nine for Falmouth.[1]

Identifying the rabbis can be complicated by the fact that the term Rav or Revd appears frequently on Jewish headstones as an honorary or courtesy title for people who were not, in fact, ordained as rabbis or registered with the Chief Rabbinate. Some were senior lay members of the congregation such as the president (*Parnas*) or the treasurer. They would have been respected men of wisdom, experience, and good character, without any special religious training, but competent in religious knowledge and practical religious matters. Such lay people were sometimes given the title *Reverend* without having any formal religious training or background in Talmudic study. In the case of others, this title would often denote some form of religious training and suitability for a limited ministry but without full ordination or recognition by the Chief Rabbi.[2] In the Penzance cemetery for instance there is only one known rabbi (B.A. Simmons, 1:8) and two reverends (Hyman Greenburgh, 2:2; and Isaac Bischofswerder, 8:3) but several other men receive the title Rabbi, sometimes in effusive terms although they are known only to have been lay members of the congregation. The example of the headstone of Henry Levin illustrates this practice:

---

[1] Susser (1993, p. 156 and 307) gives eight for Penzance and six for Falmouth.
[2] Letter from Herman Zeffertt to Keith Pearce, 17th September 1998.

His honour Rabbi Zvi, the son of his honour Rabbi Yekutiel.[3]

Some of the earliest men to have served the communities would therefore not have been rabbis in a formal sense. Care has been taken in this chapter to try to eliminate those who received the courtesy title and to include only those who are known from other documentary sources to have been employed in a religious capacity.[4]

Falmouth

As we have seen, the organisation of the earliest Jewish communal life in Falmouth was very much under the supervision and patronage of Alexander Moses. At first his efforts were focused on the development of a satisfactory economic climate which would enable the nascent congregation to become established. In those early days the community was unable to contemplate the appointment of a rabbi for some time. In these circumstances its senior members led the services.[5] In any event, such a small community could only support a rabbi if he were virtually self-sufficient with his own trade and the only name which dates from this period is that of Isaac Polack, who is known to have lived in Penryn in the 1760s and 1770s.

Nothing is known of Polack's background although his name suggests Eastern European origins. He was well educated and most certainly multi-lingual. Whether he was fully qualified as a rabbi is unclear and there is no direct evidence that he served the Falmouth congregation in any formal capacity, but his various academic skills alone would have placed him of assistance to the congregation's needs. Isaac Polack may have been only loosely attached to the congregation and not entirely committed to Judaism. On 15th February 1760 he married Mary Stoughton, a widow, also of Penryn. Whether Isaac had by then (or later) converted to Christianity is not certain, but the

---

[3] Pz. 1:5.

[4] The case of Michael Leinkram shows the problem of gaining a clear perspective on this in all cases: he appears to have been skilled primarily (or only) as a *chazan* at Penzance but his marriage certificate refers to him as a Jewish minister at this time. He did move on to other positions in Belfast and London as a rabbi, but his headstone in the Edmonton cemetery does not have the word Rav or any other reference to a religious vocation.

[5] Sarah Moses, a forceful personality and a daughter of Alexander Moses, took a prominent part in the congregation and led services in the absence of the *parnass*. She may also have done so when the men had not returned home from their work in time for the Sabbath. Unusually, she is said to have laid *tephillin* – cf. *The Jewish World*, 15th May 1903, p. 153.

wedding took place in the local church of St. Gluvias.[6] The Phillimore Parish registers refer to him as a "Jewish priest".[7] This wedding may, however, indicate a trend towards cultural rather than religious "anglicization" for the purpose of social and commercial advantage rather than full assimilation and conversion. Even if Polack did convert, it is difficult to know how seriously the issue of conversion or marrying-out would have been taken in general by the Jewish community in such isolated places, even if some cases provoked ostracism and publicity, such as that of Harriet Hyman.[8]

Polack's occupation was that of a translator and interpreter of commercial and legal documents. He was eager to promote and advance himself as a man of learning and expertise. He took full advantage of the commercial opportunities offered by Falmouth as an expanding centre for maritime trade. He realised the need for a translator and interpreter in this context. On 1st July 1776 he could afford to take out an elaborate advertisement in the Dorset *Sherborne Mercury*:

TRANSLATION OF LANGUAGES

Isaac Polack, of Penryn, in Cornwall most respectfully acquaints those Mercantile Gentlemen who have connections in foreign countries, such as France, Germany, Holland, etc. that he writes and translates into English (and vice versa) letters, invoices, bills of lading, and other incidental circumstances of commercial intercourse, stiled in either the FRENCH, HIGH GERMAN, or LOW DUTCH Languages, with the utmost propriety, accuracy, and expedition.

Also protests in the foregoing Languages carefully copied and translated for Attornies, Notaries, and Tabellions; and the greatest attention will be paid, so as to merit their kind favours. The said Isaac Polack begs leave to assure the Gentlemen above addressed, (or any other employer) that SECRECY will be the principal object attached to; and their respective commands from any part of this county assiduously accomplished at a reasonable charge.

PETITIONS, MEMORIAL, etc, drawn for disabled seamen, sailors, widows, orphans, or other persons, to any public office in

---

[6] *Phillimore Parish Registers*, vol 13, p. 87.
[7] *Phillimore*, op. cit.
[8] Susser (1993, p. 95, 238, and 243).

this kingdom, and to foreign Courts, or to their Ambassadors, Residentaries, and Ministers of State, at very moderate fees.

Dated Penryn June 27, 1776.[9]

The name of I. Polack is mentioned in the early minutes of the Penzance congregation of 1825, but it is most unlikely that this is the same person in view of the time lapse of 65 years since his wedding in 1760.

The next known minister was "Rabbi Saavill" (Samuel ben Samuel HaLevi) who served the community for some years and died on 22nd March 1814. His headstone in the Falmouth cemetery (2:11) does not refer to any formal position of leadership that he occupied but simply praises his righteousness rather than his leadership. This could imply that the use of *Rabbi* was a courtesy title.

The Rev. Moses Hyman (Rabbi Mowsha or Moses ben Hayyim)[10] is referred to as the community's *cantor* on his headstone.[11] Again nothing is known of his life but very soon after his death, his nineteen-year old daughter Harriet, who had become drawn to Christianity, announced her intention to convert. A dispute broke out within her family, fuelled by the animosity of some people within the Jewish congregation to her proposed baptism. It became so bitter that the girl ran to the Town Mayor, James ("Jas") Cornish, for protection. He was obliged to adjudicate and summoned her family, who agreed to take her back only if she stopped going to church. The domestic outcome is uncertain but her engagement was broken off. She remained resolved to convert and it was reported in the *West Briton and Cornwall Advertiser* that she was publicly baptised at the Wesleyan Methodist Chapel on

---

[9] Susser (1993, p. 95 and 293) refers to this same advert. It appeared on the same date in the *Western Flying Post*. At the time, these newspapers were the only two circulating in the south-west. Advertisements could be placed locally in Falmouth, Penryn and Truro.

[10] Born in 1765 and died 14th September 1830.

[11] Fal. 4:3. There is some confusion over the date of Moses Hyman's death. The headstone gives "Friday 22nd Ellul 5590. Alex Jacob's archive contains his own survey notes of the Falmouth cemetery (unpublished survey of 1939). He translates this date as 14th September 1830. However in his article written in 1949, published in 1953 (reprinted as chapter 3 here), he gives the date as 24th October and the year (incorrectly) as 1832. Susser in an article in the *Cornishman*, Thursday 16th July 1964, gives the month as September. He places the conversion of Hyman's daughter Harriet some six weeks later, which would roughly coincide with 7th November. However in his book *The Jews of South West England* he gives the date as 24th October 1830, cf. p. 307. He also states in the *Cornishman* article that Moses Hyman served the Falmouth community for 27 years. Since Samuel HaLevi had died only 16 years earlier, it is possible that their ministries, and at least their lives, overlapped. For further details see Susser (1993, p. 243).

Sunday 7th November 1830.[12] Evangelical activity to gain converts was common at this time as Methodism expanded rapidly. Chapels sprang up and proliferated in both the main towns and country areas alike.[13] The small Jewish congregation would have felt particularly vulnerable to such a popular and enthusiastic movement.

From 1832 to 1849 Falmouth's rabbi was Joseph Benedict Rintel. His birth certificate (issued in 1809), his *Reisepass* (1831), a six-month permit from the Hamburg authorities, and his naturalisation papers (1861) have all survived.[14] He was born in the Hanseatic town of Hamburg on 29th November 1809 to Benedict Jacob Rintel and Thérèse (née Kalman). Rintely, his father's family name, and Kalman are both Hungarian. His father's forename Benedict was a vernacular form of the Hebrew name *Baruch*. On his *Reisepass*, issued in Hamburg for a period of six months on 4th January 1831, his name is given as Joseph Benedix Rintely. He was then 21 years of age. The *Reisepass* records that he had black hair and beard, and brown eyes. This young rabbi was appointed to the Falmouth congregation in 1832. Later, he walked alongside the mayor and the Roman Catholic priest in a public parade to demonstrate for the implementation of the Reform Bill.[15] He supplemented his income by bookbinding and teaching Hebrew and German.[16] On 6th June 1838 at the age of 28, he married Fanny, a daughter of Barnet Asher Simmons. On the marriage certificate he chose to be identified by the rank of "Gentleman" rather than the profession of rabbi. The couple subsequently lived in Killigrew Street in Falmouth. Rintel was the community's *mohel*. However it is not known whether he learned this skill before arriving in England, in London itself,[17] or later from B.A. Simmons. He is mentioned in the minute

---

[12] cf. The Falmouth Methodist Register (entry no. 472) for that date records that Harriet Elizabeth Hyman of Falmouth, born on 22nd December 1811, daughter of Sally Hyman and Moses Hyman, Jewish Rabbi (deceased) was baptised, with W. Lawry officiating. Research by Eric Dawkins.

[13] By 1864 two organisations for "Promoting Christianity among the Jews" had offices in Falmouth.

[14] Documents in Godfrey Simmons' archive. His great-aunt was married to Rintel. The editors are grateful to Roger Ainsworth for translating these documents.

[15] cf. letter in *Jewish World*, 15th May 1903, p. 153. See also Jacob, chapter 3. It is possible that this relates to the petition in 1848 for a Bill to remove Jewish Disabilities and to allow Jewish Parliamentary representation (referred to by Roth in chapter 4) rather than the 1832 Reform Bill.

[16] Susser (1993, p. 248). Not only would German have been the natural means of communication for the Jewish community, it would also have helped children in their study of the Torah portion for the week which would have had a Yiddish commentary.

[17] He later became renowned in London for his skills as a *mohel*.

Joseph Rintel, Rabbi of Falmouth 1832–1849. [courtesy: executors of
the archive of Alex Jacob]

Auszug

aus dem Geburts-Register der deutsch-israelitischen Gemeinde in Hamburg.

Ao. 1809. Pag. 102.

Im Jahre /1809/ ein tausend acht hundert und neun am /29/ neun und zwanzigsten November Uhr ward hieselbst in gesetzlicher Ehe des Benedict Jacob Rintel mit Therese geborne Kalman ein Sohn geboren, derselbe erhielt den Vornamen: Joseph, —

Die Richtigkeit des Auszuges bezeugt durch seine eigenhändige Unterschrift und das beigedruckte Amtssiegel.

Extr. Hamburg den 26' October 1841.

Z. H. Hay
beeidigter Registrator

Joseph Rintel: birth certificate, Hamburg. [courtesy: Godfrey Simmons's archive]

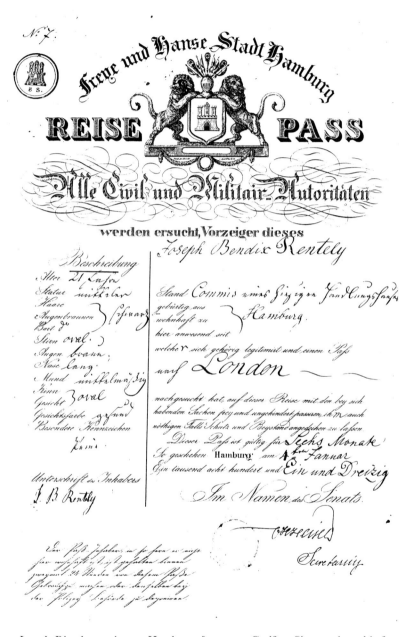

Joseph Rintel: travel pass, Hamburg. [courtesy: Godfrey Simmons's archive]

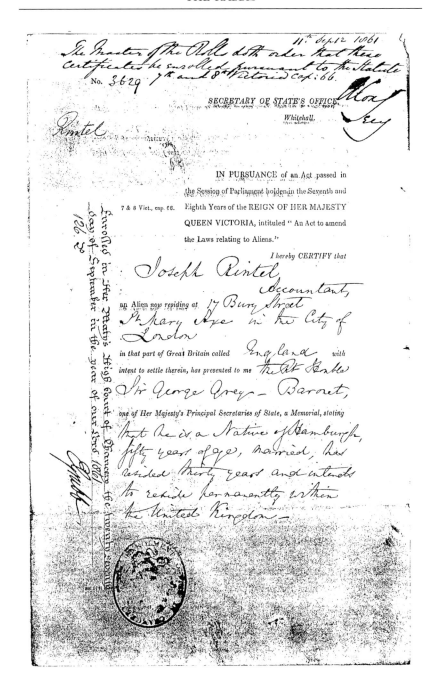

Joseph Rintel: naturalisation papers, London. [courtesy: Godfrey Simmons's archive]

books of the Penzance community because he acted as a locum there when his father-in-law suffered ill-health. He remained in Falmouth for 17 years. Local family ties and his assistance to his father-in-law allowed him to lead a settled and agreeable life in the 1840s. He kept abreast of ideas and developments in the wider Anglo-Jewish world, however, because for 1842 and 1845 he is listed as a subscriber to the Jewish periodical *The Voice of Jacob*. When he eventually left Falmouth in March 1849, the occasion was reported in the *Royal Cornwall Gazette*.[18] He had served the Falmouth congregation during the last period of its existence as a sizeable and flourishing community. It was soon to decline with rapid speed.

Rintel and his wife eventually moved to London. Rintel's brother-in-law, Moses Simmons, had already moved to London and worshipped at the Great Synagogue in Duke's Place. He was well placed to keep Rintel informed of any opportunities which might arise in the city. Rintel and his wife Fanny took up residence in Bury Street, where Moses lived, and in the same row of houses as the Chief Rabbi.

By the time of the 1851 census, Falmouth had a new rabbi. The census shows Samuel Herman from Konin in Poland, age 49, as the rabbi of the Hebrew congregation. His son, Abraham David Herman, then 23, is described as a bookbinder. However, the following year Abraham is given as the incumbent rabbi, and his father Samuel as "clergy".[19] From this time the congregation was in serious decline. In 1860 a dispute broke out between the Falmouth community and Mr. Herman relating to a delay in the payment of his salary as *shochet*. The witholding of his salary was clearly a punitive response by congregational officials to his intention to leave for another position in Sheffield. Herman saw this as a form of intimidation and he wrote to the Chief Rabbi, Dr. Adler, who wrote to the president of the Falmouth congregation on his behalf:

> Mr. Herman is leaving for Sheffield and complains you object to him leaving. I think you have no right to form an impediment to the man's promotion in life.[20]

Still less is known about the Rev. "Marks Morris of Prussia" whose appointment as rabbi of Falmouth Synagogue was announced in the *Royal Cornwall Gazette* on 5th November 1860.[21] It may be that the

---

[18] RCG, 27th April 1849, p. 8, col. 5.
[19] Information supplied by Lewis Falkson; cf. also Slater's *Royal National & Commercial Directory*, 1852, see the section "Places of Worship" and "Clergy".
[20] Susser (1993, p. 158).
[21] RCG, 5th October 1860, p. 5, col. 6.

newspaper announcement was intended to be read as "Marks, Morris" because in the 1861 census for Falmouth his name is given as "Morrice Marks" and his year of birth as 1827. He was married to Jebbeth (b. 1831). They had three children who had by that time all been born in Prussia: Charlotte (b. 1852), Willy (b. 1856) and Lena (b.1860). It is not known how long Morris remained in Falmouth, but he probably stayed until 1864 because from that year the Falmouth congregation no longer had a *shochet* and had to send to Penzance for kosher meat.

The arrival of a new rabbi, Nathan Lipman, in 1871 was particularly surprising at a time when few Jews remained in Falmouth, although there were possibly more Jews in the town or in outlying areas than the offical records would suggest.[22] Regardless of numbers, he remained until 1875 when he left for London. From 1879 to 1918 he was the *Rosh Hashochetim* or *Chief Shochet*.[23]

The last known rabbi was Samuel Orler, whose dates are not certain, but is thought to have been in Falmouth from around 1875 to 1880.[24] One of the members of the congregation, Samuel Jacob, had tried to keep some kind of communal religious life going and the synagogue open during these last years. In 1880, he finally left for London and the Jewish congregation came to an end.

The Rabbis of Falmouth

Lack of records allows only a few rabbis to be identified, with periods of office sometimes uncertain. The following rabbis served the community:

> 1760s: Isaac Polack ("Jewish Priest")
> Died 1814: "Rabbi Saavil" (Samuel ben Ha-Levi)
> Died 1830: Moses Hyman ("Mowsha" ben Hayyim)
> 1832–1849: Joseph Benedict Rintel
> 1850s: Samuel Herman, and Abraham David Herman
> 1860: Morrice Marks ("Markus Morris")
> 1871–1875/6: Nathan Lipman
> c. 1875–80 Samuel Orler

---

[22] There may have been a temporary increase in numbers. The decennial census returns were subject to errors of omission. Examples of this are given in chapter 7.

[23] He was the grandfather of the late scholar and historian, Dr. Vivian Lipman.

[24] cf. Susser (1993, p. 307). Letter from Lord Mishcon to Bernard Susser, 10th March 1993.

Penzance

In the early days of the Penzance community, members of the Hart family may have acted in some religious capacity. They had settled there just prior to the 1720s. Their influence within the Jewish community and over the Hebrew congregation was significant.[25] Several members of the family were known by the title Rabbi including Abraham Hart,[26] his son Asher Hart,[27] and Abraham Hart.[28] Although this title was one of courtesy rather than a formal one, it indicates their status and experience in leadership of the congregational affairs. They would have conducted the religious services in circumstances where it was not possible for a trained rabbi to be employed.

Between 1808 and 1811 a series of incumbents passed through Penzance, most remaining in the town only briefly. It is not known if they were all qualified sufficiently to be recognised by the Chief Rabbi. Some would have possessed knowledge in a limited area only, such as Talmudic study, or ritual slaughter, or in the skills of a cantor by virtue of a good voice, and so be of sufficient use to be hired for a short term. Roth suggests that they were hired only for a two-year period but very few stayed for the full two years. The onerous duties which the senior members expected of their rabbis may well have proved insupportable for many,[29] until the arrival of B.A. Simmons in 1811. Until then, at least eight ministers, an average of almost three a year, came and went in such rapid succession that virtually nothing is known of them. They included Rabbis Moses, Aaron, Moses Levi, Moses Isaac, and Hirsch. Roth assumes that R. Selig was the Aaron Selig who is buried in the cemetery (1:11) and who later is recorded in the minutes between 1821 and 1829, as in dispute with the congregation on at least three occasions. Rabbi Aaron may be identified with Aaron Selig, likewise Moses Levi with the Moses Isaac who was paid seven pounds and 10 shillings in wages for identical services on 30th June 1810, mentioned in the congregation's early minutes.

---

[25] Including Lemon Hart, born in Penzance in 1768, the grandson of Abraham Hart (Solomon Lazarus), who became the first president of the new synagogue when it opened in 1808.

[26] He died circa 1720.

[27] His exact date of death is unknown, but he died at some point between 1745 and 1752.

[28] Also known as Solomon Lazarus. He died in 1784.

[29] The heavy duties and poor pay which fell on rabbis in general in the south-west is covered by Susser (1993, pp. 136–159, 169). The onerous duties expected of ministers in the Penzance congregation were officially drawn up in 1817.

Roth identifies R. Feival with Philip Samuel.[30] Samuel was originally from Warsaw. It is doubtful that he was a fully trained rabbi, even though he was the son of the secretary of the Great Synagogue there and was highly educated in Hebrew. He lived in Vilna and Danzig at one point, before coming to England to escape bankruptcy and consequent imprisonment in Russia. His colourful career and his final move from Cornwall to Lisbon is told in detail by Israel Solomon. Philip Samuel was living in the Portuguese capital in January 1819 when he became re-acquainted with Israel Solomon, whose father was dying there. Solomon describes him as "from Cornwall" and that the Chief Rabbi had earlier[31] ". . . got him the place as reader in prayers at the synagogue at Penzance, Cornwall. For this he was not suited."[32] He left the post, worked as a government agent for Lyon Joseph collecting gold in Falmouth and later settled in St. Austell as a jeweller. On the advice of, and through recommendations supplied by, Lyon Joseph, he eventually went to Lisbon where he is said, by Roth, to have been one of the earliest founders of the Jewish community there.[33] He is said to have associated with the Marranos in Lisbon where he traded as a jeweller and where he died.

Barnett Asher Simmons (Abraham Issacher ben Asher, 1784–1860) was the longest serving rabbi in Cornwall. He was born in 1784 in London. On 6th June 1798 he became formally apprenticed to Abraham Jacobs, "Japanner and Painter", of Denmark Court in the parish of St. Martins-in-the-Fields, from whom he learned his trade. At the time he was apprenticed, he lived in New Court, Dukes Place, in the Parish of St. James. His indenture fee of twenty one pounds (a considerable sum at that time) was paid by his maternal grandfather Abraham Michel, also of New Court. The document was witnessed by I.I. Bing and L.J. Abrahams, and clearly signed as "Barnett Simmons".[34] Abraham Michel carried on a polishing business, catering

---

[30] Philip Samuel appears in Israel Solomon's *Records of My Family.*

[31] A date is not given.

[32] Although this might suggest that he was employed primarily as a cantor, and was unsuitable in this respect, it has also been taken to mean that he disliked his "killing" duties as a *shochet.*

[33] Lisbon has two synagogues. The main one is Sephardi and the smaller one is Ashkenazi. Israel Solomon mentions that Samuel would have met Jews from Morocco and Arabia at the Solomon's house. Even so, it is not clear in which of these synagogues he was a founding member, although it is most likely to have been the Ashkenazi.

[34] The name of B.A. Simmons' father, Asher, does not appear. He may have died because Abraham Michel was B.A. Simmons' maternal grandfather, whose will dated 1818 refers only to daughters who are not named. The original indenture document is in the archive of Godfrey Simmons.

for the needs of the many goldsmiths and silversmiths in the area with L.J. Abrahams as his partner. I.I. Bing was secretary of the Great Synagogue in Duke's Place and it would have been the synagogue where the Simmons family worshipped. B.A. Simmons' name, however, does not appear on a list of charity apprenticeships sponsored by the synagogue. B.A. Simmons' employer, Abraham Jacobs, was closely connected with the Western Synagogue in its early days. He was well known as a sign-painter and was an extremely learned man. His influence may have determined his apprentice's eventual choice to become a Rabbi.

Simmons completed his articles in 1804. Soon after, while still living in London, it is said that he was press-ganged into the Navy, and although it has been supposed that he was at the Battle of Trafalgar, no direct evidence of this has ever emerged. It is uncertain if his name appeared on the muster roll of any of the fleet which would have been registered at Greenwich. He certainly does not appear on the list of the holders of the Trafalgar medal, but as this was not issued until 1848, and had to be applied for, this is inconclusive. The tradition that he lost a finger at that famous battle is almost certainly apocryphal. The lost finger was the result of a boating accident much later in Penzance harbour.

In December 1811, at the age of 27, Simmons came to Penzance to act as rabbi and shochet, being engaged for the post by Lemon Hart. Hart must have been familiar with the tensions which characterised the Penzance congregation, especially in relation to the high-handed way in which its senior members were inclined to treat its rabbis, because he took the trouble to see that two letters of recommendation were sent. The first was from "The High Priest Solomon Hirshell" (sic.), the Chief Rabbi Hirschell, and the other was a brief personal letter from Lemon Hart to Hyman Woolf, the new president of the Penzance congregation. The letter is dated 23rd December 1811, and in it he refers to Simmons as a ". . . respectable young man. . . . I hope you will behave towards him properly, for you may rest assured that such articles are very scarce in this Market," a clear reference to the quality and range of the young rabbi's skills.[35]

In view of the fact that Simmons' early years had been shaped by living in the capital city, it is surprising that he chose to go to such a far-flung community as Penzance, even though its remote position belied its flourishing and relatively prosperous commercial and cultural life.[36] As

---

[35] Original letter in Godfrey Simmons' archive.

[36] It was the county's centre for sea trade, fishing, banking, and the surrounding mines. cf. Juliet Barker (1995, pp. 47–8).

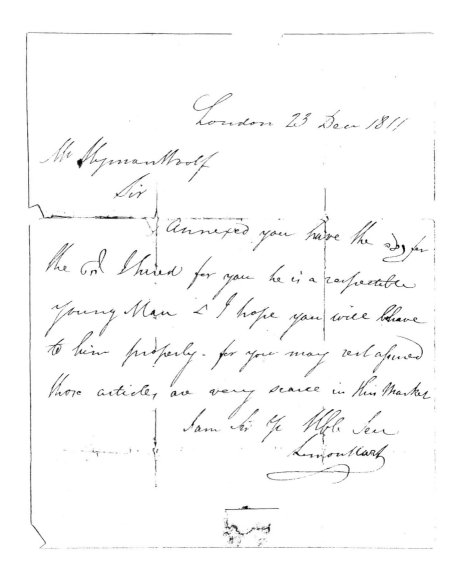

Rabbi B.A. Simmons: letter of introduction (1811) from Lemon Hart to Hyman Woolf, President of the Penzance Congregation. [courtesy: Godfrey Simmons's archive]

Lemon Hart realised, Simmons's religious and occupational versatility made him something of a desirable catch for a small Jewish community without the financial resources to employ separate individuals to carry out the functions of minister, *mohel* and *shochet*. He was the county's only permanent *mohel*; his circumcision register covering the period 1821–1847 has survived in a calf-bound book. It records a total of sixteen circumcisions: nine in Penzance, two in Falmouth and five in Truro.[37] In addition the young man was a fully qualified craftsman, capable of improving some of the internal ritual features of the synagogue.

The problems between the new rabbi and the senior members of the congregation, which came to be a repeated feature of their relations for much of the rest of his life, may have begun not long after his arrival, and Lemon Hart's admonition to Hyman Woolf was of no avail,[38] because in the years between 1811 and c.1825 at least four other men were employed for some of that period, resulting in breaks in Simmons' incumbency. Between 1813 and 1814 an Italian Jew, Elhanan Joseph Mortara, officiated at Penzance.[39] The minute book for 6th November 1815 records that the sum of £6 had been paid to Mr. Hyman Selig as coming from London and that on "Tuesday 14th November 1815 Mr. Hyman Selig left London from which time his wages begun (sic) . . . arrived at Penzance Monday 20th November 1815." He was appointed in the first instance for a year to serve primarily as a *shochet* and as a cantor, but also as a teacher of children. Two separate sums of £36 and £27, recorded in the minutes, seem to reflect these separate ritual and educational duties.[40]

By 1817 the congregation had employed Abraham Joseph as their rabbi. He had arrived in Penzance in the early 1800s and had officiated on an occasional basis soon after his arrival; however, it would seem that he moved away at some point because a note in the accounts towards the end of the last quarter of 1816 refers to expenses being paid, presumably to him (£4 10s.): "paid to [name illegible] for coming down – advanced him (5 pounds) to be paid out of his wages . . . paid him two weeks wages." Later in 1817 a contract was given to Rabbi Jacob Moses.[41]

---

[37] This includes four of his own sons and a grandson. The register is not actually complete because Alex Jacob refers to the fact that at least seven children were circumcised in Falmouth; however only two appear in Rabbi Simmons' register.

[38] Susser (1993, p. 157).

[39] He was apparently the son of Hayyim Solomon Levi Mortara, the Rabbi of Verona. cf. Roth, chapter 4.

[40] The editors are grateful to Nicholas de Lange and Herman Zeffertt for translating these sections of the minute books.

[41] He was the son of Judah Leib, a rabbinical judge of Frankfort-am-Main.

The congregation's minutes record that Rabbi Hart Symons (or Simonds) had become the communal factotum around 1818.[42] He appears to have been in Penzance at least until 1825, although he may not have officiated for the whole of that period. Nothing is known for certain of his origins. He was a man of some education and a gifted linguist. He most certainly possessed a strong and combative personality and a biting wit. He was also the author of a number of pamphlets on controversial or topical religious issues. In 1822 he entered into a literary debate over the interpretation of the Hebrew Bible with the Rev. Canon John Rogers, Rector of Mawnan. He wrote his text in Hebrew, out of principle rather than necessity, and it was translated into English by another local writer and lecturer, Solomon Ezekiel.[43] Both men were active and successful in opposing the activities of the Society for Promoting Christianity amongst the Jews which was active in Penzance and also, as we have seen, in Falmouth. Solomon Ezekiel had been able to prevent Sir Rose Price, the Society's most influential spokesman in Penzance, from establishing a branch and an office in the town. It may have been to strengthen the faith and the resolve of Jews who might become objects of the Society's attentions that Symons had written his *Letter to a Jew* in 1818, published by R. Scantlebury, in Redruth. In 1823 he had his *Arguments of Faith: Incontrovertible Answers to Sophists and Epicureans* published in and distributed from London and addressed to the Society, refuting their arguments.[44]

In 1824 a satirical pamphlet was published in Penzance under the pseudonym of J.J. Rousseau (the French philosopher and author of the controversial *Confessions*) who represented himself as "Maître de Danse, a présent malade a Penzance".[45] It was written in a brilliant parody of a Frenchman's pidgin-English, filtered through the mannerisms of how Yiddish-speaking Jews might pronounce English words. It was addressed to the Rector of St. Mary's Church, Valentine le Grice. The circumstances which lay behind and gave rise to this pamphlet are not clear, but le Grice, who had come to Cornwall from Essex, had married well into the prosperous and landed family of Sir Rose Price of Trengwainton, near Madron. Le Grice subsequently secured the incumbency of St. Mary's where his position would have been ideal for promoting the views of the Society for the conversion of the Jews. He regularly published his sermons and other pamphlets for the edification

---

[42] Roth has identified Hart Symons with B.A. Simmons. This is inaccurate. They are two different people who were not related to each other.

[43] *Bibliotheca Cornubiensis* B.C. Vol i (1874) p. 145.

[44] Susser (1993, pp. 244–5).

[45] The complete text is to be found in appendix 5.

and interest of the local populace. Hart Symons had sent him a Hebrew text (possibly of a previous publication), refuting or taking issue with his views. It is not known how, or if, le Grice responded to this, or if the matter became a *cause célèbre* in Penzance, but the *Letter of Condolence* was subsequently published by Symons, and then included by le Grice himself in one of his own collections.[46]

The Letter of Condolence is remarkable from a literary point of view for the perfect taste and judgement which Symons shows in the use of the satirical genre. It is noticeable that he achieves his effects by satirising le Grice as the social-climber with his pretentious French surname and its aristocratic associations, who lived in some comfort, with his enviable garden, somewhat detached from the town he "served", and who could not readily understand the Jew's Hebrew book. At the same time, in the person of the multi-titled "*Maître de Danse*", he creates a picture of the reactionary absurdity of those who might sympathise with the stereotypes of the Jew which "Rousseau" expresses, and also be appalled and enraged to the point of apoplexy at the temerity of a Jew who dared contradict a Christian "*Curé*". The *Letter* shows clearly that the rabbis were often very well-educated men. It shows the confidence and boldness of a Jew who is proud and secure in his religion and his identity. It also highlights the liberal tolerance of the society in which the Jews found themselves in Cornwall.[47]

It is difficult to assess the the significance of the re-publication of the *Letter* in le Grice's own collection. It could point to his naivety in being taken in by it, supposing the real Frenchman J-J. Rousseau to be an ally, but it could equally suggest that he saw the joke. Whatever the case may have been, this particular rabbi had certainly raised the profile of the Jewish community before he left.

The periods of interruption in B. A. Simmons' incumbency were sometimes the result of dissatisfaction, possibly on both sides, and also of the ill-health which he experienced in later life, especially from 1846 onwards. He was not so much suspended from his duties, but "suspended" himself by walking out in the wake of some dispute or other. Simmons accepted or endured these breaks and remained

---

[46] cf. Le Grice, 1824, Morrab Library.

[47] Non-conformism was on the ascendancy in the county at this point in the eighteenth century. Only twelve years before, in 1812, the Wesleyans had broken away from the Church of England. The first, very large, Methodist church was built in Chapel Street in 1814 only a few hundred yards from St. Mary's. The Methodist family, the Branwells, had built both Penzance synagogues and were also instrumental in the building of the Methodist church. cf. Barker (1995, p. 49). The Branwells had business and masonic connections with local Jews such as Lemon Hart.

available if and when the congregation should decide to re-appoint him. That he was prepared to do so for many a decade, when other rabbis were moving on quickly to seek better opportunities and more amenable situations elsewhere, most certainly ran counter to the pattern set by most of the rabbis in Cornwall. In total he was to spend 44 years in the town in this way, with only a three- or four-year break in south Wales after his retirement, eventually returning to Penzance.

In 1813 Simmons wrote to the then Chief Rabbi, Solomon Hirschell, asking permission to marry Blumah (Flora) Jacob of Redruth,[48] one of the many children of Moses Jacob. In this letter, to jog the Chief Rabbi's memory, he reminds him that his nickname was *Little Bera*, being short in stature (a family attribute that has come down the generations in the Simmons family). With a new wife and the prospect of a family,[49] he turned at some point to setting up some kind of small shop as an alternative and occasional source of income. He could calculate that he would always find himself in demand as a rabbi eventually and he could be in a position to make himself indispensable to the little congregation as the need arose. From 1818 to 1854, he was the congregation's most frequently employed incumbent, even though disagreements continued and ill-health intervened. While he was on hand as *shochet*, there was no need for the congregation to look elsewhere or to import the necessary supplies of kosher meat. That the congregation came to rely on him almost exclusively is indicated by the fact that he was formally reprimanded when he occasionally neglected to butcher sufficient meat for the Friday Sabbath eve, and that when he fell ill, kosher meat had to sent for from Falmouth. Even though his skills as a *shochet* became a matter for criticism, because he was required to go to London on at least one occasion to be checked by the Chief Rabbi on slaughtering, he returned with a completely satisfactory report.

---

[48] Two fine family portraits of the rabbi and his wife hang today in the Penlee House Art Gallery & Museum in Penzance. They were painted by R.A. Pentreath, member of The Royal Academy, to celebrate the rabbi's 50th birthday.

[49] Flora Jacob was born in Redruth in 1790. Her parents, Moses Jacob and Sarah Moses, had previously lived in Falmouth but had moved to Redruth in 1766, where they remained. Flora Jacob is described on her *ketubah* (marriage) document as "of Falmouth", reflecting her parents' original town and the Falmouth congregation to which the Jacob family was affiliated. B.A. and Flora Simmons lived in Market Jew Street (up to 1848), and subsequently moved to Leskinnick Terrace (in 1849) and eventually to the Rosevean area of town (in 1859). They had eleven children (see Appendix 3), including Pessia who died in the cholera epidemic of 1832. She is buried in the Penzance cemetery (5:2).

To

London May 31. 5597

M͞r Wolf President

Sir/

 I acquaint you herewith that on the first morning when I saw M͞r Simmons I appointed him immediatly to begin his examination but being rather fatigued from his journey detained him untill this morning when he finished his examination both with the knife and serging in Whitechapel and he is capprable of the situation

 I remain with wishing you every happiness your wellwisher &c.

[Hebrew signature]   Hirsch

Rabbi B.A. Simmons: report from Chief Rabbis Hirsch (1836) concerning his satisfactory examination as a shochet. [courtesy: Godfrey Simmons's archive]

Numerous tensions within the Penzance congregation persisted for much of Simmons's tenure. The congregation's minute book allows glimpses of a fractious and occasionally very tense atmosphere amongst the synagogue's administrators, worsened, no doubt, by continuing difficulties of financing the community's religious needs from such limited resources. Too much came to be expected of the incumbent minister because in his duties as *shochet* alone he was expected to slaughter twice a week in the winter months and three times a week in the summer.[50] It would seem that the senior members who administered the congregation's affairs were themselves over-bearing and domineering, and their failure to retain other incumbents for more than very brief periods would suggest a failure on their part to create good relations with their ministers, on whom they placed unreasonable demands. The minute book records various occasions when Simmons was reprimanded for dereliction of duty, incivility and even physical assault upon a member of the congregation, suggesting that he had a fiery temperament.[51] He was suspended from his duties on at least one occasion, although for how long is unknown. Whether these criticisms were justified or not, we cannot be certain. His salary was inadequate and was often a fundamental bone of contention. To supplement his income Simmons ran a small huckster's shop at 21 Market Jew Street where he sold crockery and other small household and personal items, including clothing. He may also have carried out book-binding.[52]

The tense relationship between Simmons and the Penzance congregation was not unique.[53] The ministers, who were often better educated men than their congregants, whose servants they were, could find themselves treated as such. Whether or not the complaints, resignations and re-engagements of B.A. Simmons reported in the minute book were justified, it is certain that steps were taken to ensure that the rabbi was not overpaid. At a meeting on 13th April 1845, it was resolved that his salary should be 32 pounds and 10 shillings per annum: "which sum is to include all prerequisites and grants."[54] Having made application for a salary increase, he was granted a salary

---

[50] Susser (1993, p. 149).

[51] cf. Penzance minute books, 17th & 20th June 1852 (Letter to the Chief Rabbi); and 10th & 24th July 1853.

[52] There is an original stock-list from B.A. Simmons' shop in the archive of Godfrey Simmons. There is also a range of hand-bound vellum pocketbooks in the archive.

[53] cf. Susser (1993, pp. 157–9) where he gives examples of disputes at Exeter, Plymouth and Falmouth. In each case the incumbent minister was supported by the intervention of the Chief Rabbi, Dr. Adler.

[54] Pz minute book, 1845.

of 37 pounds and 10 shillings at a meeting in March 1847. Later during a period of poor health, he made application for a charity grant from the congregation. This would suggest that he was not in receipt of a salary at this time. At a meeting held on 13th April 1851, the members voted to give him the sum of 10 shillings – not an over-generous amount even in the days when money was worth its face value. After a resignation in June 1852, he was re-engaged in the same post at a reduced salary of "30 pounds per annum, including all grants, education excluded."[55] The "article" (as Lemon Hart had previously referred to Simmons in his letter of recommendation) had become significantly devalued in this particular "market." It is difficult to understand why Simmons was prepared to endure this for a period of 43 years when he could have moved to another post; especially after his children had left the town. Genuine attachment to the locality and its people could have played a part, particularly since his wife Flora had lived in the county all her life.

B.A. Simmons was not the only minister or member to be the object of disapproval and reprimand. Faults no doubt existed on both sides, and Simmons' chronic poor health, subsequent indisposition and inability to sustain his duties did not help. On a number of occasions his son-in-law Rabbi Joseph Rintel of Falmouth acted as a locum,[56] even though Rintel was not formally employed at Penzance. Simmons certainly did not serve continuously for the whole of the period 1811–1854, and was dismissed but later re-employed. By the time Simmons retired in 1854 the decision to leave Penzance had been made. The couple went to live with a married daughter in Merthyr Tydfil. He was replaced from 1854–7 by Solomon Cohen, whose wage was 14 shillings a week.

The domestic arrangement in Merthyr was not an unqualified success. Simmons and Flora may have missed the town of Penzance where they had spent so much of their life. In 1857, they returned to Penzance to take a cottage in the peaceful Rosevean area just outside the town centre. In a letter to a member of the family,[57] the rabbi described how he would go to the cemetery to say his prayers each day. Obviously relations with the Jewish congregation could not have been so bad that they would not countenance re-employing Simmons once more as their rabbi. He was re-engaged on a renewable 12-month contract. He served two final years there from 1857 to 1859. He died in 1860 at the age of 76 years and was buried in the cemetery of the

---

[55] Pz minute book, 1852.
[56] Simmons also did the same for Falmouth.
[57] Godfrey Simmons's archive.

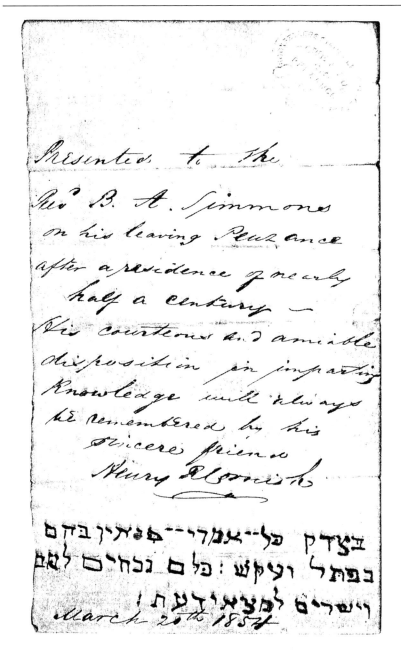

A presentation gift to B.A. Simmons on his leaving Penzance in 1854, from his Gentile friend, Henry Cornish. [courtesy: Godfrey Simmons's archive]

community which he had served for so long. The *Cornish Telegraph* referred to him as "highly esteemed and respected by his own friends and neighbours in this place."[58] A few days later on 8th December, the newspaper published an anonymous tribute in the form of a letter from a local non-Jew, entitled paradoxically "The Christian Jew", which for its day suggests the genuine respect and affection with which he came to be held in Penzance:

> SIR – I observed in the obituary of your last week's paper the report of the death of the Rev. B.A. Simmons – for nearly half a century the Rabbi of the Jewish congregation in this town.
>
> He was a man much to be admired for his uprightness of character; well read in the writings of his profession, yet without bigotry, or bitterness towards those holding religious opinions differing from his own; and an example for many professing Christians of this day in this respect.
>
> I as an old friend of his, though of another creed, have often wished in my heart that a man so estimable had professed Christianity. He rested firmly on the promise made to Abraham and his seed. Sir, yours respectfully, HOMO. – Penzance, Dec. 8th, 1860.

No such record has been found of any printed tribute to him from the Jewish community. His widow Flora returned to Merthyr Tydfil in the same year to live with her daughter, where she died on 2nd December 1874 at the age of 84. She is buried in the Jewish cemetery there.

The Rev. Hyman Greenberg, also known as Samuel Hillman, was engaged by the congregation in 1859. He was a young man of 21 when he came to Penzance. Whether he had completed training in all of the skills required to become a rabbi is not known, but he may have undergone Talmudic study and possessed sufficient religious knowledge to enable him to fulfil the congregation's ceremonial needs. He gave at least one discourse in the synagogue on the Sabbath preceding the Passover of 1859 and wore a newly-acquired clerical hat to make the services more dignified.[59] Roth suggest that he also acted as a secretary which in itself would require a reasonable education. That he did so voluntarily, according to Roth, and was "a very good type" suggests that his youth and relative inexperience allowed him to be

---

58 *Cornish Telegraph*, 5th December 1860.
59 Reporting on the annual meeting on 1st April 1860, the Penzance minute book says: "a vote of thanks was proposed and carried unanimously to Mr Greenbourgh for his able and instructive lecture . . . Mr Levin has presented . . . a clerical hat to be worn by the rabbi on all the religious occasions."

Portrait of Rabbi B.A. Simmons. [courtesy: Bernard and Godfrey Simmons's, on loan to the Penlee Art Gallery & Museum, Penzance]

B.A. Simmons's headstone.
[courtesy: Gordon Brown]

Flora Simmons's headstone.
[courtesy: Godfrey Simmons]

Portrait of Flora Simmons.
[courtesy: Bernard and Godfrey
Simmons, on loan to the Penlee
House Art Gallery & Museum,
Penzance]

adaptable and pliable to the requirements of the senior members of the congregation. He remained in the post for three years and died tragically young at the age of 24 in 1861.[60] He is buried in the Penzance cemetery.[61]

Rabbi Lupshutz filled the post briefly from 1861–62. He was replaced by Mr Spero (Spiro) who was engaged in 1863 at £1 per week. The minutes record that one Friday evening he left to go to Plymouth without any warning or prior notice, leaving the congregation on the eve of the Sabbath.[62] He was severely reprimanded and on 1st October 1865 had his salary reduced. He resigned some six months later on 9th April 1866.[63] Soon afterwards Mr. Rittenberg is noted in the minutes as the incumbent minister.[64] There were in fact several rabbis living in the town about this time. On 22nd November 1865, when Spiro was the official incumbent rabbi, soon after the reduction in his salary, Rittenberg and I. Rubinstein co-officiated at the marriage of George Goodman of Glamorgan to Rose Joseph, a daughter of Henry Joseph. The presence of Rabbi Rubinstein at the Goodman-Joseph wedding is somewhat surprising in that he is not recorded as the official incumbent for Penzance until 1886–1887, and so it appears that he had been resident in the town for some considerable time, unless in the meantime he had left for another post and returned in 1886. Rittenberg stayed in his post for several years and he too had his salary reduced by the withdrawal of an annual allowance.[65] However, it is not clear from the minute books if this was the result of financial restrictions or for disciplinary reasons.

The arrival of Rabbi Isaac Bischofswerder in the late 1860s with a large family breathed fresh life into the congregation and certainly gave it some stability. He was appointed around 1868, because he officiated at his first wedding on 9th June 1869. He served the congregation for 21 years until his retirement in 1886.[66] He remained in the town for 30

---

[60] Not in 1863 as suggested by Susser (1993, p. 156).

[61] Pz. 2:2. His headstone refers to "Samuel Hillman, the son of our honoured Master and Teacher Rabbi Simeon Greenberg". This would suggest that Simeon Greenberg was at some time a member of the congregation, although his name does not appear in the minute books, and so it may be assumed that, even if he was a trained rabbi, he was never appointed as an incumbent.

[62] 31st July 1864.

[63] Not 1863 as again suggested by Susser (1993, p. 156).

[64] Pz minute books, 14th April 1867.

[65] Pz minute books, 14th April 1867.

[66] cf. *The Cornishman*, August 1889. It is unlikely that he did so continuously throughout that period. Although the first mention of Isaac Bischofswerder in the minute book is in 1874, and he did retire in 1886, he had officiated at a wedding as early as 1869, and the *Cornishman* (August 1889) refers to his ministry of 21

years until his death in 1899. He did not serve continuously throughout this period and after 1886 he was in poor health. He had come to England from 'Vandsburg' (Bromburg) in Prussia in the 1860s.[67] This had been the place of his birth in 1822. He married Rahle Weile, also a native of Prussia.[68] The marriage would appear to have taken place in Germany because no marriage certificate has been traced in England. Isaac had seven children all born in Germany between 1852 and 1863. They were: Yette (Henrietta), Marcus, David, Morris, Marks (Markus), Saby and Augusta. The eldest son Marcus and his wife Sarah came to England with two of his brothers, David and Morris. Having settled here, they then brought over Isaac and the rest of the family. It is not known exactly when the Bischofswerder brothers came to Penzance or when the rest of the family arrived in the town.[69]

Isaac Bischofswerder officiated at his first Jewish wedding in Penzance on 9th June 1869: that of Aaron Beirnstein of Dowlais in south Wales to Esther Joseph, a daughter of Henry Joseph. He officiated at another wedding on 31st August 1870 of Abraham Freedman of Abedare to Kate Joseph, another daughter of Henry Joseph. However, it was not until April 1874 that he is first mentioned in the minute books for the congregation. The salary that he received was not generous at some 47 pounds per annum. He soon requested an increase which was granted to 52 pounds. The congregation must have been satisfied with their new rabbi to allow this. Finance had become a growing problem for the congregation in the latter part of the 19th century. When Isaac fell ill in 1875, the minutes of 19th April that year record that they agreed to settle a bill of 1 pound 2 shillings and 6 pence on his behalf for his treatment by Dr Harvey. Isaac Bischofswerder, like rabbis before him, would have needed a small shop or business to supplement his income. His sons certainly became well established in the town and were very successful in business.[70] They could afford to live in some

---

years. (His headstone in the Penzance cemetery, 8:3, reads in Hebrew: ". . . was Cantor and Shochet here for more than twenty years . . .").

[67] Now Bydgoszcz in Poland, between Gdansk and Warsaw.

[68] She was born c.1830. She was the widow of Solomon Weile and had a daughter Berthe from that marriage.

[69] Much of the information about the Bischofswerders and the photographic records have been provided in letters and other documentary material by various descendants, including Lilly, Sheila and Ivan Segal, and David and Victor Bishop. The editors are also grateful to David Samuelson and Harold Dunman for access to relevant sections of the text of their book, currently in preparation, entitled *Bertie, the Life and Times of G.B. Samuelson.*

[70] They were involved in a range of commercial ventures. Their descendants have become established in the jewellery and wine and spirit businesses in various towns and cities in the north of England and Scotland. Their success and their numbers

style in a very large and imposing house which still stands in the Alverton area of the town. Isaac Bischofswerder later moved into a newly-built town house at 9 Belgravia Street, where his wife died.[71]

In 1875, there occurred one of the most serious accidents at sea in living memory, when the German mail-steamer *Schiller* (at that time one of the largest vessels afloat) left New York on 28th April, scheduled to arrive in Plymouth on 8th May. The ship foundered on the Retarrier Ledges off Scilly on 7th May.[72] Nearly 350 lives were lost, and only 37 people survived. The incident was reported extensively in the Cornish and national press from 10th May, and shocked the local community in west Cornwall. The Board of Trade Enquiry and the coroner's inquest went on for many months. It fell to the local Collector of Customs and Receiver of Wrecks, J.T. Handley,[73] to supervise the enormous task of recovering and recording all the bodies and property found on them, the cargo and other salvage, and he did so meticulously,[74] with the result that almost all the gold and cargo were recovered. Newspapers reported services of burial and remembrance in various local churches, including a formal service at Paul attended by Handley and many dignitaries and representatives of local organisations. The names of the victims and those of the the survivors were published in various reports, and from these it seems likely that some of the passengers were Jews. There is no mention in the newspaper reports, however, of Isaac Bischofswerder (who, as we have seen, had recently been in ill-health) or any other member of the Jewish congregation being involved with any of the relatives of the dead, or officiating at any

---

(Marcus and his wife Sarah had 17 children) kept the synagogue and its finances going until 1906. The sons were in a position to invest in the Bolitho Bank which may have eased the congregation's financial situation.

[71] David Samuelson *et al*, p. 9. Editorial note: according to Penwith District Council records, the houses in Belgravia Street were not built until the mid- to late nineteenth century.

[72] A comprehensive account of the wreck can be found in Larn (1971, pp. 38–41). Of the many newspaper reports, the following are perhaps the most detailed: *Western Morning News*, 10th May; *Falmouth Packet*, 15th and 22nd May (the latter reporting the account from *The Times* of 12th May); *The Cornish Telegraph*, 12th and 19th May; *The West Briton*, 10th, 12th, 17th, 20th, 27th May; 3rd, 7th, 10th, 17th June; and 5th July. Reports continued until the end of the year and beyond.

[73] Board of Trade Telegram, 14th May 1875, PRO KEW: CUST 68/163 (all PRO Kew references from Peter Towey's research); *Cornish Telegraph*, 12th and 19th May; *Falmouth Packet*, 15th May.

[74] PRO Kew: Lloyd's List, from 11th May to 31st March 1876; CUST 68/158 Isles of Scilly: Wreck letter book 1857–1886; CUST 68/163 Isles of Scilly: Board of Trade Letter books 1868–1908; *SS Schiller* Droit (Recovered Property) Book. (Handley also applied salvage procedures so rigorously that he provoked bitter protests against him, especially by the men of Newlyn.)

Rachel and Isaac Bischofswerder, c.1880. [courtesy: Harold Dunman &
David Samuelson]

Amy Bischofswerder, right, one of Isaac Bischofswerder's numerous grandchildren, and daughter of Morris and Julia Bischofswerder, with her Gentile friend Gertrude Kate ('Daisy') Uren, c.1903. [courtesy: Graham Rogers]

ceremony for them, and there were no burials in the Jewish cemetery at this time.[75]

On 9th February 1876, at the age of 21, Henrietta Bischofswerder married Rabbi Elias Pearlson, age 23, from Newcastle and moved there.[76] He became the rabbi in Newcastle and they later moved to Hull.[77] Eventually a grandson of Isaac Bischofswerder, Michael the son of Marcus and Sarah Bischofswerder,[78] also moved to Hull. From his Cornish roots, his house was given the name St Michael's Mount. Marcus and Sarah later joined their family there.[79] On 5th February 1884, at the age of 27, Morris Bischofswerder married Julia Joseph the daughter of a prosperous local pawnbroker, Henry Joseph of Queen's Square.[80]

On 10th March 1886 at the age of 55, Isaac Bischofswerder's wife died.[81] Although he may also have been in poor physical health for some time, this blow prompted the rabbi to hand in his resignation, on the grounds of ill health, a few days later on 14th March. For the next year Rabbi Isaac Aryeh Rubinstein from Northampton became the

---

[75] It has been supposed that Isaac Bischofswerder was the Receiver of Wrecks in 1875 (which was clearly not the case: the name *Bischofswerder*, or any likely variant of it, is entirely absent from the newspaper reports to the end of 1875, and from the Board of Trade records at PRO Kew), and that in this capacity he became wealthy through the dubious acquisition and re-sale of salvage from the wreck. It should be noted that small items found on the bodies were not classified as salvage by the Board of Trade (although Handley still recorded them), and that after all attempts had been made to trace the legal owners of the cargo and other salvage recovered (except bullion), it was de-classified and placed for *lawful* re-sale with a local marine-store dealer, at which time any member of the public could have come into possession of it, or apply for rights of salvage. Even so, a legal injunction was placed on some Sennen fishermen who had recovered a quantity of dollars from the wreck of the Schiller, as late as January 1876. cf. information from Tony Pawlyn and Peter Towey.

[76] Henrietta's age, clearly stated on the marriage certificate, would make her year of birth 1855. However, Samuelson (op. cit., chapter 2:6, p. 10) gives the year as 1850/1 on a genealogical tree. The editors have assumed that this is an error in that the other Samuelson dates (for Morris and Marcus/Marks) are consistent with marriage certificate details.

[77] Their son Gustav became a professional pianist. He was also a gifted linguist and is said to have written a book on Jewish history at the age of 18.

[78] Michael was born in 1899.

[79] Letter from Ivan Segal to Keith Pearce dated 9th September 1998 in which the writer recalls: "I remember going to Michael's house which was huge by any standards. . . . My grandmother always had a pronounced Cornish accent . . . and made . . . Cornish pasties."

[80] She was aged 33 at the time of the marriage.

[81] She was known locally as Rachel.

minister. He had been living in Penzance as early as 1865 because, as we have seen, he officiated at a wedding in that year. He was Russian by origin. He arrived in Penzance to be mystified by the scale of the congregation's decline and the exodus of Jews from the locality. In contrast to the restrictions, persecution and prejudice which were familiar to him in Russia, he marvelled at the open, tolerant and affluent society where opportunities seemed to flourish. Nowhere was this more so for him than in Penzance. Writing home in 1886, he says:

> Many Jews flourished here in abundant plenty and some acted in a representative capacity in local and national government equally with Christians. Moreover those who live here today live on the fat of the land and enjoy unhindered and uninterrupted peace. In spite of this, our brethren have forsaken this place. . . . Why, I know not. It is a riddle without interpretation . . . they leave a blessed land . . . without any compelling reason.[82]

Susser refers to the typical character of this "panegyric" of East European Jewish immigrants extolling the opportunities to be found in their new country of residence. Rubinstein's letter was printed in the Russian-Jewish journal *Ha-Melitz*. The Russo-Jewish Committee responded by advertising the reasons why Jews should not leave the East End of London for the provinces; including problems of isolation, fear of prejudice, language barriers and lack of opportunities for Jewish education. These reasons, although significant, do not entirely answer Rubinstein's questions. It is unlikely that the Cornish Jewish population, even at its highest, was more than 50-60 people in each of Penzance and Falmouth. If one removes from this the children, then there was little room for intra-marriage (exclusively between Jews, especially within the same congregation). Most Jewish marriages in Penzance were to Jewish partners from outside the area, resulting in migration from Penzance. As the next chapter will show, conversion or marriage to non-Jews was not uncommon. The modest size of the Cornish Jewish congregations made them intrinsically non-viable in the long-term without a continuous and increasing influx of new members.

In 1887 Isaac Rubinstein left Penzance with a testimonial to take up a position at Cardiff and was succeeded by Michael Leinkram.[83]

---

[82] Susser (1993, pp. 42–44 & 279) quotes from this letter at greater length.

[83] Much of the information on Michael Leinkram has been provided in letters and supporting documents by his descendants: Esther Fishman, and Mr. and Mrs. Stuart Raine.

Leinkram's exact date of birth is unknown but he was born in Krakow (Cracow) in Poland some time between 1852 and 1854. His birth name was Mikael ben Schloma, the son of Solomon Leinkram.[84] Michael was one of four sons, some of whom emigrated to America. When Michael emigrated to England, his father remained in Poland. The East End of London contained a large Polish-Jewish community in the late nineteenth century and so Michael was able to live with a Polish family at 6 Wentworth Street, Spitalfields.[85] He later married their daughter, Esther Riesenfeld, at the Sandys Row synagogue.[86]

Michael was appointed to Penzance at the age of 33, just before returning to London where he married Esther Riesenfeld on 7th December 1887. He was described as a "Jewish minister".[87] Esther was illiterate and gave her mark on the marriage certificate instead of a signature. Within the first year Esther was expecting their first child. On 23rd September 1888, the congregation put aside a sum of two guineas for the rabbi: "on account of his wife's coming accouchement."[88] It seems that the couple lost this baby because family records do not show a first-born child for several years. In 1890, the finances of the dwindling community were such that the services of a rabbi were formally dispensed with, although Leinkram continued with some duties. In fact he was to officiate at the last Jewish wedding in the town; namely that of Marcus Bischofswerder to Emma Hawke on 12th June 1892. Michael Leinkram was also blessed with a fine voice and for a period went to America,[89] where he worked as a singing teacher. He is said to have been offered a position at the New York Opera, which out of religious principle he declined because it would have necessitated performances over the Sabbath.

It is not known how long he remained in America or indeed if he made several visits over the next decade. The couple may have returned to London at some point, but by the early 1890s they were back in Penzance where their son Maurice was born in 1892. A second son Blazelle Bear Leinkram, known as Samuel or Solly (Solomon), was born around 1894.[90] The third child Sarah, known as Sadie, was born some two years later and was the survivor of twins. In all, Michael Leinkram lived intermittently in Penzance from 1887 to 1896. By 1898 he had

---

[84] Solomon Leinkram was known as Solly Barnett. He was a teacher by profession.
[85] He lived with Moses (Morris) Riesenfeld who was a tinker and had a daughter called Esther.
[86] Rabbi V. Rosenstein officiated at their marriage.
[87] His father had already died by this time.
[88] At the half-yearly meeting – cf. Pz minute book 1888.
[89] He had two brothers already in America.
[90] He was named after his grandfather.

Rabbi Michael and Esther Leinkram, c.1910. [courtesy: Esther Fishman, and Gail & Stuart Raine]

been appointed as a minister in Belfast.[91] He became a minister in Woolwich from 1906 where he was described as a draper and general shopkeeper. He was buried on 26th November 1923 at the Edmonton Federation Cemetery in north London. His wife Esther died in 1930 and is buried next to him.

At this time Isaac Bischofswerder, albeit retired, remained in Penzance and was available to assist with ministerial duties on an occasional basis. The affairs of the congregation were by now almost entirely in the hands of the Bischofswerder family which had grown to a sizeable dynasty. In August 1889 the bar mitzvah of one of Isaac's numerous grandchildren, Harry, took place in the synagogue.[92] Rabbi Michael Leinkram officiated. A few years later the marriage of Isaac's youngest son Marks (Marcus) to Emma Boramlagh Hawke took place at 22 Rosevean Road, which the couple made their home.[93]

The Bischofswerder contribution to the life of the town was by now considerable. However, the size of the family as well as the prolifera-tion and repetition of family forenames down through the generations (until the present) make precise identification of individuals difficult. There were at least four "Harrys" distinct from the 13 year-old boy whose bar mitzvah has been mentioned. The infant son of Marcus and Sarah Bischofswerder, David Harry, died at the age of 14 days in July 1881 and would have been buried in the Penzance cemetery (although his grave was unmarked), along with David and Helena Bischofswerder's children Malkah (Millie) and Sarah Zillah (Cicilia). Malkah had died in the previous year at the age of 11 weeks and Sarah at 14 months old in March 1891. A Henry (Harry) was born to Morris and Julia Bischofswerder in 1885, and another Harry to Marcus and Sarah on 17th July 1892. The former appears on the 1891 census, age 6, and the latter in a private family birth register.

Yet another Harry, whose date of birth is unknown, became a wealthy man. He took a civic and philanthropic interest in the affairs of the town, building the Jubilee Hall in 1887 for the use of the public. He was also concerned about the poor of the town and for some years in the 1890s, he and his wife provided an annual New Year's Day dinner,

---

[91] It was here that his daughters Crozy (Caroline) and Gertrude were born in 1898 and 1904 respectively.

[92] This Harry would have been a son of David and Helena Bischofswerder. The occasion is described in the *Cornishman*, August 1889, where Isaac is referred to as the grandfather, and Marcus and Morris as uncles. Information concerning the latter Harry who appears in the 1891 census has been taken from Graham Rogers' research.

[93] Marks was 39 at the time of the marriage. Emma, aged 27, was the daughter of a local policeman, the late Thomas Hawke.

including a post-dinner celebration where those who had served the poor became his guests. The couple were well known in the town for their kindness and generosity.[94] It is likely to have been this Harry who, briefly between 1891 and 1892, had a financial interest in a local tin-mine which was re-opened and re-named as "Wheal Helena". This secured its future as a mine at the time and provided local employment for those who returned to work in it. He was the "Mr Bischofswerder" together with "Miss Hetty" who were reported in the *West Briton* on 29th October 1891 as attending the very grand occasion of the re-starting of the pumping engine at the mine. This was heralded by the Penzance Season Band, followed by a champagne dinner for 150 guests.[95] This venture did not have a fortunate outcome, leaving Harry Bischofswerder's finances severely damaged in the process. He eventually left Cornwall to make a new start in Birmingham where he settled in Selly Oak.[96]

On 18th October 1899, Rabbi Isaac Bischofswerder died at the age of 77. Over a period of time most of the family members moved away. Morris remained in Penzance to try to keep the synagogue open. By the beginning of a new century, it had become obvious that the congregation was no longer sustainable. The synagogue was used for the Sabbath and then eventually only for the High Holy Days and Festivals. Business meetings were conducted in Morris's home. Finally in 1906 the synagogue was sold. On 20th April 1911, Morris lost his wife Julia. By 1913 he had left the town. There are today at least five impressive graves in the Penzance cemetery, taking up much of the area at the front of the burial ground. They are a reminder of the importance which Rabbi Isaac Bischofswerder and his family had in the life of the declining congregation and the life in the town.

The Rabbis of Penzance

1700s: Asher Hart (died c. 1745–1752); Abraham Hart (Solomon Lazarus) settled in Penzance, died 3rd July 1784

1808–1811: a series of ministers followed in rapid succession:

---

[94] Susser (1993, pp. 203 and 319).

[95] Barton (1974, pp. 120–121). Susser (op. cit., pp. 203 & 298) refers to Harry as the proprietor and as owning the mine. He also states that Wheal Helena was: "An alternative name for Tregurtha Downs Mine near Marazion. It was the last survivor of a brief upsurge of interest in mining in 1881, and was closed in 1895" (p. 319, n. 109).

[96] Information supplied by a descendant, David Bishop in Glasgow.

Errata

The Editors have identified important information from public records, too late for amendments to the text of chapter 6.
(C= census; R= Registrar's birth & marriage records.)

p.185: Isaac Bischofswerder had five sons and two daughters from his first marriage. Their names are correct as given, except that *Marks* (1871C) was *Max* (1881C), not a second Marc(k)us, and *Saby* (or *Laby*, 1871C script unclear) was a family name for *George* (1881C), the youngest son. *Max* did not marry Emma Hawke (in 1892R) but moved to Plymouth, where in 1884R he married Catherine Jacobs. The couple are buried there (as *Bishop*) in the Gifford Place cemetery.

pp.185–6: Isaac Bischofswerder and his family did not own or occupy the Alverton house (*The Hollies*) at this time as implied. In 1871C and 1881C the family were living in a small house at 6, Belgrave Terrace (later Belgravia Street). In 1881C David Bischofswerder and family were at No.19, in the same street, and Isaac's daughters were living at Elswick, Northumberland. By 1891C David Bischofswerder and his family (with the widowed Isaac) were the sole occupants of *The Hollies*, and in that year Morris and Marcus are shown in the census as living in modest houses, at 8, Cornwall Terrace and 22, Rosevean Road respectively.

pp.191 & 193: Emma Hawke was living with the Bischofswerder family (recorded as *servant*) in 1881C, and by 1891C with *Marcus* (the eldest son) at Rosevean Rd. (The census records her as *Emma*, Marcus's *wife*.) By this time she had borne six children. She converted to Judaism and married Marcus in 1892R. She was subsequently known as *Sarah*, and further births were registered under "*Sarah Bischofswerder, formerly Hawke*". From 1895 to 1903, their family alternated between Plymouth and Penzance, eventually moving to Hull. (The statement, on p.185, that Sarah had come to England with Marcus as his wife, is, therefore, incorrect.)

pp.193–194: Contrary to earlier sources (e.g. Susser, 1993, pp.203, 298 and 319) a *Harry* Bischofswerder did not build the Jubilee Hall (in 1887), own the *Wheal Helena* mine (1891), or host New Year dinners for the poor (1891/2). Isaac's son, *David*, is clearly and consistently identified as the benefactor in each case by the following reports, with his wife *Helena*, son *Harry*, (whose age is given as 14 in 1891C), and daughter *Hetty* (Esther, ref. 1891C), receiving incidental mention: *Cornishman*, 11th Aug. 1887, p.3; *West Briton*, 29th Oct. 1891, p.2; *Royal Cornwall Gazette*, 21st. Jan. 1892, p.4. (*The Jewish Chronicle* alone, 15th Jan. 1891, states incorrectly that Harry hosted the dinner, and refers to Harry as the son of David Bischofswerder, *"proprietor of the Wheal Helena mine"*. In context, the latter phrase could be mistaken as referring to Harry.)

The Editors regret these inadvertent errors, and hope that there may be an opportunity in a revised edition of *The Lost Jews of Cornwall* to amend and expand the material on the Bischofswerder family.

Keith Pearce & Helen Fry (November 1999).

Rabbi (i)   Moses
  (ii) Feival (Philip Samuel)
  (iii) Selig
  (iv) Aaron
  (v)   Moses Levi   (v) and (vi) may be the same person
  (vi) Moses Isaac
  (vii) Hirsch

1811–1859: Barnet Asher Simmons; his period of office was not continuous

1813–1814: Elthanan Joseph Mortara

1815–1816: Hyman Selig

1817: Abraham Joseph

1817–1818: Jacob Moses (Moses ben Judah Leib)

From 1818: Hart Symons (Simonds)

1849: Joseph Rintel from Falmouth acted as locum

1854–1857: Solomon Cohen

1857–1859: Barnet Asher Simmons

1859–1861: Hyman Greenberg (Samuel ben Simeon, also known as Samuel Hillman)

1861–1862: R.A. Lupshutz

1863–1866: Marcus Spero (or Spiro)

1866–c.1868: M. Rittenberg

c.1868–1886: Isaac Bischofswerder

1886–1887: Isaac Aryeh Rubinstein

1887–c.1896: Michael Leinkram, may have left Penzance for a while from 1888

1887–1890: Isaac Bischofswerder resumed duties over the dwindling community

1890: The services of a rabbi were formally dispensed with

1892–1896: M. Leinkram was available for some duties

The People

Godfrey Simmons and Keith Pearce

PART 1

The Jews who lived in Cornwall in the eighteenth and nineteenth centuries can be traced from a wide range of sources; these include commercial and trade directories, census returns, newspaper reports, marriage certificates, cemetery headstones, published studies such as Brown's on the Cornish clockmakers, Osborne's on freemasonry, masonic members' directories, and customs and shipping records. The names of many of the people recorded in this chapter have already been mentioned in previous chapters. Here we will concentrate on the residence and occupations of Jews in Cornish towns.

Itinerant Jewish pedlars and hawkers were frequent visitors to the county.[1] Some put down roots in Cornwall even before any significant Jewish settlement began in either Penzance or Falmouth. It was the establishment of Jewish shops in the towns, however, which marked the beginning of Jewish communal life. Settled Jewish life necessitated the acquisition of two cemeteries, one in Falmouth and one in Penzance, and the founding of the two synagogues. This gave the Jewish residents a congregational focus.

The total size of the Jewish population in Cornwall at any one time is difficult to estimate. Physical and documentary evidence can prove to be of a limited and superficial value. For example, the cemeteries each contain about 60 graves, but no inference can be drawn from this because these numbers are cumulative over two centuries. Some children and relatives moved elsewhere, so that migration and emigration became unsettling factors which changed the total numbers periodically. Trade directories can be helpful but they give only the names of the owners of the business and take no account of their families.

Decennial census returns have been used in this chapter to identify many of the Jewish people in Cornwall. The census returns provide an overall computation from the size of each household where each adult

---

[1] Naggar (1992, pp. 22 & 28–30).

and child is named, together with details of age, occupation, and place of birth. There is room for error when using census returns to collect particular data. Although names and families appear on the original census returns, even the expert researcher can miss them amongst the mass of information in which they are contained. The early census returns, particularly for 1841, are often in illegible handwriting, making names difficult to decipher. Moreover, it is not always obvious that a particular name is that of a Jew. Likewise, some names are mistakenly taken as being Jewish when in fact they are not. Census returns and subsequent published accounts cannot always be taken as entirely accurate. Sometimes names are missing from the original returns where particular families were known to have been living in that place at the time. Sometimes there were circumstantial factors or procedural errors at work when the original census data was compiled, leading to names being omitted from the official census returns. For example, in 1861 Esther Falkson's name does not appear on the official census[2] even though it is known that she was living in Well Lane at the time of her death in 1863.[3] It is possible that she was away from Falmouth when the census was taken. If so, this would highlight a circumstantial variable not subject to the control of the census collector at the time. However, it would require the physical absence of whole families to explain their statistical omission from the data. If individuals were in fact present at that time, it simply serves to emphasise the potential for procedural error. The joint work of several researchers (and perhaps at least one with a very personal family interest and knowledge) would be necessary to cross-check the registers to be certain of exactitude. Family size varied considerably and so the nominal estimate of the Jewish population of a town from a speculative average would be misleading. Census returns do not assist here either. For example, in 1851 in Penzance, Henry Joseph's family consisted of nine children whilst Rabbi B.A. Simmons shows none. The latter, in fact, had had 11 in all and most of them had left the town over time, although one had died in 1832, and two, Sarah and Simon, were living in the Joseph household as employees. It is, therefore, the factor of when and not where the census is taken which conspires to frustrate any estimate of population size.

There is no doubt that private research into family history and also expert genealogical research, such as that of Anthony P. Joseph, into the Cornish Jewish families and their descendants, play a very

---

[2] PRO ref.RG 9/1565.

[3] cf. her death certificate, information from which has been provided by Leslie and Naomi Falkson.

important role in any attempt to reconstruct a comprehensive profile of the population. The genealogies of the Cornish Jews are very complex with frequent intra-marriage between Jewish families and the proliferation of identical names. This means that the risk of confusion, duplication and mistaken identity is high if the exercise is not conducted by a specialist with experience. Indeed, a separate publication by such an expert on the genealogy of these families would be a valuable complement to this book, which can only try to give a representative picture and not a definitive record of the population.

From the foregoing, it would seem that the only method which can be used is a synthetic one, where information is drawn from a number of co-existing but disparate sources, and compiled to give at least some overall historical impression of the extent of the Jewish presence in Cornwall during the period from the early eighteenth to the late nineteenth centuries. Taking the 1820s to the 1840s to represent what seems to have been the peak of the Jewish communities, then it is unlikely that there were more than a dozen families (50 to 60 individuals, adults and children) in each of Falmouth and Penzance, with a few Jews in other towns. From the mid-nineteenth century these numbers declined steadily. Even if they cannot provide a definitive indication of size, this at least is the demographic pattern which the trade directories, the census returns and the marriage registers would suggest.

Marriage and Conversion

Marriage to non-Jews or conversion to Christianity can also confuse the issue and may have been more widespread than the available evidence suggests. Several examples of this have been given in the previous chapter, including the marriage of Isaac Polack of Penryn to Mary Stoughton, the conversion of Harriet Hyman, the family of Henry Moses of Falmouth and the family of John Levi in Truro. Gabriel Abrahams and Thomas Levi, both of whom were from Falmouth, converted to Christianity. On the 8th April 1791 William Cohen, born in June 1783, was baptised in Falmouth at the age of eight. His parents were Moses and Betsy Cohen. In the baptismal register, William is stated to have been "formerly a Jew".[4] Rose Cohen,

---

[4] cf. letter from Wilfred S. Samuel of the Jewish Museum to Alex Jacob, dated 12th May 1939. Letter in the Jacob archive. See also *Register of Baptisms, Marriages, and Burials of the Parish of Falmouth 1663–1812*, part 1, p. 464 (The Devon and Cornwall Record Society, 1914).

aged 47, and her four children were residents in Falmouth in 1851.[5]
On 22nd February 1822, the four children of Jacob and Elizabeth Levy
were all baptised in St Mary's Church, Truro.[6] They were called
Charles, Anna, Jacob and Elizabeth, born between 1813 and 1822. On
11th August 1840 at Budock Parish Church in the district of Falmouth,
Henry Moses of Budock, then aged 37, married Johanna Bristo of
Budock, a widow aged 29. She was originally from Hayle and a
daughter of John Richards, a miner. Henry Moses was a hawker and
traveller.[7] The two witnesses to the marriage were both non-Jews: the
bride's father and Mary Ann Polglase. The 1851 census takes this
Henry Moses to have been Jewish. By this time he had moved with his
wife, their four sons and a daughter to Porham Lane, Falmouth and
were able to accommodate a servant girl, Eliza Martin.[8] These people
could be regarded as Jewish from a genealogical, if not a strictly
religious, viewpoint. Whilst this approach has its merits and advantages
for historical research, it is not entirely free of interpretative and
evaluative problems. There are issues relating to the development of
the law governing the registration of marriages and also to any assess-
ment of the attitude and practice of Jewish congregations towards inter-
marriage (especially in a church), as well as the baptism of Jewish
children and the subsequent religious practice of the Jews concerned.
Moreover, church marriages involving Jews do not in themselves
provide proof of conversion.

There are two extensive passages in Susser which merit careful
study.[9] He outlines the fact that the marriage of a Jew to a non-Jew is
not only contrary to Jewish law, but, because Jewish identity is defined
by matrilineal descent, the children of a non-Jewish mother would not
be regarded as Jews, and that, unless the mother converted to Judaism,
the extensive home ceremonials could not be celebrated adequately. In
so doing he introduces, although he does not explore, the complicating
factor that the view taken by a Jewish community of inter-marriage
might differ according to whether the Jewish partner involved were
male or female. These issues of *principle* and practice are contrasted,
however, with various examples from the eighteenth and nineteenth

---

[5] cf. 1851 census returns for Falmouth.
[6] cf Susser (1993, p. 243); and St Mary's Parish Register, Truro, p. 654.
[7] Source: A non-facsimile copy of the certificate from the archive of Alex Jacob.
     Henry Moses was most likely a grandson of Alexander Moses, in which case his
     father was the same Philip who is buried in the Falmouth cemetery (2:2) and who
     died in 1831. His father Philip is mentioned on the marriage certificate but did not
     sign it as a witness.
[8] Susser, 1851 Census.
[9] Susser (1993, pp. 236–237).

centuries of inter-marriage and church weddings which reveal a complex pattern of *attitude* and practice. Susser stresses that a church marriage between a Jew (who had not converted or been baptised) and a Christian was legal: Manasseh Lopes married Charlotte Yeats near Windsor in 1795, but did not abandon his Judaism until 1802. Church marriages involving Jews are not, therefore, conclusive evidence of conversion.

Furthermore it cannot be taken as axiomatic that such a marriage would lead to automatic estrangement from or expulsion from the Jewish congregation. Although it might lead to exclusion from certain synagogal rites, it did not invariably lead to the loss of all contact. The following passage deserves to be quoted in full in this context: ". . . Samuel Ralph was married more than once in church and yet had a Jewish burial.[10] Isaac Gompertz . . . married Florence Wattier in church in 1818 and baptised all his children at birth; yet he was buried in the Jewish cemetery at Exeter."[11] Susser even finds an example of a clear case of conversion, that of Moses Ximenes who was baptised in 1802 and yet remained on friendly terms with the practising Jews of the Lousada family. It would seem that church marriages involving Jews were common in the eighteenth century and may even have been tolerated by some congregations. If Jews, (in Susser's words) "strongly desired to be accepted", such as Abraham Franco did in a letter of application to the Plymouth congregation in 1829 on behalf of his non-Jewish wife and *Familie Particular*,[12] they might be accepted although it is not known if Franco's application succeeded, and the Plymouth congregation had certainly instituted a rule against church marriages long before this, in 1779.

Church marriages involving Jews would, however, carry the risk that the children and the Jewish partner would be baptised or formally converted in the future, if not at the time. There was a conflict of loyalties at the very least (subsequent church attendance would have been an obvious test) and an inevitable long-term loss of members from the Jewish congregations. Some Jews may have undergone church marriage or had their children baptised for reasons of security rather than religious belief. Jewish experience of the perils and pogroms suffered on the Continent and a desire to ensure the safety and future of their children, even in what appeared ostensibly to be a tolerant and welcoming country, may have played its part. This could be seen as *Anglicization* rather than conversion and could be interpreted

---

[10] He was buried in 1867, although not in the main part of the Plymouth cemetery.
[11] Susser (1993, p. 190).
[12] Susser, op. cit., pp. 227, 237, 325.

as adaptation and adjustment rather than apostasy. Moreover, subjective perception and objective appearance may not have coincided in all cases and the dynamics may have differed from the mechanics of the event. Even so, such church marriages and baptisms are highly suggestive of a compromise which would often lead to the abandonment of Judaism and they are indicative of conversion, especially as marriage law at this time recognised the legality of Jewish marriage in synagogues.

Since the sixteenth century, the lack of uniformity and completeness in the administration and recording of marriages and deaths had been recognised as a problem. Various attempts had been made to address this.[13] Apart from a brief period during the Commonwealth when the first attempt at civil registration was introduced, responsibility for record-keeping had rested with Anglican clergy. Roman Catholic churches continued to grow and the non-conformist churches spread rapidly in the seventeenth and eighteenth centuries, such that the need for effective centralised registration and regulation was pressing. In addition to this, there was an alarming growth in the number of unregulated, clandestine marriages which often took place (without proper safeguards of parental permission, witnesses or registration) not in places of worship but in houses and taverns, sometimes with unscrupulous clergy officiating. The legal implications for legitimacy and inheritance were considerable and these irregular marriages became so prevalent that in 1754 Lord Hardwicke's Marriage Act was passed to enforce strict marriage regulations. The key requirements were:

(i) banns must be proclaimed in the parish church or
(ii) a licence obtained;
(iii) the marriage could only take place in the Anglican parish church in the presence of at least two witnesses;
(iv) the marriage must be registered in the parish register;
(v) the only legal proof of marriage was a certificate from the register, and
(vi) all non-conformists, including Roman Catholics, had to marry in the parish church, making it impossible to be married legally outside the Church of England.

---

[13] Much of what follows has been drawn from official information provided by Rita Collier, Superintendent Registrar of Marriages, Penzance (26th January 1999) and from Dianne Pryce of the Office for National Statistics, Southport (9th February 1999).

Quakers were excluded from the Act. Crucially, Jews were also exempt so that marriages in a synagogue were recognised as legal. The exemption of these two groups was an acknowledgement of the scrupulous manner in which those congregations were accustomed to publicise, celebrate and register their marriages. The Act did require that if a Jew was to marry a person who had been baptised in the Church of England, this marriage *had* to take place in the parish church even if the Jew did not convert through baptism.

In July 1837 a compehensive system of civil registration of all births, marriages and deaths was introduced in England and Wales together with the facility for civil marriage in a register office. Synagogues were not required to be registered for marriages partly because of their good record-keeping but also because Jewish law allows Jews to marry in a private location, such as the family home, provided the secretary from the bridegroom's synagogue is present at the wedding. From 1837 all previous marriages (including Jewish) were to be sent for registration to the Registrar General and all subsequent marriages were to be registered either in parish churches, non-conformist or Roman Catholic churches, synagogues and with the local register Office, from where they would be sent for centralisation at the regional or county record office.

Unlike Roman Catholics and non-conformists, who had been placed in a situation of compromise and ambivalence by the law, it had not been a legal requirement for Jews to marry in the local Anglican church or have a marriage registered there before 1837, and most certainly not after that date when marriage in a register office became available as an alternative on a civil basis. However, these advantages had applied to Jews who married Jews. Where a Jew wished to marry a Gentile who was not willing to convert to Judaism, then the marriage would have taken place in the parish church as a matter of course.[14] From 1837 a Jewish-Gentile marriage could take place in a civil context, although this would not eliminate the social pressure and preference from the Christian party and their family that it should take place in a church, as a social if not legal necessity. It is questionable, therefore, whether a Jewish-Gentile marriage in church signifies conversion on the part of the Jew, in that the event could have been undertaken to secure the legality of the marriage where a Jewish ceremony was not possible. What is crucial is that these marriages can only be taken as conversion by the Jew if information

---

[14] Susser, op. cit., pp. 237–8. He points out that most of the known converts to Judaism in the south-west were women. Conversely most of the church marriages were between Jewish men and Gentile women.

other than the mere fact of the location is available; for example such remarks as "formerly a Jew" as in the case of Henry Moses, or a baptism as in the case of Abraham Levi. The subsequent baptism of children does not in itself prove conversion by or even the complete abandonment of Judaism by the Jewish partner, although it is highly suggestive of a distinctive move towards conversion or assimilation into a predominantly Christian culture. Clearly a judgement needs to be made whether to include as a Jew anyone who was married in church or had their children baptised during this period. Where a person is known to have been of Jewish descent, even if they no longer associated with the Jewish congregation, they have been included in this chapter.

Despite the reforms of 1837, the accuracy of official registers in computing the size and profile of the Jewish population of Cornwall remains doubtful and is problematical. Between 1838 to 1892 there are 17 official Jewish marriages for Penzance (where one or both parties were Jewish and where the synagogue records would have been copied to the local registrar) and yet a copy of the certificate of a marriage in 1862, that of Frederick Lazarus to Emily Cock, exists in the family today. Most of the Jewish marriage registers for Falmouth have been lost as a result of their transfer to the Records Office at Exeter where they were eventually destroyed during the Second World War. With those records has been lost the demographic information which could have been drawn from them.

Trades and Occupations

The occupations followed by the Jews in Cornwall were largely defined by the requirement that their trade and skills should be relocatable. Some people remained for several decades and their names are to be found in the directories from the earliest to some of the later editions: Joseph, Abrahams and Jacob families of Falmouth, and the Woolf, Joseph and Levin families of Penzance are examples of these, and some of their members are buried in the two cemeteries. Others, for reasons of marriage or self-improvement soon moved away; for example the trade of a jeweller and watchmaker, a pawn-broker or general dealer in clothes or hardware could be transferred and taken up in any place.

Some became more specialised and adapted to the special oppor-tunities of the town as a tinman,[15] or as a sideline, a dealer in

---

[15] For example, Solomon Ezekiel of Penzance.

mineralogical specimens.[16] Some became established in a flourishing family business, such as the merchant Lemon Hart in wines and spirits and in sea-trading and imports, or the Oppenheims in what was for its day a superstore for household goods. The Harris family became jewellers by royal warrant in Truro. The success and relative wealth of the Bischofswerders in local business in Penzance has been mentioned in the previous chapter. Not only did that family own a large family town-house, but one, Harry, had financial interests in a tin-mine. Gabriel Abrahams of Falmouth became a money broker and naval agent, and at least one of the Jacob family of Falmouth had wide-ranging investments in mining and shipping.

---

[16] For example, Moses Jacob of Redruth.

PART 2

Falmouth

Reference has been made in several of the previous chapters to the importance of Alexander Moses ("Zender Falmouth") in establishing the Jewish congregation and providing the community with an economic system from which it could expand. He had been born circa 1715 in Alsace, where he married Phoebe. He is said to have come to Cornwall around 1740 at the age of 25.[17] He was a silversmith and recruited pedlars and hawkers both to work for him in return for loans and also to make up the necessary *quorum* for the Sabbath celebrations:

> . . . hawkers would gather at his large brick house (at that time considered quite a luxury). They ate together and said prayers on Saturday . . . and on Sunday they would make up their accounts, pay back loans, and be furnished with more goods for their packs . . . (in a footnote: . . . very heavy loaded box called a *marsh* . . . German patois name for a Buckle . . .). Zender also paid for some of their licences, but only if the hawker agreed to change his original (i.e. *foreign*) name to an English Jewish one, which then became his family name.[18] Later . . . (Zender) might introduce them to suitable young girls to marry. As the pedlar saved money, he would buy a shop . . . and in his turn employ pedlars to sell his goods in the country. In this way, small Jewish communities grew up all over England and Scotland.
>
> Other pedlars would travel around Cornwall on pack-horses, lodging at specific Inns, where each innkeeper kept the key to a cupboard containing only kosher cooking utensils. On arrival, the pedlar would find on the frying pan the name of the previous pedlar who had used it, together with the date and a Torah text in Hebrew from the Sedrah, all inscribed in chalk. Before the pedlar left he would wash up, write his own name on the frying pan, with the date and a Torah text in Hebrew, from the current week's *Sedrah*, so when the next pedlar arrived he could be sure that everything was kosher.[19]

---

[17] Letter from David Lang to Godfrey Simmons, 8th January 1999.

[18] For example, Israel Behrends became Israel Solomon, and Issachar Baer (or Bernard Beer) became Barnet Levy.

[19] Naggar (1992, pp. 30–31). This book contains a wealth of information on the life and importance of Jewish pedlars in the eighteenth and nineteenth centuries.

Moses, Levy, Jacob & Solomon of Falmouth

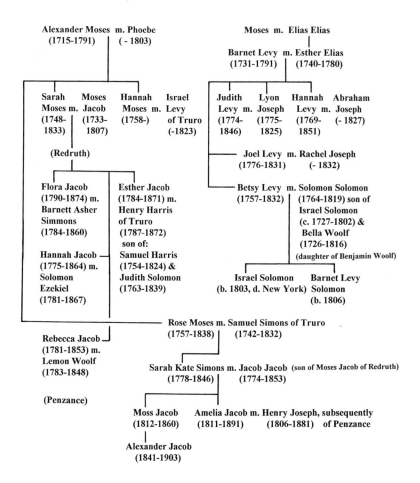

Source: Anthony P. Joseph (abridged).

Alexander Moses was helped by Benjamin Woolf (sometimes given as Wolf or Wolfe) in founding the first congregation. Woolf, who is mentioned in Israel Solomon's *Records of my Family*, had come from Holland and arrived in Falmouth, via Penzance, at about the same time. Barnet Levy (c.1731–1791) arrived in Falmouth around 1770 with his newly-wed wife, Esther Elias,[20] after a three-hundred mile journey on horseback from London. His story is also told in some detail by Israel Solomon. He became one of Zender's protégés. Judith Levy (1774–1846), a daughter of Barnet Levy and Esther Elias, married Lyon Joseph (1775–1825) who became a prosperous merchant. Lyon Joseph was instrumental in having a new synagogue built in 1808 at the top of Smithick Hill, so that (it is said) even while he was praying, he could keep an eye on his ships and any new arrivals in the harbour.[21]

The Jacob Family

It is not known when the Jacob family first came to Falmouth, but Moses Jacob (1733–1807) was the child of one of these early settlers, and his year of birth would suggest that he may even have been born in Falmouth. He married Sarah, one of Alexander Moses' daughters, and although he may at first have been dependent on his father-in-law's franchise, he eventually became commercially independent and settled in Redruth. His story is told later in this chapter.

By the 1840s the Jacob family had become sufficiently prosperous to engage in a range of business opportunities. A ledger of speculative investments made by a member of the Jacob family from 1844 to 1867, written in the same hand throughout, still exists in the archive of the late Alex Jacob.[22] The name of the investor is not inscribed in the book at any point but clearly it is a member of the Jacob family. These investments were considerable and wide-ranging. Rail transport was expanding rapidly and there are accounts for the Cornwall Railway (1845–67), the Midland Railway (1848–52), and the Oxford and Worcester Railway (1848–57). Most of the investments, however, were in Cornish enterprises, such as shipping and mining.

---

[20] Esther Elias: c. 1730–1780.

[21] David Lang, ibid.

[22] The editors are grateful to the executors of the Jacob Estate for making this account book available, and also to Tony Pawlyn of the Maritime Museum in Falmouth for his analysis of the information on the Jacob shipping interests in this chapter. Of relevance is a letter to Godfrey Simmons from Tony Pawlyn dated 8th December 1998.

The investor was much involved in Falmouth's maritime affairs. Between 1858–1865 he invested in the tugs the *Dandy* and the *New Dandy*. The first was a late contemporary of the *Sydney* (first registered at Falmouth in 1848) which was used between the creek port of Devoran to carry tin via the Redruth-Devoran railway. The *Sydney* was not a powerful boat and contributed to the wreck of a big full-rigged ship the *Northern Empire*,[23] which was in Falmouth en route for London awaiting orders to which port to discharge her cargo of guano. On the night of Tuesday 2nd March 1858 the tug *Sydney* was used to move the larger ship out of its berth; however, when the ship's anchors were up, the tug could not hold her and the ship was wrecked against the rocks. It was later salvaged and sold for £1,200. The accounts relate to the salvage of the *Northern Empire*, from which he made a profit of 5% (£90) in 1859.

The first *Dandy*[24] had been built for Edmund Hancock and others, one of whom was the Jacob investor. The ship was about 91 feet long and had a similar power to the *Sydney*. The owners ran the ship for five years, gaining about 32% profit at the end of that time (c.1858–65). The second *Dandy* mentioned in the accounts replaced the first in 1863. This was a bigger iron tug, about 106 feet long and 126 tons with more powerful engines. His investment records for this tug only go up to 1866. Between 1856–67, Jacob family investments were made in the *Baroness*, a 353-ton ship built at Sunderland in 1851 and registered in London. The principal owner was called Robinson, and through the 1860s the ship made voyages to the Mediterranean, Aden, and Port Said. The account book contains a note of insurance received at Gibraltar, reflecting this use of the ship. The vessel only paid her way from 1860 with a gross return of 385 pounds over the 11 years.

There were also shares in the Falmouth Docks Company. These were a long-term investment and directly helped to secure the future of the port. The Jacob accounts do not record any significant return, although the account book only covers the period 1858–62. The Docks Company built three breakwaters, two dry dock basins and twelve warehouses, and the work was completed in 1865. However, income alone was insufficient to sustain the work and 74,500 pounds had to be secured on loan from the Public Works Commissioners. A serious storm in 1867 caused considerable damage and by 1883, the Falmouth Docks were in arrears of their repayments. The Commissioners eventually took possession of the works as mortgagees. It is

---

[23] The *Northern Empire* had been built in 1854.

[24] It first appears in the Parliamentary *Returns of Steam Boats* from 1859.

Great Condurrow Mine, Camborne: the new engine house on Woolf's shaft in 1906.
Condurrow Mine, in which the Jacobs family had investments, was on or near this
site.[courtesy: The Royal Institution of Cornwall, Truro]

Swan Pool Mine, Falmouth, c.1850, in which the Jacob family had investments.
[courtesy: the Cornish Studies Library, Redruth]

Alexander Jacob of Falmouth (left) with three Cornish miners, c.1859.
[courtesy: executors of the archive of Alex Jacob]

doubtful if the Jacob family along with the original shareholders ever received any significant returns from this investment. Apart from investing in harbour and port enterprises, between 1844 to 1866 the investor was also a shareholder in a number of tin mines. His largest investment was in Condurrow mine (of Camborne) of £2,407 in 1844. He also held shares in various other mines including Tolgus, Trevan, North Fowey, Consols, Bosore, Clinton, Wheal Bassett, East and South Bassett, South Wheal, Buller, Swanpool and Wendron.

Another member of the Jacob family, Alexander Jacob also became involved in the mining industry. In 1859 he went to British Columbia as a prospector, accompanied by three Cornish miners. A photograph of Jacob with these three Cornish miners has survived, probably taken just before they left for Columbia. This may not have been a successful venture because Alexander returned to England around 1861. He lived for a time in Birmingham and then moved to London where he died on 3rd May 1903.

Trades and Occupations

The names of the Jews who traded in Cornish towns in the eighteenth and nineteenth centuries can be compiled from various sources, including the published trade directories of the day. The appendix at the end of this chapter explains the abbreviations which are given with each person. The names appear here in approximate chronological order, in that the source references allow each person to be placed as working in the respective town at the time or during the years given in the directories.[25] For Falmouth these are:

Barnet Levi(y): silversmith (Ja. 1776; p. 317). Formerly in St. Austell (see pp. 65 and 68).

Benjamin Wolf: pawnbroker (Un. 1793–98).

Alexander Moses: pawnbroker (Un. 1799).

Frances Polack: shopkeeper (Penryn) (Un. 1799). This could be a relative of Isaac Polack also of Penryn.

Levy Barnes: pawnbroker (Un. 1799). It is not certain that he was Jewish.

---

[25] The editors are grateful to H.C. Faulkner of Illogan, Redruth for information on some of those listed in this section and especially for making available his research into the 1841, 1851 and 1861 census returns for Falmouth. Thanks also to Eric Dawkins of Penryn for his material.

S. Jacobs: watch & clockmaker (from Penzance) (Br. c. 1800).

Solomon Ezekiel: tinman (later at Penzance) (Ho. 1811).

Gabriel (George) Abrahams: druggist (Ho. 1811), money broker, Church St. (Pg. 1823/4) and naval agent, Fish Strand (Fal. 1815; Pg. 1830); coin & bullion merchant (*Philip's Panorama of Falmouth*, 1828). Gabriel Abrahams was born in Germany in 1763, and came to England about 1791. He was of Jewish descent but converted to Christianity soon after his arrival in England. On 31st March 1817 he gave evidence in relation to an unpaid loan at the trial of Robert Sawle Donnall at Launceston for the murder of his mother-in-law, Elizabeth Downing. He married Jane Lovely Symons in Falmouth Parish Church on 16th May 1819 and their three children were all baptised in the same church. As one of the only two money agents in Falmouth he would have been an influential figure in the town.[26]

Lyon Joseph: merchant (Ho. 1811).

Lyon J. Joseph was born in Falmouth in 1827. By the time of the 1851 census he had moved to 25 Bull Street, Birmingham where his occupation was given as commercial traveller.

Jacob Levi: watch & clockmaker, later at Truro (Ho. 1811).[27]

Jacob Jacob & Co. pawnbroker, cabinet makers & upholsterers, Market Street (Fal. 1815; Pg. 1823/4/30).

Abraham Joseph: clothes dealer, pawnbroker and watchmaker, Market St. (Ho. 1811; Fal. 1815; Pg. 1823/4/30; Br.1827).

Judith Joseph: earthenware dealer, Market St. (Pg. 1823/4).

Kitty Solomon (Jacob): milliner, Church St. (Pg. 1823/4).

Moses Lazarus Lawrence: money broker, Church St. (Pg. 1823/4; Philp 1828).

Samuel Harris: printer & stationer, watch & clockmaker, High St. (Ho. 1811; Pg. 1823/4; Br. 1823). This is the father of Henry Harris, later in Truro, who also traded as a watchmaker in Falmouth in High St. (Trathan's History, 1815, p.84).

---

[26] From the family records of H.C. Faulkner.
[27] It is not known if there was any family connection with the Benjamin Levi who was reported as receiving stolen silver from Ruth Goodman in Falmouth in 1852. cf. *Royal Cornwall Gazette*, 22nd October 1852, p. 5, col. 5.

Joseph Joseph: watch & clockmaker, Market Strand. (Pg. 1823/4; Br. 1823).

Isaac Symons & Co.: china, glass & earthenware dealers, Market St. (Pg. 1830); bullion dealer, Church St. (1884 Census). Isaac Symons (b. 1796) was married to Rosetta (b. 1800). They had nine children: Hanna (b. 1823), Eliza (b. 1824), Julia (b. 1825), Solomon (b. 1827), Frederick (b. 1828), Walter (b. 1829), Sarah (b. 1835), Harriet (b. 1838) and Rebecca (b. 1840).

Isaac Isaac & Co: clothes dealers, High St. (Ludgate Hill). (Fal. 1815; Pg. 1830; 1841 Census). Isaac Isaac was born in 1786 (not in Cornwall), and was married to Judith (b. 1796). There were five children: Betza (b. 1821), Harriet (b. 1826), Abraham (b. 1828) who became a shoemaker, Amelia (b. 1829) and Sarah (b. 1832).[28]

Abraham Aaron: merchant (c.1830-40; ref. Pz. Marriage Register no. 5).

Sarah Abraham: grocers & tea dealers, High St. (Fal. 1815; Pg. 1830).

Abraham Davidson: watch & clockmaker, High St. (Pg. 1830). He was born in 1801, and married Rosetta (b. 1806). They had four children: Isaac (b. 1830), Eliza (b. 1832), Henry (b. 1834) and Arabella (b. 1836).

Isaac Heilbron: merchant, and Jonas (Joseph) Heilbron: jeweller (c.1830–40; ref. Pz. Marriage Register no. 6).

Henry and Barnett Joseph: watch & clockmakers, jewellers & silversmiths, Market St. (Pg. 1830).

Garson Elias: itinerant pedlar. A gold ring was stolen from him (*Royal Cornwall Gazette*, 12th April 1844; p.3, col.5).

John (Jacob) Jacob: clothier to "Nobility, Gentry & Clergy", Bells Court. (Pg. 1844; Sl. 1852–3; 1841 & 1851 Census). Jacob Jacob was a son of Moses Jacob and Sarah Moses. He had been born in Redruth in 1774, and was married to Sarah Kate (Kitty) Simons.[29] At the time of the census returns, Jacob's unmarried sister Amelia lived with the family. Jacob and Sarah's daughter Rebecca married Morris Hart Harris, son of Henry Harris of Truro.[30]

---

[28] There is a Lazarus Isaac, born 1816, also listed as a salesman in the census.
[29] The census date for her birth, 1781, does not agree with the genealogical date which is generally accepted as 1778; cf. Anthony Joseph, ibid.
[30] See the section on Truro in this chapter, and chapter 5: Falmouth cemetery (5:2 & 5:3) for details of their family.

Moss Jacob Jacob(s): fancy repositories, clothes dealer & pawnbroker, Market St. (Pg. 1844; Sl. 1852–3). Moses Joseph (b. 1826, Devonport) resident shop assistant: (1851 Census). Moss Jacob Jacob had been born in Camborne in 1813. He was married to Frances who was born in Portsmouth in 1812. They had six children: Samuel (b. 1838), Hannah (Anne, or Annie, b. 1840), Michael (b. 1841), Alexander (b. 1842), Lawrence (b. 1844) and Sara (b. 1850).

Moses Jacob: pawnbroker, hardware shop, Market St. (Pg. 1844; Wi. 1847).

Lewis Falkson: jeweller, optician, watch & clockmaker, High St. (Ludgate Hill). (Pg. 1844; Wi. 1847; Sl. 1852–3; Br. 1852). He was born in London in 1787 and later married Esther (b. 1791 in Truro). The 1841 Census shows a Mary Palmer living with the Falksons. She was probably a servant or shop assistant. Lewis Falkson died of dysentery, a victim of the 1852 cholera epidemic. His wife continued to live in Falmouth at Well Lane, a run-down area of the town, where she died in 1863.[31]

Jacob Schwerer: jeweller, watch & clockmaker, Market St. (Pg. 1844; Br. 1844).

Lazarus Isaac: salesman, High Street. (1841 Census).

Isaac Isaac: shell dealer. (Pg. 1844).

Berenger & Schwerer: watch & clockmakers, Market St. (Wi. 1847). Their business partnership became located in several Cornish towns. Berenger, who was from the Black Forest, was not Jewish. Jacob Schwerer (as above) was Jewish and married into the Jacob family.

Grace Davidson: milliner, 146 Porham St. (from Kent; Susser: 1851 Census).

Simeon Silverstone: stationery traveller, 51 Killigrew St. (from Poland; Susser: 1851 Census).

Solomon Simmons: pedlar, 209 Fish Strand (from Truro; Susser: 1851 Census).

Rose Cohen: pedlar's wife, 14 Killigrew St. (1851 Census). She is listed as married, rather than widowed, and as the head of household. Her husband was an itinerant pedlar, only loosely based in Falmouth, and his name does not appear. Rose had been born in 1804 in Falmouth,

---

[31] The editors have received some of this information from the family records of Leslie and Naomi Falkson.

but had lived in Penzance at some point. There were four children: Hannah (b. 1837 in Penzance), who was a milliner's apprentice, Sarah (b. 1838 also in Penzance), Phoebe (b. 1839 in Falmouth) and Josiah (b. 1841 in Plymouth).

Joseph Abraham: sugar boiler, Fish Strand. At the time of the 1861 Census, he lived with George and Alice H. Lemon of Scotland, but it is not certain if the Lemons or the Abrahams were Jewish. Joseph Abraham had been born in 1837 in Penryn and had married Isabella Lemon (b. Penryn, 1840) who was a dressmaker. There were two children: John (b. 1859, in Penryn) and William (b. 1860, in Falmouth).

Nathan Vos: ships' chandler, Arwenack St. (1861 Census); innkeeper of the Marine Hotel (1871 Census). He had been born in Holland in 1833, and he died in 1913, his burial being the last in the Falmouth Jewish cemetery. He was married to Mary (1841–1914), and had three children: Frederick (b. 1868), Henry (b. 1870) and Rosalie (b. 1873). Mary Ann Vos also ran a public house, the Greyhound (Kelly, 1883). Nathan Vos was a freemason.

William Isaac(s): carver & turner, Wellington Terrace. (Wa. 1864). He was born in 1830 in Truro, and was married to Susan (b. 1837 in Falmouth). Their son Frederick was born in 1860 (1861 Census).

Samuel Jacob: jeweller & silversmith, Market St. (Wa. 1864; Tregoning (1865) p. 72).

Moses Jacob Jacob: watch & clockmaker, dealer & pawnbroker, 19-21 Arwenack St. (Br. 1854; Po. 1862). Tailor & outfitter, jeweller & silversmith, Foreign Money & Exchange Office (Wa. 1864). In the Post Office Directory of 1873 he is called "Moss Jacob".

Samuel Marks: auctioneer & commission agent. Furniture, glass showroom; upholstery & French polishing, Market St. (Wa. 1864).

Sam Abrahams (Fisher & Abrahams): furniture, pictures & looking-glasses, 10 High St. (K. 1889).

Thomas Henry Moses: hawker/broker, Porham Lane (1851 Census), Allen's Yard (1861 Census); with Thomas King Moses, as shopkeepers, and Philip Henry Moses, basket-maker, all of 46 Smithwick Hill (K. 1889). The family may have been of Jewish descent.[32] The eldest son Philip (above) was born in 1842 and was blind. There is only one

---

[32] The marriage of Thomas Henry Moses (b. 1804, in Falmouth) to a non-Jew, Johanna Bristo of Hayle, at Budock Parish Church on 11th August 1840 has been mentioned in the previous chapter.

baptism in the Falmouth Parish Church Register of Elizabeth Ann Moses on 13th November 1844. She became a dressmaker. It seems likely that the family were Christians. There were five other children: John Alexander (b. 1849), a shoemaker, Thomas King (b. 1851), Joseph (b. 1853), William Adolophus (b. 1855) and Richard (b. 1857).

Barnet Falk (Barnes Falck) has sometimes been taken for a Jewish resident of Falmouth. He is listed in the trade directories as a sailmaker (Un. 1799) and a ship owner (Fal. 1815). Both *Barnet* (Barnet Levy) and *Falk* (the Falksons) are familiar Jewish names from this period. An Isaiah Falk Valentine, a money changer and shochet from Plymouth, who had originally come from Breslau, was murdered in Fowey in 1811.[33] He had been invited to Fowey by William Wyatt, landlord of the Rose and Crown Inn. Valentine's body was later found in the river. Wyatt was convicted of his murder and hanged.[34] Isaiah Valentine may have been related to Martin Valentine, described as a "Cheap John" of the "travelling pack-man fraternity", who died at the Town Arms public house in Camelford in June 1844 and whose body was taken for burial at the Jewish cemetery in Plymouth.[35] Even if the Falks, who had come to England from Denmark, were of Jewish descent, members of the Falk family across five generations were married, baptised and buried in the parish church in Falmouth.[36] The Falks were members of a Trinitarian (Christian) masonic lodge.

Nathaniel Schram: dealer, herbalist, Ludgate Hill (1841 Census) subsequently at Truro and Plymouth 1851 Census), was born in the Hague, Netherlands in 1804. His wife, Anna, was born in Gwennap near Redruth in 1816. Three of his five children bore common Jewish forenames: Jacob (b. Falmouth 1842), Henrietta (b. Truro 1845) and Abraham (b. Plymouth 1851) but it is not known if the family was Jewish. There were two other children: Angelina (b. Truro 1843) and Marianna (b. Plymouth 1849). Susser makes no mention of a Schram.

Also uncertain is Emanuel Asser: pedlar. Boarder at Mulberry Square (1861 Census), who had been born in Amsterdam in 1806; and Joseph Pfaff: jeweller, High St. (Wa 1864).

The following were born in Falmouth:

---

[33] Susser (1993, pp. 36, 151 & 165).
[34] Douch (1966, p. 62).
[35] *West Briton*, June 1844.
[36] H.C. Faulkner's research into parish registers.

Tobiah Meyers in 1788: she married Israel Meyers, b. 1791 Bavaria. They lived in Plymouth (1851 Census), where all of their children were born: Bessy (b. 1833), Meyer (b. 1836), Isaiah (b. 1838), Rebecca (b. 1843) and Jacob (b. 1845).

Eliza Lazarus in 1815: she married Isaac Lazarus, b. 1817 Exeter, where the couple lived (1851 Census) and where their children were born: Lewis (b. 1845) and Julia (b.1847).

Bernard Ezekiel in 1815: he married Priscilla, b. Bath 1827. Their son John was born in Redruth in 1840. The family moved to Plymouth (1851 Census) where the other children were born: Elizabeth (1843), Moses (1845) and Benjamin (1849).

Moses Levi Jacob in 1819: he married Sarah, b. Portsmouth 1825. They moved to Birmingham (1851 Census) where their daughter Eleanor was born in 1850.

Lyon J. Joseph in 1827: he later moved to Birmingham (1851 Census).

Marriages

The destruction of much of the Falmouth records during the Second World War (including those marriages conducted in the synagogue or in Jewish homes) means that only a fragmentary and tentative outline of Jewish marriages, or marriages involving Jews in or from Falmouth, can be made.

1. 15th February 1760. Isaac Polack to Mary Stoughton, both from Penryn. (Phillimore Parish registers.)

2. December, 1763. Eleazar Hart, of Penzance, to Rebecca Wolf, of Falmouth. (Susser, pp. 32 & 276; Anthony Joseph ibid. chart A, p. 26, facing).

3. 12th June 1805. Jacob Jacob to Sarah Kate Simons, at Truro. (Archive of Alex Jacob).

4. 10th November 1825. Thomas Levi (son of Abraham and Rebecca Levi) to Ann Paskoe, in Falmouth Parish Church. Thomas was baptised the same day. (Archive of H. C. Faulkner).

5. August 11th 1840. Henry Moses, of Falmouth, to Joannah Bristo, of Hayle. (Budock Parish Church).

6. 31st July 1844. Morris Hart Harris to Rebecca Jacob, at Falmouth. (Archive of Alex Jacob).

The Decline of Falmouth's Jewish Community

By the 1840s there may have been as many as 50 Jewish families in Falmouth but this was the community's peak, soon to decline with surprising speed. Reasons for the community's demise were various and consecutive. The removal of the packet boat service in 1850 was a major economic disaster for the town. "Falmouth, with its deep harbour, was the main port in the west of England. It was the main packet station for the mail. Large ships would make it their first call, drop anchor and send runners to Lloyd's of London and await instructions from their owners as to the disposal and collection of cargo."[37] After this the Jewish community continued but it did so with ever-diminishing numbers. The train of causation which underlay the community's decline was complex, however, but can be traced through a series of earlier and later physical and economic disasters.

In 1832, the national cholera epidemic reached Cornwall.[38] Penzance and Newlyn were affected with particular severity.[39] Newlyn was placed under strict quarantine and a fever field was set aside in the nearby village of Paul to segregate and bury the victims. The epidemic is mentioned on the headstones of two girls buried in the Penzance cemetery (row 5:2, Pessia, and row 6:7, Ruth). They are the only known Jewish victims of that epidemic. In 1833 the epidemic swept Falmouth and Helston, and within four months over 90 victims were recorded, although it is not known how many of these, if any, were Jews or how many people died of secondary illness precipitated by the cholera.

Cornwall experienced another outbreak in 1849, with the highest mortality being at St. Germans (236), Liskeard (132), St. Austell (135) and Redruth (133). In Penzance, out of a total population of 50,144, there were 22 deaths, and in Falmouth with a population of 21,700, there were 73 deaths. In both Penzance and Falmouth, there were aggravating topographical factors. Both towns are built on gradients rising from sea level. Together with inadequate sewerage systems this allowed raw effluent to flow downhill contaminating the otherwise pure water-wells.[40] Fatalities may have hit the small Jewish community in

---

[37] Dunitz (1993, p. 31).

[38] It has been described comprehensively by John Rowe and C.T. Andrews in their paper, "Cholera in Cornwall" in *The Journal of the RIC*, vol 7, part 2, 1974. cf. pp. 159–162.

[39] The Penzance epidemic is described by G.T. Clark, *Report . . . Sanitary Condition . . . of Penzance* (HMSO, 1849, s.21, p. 6). See also Pool, op. cit., p. 121.

[40] Archive of Eric Dawkins: from information supplied by Leslie and Naomi Falkson, 26th May 1993.

Falmouth: High Street fire, April 1862.

Falmouth: Market Street fire, January 1870. [both pictures courtesy:
Historical Research Unit, Royal Polytechnic of Cornwall, Falmouth]

219

Falmouth disproportionately, and some may have been prompted to leave, if only out of fear of recurrence.

In 1857 a telegraph service was introduced with the result that ships no longer had to wait in the harbour for instructions from London, which could take at worst several weeks, to the obvious advantage of local tradespeople. From 1859 some Jews left for the Gold Rush territories in America, for example: Alexander Jacob to British Columbia, and Lionel and Josephus Joseph to California and Hawaii, the latter eventually buying land for building development on Vancouver Island (Alex Jacob).

Finally two great fires, the first in High Street on 12th April 1862, destroyed 30 houses and the second broke out in Market Street on 5th January 1870. These were the main commercial areas of the town where Jews had carried on their businesses from some of the shops and premises. The former fire was particularly devastating as it destroyed the centre of the main street which was so narrow (barely a cart's width) that the flames spread quickly. The Town Council resolved that the reconstruction should include the widening of the entire street and proceeded on the compulsory purchase of properties on both sides of the street, paying minimal sums to the residents and shopkeepers based on land values only without regard for loss of trade.[41]

The first direct rail link between Truro and London opened in 1863 and the proximity of Falmouth to Truro enabled many of the remaining Jews to leave, mainly for Bristol, Birmingham, Plymouth and London. This, together with the fire of 1870, heralded the end of the Jewish community. The cumulative and unrelenting weight of these successive blows between 1850–1870 produced effects felt in the Jewish community in Penzance and no doubt played a part in the eventual decline in numbers there. The two communities were inter-related both through marriage and the sharing of resources, such as kosher meat when necessary. That Penzance lasted until the end of the century was due largely to the fact that it was more isolated, suffered no comparable disasters on such an unrelenting scale during this period, and possessed its own economic hinterland.

In Falmouth, Samuel Jacob kept the synagogue open for services up to 1879, but in 1880 he left with his family for London after carrying out repairs to the building, which subsequently fell into serious dis-repair. And so the Jewish congregation ceased and with it, communal life in Falmouth dwindled to a handful of traders: Moss Jacob, Sam

---

[41] cf. archive of Eric Dawkins; information supplied by Leslie and Naomi Falkson, op. cit.

Abrahams, Mary and Nathan Vos, the latter dying on 23rd October 1913. His burial was the last to take place in the former congregation's cemetery near Penryn.

PART 3

Penzance

The previous chapter has referred to the earliest known burial in the Penzance Jewish cemetery as having taken place in 1741, and that this in itself implies a Jewish presence in the town for some years before that date. The Harts from Weinheim in the Rhineland, Germany represent some of the earliest settlers, arriving about 1720.[42] The family lived for generations in Weinheim near the Rhine, where they became known as Altstadter. Asher Altstadter and his son Abraham Altstadter both died in Germany.[43] It is not known for certain if Abraham's son, Asher (died circa 1745–1752) came to Penzance with his family, but this particular Asher had a son also called Abraham who did arrive in the town around 1720. He would have been a very young man at the time, possibly still a child, but eventually adopted the surname *Hart*, although he was known locally as Solomon Lazarus. He died on 3rd July 1784 and is the first Hart of whom we have documentary evidence.[44]

---

[42] The eminent genealogist Sir Thomas Colyer-Fergusson is believed to have compiled an annotated family tree of the Harts in the early part of this century from information which he may, in part, have received from descendants of the Harts then living in London. A copy of these documents, apparently in Colyer-Fergusson's handwriting, was passed to Godfrey Simmons by Anthony P. Joseph some years ago. The details given in this introductory paragraph are drawn directly from these documents as a tentative reconstruction of the family's origins. The Colyer-Fergusson Collection is owned by the Jewish Historical Society of England, and was formerly placed on long-term loan deposit at University College, London. It is now in the safekeeping of the Society of Genealogists where it is on indefinite loan. The editors are grateful to the Society of Genealogists for permission to draw extensively on Colyer-Fergusson's family tree of the Harts in this book.

[43] Asher Altstadter died some time before 1682 and Abraham Altstadter died between 1710–1720. It is not certain that the Harts had been known as *Altstadter* in Germany in the seventeenth and eighteenth centuries because Colyer-Fergusson states only that: ". . . the present name of the family in Germany is Altstadter", and does not give a surname for the family before Abraham Hart (b. 1784).

[44] It was common to alternate between the Hebrew names by which a person may have been known in the privacy of the Jewish family or in the context of the synagogue ritual. It was common practice to use societal names in the wider community. Usually, but not always, the former is of Hebrew and/or foreign origin (e.g. German) and the latter an Anglicised version. Hence the name *Lemon* is sometimes spelt *Leman* as the vernacular of the Hebrew *Laemle* (meaning: consecrated or devoted to God. In Christian versions of the Hebrew Bible/Old

Abraham Hart traded in Penzance under the name of Solomon Lazarus. In his ledger, the west Cornwall historian the Rev. William Borlase records between 1756 and January 1759:

> Recd from a Jew a toothpick case Birmingham enamel . . . the same Jew has an eye glass case abt 7/6 sent to be set in silver etc. to London.[45]

In his private accounts (1734–1772),[46] Borlase had also referred to his dealings with an unnamed Jew:

> 30th December 1748: to a Jew for knives . . . 8 shillings.

From then on, entries relate specifically to dealings with the Harts:

> 30th November 1765: to half a dozen knives and forks from Sol. Lazs. 10 (shillings) and 6 (pence).
> 28th January 1757: To Solomon Lazarus for 4 silver salt shovels (8s.) and a screw (1s.) . . . 9 (shillings).
> July 27th 1758: Paid Solomon Lazarus for a pencil cap . . . 2 (shillings).
> April 23rd 1759: Paid Solomon Lazarus for two razors . . . to be returned if not liked . . . 2 (shillings).

William Borlase obviously needed to be quite satisfied with products before he eventually accepted them as goods. Abraham Hart is also described as a goldsmith (see later). The Borlase papers make no further reference to him after 1759.

Abraham Hart had a number of children,[47] including Lazarus Hart who was known as Eleazar or Kazanes.[48] His name first appears in Borlase's accounts on 21st May 1764 when Borlase paid him a guinea

---

Testament as *Lemuel*). Its use may also have derived from local, non-Jewish associations (see later). The use of a familiar Biblical name, unrelated to the person's Hebrew name, which he would be known by and which was often used by non-Jews themselves was also common; for example, Solomon or Samuel.

[45] Ledger in the Morrab Library, Penzance, p.115. Presumably these unnamed Jews were itinerant pedlars. (Rev. William Borlase was the first clergyman in Cornwall to be admitted as a member of the masons, at the Falmouth Love and Honour Lodge, on 26th September 1751: (Osb. FM p. 266). See later pp. 269–270.)

[46] They are to be found in the Royal Institution of Cornwall Library, Truro, pp. 56–96. Information from research by Godfrey Simmons. The editors are also grateful to Leslie Douch for some of this information.

[47] The only known names from genealogical records are: Mord(e)chai (b. 1736), Madel (b. 1743), Edel (b.1747), Anna (b. 1750), and Lemel (b. 1755). Source: Colyer-Fergusson, op. cit. and Anthony P. Joseph.

[48] He was born in 1739 and died 5th October 1803.

". . . for exchanging a watch upon six months tryal, and buckles."
The watch was part-exchanged on 18th July 1765:

> Pd Mr. Lazarus Hart besides one guinea pd him May 21st 1764,
> for changing a watch in part. He to warrant the watch now taken
> in exchange for two years from this date, and then to receive one
> guinea more. . .as per rect. 1. 10. 0 . . . pd . . . Do for 1/2 pd of
> tea for Mrs B. Handkerch 3/10 a screw and key 1/6 . . . 14/4.

On 16th August 1767: ". . . pd. Lazarus Hart for screw and cane in
full of all . . . 3/6." and on 29th January 1770: "To Mr. Lazarus Hart
for Billy's buckles 14/6 . . . 2 large tea spoons 10/6 . . . 1 (pound) 5
(shillings)." The offending time-piece, or a successor, was eventually
returned to Hart on 21st August 1770:

> Return'd my watch to Mr. Lazar. Hart being long Complain'd of
> for not going to contract. pa: 80 and promised to be sent to the
> maker.

On 12th February 1772 a similar experience with a pair of spectacles:
"Pd. Mr. Laz. Hart for spectacles silver sett but returned as not suiting
. . . 1/6."

It was Lazarus Hart who developed the family business. The
eighteenth century was a time when there was much interest in the
West Indies, and a number of families connected with the West Indies
trade came to settle in the south west. Among them were the Prices of
Trengwainton, Penzance; and further up-country the Lopes family,
who had been long established in Jamaica, put down new roots in
Roborough, Plymouth.[49] The Lemon and Daniell families of Truro,
among others, had Jamaican interests, and one of the Lemons had
been manager of the tin-smelter at Chyandour, Penzance. In view of
the Harts' shipping interests and the links between the tin producers
and the shippers, it is quite possible that Lazarus Hart was in touch
with this member of the Lemon family. From this local association,
Lazarus Hart and Hyman Woolf could have adopted this prestigious
surname as forenames for their sons.[50]

The Hart and Woolf families became related through marriage.
Benjamin Woolf and his wife had come to Penzance from Holland
(circa 1820–30) and later moved to Falmouth. Their daughter
Rebecca Woolf married Eleazar (Lazarus) Hart (in Falmouth in
December 1763), and their son Hyman Woolf (who remained in

---

[49] Susser (1993, pp. 35, 38–9, 225, 236, 257–8 & 328).
[50] Lemon Street and Lemon Quay in Truro are named after the Lemon family. The
archives of Allied Domecq plc. record Lemon Hart's name as *Lehman*.

Penzance) married Lemon Hart's sister, Eddle Hart, a daughter of Lazarus Hart and Rebecca Woolf.[51]

United Rum Distillers[52] suggest that Abraham Hart had started trading in the import of rum in Penzance in 1720 and that he is believed to have visited Jamaica during the 1750s.[53] Whenever it began, the importance of rum to the Hart's business was soon established and Lazarus Hart's interest widened to include ship-owning, in which capacity he was known as *Kazanes Heart*.[54] In the Penzance shipping registers he is given as a shopkeeper and one of five partners co-owning the *Nancy & Betsy*,[55] registered at Penzance on 7th April 1787 as a 78-ton brigantine, 61ft long, 17ft 8 ins. breadth, and 10ft deep in the hold.[56] On 18th November 1791 the vessel was issued with a plantation certificate by Penzance Customs House for an intended voyage to Jamaica.[57] The last heard of this venture was that the ship foundered near Lundy about 15th February 1793 while on passage between St. Ives and Swansea. To be lost so near to her home

---

[51] Colyer-Fergusson does not give a sister of Lemon Hart with the name Eddle, but only an aunt Edel (b. 1747); however Joseph (1975, facing p. 26) does give Eddle as Lemon Hart's sister. His other sisters were Rebecca and Leah.

[52] This was the company which once owned the LEMON HART ® rum Label. LEMON HART ® rum is still produced under its own name as a registered trade mark of Allied Domecq Spirits & Wine Limited. The editors are grateful to the Company for various information from their records and permission to reproduce the portrait of Lemon Hart, the LEMON HART ® rum label, and other illustrations commissioned by United Distillers as promotional material: all supplied by Allied Domecq from their archives.

[53] From information contained in letters from Joanne Liddle of Allied Domecq to Keith Pearce, 4th & 10th February 1999 summarising records from their archives. This included a promotional booklet entitled *Rum: Discover the World of Rum: The Story as Told by United Rum Distillers*.

[54] The information on ships and ship-owning in this chapter, as well as some other material, has been provided from extensive research by Tony Pawlyn, a trustee of the Cornwall Maritime Museum at Falmouth where it is intended to establish a maritime research library.

[55] Merchant Shipping Registers, Penzance (CRO, MSR, Penzance 1786–1823).

[56] It had been newly built at Mevagissey. The other owners were Thomas Love (a merchant), John Stone, Thomas Branwell and William Woolcock, all described as "Gentlemen". The first two were from Penzance and the last from St. Mary's, Scilly. The proportion of shares held by each is not recorded.

[57] The Penzance Custom House out-port letter books do not contain the original documents, but are contemporary fair copies made by the Customs House clerks. They exist in a very extensive range of 200 unnumbered folio volumes, copied roughly in date order. They appear to be the original copies kept at Penzance. They can be found at the Public Record Office at Kew where the Cornwall books are filed under PRO.CUST 66–69. The Penzance books are numbered PRO.CUST 68. The *Nancy & Betsy* plantation certificates are to be found as PRO.CUST 68/13 & 68/15.

port was a stroke of misfortune as she had made voyages to Jamaica via Newfoundland, where rum was drunk by the fishermen. This was a serious financial set-back for Lazarus Hart.

Problems had not been confined to overseas trade. Earlier in 1790 Hart had sent 24 Tea Waiters by land carriage to Mr. William Basley of Padstow for auction. Only three were sold and Basley returned the unsold balance on the *Mary* sloop from Cork, bound to Plymouth by way of Padstow and Penzance. He fell foul of the Customs House and was accused of trying to avoid duty on imported goods:

> To the Honble Commissioners of His Majesty's Customs. The Humble Petetion of Lazarus Hart of the Town of Penzance in the County of Cornwall, Shopkeeper:-
>
> Most humbly Sheweth,
> That your petitioner is a dealer in most kinds of Birmingham and Sheffield wares, and being over Stocked in Japan'd tea Waiters, forwarded by Land Carriage the 19th June last, Twenty four tea Waiters for sale to Mr. William Basley of Padstow, in said County (he being an Auctioneer) with an order to said Mr. Basley to return such part thereof as did not meet with a Ready Sale, supposing by; and Conveyance as forwarded to him. . . . The said Mr. Basley, meeting with an Opportunity by the Mary sloop Captain William Corbett with whom he was acquainted, from Cork bound to Padstow, Penzance & Plymouth with Provisions, ignorantly shipped 21 on said vessel of the said Tea Waiters (having sold three only) with a view to save land carriage, not dreaming any manner of danger, in such trifling Matters, knowing the goods to be realy and bonafide the Manufacture of Great Britain, such is the Real Truth of the whole Transaction without Reserve, and it was not by any Means to defraud the Revenue; In Tender consideration of the premises, your Petitioner most humbly Hopes your Honrs will take this into your most serious Consideration and not blend the honest Dealer who had no manner of Intention to defraud Government, with the Smuggler; but restore the said Twenty one Waiters to your Petitioner, who shall every pray,
>
> Laz.s Hart.
>
> Lazarus Hart maketh Oath
> That the Contents of the above
> Petition are True.
> Sworn at Penzance the 10th May 1790, before me,
> J. Batten Jn.r Mayor.[58]

---

[58] PRO.CUST 68/14.

On 21st May the Commissioners insisted on proof from Hart to support his petition:

> The Collector and Comp.r Penzance are to State what proof has been submitted to them to shew that the contents of the Former Petition is True and particularly that the Waiters are of British Manufacture and also to report their Observations on this Petition.
>
> By Order of the Commissioners
> M. Hutson.

Hart was able to satisfy these requirements because he was exonerated. On 1st June 1790 the Customs Officers at Penzance issued a statement withdrawing their previous accusations:

> We beg leave to report that the proof Submitted to Us to Shew that the Contents of the former Petition were true, was by the petitioner Offering to Swear to it (which he has since done) producing at same time his Invoices, from his Correspondent at Birmingham, on the first purchasing of said Waiters, likewise his Correspondence with Mr. Wm. Basley at Padstow, and by our own together with several others examined the Waiters, and we verily believe that they are of British Manufacture, & that no Fraud was intended.
>
> Custom Ho. Penzance.
> J S Coll.r
> J W Comp.r

A few years later, Lazarus Hart had decided to wind up his business in Penzance. The reasons are not known, but in view of the fact that he continued to trade in the town until 1803, it could be that the desired sale was not forthcoming or that he re-considered. The following advertisement appeared in the *Sherborne Mercury* on 6th May 1793:

> NOW SELLING: at prime cost, the entire stock of Mr. Lazarus Hart of the town of Penzance, who begs leave to recommend the same to the public in general, as well worth their attention; consisting of silver tankards, quarts, pints and half-pints; coffee-pots and waiters; tea-pots; quart, pint and half-pint goblets; skewers, polished and common; plain and engraved table and tea-spoons; milk-urns, punch-ladles, sugar-tongs etc. and a great variety of silver shoe-buckles; new and second-hand watches, plated candlesticks, bread baskets, dish-crosses, sugar and cream pails, and a great variety of plated shoe and knee-buckles; some articles in the jewellery line; knives and forks, scissors, razors etc. Also a large quantity of 7/8ths and yard-wide Irishes, printed

cottons and chintzes; nankeens, muslins, duroys, velverets, stockings, silk handkerchiefs, black sattins, and some umbrellas. Also a
large stock of new and second-hand sea and landsmen's cloaths.
Any person in trade inclinable to buy the stock will meet with
encouragement, and may have the house, which is well situated
in the market-place, and an established shop in the above line for
these many years past.

Old gold or silver taken in exchange, at its full value.[59]

No more is known about Lazarus Hart's business affairs until 1801
when he registered a complaint with the Customs and Excise against
John Julyan, a tide waiter (customs officer) at Penzance.[60] Writing "as
a man of honour . . . with the greatest respectability" Hart com-
plained of the ". . . constant insults and turbulent conduct of John
Julyan . . .", and reported to the Commissioners that Julyan ". . . kept
an open shop in this town and deals in Excisable goods in the name of
a third party whose name (was) not known in Julyan's house, in the
town of Penzance, or in the neighbourhood." Hart also stressed that
he was complaining under his own name and not as an anonymous
informer. The complaint was duly investigated and the Commissioners pointed out that by an Order dated 6th June 1799, Julyan had
been given permission for his wife to carry on a business "provided it
did not interfere with his duty". The report went on to state that
Julyan had been "searching round a cart which said Hart keeps for
conveying (as he says) goods to his customers" and then alleges that
Julyan had "positive information" that Hart was "concerned with this
illegal traffic".

Julyan was clearly a man to be reckoned with. As a tide waiter he
was part of the waterguard which was responsible for checking loaded
vessels or vessels afloat for contraband. (The land waiters on the other
hand were responsible for checking goods on the quays before they
were loaded into ships, or after they were discharged). Julyan was first
appointed as a boatman in February 1786 and after two years trial, he
received a commission as a boatman. He was a very active officer who
took part in a number of seizures and incidents. He was promoted to
the position of landing and coast waiter duties in March 1789 when he
was sent to Plymouth for training. In his new role he would have

---

[59] As there is no mention in this advertisement of Lazarus Hart's interest in the wine
and spirit business, it can be assumed that his shop was secondary to his main
source of income as a wine and spirit importer and merchant, as well as his
shipping interests. The editors are grateful to Leslie Douch for providing this
material from his research.

[60] PRO.CUST 68/18.

responsibility for both seaside and landside searches. The Penzance officers did not enjoy a very high reputation and a number were dismissed for a variety of irregularities, although they were very rarely prosecuted for dereliction of duty. Since Julyan held office for twenty years or more, he must have been considered a satisfactory officer.[61]

It would seem that the Hart complaint was not upheld and matters went no further. When one considers the allegations and counter-allegations, one is left with the feeling that Hart's complaint was not only ill-judged but may well have been a case of "the pot calling the kettle black". As a way of settling personal accounts it may have been seen as necessary to discourage such complaints if only because it could have endangered a well-established Cornish way of life.

Lazarus Hart died at the end of September 1803 and on 3rd December his shop goods and unredeemed pledges due to him were advertised for sale by auction in the *Royal Cornwall Gazette*:

Unredeemed Pledges
FOR SALE BY AUCTION
ON THURSDAY the 15th instant, by Ten o'clock in the Fore-noon, at the Dwelling-House of the late MR. LAZARUS HART in Penzance.

A GREAT variety of UNREDEEMED PLEDGES, whereof the term of 12 months and one day are expired. Also the whole of his SHOP GOODS, consisting of Cloths, Beavers, Checks, Striped Cottons, ready made Men's and Women's Cloaths, Silver and Plated Goods, Watches, Hardware, &c., &c.,well worth the attention of the Trade and the Publics' in general.
NB. The Pawnbroker's Business will be carried on as usual, in the same House, by his family – Groceries sold Wholesale, as cheap as in London or Bristol.
All Persons indebted to the Estate of the said Mr. Lazarus Hart, are destined to pay the same forthwith to Mr. LEMON HART, Wine Merchant, in this Town; the Administrator.
Penzance, 1st.Dec.1803.

Letters of Administration had been granted to his son Lemon Hart on 13th October 1803; the estate being valued at £3,600 according to the commission executed before the Clerk Master of the Archdeaconry of Cornwall. For Lemon Hart,[62] 1803 became a year of tragedy. Not only did he lose his father, but also his wife, Letitia, in

---

[61] Letter from Tony Pawlyn to Godfrey Simmons, dated 8th December 1998.
[62] His Hebrew name was Asher Laemle ben Eleazar (Nov. 1768–13 Oct 1845).

a fire at their home on 2nd October.[63] The event, and the shocking circumstances leading up to her death, were reported locally and were felt to be so dramatic as to be re-printed 65 years later in the monthly journal *One and All* in November 1868:

> ACCIDENTS SELDOM COME ALONE, EVEN IN PENZANCE.
> Sunday evening, Oct. 2nd, 1803, as Mrs. Hart, wife of Mr. Lemon Hart, spirit merchant, Penzance, was in an upper room alone, with a candle, her clothes unfortunately caught fire, and burnt her in a shocking manner. She was pregnant, has since been prematurely delivered, and now lies in a situation so deplorable, that her life is depaired of. In addition to this calamity, Mr. Lazarus Hart, father of the above-named Mr. Hart, died a few days ago in a fit of apoplexy. (Mrs. Hart died Monday, Oct. 10th).

Letitia Hart is buried in the Penzance cemetery, but her exact grave is unknown because no headstone has survived.

It was not long however, before Lemon Hart, with the responsibility and prospect of bringing up his children on his own, had found a new wife. It may be that matters of business already took him to London, and on 29th July 1804 he married a widow, Mary Solomon,[64] the daughter of Lazarus Solomon of Prescott Street, Goodmans Fields, London.[65] What is clear is that Lemon Hart's personal connection with London was well established some years before his move from Penzance.

---

[63] Lemon Hart's wife, Letitia (or Letty) Michael of Swansea, remained unidentified until a letter was recently discovered in the miscellaneous papers of Cecil Roth in the Brotherton Library in Leeds which gave her name. The letter was addressed to Roth, dated 25th February 1955, from Geoffrey H. White, editor of *The Complete Peerage*, and a descendant. Information provided from Evelyn Friedlander's research. Roth in chapter 4 mentions an "F. Michael of Swansea" who had become attached or affiliated to the Penzance congregation. There is a donation of £1. 1s. recorded in the early Penzance accounts of 9th October 1808 as given by F. Michael of Swansea. It can be assumed that this was a relative of the late Letitia Hart, most likely her nephew Frederick David Michael (1780-1870). This information has been provided by Anthony P. Joseph and Godfrey Simmons.

[64] In his will, proved 1847, Lemon Hart refers to a stepson, Benjamin Slowman. Mary's previous husband may have been Slowman; alternatively it may be a transmutation of Solomon.

[65] *One and All*, November 1868 and *Collectanea Cornubiensia*, cc. 325 (1890), RIC Truro. cf. also a letter from Wilfred Samuel to Alex Jacob, dated 14th March 1955 in the Jacob archive. As with Lemon Hart's first wife, Letitia Michael, Mary Solomon was not from Penzance, and she had lived in London before coming to Penzance in 1804. The couple moved to London in 1811.

The Hart Family
(with some Woolf & Jacob connections)

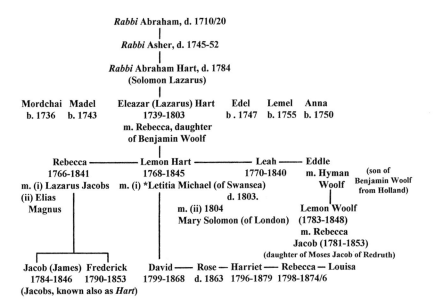

Rabbi Abraham, d. 1710/20

Rabbi Asher, d. 1745-52

Rabbi Abraham Hart, d. 1784
(Solomon Lazarus)

Mordchai	Madel	Eleazar (Lazarus) Hart	Edel	Lemel	Anna
b. 1736	b. 1743	1739-1803	b. 1747	b. 1755	b. 1750
		m. Rebecca, daughter			
		of Benjamin Woolf			

Rebecca ———————— Lemon Hart ———————— Leah ——— Eddle
1766-1841   1768-1845   1770-1840   m. Hyman   (son of
m. (i) Lazarus Jacobs   m. (i) *Letitia Michael (of Swansea)   Woolf   Benjamin Woolf
(ii) Elias   d. 1803.   from Holland)
   Magnus   m. (ii) 1804   Lemon Woolf
                                Mary Solomon (of London)   (1783-1848)
                                                                      m. Rebecca
                                                                      Jacob (1781-1853)
                                        (daughter of Moses Jacob of Redruth)

Jacob (James) Frederick   David —— Rose — Harriet — Rebecca — Louisa
1784-1846   1790-1853   1799-1868 d. 1863 1796-1879 1798-1874/6
(Jacobs, known also as *Hart*)

Source: Colyer-Fergusson & Anthony P. Joseph (abridged).
   *Roth Collection, Leeds.

231

Lemon Hart of Penzance: artist and date unknown. [courtesy: Allied Domecq plc]

Lemon Hart's headstone in the Brady Street Jewish cemetery, London. [courtesy: Michael Shapiro]

During his father's lifetime Lemon Hart had already pursued business interests of his own. Lemon *Heart* is recorded as one of six co-owners of the 52-ton sloop *Amelia* which was registered at Penzance on 28th May 1802.[66] The other owners were John Mathews (shipwright of Penzance), Arthur Hampton, Joseph Nicholls and William Richards, "Gentlemen" all of Penzance, and John McFarland (a victualler of Plymouth).

The *Amelia* was a French prize taken by HMS *Amelia*. Her new owners employed her in the general coastal trade, mainly sailing between Penzance and Swansea as a collier. In February 1806 she was employed as a temporary tin-ship to carry tin between Penzance and London, but on her first run she was re-taken by the French off Portland Bill on 24th February of that year.[67]

On 28th January 1804, in a lengthy advert for the sale of the Dutch brig *Flora* and her cargo, Lemon Hart is named as the broker conducting the sale on behalf of the Admiralty. On 12th November 1805, Lemon *Heart* became the first named partner in another ship the *Speculation*, a 57-ton sloop newly built at Penzance, similar in dimensions and capacity to the *Amelia* of 1802. The other co-owners were Joseph Branwell (butcher), John Mathews (shipbuilder of Penzance), and three men from St. Ives: James Halse (gentleman), William Ninnis (cabinet maker) and Richard Banfield (merchant). The named owners later sold the vessel to William Bryant, her former master, who is recorded as her sole owner when her port of register was transferred to St. Ives on 17th October 1808.

Not only did Lemon Hart continue his father's business which prospered under his direction, but his own wine and spirit trade was well established by 1804. He played an active role both in the religious community as the first president of the Hebrew congregation's new synagogue but also in the wider society of Penzance. The latter years of the eighteenth century and the early years of the nineteenth were times when the fear of invasion from France was ever-present. Hart served in the Ludgvan and also the Mount's Bay Volunteers as an officer. The Ludgvan Pioneers detatchment was raised in 1798 with Captain Lemon Hart as their commander, although he later resigned in favour of Captain John who had transferred from the Marazion Rangers.[68]

---

[66] 49ft. long, 16ft. breadth, with 8ft. 8 ins. depth in the hold.

[67] Another *Amelia*, also a French prize, followed in June 1807 but Lemon Hart was not one of her owners.

[68] Susser's information on p. 253 of his book is largely drawn, as he acknowledges on p. 331, from C. Thomas (1959, pp. 11–12). This was drawn to Susser's attention by Godfrey Simmons. Susser: "Pioneers were small corps designed to assist in such work as blocking roads, building defences and constructing batteries."

When the Ludgvan and Marazion groups merged, Lemon Hart left and became a first lieutenant in the Mounts' Bay Fuzileers,[69] although he returned to the re-named Ludgvan and Marazion Volunteers in 1800. Jacob Hart, Lemon's nephew, was also involved in these activities and was appointed to be Ensign of the St. Ives Volunteers in November 1803.[70] Members of several well-known West Penwith families served in these groups at that time and changing between the various volunteer bodies was by no means uncommon. It is also perhaps an indication that Lemon Hart moved with ease and tolerance between his congregation and the wider community that at least three of his children married Gentiles.[71]

Lemon Hart's son David (1799–1868)[72] married a Gentile, Cornish girl, Mary Pidwell on 3rd January 1831.[73] David and Mary Hart lived at Park House (or The Park), Leytonstone in East London, not far not far from the location of his father's business interests along the stretch of the river from Tower Hill to Deptford. David Hart traded in London as a wine merchant, becoming a wealthy man able to buy land in Leytonstone and Harrow Green. He also became Overseer of the Poor in 1860.[74] David and Mary had numerous children[75] and must have returned to Cornwall to visit, where one son Charles was born in 1846. Of David Hart's sisters, two married Jews: in 1820, Rebecca

---

[69] This was a two-company corps which had been established in 1787.

[70] *The Royal Cornwall Gazette*, 12th November 1803 reporting from the War Office announcement of 8th November in the *London Gazette* of a widespread fear of a French invasion. Tony Pawlyn, ibid.

[71] Susser, op. cit., pp. 236 & 323; cf. also *Jewish Chronicle*, 17th June 1881.

[72] David Hart had been born in 1799 and so he would have been taken to London by his father in 1811.

[73] Colyer-Fergusson's family tree of the Harts refers to Mary Pidwell as "of Falmouth", and a "Joseph Pidwell, linguist" does appear in *Warn's Trade Directory for Falmouth* (1864, p. 94) in Killigrew Street. The editors have been unable to trace a record of the marriage of Hart and Pidwell in either the Falmouth or Budock Parish registers. The Waltham Forest records refer to Mary, aged 49 in 1863, as born in the Parish of Paul, near Penzance (cf. directories of 1848 & 1863) but again, no marriage record has been found at the CRO, Truro. Much of this information has been provided by Josephine Parker, archivist of the Waltham Forest Archives in a letter and enclosures to Helen Fry, 26th February 1999; and letter to Keith Pearce dated 23rd March 1999 from Christine North, County Archivist, CRO, Truro.

[74] Park House had extensive grounds, stabling and two tenant-cottages. The household was a large one with a cook, parlour maid, housemaid, poultry-girl, nurse and a man servant – all in residence. Whereas most of the domestic staff in the 1861 census were drawn from London and its environs, at least two (Susan Bassett and Henry Johns) had come from Cornwall, Falmouth and Mylor respectively.

[75] Colyer-Fergusson gives 13.

(1798–1874) married Walter (d. 1828), a son of Jacob Levi; and then in 1834 she married her first cousin, Frederick, a son of Lazarus (Isaac) Jacobs;[76] in 1824, Rose Hart (1824–1863) married Jacob Michael of Swansea (d. 1882). Harriet (1796–1879) and Louise (dates unknown) married non-Jews in churches in London: in 1830, Harriet married James McTernan; and in 1832, Louise married Samuel Amos of Evesham (who may have been a convert to Christianity).[77]

In the early 1800s Lemon Hart's business affairs had continued to prosper, and by 1804–1807 (or soon after), it is said that the Lemon Hart firm was established with Lemon Hart rum® as his own name-sake brand, and that he was appointed as a victualler to the Royal Navy.[78] His success as an importer of wines and spirits encouraged him to expand his interests by setting up a branch of his business in London, whilst at the same time remaining in Penzance. To achieve this aim, on 11th October 1806 he drew up a deed of partnership with his nephew, Jacob James Hart (1784–1846), a great-grandson of Abraham Hart and a son of Rebecca Hart (1766–1841) who had married Lazarus Jacobs. The partnership was to be for 14 years from 1st January 1807. Jacob was to act as managing partner and to reside at the premises of the London business where he was to devote his whole personal labour, time and attention to the enterprise. Jacob was also bound to travel as and where directed by his uncle until such time as the partnership could afford to employ staff for that purpose. Lemon Hart, on the other hand, was obliged to act in the business only if he so wished. The initial capital to start the business amounted to £5000, a considerable sum for that time. That all of it was subscribed

---

[76] Colyer-Fergusson gives Rebecca's date of death as 1866; Anthony Joseph gives it as 1864.

[77] Susser, op. cit., pp. 236 & 323; *Jewish Chronicle*, 17th June 1881.

[78] cf. Joanne Liddle (op. cit.,) and Roth (Chapter 4, op. cit.,). Geoffrey Green (op. cit., p. 147) implies that the Lemon Hart firm became purveyors of rum to the Navy at a later date, from the time of Lemon Hart's move to London in 1811. In fact Lemon Hart's appointment as a victualler and the identity of the Naval officials involved in the original and ongoing contractual arrangements have not as yet been confirmed from independent documentary sources despite extensive searches of the official Naval records held at the PRO Kew (ADM 109–111; 111/ 270 & 284; 112/160–1, 197–8 & 212; & 113) and the National Maritime Museum, Greenwich (ADM: C 729–731 & DP 31 A&B.): research by Peter Towey. Rum had been supplied to the Navy from various sources for many years prior to 1804, and Lemon Hart may have been one of these earlier suppliers, but he was by no means the first. *Hart, Hart & Co* were successively at 59, Fenchurch St., Lower Thames St., Water Lane and Tower St. In the Hart business and estate papers 1806–1848, there is an authenticated copy of the co-partnership agreement between Lemon Hart and his nephew Jacob (Ms. 10,622, Guildhall Library, London): research by Michael Gandy, December 1997.

by Lemon Hart himself was a clear sign of his success and financial strength as well as his confidence in the venture. Jacob undertook to put in his half-share as soon as his financial situation permitted. The deed of partnership also demonstrated quite clearly Lemon's determination to be in control of the future direction of his business. The London business must have been a success because Lemon Hart left Penzance for the capital city around the middle of 1811. At some point he became resident at Fenchurch Street in the City, near Tower Hill and the river. Eventually he moved his company to the West India Docks, up-river from Greenwich. This was at a time when shipments of rum and sugar coming into the country had a high risk of being plundered. To remedy this the Government had had the West India Dock built some years earlier in 1802 in the style of a fortress with guards manning the walls to protect the ships.[79]

Lemon Hart left his nephew Lemon Woolf to look after his Cornish interests. Lemon Woolf already had his own well-established wine and spirit business in Penzance in Market Jew Street.[80] At some point Jacob James Jacobs adopted the surname *Hart* and, as Jacob James Hart, remained employed in the London business for some years.[81] He became well connected as a result of contacts made through supplying wine to the London clubs and enjoyed the friendship of the young Lord Palmerston, through whose patronage he was eventually appointed Consul-General to the Kingdom of Saxony.[82]

Lemon Hart and his wife eventually retired to Brighton, where he died in 1845. He is buried in the Brady Street Jewish cemetery in London. The direction of the firm was left in the hands of his son, David. As a measure of his success, by the year 1849 the Royal Navy is said to have been taking rum from the Harts at the rate of 100,000 gallons a year.[83] Lemon Hart's name is not likely to be forgotten as Lemon Hart® rum is still produced under its own label. Anyone drinking it today, drinks to a name with more than two and a half centuries of history.

---

[79] Joanne Liddle, op. cit.

[80] The complexity of the family relationships which resulted from inter-marriage between the Cornish Jewish families mean for example that Lemon Woolf is sometimes described as Lemon Hart's cousin.

[81] Green (1989) p. 147) incorrectly identifies Jacob as Lemon Hart's brother. Genealogical records show Lemon Hart as Eleazar (Lazarus) Hart's only son. Another of Lemon Hart's nephews, Frederick Jacobs (1790–1853), Jacob James Jacobs' younger brother, who had married Lemon Hart's daughter Rebecca (as her second husband), is said to have subsequently joined his brother Jacob in London in a partnership. His date of death (as 1853) is not certain.

[82] Jacob Hart is buried in the Penzance cemetery (5:3).

[83] Green (op. cit., p.147).

Before Lemon Hart left Penzance, he donated a number of religious artefacts to the synagogue and handed over the role of president of the congregation to Hyman Woolf,[84] the father of Lemon Woolf. Hyman supervised and maintained the communal *mikveh* which was attached to his house in Causewayhead, where there was an underground stream. Hyman did not enjoy good health in his later years. His son sometimes substituted for him at the congregation's administrative meetings and on occasions signed the minutes for him. Lemon Woolf, who was married to Rebecca Jacob, a daughter of Moses Jacob of Redruth, eventually became the third warden and together with Henry Joseph negotiated the cemetery leases.

Lemon Woolf owned a wine and spirit business in Market Jew Street[85] and another in Chapel Street. He also occupied another premises in Causewayhead as a pawnbroker. In his journal between 1816–17, the Mayor of Penzance, sitting in his judicial capacity as a magistrate, recorded a number of occasions when Lemon Woolf came before him.[86] Woolf had become sufficiently wealthy to employ at least one servant who entered into a legal dispute with him. On 29th November 1816 she laid a complaint before the Mayor at the Guildhall that Woolf had refused to pay her wages. The Mayor found that the girl had left the service of the family without warning and so dismissed her complaint. "Mr. Woolf stated that he would still pay her the amount on proper apology, otherwise give it to the poor."

These same journals reveal the only recorded incident which could be viewed as a form of harassment of the Jewish congregation. On Monday 22nd September 1817, Woolf and Symmons[87] made a complaint against "boys for disturbing the Syn.", and the next day the Mayor granted a summons against John Noy and Mark Row. The matter was heard on the 24th, when the two complainants stated that the boys had thrown "an iron bullet" into the synagogue. Row confessed that he had given the bullet to Noy ("an idiot") and told him to bowl it against the door which was . . . (as a result) . . . broken. "The prosecutors proposed that the parents of Row should be charged to chastize him severely and that he should sign an acknowledgement of his guilt, sorrow, etc. . . . which was ordered accordingly." The interest in this incident is clearly that the two Jewish complainants

---

[84] Details of these ritual artefacts are given in chapter 9.

[85] The shop continued to be a wine and spirit business and was trading as Davey until it closed in the early 1980s.

[86] *Bibliotheca Cornubiensis*, vol 3, c.c. 1510, 1534, 1563–4.

[87] This is referring to B.A. Simmons, the rabbi.

were treated with the respect and impartiality which was due to any members of the community.

On 18th November 1830, Lemon Woolf became involved in a civil suit when Abraham Joseph,[88] a former rabbi or reader at the synagogue, was made bankrupt. Abraham Joseph (1799–1868), who was the third son of Joseph Joseph (1761–1845), was married to Lemon Woolf's daughter, Eliza (d. 1850), known as "the beautiful Miss Woolf of Penzance". Woolf had made a written guarantee on 23rd May 1827 to cover Joseph's account for porter with a firm of brewers and was as a consequence sued upon his guarantee. He pleaded in court that the brewers had given Joseph further credit without reference to him (Woolf). The jury stated that "as practical men" they considered this should not release Woolf, but on Appeal, the decision was reversed. The case of *Coombe v. Woolf* became a leading authority on the law of guarantee into the twentieth century.

Trades and Occupations

Solomon Lazarus (Abraham Hart): goldsmith (Ja. 1757–64: p. 319).

Solomo(a)n Solomon: silversmith, (c. 1781; PRO. CUST. 68/11). On 13th June 1781 he made a voluntary deposition before the Penzance magistrates, John Price and Samuel Borlase, in a Customs case. He is described as ". . . being one of the persons called Jews . . .", and that he had ". . . sworn on the Pentateuch . . ." The case concerned an incident ". . . about the latter end of May or the Beginning of June . . ." involving a Francis Bradley, a Tidewaiter in his Majesty's Customs of St. Michael's Mount, who had approached Solomon to ask if he dealt in indigo, to which Solomon confirmed that he did. It was agreed that Bradley would bring between 150 to 200 lbs. of indigo

---

[88] A letter from Stephen Pyke to Alex Jacob, dated 13th April 1949, gives Abraham as the bankrupt. But a letter from W. S. Jessop of Chicago to Cecil Roth dated 20th July 1948 (in the Roth Collection, Leeds) states that it was his father Joseph Joseph who was involved in the Woolf case. Pyke notes that Woolf signed the guarantee as *Leman*. (It should be noted that the Henry Joseph who is buried in the Penzance cemetery, 6:5, who was a prosperous pawnbroker in the town and a prominent member of the Hebrew congregation, was not related to Abraham Joseph of Penzance, but was a son of Abraham Joseph of Falmouth, who had married Hannah Levy (Pz. 1:2), daughter of Barnet Levy of Falmouth. Henry Joseph of Penzance was, therefore, a grandson, not of the Joseph Joseph above, but of Joseph Joseph of Alsace who died in London. Henry Joseph of St. Austell (Fal. 2:4; d. 1803) was a son of Joseph Joseph of Alsace.)

Oppenheim's advertising board, Penzance c.1890.

Levin's upholstery store (Lavin's), c.1880. [both pictures
courtesy: Penlee House Art Gallery & Museum]

239

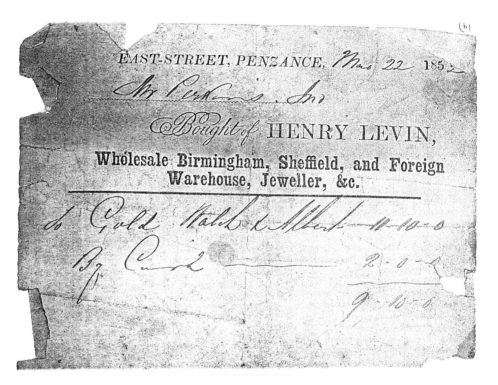

Jewellery receipt for a 'Gold Watch & Albert', 1852 from Henry Levin. [courtesy: Ron James]

Above: Oppenheim's furnishing stores, Penzance, receipt dated January 28th, 1869. [courtesy: John Bodilly]. Following pages: front page advertisement from an original of the first issue of the *Cornishman* newspaper, July 18th, 1878 [courtesy: Eileen Nethercotte], and advertisement c.1880 [courtesy: the *Cornishman*]

ESTABLISHED 1836.

ISRAEL OPPENHEIM,

Cabinet Maker, Upholsterer,

DRAPER, CARPET FACTOR,

COMPLETE HOUSE FURNISHER, AND CONTRACTOR.

SHOW ROOMS AND OFFICES:—

3, 4, & 8 MARKET JEW STREET,

and Bread Street, PENZANCE.

DEPARTMENTS.

Iron and Brass Bedsteads
Chest Drawers, and Wardrobes
Washstands and Toilet Tables
Wood Bedsteads
Dining, Loo, and other Tables
Chiffonniers and Sideboards
Easy Chairs and Couches
Chairs of every description
Toilet and Chimney Glasses

Gilt Cornices, Poles, &c.
Bedding, Carpets
Mattings, Drapery
Blankets and Quilts
Linens, Damasks, &c.
Furnishing Ironmongery
Fenders and Fire Irons
Cutlery, Trays, &c.
Toilet Sets

AND EVERY REQUISITE FOR COMPLETELY FURNISHING A HOUSE THROUGHOUT.

Best Quality Venetian Blinds, Painted any Colour, 8d. per Sq. Foot.

SALESMEN SENT TO ANY PART TO WAIT ON CUSTOMERS.

GOODS DELIVERED FREE BY OWN VANS WITHIN 20 MILES.
All Goods sent Carriage Paid to any Railway Station (no Charge for Packing).

AN ILLUSTRATED CATALOGUE SENT POST FREE ON APPLICATION.

WHOLESALE & EXPORT ORDERS PROMPTLY EXECUTED.

Factory: Bread St., PENZANCE.

to Solomon ". . . a few evenings after about twelve O'Clock at night . . ." This did not happen, and the next Sunday Solomon was summoned by Bradley to meet him at the "House of Christ.r Ellis an Innkeeper" in Penzance, where John Dale and Richard Hill, said to own the indigo, promised Solomon that they would bring it to his house a few days later. This appointment was also not kept, and Solomon later heard that a quantity of indigo had been stolen from the brig Neptune, then moored in the harbour of the Mount. Solomon went to the ship's master, Barend Terkelsen, and relayed his story. Solomon's deposition led to the three men being committed to the Common Gaol on 2nd July to await trial at the next assizes, but "through some mistake of the Attorney for the Prosecution" the case collapsed.[89]

Thomas Solomon: who may have been Jewish. Notice from the Exeter Gazette of 22nd October 1793: "Penzance, Cornwall – To be Sold by Public Auction at the Star Inn . . . October 22nd . . . All the Stock in trade of Thomas Solomon, deceased; consisting of a variety of gold and silver watches, jewellery, plate, and hardware, quite new and of the most modern taste – Mr. Thomas Branwell, his Executor in Trust." He was also a watchmaker (Br. 1793).

Solomon Jacobs: watchmaker (Br. 1803)

Henry Ralph: Navy agent 1809 (Green, 1989, p. 147)

Levi Jacobs: watchmaker (Br. 1823)

Lemon Woolf: pawnbroker, Market Place; wine & spirit merchant, Chapel St. (Pg. 1823/24/30); wine & spirit merchant, East St. (Pg. 1844), Market Jew St. (Wi. 1847)

Sophia Jacob: clothes dealer, Chapel St. (Pg. 1830)

Henry Levin: clothes dealer, Chapel St. (Pg. 1830); fancy repositories, East St. (Pg. 1844); . . . & marine store dealer, jeweller & hardware, Market Jew St. (Sl. 1852/3)

Joseph Joseph: watch & clockmaker, jeweller, Market Jew St. (Pg. 1830)

Henry Levy: watch & clockmaker, jeweller, Alverton St. (Pg. 1830)

---

[89] He was probably a member of the Solomon family mentioned in *Records of My Family*.

Aaron Selig: watch & clockmaker, Market Jew St. (Pg. 1830)

Moses (M.B.) Simmons: cabinet maker, carver & gilder, East St. (Pg. 1844; Wi. 1847)

Samuel Oppenheim: clothes dealer, East St. (Pg. 1844); Slop Warehouse, Market Jew St. (Wi. 1847); clothes dealer, Market Jew St. (Sl. 1852/3); clothier, 3, Market Jew St. (Co. 1864). Samuel's son, Israel, continued the family business. He also invested in the local tin-mining industry, losing most of his money as a result of a collapse in the market. He eventually moved to Bristol.[90]

Benjamin Selig: clothes dealer, and watch & clockmaker, North St. (Pg. 1844; Br. 1844); . . . & china and glass warehouse (Wi. 1847). Watch etc. . . . (Sl. 1852/3). He was married to Catherine and they had two children, Aaron and Lemon. A shop assistant, Phoebe Jacobs, lived with them (1851 Census). The family eventually emigrated to New Zealand.

Phoebe Simmons: clothes dealer, East St. (Pg. 1844)

Henry Joseph: pawnbroker, Market St. (Pg. 1844; Sl. 1852/3); Chapel St. (Queen's Sq.) (Wi. 1847); 5, Market Jew St. (Co. 1864). The Penzance cemetery section (6:5) of chapter 5 gives details of the Joseph family.

It can be seen from the Samuel Oppenheim and Henry Joseph entries in *Coulson's Directory* above that from the 1860s, house and premises numbers begin to be used for some of the chief business and residential streets. It is likely that it took some time for these to settle into a coherent system of numbering as the postal service and new building expanded rapidly. The numbers for Penzance in *Coulson's Directory* for 1864 are street-specific. Around 1878, George Bown Millett attempted an historical reconstruction of the buildings and businesses in the town centre from the beginning of the century, allocating numbers to each site. These numbers are not based on the postal system but upon his own plan and are conjectural. Millett referenced each of his numbers

---

[90] Letter from David M. Jacobs to Keith Pearce, dated 2nd January 1989. David's maternal grandmother was Israel Oppenheim's daughter Annie (later Salanson) who was born in Penzance in 1868. Israel Oppenheim later moved to Bristol, where his daughter Annie played a significant part in the Jewish Social and Debating Society; cf. *Jews in Bristol*, Judith Samuel (1997, pp. 148–150 & 169). Samuel Oppenheim's (only) son Israel married Mathilda, daughter of Barnet Lyon Joseph of Falmouth. cf. letter from Anthony P. Joseph, 26th March 1999.

to the town centre as a whole as "Market Jew St." irrespective of the separate names by which the streets had come to be known. The locations on his plan would, however, seem to coincide with the other directory addresses and a copy of his plan and extracts relating to Jewish shops is attached to the end of this section.

Morris Hart Harris: watch & clockmaker, Chapel St. (Pg. 1844); watch & clock dealer . . . "advertises American clocks at 17/6d each" (Br. 1844); jeweller, silversmith, watch & clock repairs, china & glass, Chapel St. (Wi. 1847).

Alexander Levin: watch & clockmaker, & dealer in china, glass etc., & marine stores (Wi. 1847). He eventually moved to Birmingham.

Samuel Jacob: jeweller, 9 Leskinnick Terrace. (1851 Census). He was a son of Moses Jacob of Redruth. Samuel Jacob was deaf. He was married to Sarah, or Sally, Levy of Truro. Their daughter Bettsey, who was deaf and dumb, was a dressmaker.

Rabbi B.A. Simmons: Slop Warehouse, Market Jew St. (Wi. 1847). He lived at 16 Leskinnick Terrace (1851 Census) with his wife Flora, a daughter of Moses Jacob of Redruth. An elderly relative, Kitty Simons from Redruth and a servant called Grace Read lived with them in 1851.

Solomon Teacher: hardware & jeweller, Market Jew St. (Wi. 1847; 1851 Census). He was from St. Ives and lived at 35 Leskinnick Terrace, Penzance with his wife Maria, daughter of Aaron and Hannah Selig and brother of Benjamin (above). Solomon and Maria Teacher's daughter, Annah (b. circa 1850), and a servant called Jane Caday, lived with them. There were also two sons, David (b. 1854) and Solomon (the latter born in the same year as his father died, 1856, and named after him). David Teacher also named one of his sons Solomon. Solomon Teacher took an active part in congregational affairs and is mentioned in the minute books on several occasions, including his proposal (which was narrowly defeated) that Rabbi B. A. Simmons should be dismissed without notice. By 1856 the Teacher family's finances were strained, and at a meeting on 13th April 1856, the congregation paid out £2 16s. 9d. for Solomon Teacher's funeral expenses. They also paid £2 15s. 6d. for Mr. Staalhagen (sic. Rev. Myer Stadthagen of the Plymouth Congregation from 1829-1862) to come to Penzance to circumcise "Mrs Teacher's child", Solomon. (The congregation paid £1 15s. 6d. for the funeral of Joseph Barnet, also from St. Ives, at the same time.)

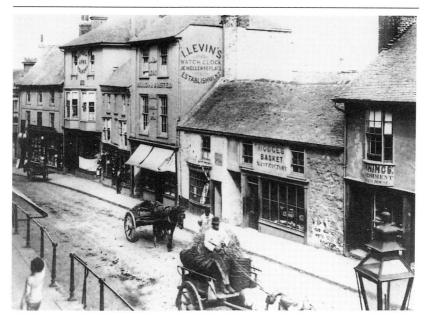

Israel Levin, jeweller, Market Jew Street, Penzance c.1880.

Market Jew Street c.1890, with Oppenheims' store to the right. [both pictures
courtesy: Penlee House Art Gallery & Museum]

247

I. LEVIN'S
WHOLESALE & RETAIL
Watch, Jewellery, and Plate Establishment,
102, MARKET-JEW-STREET, PENZANCE.

Gold and Silver Watches, Gold Alberts, Neck Chains, Lockets, Ladies' Rings, Gents' Rings, Brooches, Ear Rings, and Scarf Pins. SILVER & ELECTRO PLATE.
A LARGE ASSORTMENT OF
PLATED AND JET JEWELLERY, CUTLERY, &c., &c.
SILVER WATCHES, 25s. GOLD WATCHES, 3 GUINEAS.

Advertisement for Israel Levin's jewellers, from the *Cornishman* newspaper, July 18th, 1878. [courtesy: Eileen Nethercotte]

Rabbi Isaac Bischofswerder of Penzance (extreme right) with family and friends c.1889. [courtesy: Victor Bishop of Norwich]

Solomon Ezekiel: tinman, (Co. 1864). He has been referred to earlier in the previous chapter, and was born in Devon (either at Exeter or Newton Abbot) in 1786. He had moved to Falmouth by 1811 where he is listed in Holden's directory for that year as a tinman. He later moved to Penzance where he lived in Causewayhead and traded as a plumber and coppersmith. He was married to Hannah Jacob (Penzance cemetery, 6:5). Solomon was involved in the wider community as a member of the Highways Committee (1845) and also became something of a local scholar and lecturer, publishing several pamphlets. He successfully prevented a local landowner, Sir Rose Price of Trengwainton, from establishing in Penzance a branch of the London Society for Promoting Christianity among Jews, which he countered by founding the Penzance Hebrew Society for the Promotion of Religious Knowledge.[91]

Israel Levin: marine store dealer, Levin's Court & 102 Market Jew St. (Co. 1864). The son of Henry Levin, above.

Marcus Spiro: rabbi, 2 New St. (adjacent to the synagogue); (Co. 1864)

Berenger & Schwerer: watch & clockmakers, 17 Market Jew St. & 27 Market Place; (Br. 1856). They appear in several Cornish towns. The latter was Jewish, the former was not. It is doubtful if the following Penzance clockmakers were Jewish: Samuel Shortman (1823), Henry Sleeman (1833), Nicholas Daniel (1844), Matthew Kistler (1844), Michael Daniel (1847), George Kistler (1856/73), Matthias Kistler (1873).

Kelly's Directories (1883–1910):[92]

Rev. Isaac Bischofswerder: Jewish minister, 9 Belgravia Street (1883)

David Bischofswerder: pawnbroker and jeweller, 13 & 14 Market Jew Street (1889); tobacconist, 111 Market Jew Street (1889); Home: Alverton Road.

Morris Bischofswerder: secondhand clothes dealer, 118 Market Jew Street (1883); Home: 8 Cornwall Terrace (1889). General dealer (1891). Jeweller, 118 Market Jew Street (1902/1906/1910). Home: 47 Morrab Road.

---

[91] Susser, 1993, pp. 208–9.
[92] From research by Graham Rogers, 1999.

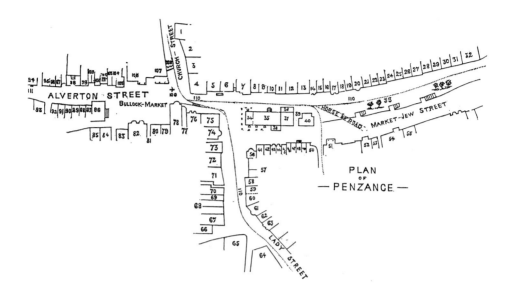

PLAN
OF
— PENZANCE —

B A Simmons	Rabbi	21 "Market Jew St." Mi. 1878/80
Oppenheim	Furniture Trader	22
Henry Joseph	Pawnbroker	24
Oppenheim		27
Lemon Hart	Wine & Spirit Merchant	47
Joseph	Pawnbroker	49 (possibly as 24)
Simmons	Old Clothier	56 (Phoebe Simmons?)
Ol(i)ver & Simmons	Drapers	59/60
Harris	Jeweller	62
Lemon Woolf	Spirit Merchant	70

George Bown Millett: "Plan . . . abt 1805 . . . of the Centre of Old Penzance and the Names of some of the Several Persons who occupied houses and shops . . . from about the commencement of this century to the present time. This list does not pretend to completeness or much accuracy . . . but it may be . . . an aid to memory."

Penzance Marriage Registers, 1838–1892[93]

There were 18 Jewish marriages during this period. Of these, two were between a Jew and a Gentile where both partners were living locally at the time. Only four marriages were between partners who both lived in Penzance, and four were between members of the Penzance and Falmouth congregations. The remaining eight marriages were between Penzance residents and partners from outside the locality. This in itself would indicate the trend for marriage to result in migration from the town. The synagogue was used for nine of the marriages, eight were in the family homes, and one took place at the register office. The abbreviation *ofa* indicates that of *full* age appears on the certificate; *Ma.* that the register indicates that the couple were "married by . . .", who signed the certificate.

1. June 6th 1838. Joseph Benedict Rintel, Jewish Rabbi (of Falmouth) age 28, son of Benedict Jacob Rintel, Gentleman, married Fanny Simmons, 24, of Penzance, daughter of Rabbi Barnett Asher Simmons.
   Witnesses: I. Jacob and Henry Levin. (House) Ma. Rabbi Barnett Simmons.

2. January 23rd 1839. Samuel Oppenheim, age 34, son of Nathan Oppenheim, Merchant, married Elizabeth Levy, 38, daughter of Israel Levy, Jeweller. Both parties of Penzance.
   Witnesses: Henry Levin and Lemon Woolf. (Synagogue) Ma. B.A. Simmons.

3. June 9th 1841. Bella Woolf, 24, daughter of Lemon Woolf, Merchant, married Markis Levy, 29, Silversmith, of Plymouth, son of Abraham Levy, Merchant.
   Witnesses: Henry Joseph and Benjamin Selig. (House) Ma. B.A. Simmons.

4. May 10th 1842. Amelia Woolf (ofa), of Penzance, daughter of Lemon Woolf, Merchant, married Phillip Solomon (ofa), Hardwareman, of Newcastle-on-Tyne, son of Isaac Solomon.

---

[93] Secondary copies of these marriage certificates have been drawn from the archive of Godfrey Simmons. The editors are grateful to John Lee, Marriages Section of the General Register Office for National Statistics, Southport for permission to use the personalised data contained in these documents: letters to Keith Pearce, 12th October & 18th November 1998; also to Rita Collier the Registrar at Penzance who has provided information on these marriages.

Witnesses: Josiah Solomon and Lemon Woolf. (House) Ma. B.A. Simmons.

5. June 10th 1846. Moses Barnett Simmons (ofa), Gilder, of Penzance, son of Rabbi Barnett Asher Simmons, married Rosa Aaron (ofa), of Falmouth, daughter of Abraham Aaron, Merchant. Witnesses: Jonas Heilbron and Benjamin Aaron Selig. (House) Ma. B.A. Simmons.

6. August 5th 1846. Jonas Heilbron (ofa), Jeweller, of Falmouth, son of Isaac Heilbron, Merchant, married Phoebe Simmons (ofa), of Penzance, daughter of Rabbi Barnett Asher Simmons.
Witnesses: Henry Joseph and Benjamin Aaron Selig. (House) Ma. B.A. Simmons.

7. November 11th 1846. Solomon Teacher, age 35, Shopkeeper, of Penzance, son of Markus Teacher, Merchant, married Maria Selig, age 32, of Penzance, daughter of Aaron Selig, Watchmaker. Witnesses: Henry Levin and Moses B. Simmons. (Synagogue) Ma. B.A. Simmons.

8. September 1st 1847. Benjamin Aaron Selig, age 33, Jeweller, of Penzance, son of Aaron Selig, married Catherine Jacob, age 26, of Falmouth, daughter of Samuel Jacob, Jeweller.
Witnesses: Henry Levin and B.A. Simmons. (Synagogue) Ma. B.A. Simmons.

9. June 12th 1850. Hyman Feinburg (ofa), General Merchant, of Newport, Wales, son of Moses Feinburg, Merchant, married Catherine Simmons (ofa), of Penzance, daughter of Rabbi Barnett Asher Simmons.
Witnesses: Jonas Heilbron and David Levin. (Synagogue) Ma. B.A. Simmons.

10. August 21st 1850. Charles Goodman, age 23, Painter & Glazier, of Newbridge,[94] Lamorna, son of George Goodman, Jeweller, married Amelia Jacob, age 28, of Penzance, daughter of Samuel Jacob, Jeweller.
Witnesses: Solomon Teacher and Simon B. Simmons. (Synagogue) Ma. B.A. Simmons.

---

[94] This is not the Newbridge to the west of Penzance, but the town of the same name north of Cardiff. Presumably, Goodman was living at the time of his marriage at Lamorna, several miles to the south of Penzance, on the Land's End peninsula.

11. May 8th 1853. Ephraim George Goodman, age 26, Glazier, of Merthyr Tydfil, Wales, son of Harris Goodman, Pawnbroker, married Phoebe Jacob, age 24, of Penzance, daughter of Samuel Jacob, Jeweller.
Witnesses: Benjamin Aaron Selig and Solomon Ezekiel. (Synagogue) B.A. Simmons.

This was the last marriage conducted by Rabbi B.A. Simmons before his retirement.

12. July 24th 1861. Frederick Lazarus,[95] age 24, Licensed Hawker, of Penzance, son of Jonas Lazarus, deceased, Licenced Hawker, married Emily Cock, age 22, Domestic Servant, of Penzance, daughter of Thomas Cock (deceased), Farmer.
Witnesses: William Noy and John Easton Tonkin. (Register Office) Ma. John Trythall (Registrar).

The marriages given here as 13 to 18, are Nos. 12 to 17 in the Penzance Register of Jewish Marriages.

13. November 22nd 1865. George Goodman,[96] age 37 (widower), Pawnbroker, of Pontypridd, Glamorganshire, son of Harris Goodman, Pawnbroker, married Rose Joseph, age 27, of Penzance, daughter of Henry Joseph, Pawnbroker.

---

[95] This is the first recorded marriage of a Jew to a Gentile. (From David James, great-grandson of the couple, who has provided marriage and birth certificates and the information that Frederick Lazarus was Jewish. cf. Letter to Keith Pearce, 3rd September 1997). Frederick Lazarus may have been an itinerant hawker who resided in Penzance only briefly. It is not known if he was related to the Hyman Lazarus who is mentioned in the Penzance congregation's minute books (in 1843 & 1845) or to the Isaac Lazarus who donated 4 shillings or the ". . . Lazarus", whose donation of 1 shilling and 7 pence is recorded in a copy of the original handwritten accounts for the acquisition of a new *Sifre Torah* in 1828. It should be noted that the Penzance Register of Marriages does not include this certificate amongst its Jewish marriages. Although this may suggest that Frederick was not Jewish, it could be that it was not recorded with the others because Lazarus did not declare his religion, or that he, as an itinerant, had no affiliation with the Penzance congregation. There was certainly no Jewish witness to the marriage. On 23rd August 1862 the birth of Frederick and Emily's daughter, Annie, was registered in Redruth where at the time they were living in Penryn Street. Frederick Lazarus gave his mark in place of a signature on both certificates; Emily signed her name on the marriage certificate.

[96] It is not known if George Goodman or any of his family had been resident in Cornwall for any length of time. A Ruth Goodman was charged with handling stolen silver to Benjamin Levi, at Falmouth, in 1852. cf. *The Royal Cornwall Gazette*, 22nd September 1852, p. 5, col. 5. Goodman was a common name amongst the Jews of South Wales.

Witnesses: Henry Levin and Michael Jacob. (House) Ma. Rabbis Rittenberg and I. Rubinstein.

14. June 9th 1869. Aaron Harris Mark Beirnstein,[97] age 21, Pawnbroker, of Dowlais (Merthyr Tydfil), Wales, son of Abraham Beirnstein, Pawnbroker, married Esther Joseph, age 26, of Penzance, daughter of Henry Joseph, Pawnbroker.
Witnesses: Henry Levin, Jonas Levy, A. Abelson and Henry Joseph. (House) Ma. Rabbi Isaac Bischofswerder.

15. August 31st 1870. Abraham Freedman, age 28 (Widower), Pawnbroker, of Aberdare, son of Samuel Freedman, Pawnbroker, married Kate Joseph, age 23, of Penzance, daughter of Henry Joseph, Pawnbroker.
Witnesses: B.H. Jos(eph), Henry Levin, Abel Abelson and Henry Joseph. (House) Ma. Isaac Bischofswerder.

16. February 9th 1876. Elias Pearlson, age 23, Rabbi, of Newcastle-on-Tyne, son of Abraham Pearlson, Hebrew Teacher, married Henrietta Bischofswerder, age 21, of Penzance, daughter of Isaac Bischofswerder, Rabbi.
Witnesses: Henry Levin, Marcus Bischofswerder and Henry Joseph. (Synagogue). Ma. Isaac Bischofswerder.

17. February 5th 1884. Morris Bischofswerder, age 27, Clothier, of Penzance, son of Isaac Bischofswerder, Jewish Minister, married Julia Joseph (ofa), of Penzance, daughter of Henry Joseph (deceased), Pawnbroker.
Witnesses: B.H. Joseph, David Bischofswerder and Israel H. Levin. (Synagogue) Ma. Isaac Bischofswerder.

18. June 12th 1892. Marcus Bischofswerder, age 39, Jeweller, of Penzance, son of Isaac Bischofswerder, Retired Rabbi, married Emma Boramlagh Hawke, age 27, of Penzance, daughter of Thomas Hawke (deceased), Policeman.
Witnesses: George Bischofswerder, J. Myers, David Bischofswerder and H. Bischofswerder. (House) Ma. Rabbi M. Leinkram.

This was the last Jewish marriage recorded in Penzance at a time when the Jewish congregation was in terminal decline. It was only the second marriage to a Gentile, and the only one in which a

---

[97] The bridegroom wrote his name in Hebrew and it was transcribed onto the certificate as Aaron Mark Beirnstein Harris, but he signed in English script as Harris Mark Beirnstein.

rabbi is known to have officiated. Unlike the other two Bischofs-werder family marriages, it did not take place in the synagogue and Isaac Bischofswerder, who was by now in poor health, may not have been present. He did not sign the certificate as a witness.

The Branwell Family

The Branwells of Penzance were not a Jewish family but, along with other influential Christian families in the locality, such as the Barham, Bolitho, Borlase and Rogers families, they were supportive of the Jewish community and helped them become established in the town. Their reasons may not have been entirely without financial self-interest but their role in facilitating the provision of land for the development of a burial ground and the building of both synagogues was crucial.

The Branwells, who lived at 25 Chapel Street, were involved in the leasing and building of both the first and second synagogues. They were a prosperous Methodist family and in 1814 they also built the town's first purpose-built Wesleyan chapel, opposite the Turk's Head Inn in Chapel Street. They were also freemasons in the same Redruth Lodge, the Druid's Lodge of Love and Liberality, as were several of the leading members of the Jewish community, including Lemon Hart and Lemon Woolf. Richard Branwell (1744–1812, or his son Richard, 1771–1815) appears as a member in 1808, and Thomas (b. 1801) in 1826.[98]

Thomas Branwell (1746–1808) was a prominent member of the Town Corporation and a successful grocer and tea merchant who was involved in the import trade. He owned bonded warehouses and cellars on the Quay where imported luxury goods (tea, brandy, wines and snuff) were processed through the Customs House before being sold in his shop in the Market Square. He had also invested in property around the town, including the Golden Lion Inn in the same square and a brewery.[99] These business interests would also have

---

[98] Osborne (1901, pp. 82 & 112). Thomas Branwell (1746–1808), Maria Branwell's father, had married Anne Carne (1743–1809) in 1768. The Richard Branwell above was either Maria's paternal uncle, or his son, her cousin. The Thomas Branwell (b. 1801) would have been her maternal nephew, the son of Benjamin Carne Branwell (1775–1818). cf. Pool (1990).

[99] Barker (1995, pp. 48–49). The Branwells were also responsible for a number of important buildings in the town, including the former Assembly Rooms in Chapel Street (now incorporated into the Union Hotel), the Masonic Lodge (very near the synagogue) and Branwells Mill at Gulval. They also owned land in the Leskinnick area of the town. cf. Peter Pool (1990).

brought him into contact with Lemon Hart and Lemon Woolf. Lemon Hart owned warehouses and was involved in the import of Jamaica rum. As we have seen earlier, Thomas Branwell acted as executor in trust to the estate of Thomas Solomon, a former jeweller, in October 1793.

The Penzance of the late eighteenth and early nineteenth century was a far more prosperous and cultured town than its far-flung location might suggest. Sea trade, fishing and tin-mining had made it the most important banking centre in Cornwall. The Bolitho family bank held substantial investments for the Branwells as it did for most of the other traders in the town,[100] including Jewish traders, and hence it is likely to have been involved in the Jewish congregation's financial arrangements.

Thomas Branwell had married Anne Carne, a Penzance silver-smith's daughter. They had eleven children in all, at least three dying in infancy,[101] and possibly two others in childhood. Soon after the second synagogue had been built, Thomas Branwell died in 1808 and his wife died the following year. Their son Benjamin continued his father's businesses and became mayor in 1809. By 1841 the Branwells were still carrying on a flourishing and expanding business in the town.[102] There were four daughters, including Maria who was born in 1783 and who (in 1811) moved to Yorkshire to live with her aunt, Jane Fennell, to work in the Methodist boarding school run by Jane's husband, the Rev. John Fennell. There, Maria met and married the Rev. Patrick Bronte, the minister of Hartshead, and they became the parents of the famous Brontë sisters.[103] It is not surprising, therefore, that the Branwell family with its free-thinking non-conformist tradi-tion, closely involved with and sympathetic towards the Jewish com-munity of Penzance, should have produced the independent-minded sisters who, for their day, were radical novelists.

---

[100] Barker, op. cit., p. 49.
[101] Barker, op. cit., p. 48.
[102] Barker, op. cit., p. 844, note 72.
[103] Barker, op. cit., p. 51ff.

PART 4

Truro and Towns of Minor Settlement

Truro

It has been mentioned previously that there was a small Jewish population in Truro comprising at any one time no more than a few families. Susser gives 14 families for the period 1748–1844.[104] Before the early 1800s, trade directories suggest isolated individual names, but it is during the period circa 1820–1850 that Jewish family businesses are most frequently mentioned. Any significant Jewish presence in Truro was comparatively short-lived from the late eighteenth to the mid-nineteenth century. Even though such a small community would not have had a rabbi, it did have a *shochet* for a period in the 1820s.[105] The small Jewish burial ground, established some time around 1780–1800, was abandoned by the 1840s and is no longer to be seen. No documentary evidence of a synagogue in the town has been found. Nevertheless, worship could have taken place in private homes, but Jews would have looked to Falmouth as the nearest established congregation where family ties through marriage and business would draw them. Similar links existed with Penzance.

Trades and Occupations

Levy Emanuel: silversmith. (Lipman, Plymouth Aliens List: AR 30; Su. 1748–63)[106]

Isaac van Oven: spectacle-maker. (AR 20; Su. 1771–85; b. 1730)

---

[104] cf. Susser, op. cit., Table 10, p. 51. Although it is not clear how he has arrived at his figures for the towns listed, these are probably minimal estimates based on references compiled by the author over time. Source references are not given on the table for any of the totals.

[105] cf. Chapter 4, edit 14.

[106] Some of these references (Su.) were given by Bernard Susser in a letter to Godfrey Simmons, dated August 1994, extracted from his Ph.D. thesis prior to the publication of his book. For Truro and some of the other Cornish towns see Susser, 1993, chapter 2 on "Towns of Minor Jewish Settlement . . .", pp. 47–51.

Solomon Simons, born in Truro, 1778 (Su.) Later in Falmouth (1851 census)

Sally (Sarah) Levy (later Jacob), born in Truro, 1783 (Su.). Later in Penzance, (1851 census)

". . . son of Libche, Truro, shoemaker." (Su. 1796: referenced by Susser as "a scrap of paper (in Hebrew) inserted in a note-book").

"Alexander, son of Samuel, of Truro". (Su. Plymouth Hebrew Congregation Account-Book, 1815–22)

Israel, ben Naphtali Hirsch, Truro (c. 1836). His occupation is unknown. (Su. ibid. p. 218)

The Levy Family

A "Levy" who was a jeweller appears in Truro from the 1780s (Ba. 1783; Un. 1799), and a Sally, or Sarah Levy, was born in the town in 1783 (Su.), later moving to Penzance (1851 census). "Levi" or "Levy" is a familiar name, and it cannot be certain that the Truro Levys were inter-related. There were at least three people named "Levi" trading in Truro: Israel Levi, clothes dealer, who was trading at 4 High Cross St. by the 1820s, (Pg. 1823/4), Henry Levi (known as Levin), a clothes dealer at East Bridge St. (Pg. 1823/4), and Jacob (John) Levi, a watch & clockmaker, at 5, King St. (5, St. Nicholas St.), (Pg. 1823/24/30; Wi. 1847).

Jacob Levi(y) was married to Elizabeth, and their four children were Charles, Anna, Jacob and Elizabeth, born between 1813 and 1822, baptised on 22nd February 1822 in St. Mary's Church,[107] which was subsequently demolished for the building of the cathedral. Jacob and Elizabeth had another son, Henry, after 1822. The eldest son, Charles was a watch & clockmaker, and jeweller in Kenwyn Street. (Pg. 1844; Sl. 1852/3) and at 6 King Street. (Br. 1844). On 11th April 1845, the *West Briton* reported that Charles Levy was to open a further shop at 29 Boscawen Street. On 29th January 1846, he relinquished these premises but continued to trade in Kenwyn Street, where he sold ironmongery, toys, carpenters' and masons' tools, musical instruments, and American and bracket clocks (Br.). He also traded as a silversmith (Wi. 1847), and another ". . . Levi", and a John Levy (Charles' brother Jacob) were cabinet makers in the same

---

[107] St. Mary's Church Register, p. 654, Su. The role palyed by Jacob Levi in the establishment of a municipal cemetery in Truro has been mentioned in Ch. 5.

street (Wi. 1847). *Kelly's Directory* of 1856 indicates that this was a versatile family business, listing Charles, now as a cabinet maker at 7 Westbridge, and another brother Henry as a jeweller, silversmith, and the proprietor of a musical instrument warehouse in King Street, (Slater, 1852/3, also lists him as a watchmaker). Kitty Levy was a clothes dealer in Calenick Street. (Su.).

The Harris Family

Henry Harris: watch & clockmaker, 2 Lemon St. (Pg. 1823); jeweller, 8, Lemon St. (Pg. 1830/44; Br. 1844); silversmith, silks & haberdashery (Wi. 1847; Sl. 1852/3). Henry Harris was the son of Samuel Harris and Judith Solomon, both of whom are buried in the Falmouth cemetery (3:12 and 4:7). The Harris family had originally come from Germany. Samuel Harris came from London to Falmouth around the mid- to late 1700s, and traded there in High Street as a watchmaker until his death in 1824.[108]

Judith Harris died on 5th March 1839 at the family home in High St. and she was described on her death certificate as the "widow of a merchant".[109] Henry Harris married Esther Jacob (a daughter of Sarah Moses of Falmouth, and Moses Jacob of Redruth) in 1819. By 1823 they had moved to Truro where Henry established a successful business as a jeweller in Lemon Street where Esther ran a lodging house from the same premises.[110] In 1833, Henry Harris was appointed by warrant as Jeweller to William IV,[111] and this was subsequently renewed "to be her Majesty's Jeweller in ordinary at Truro" by Queen Victoria in 1837.[112] Henry and Esther Harris had seven children, one of whom (Simon) died in infancy. There was another Simon, Jacob, Morris Hart and Samuel, and two daughters, Arabella and Phoebe. In the early 1850s Henry and Esther Harris

---

[108] A copy of James Trathan's *The Ancient and Modern History of Falmouth* (1815) in the archive of Godfrey Simmons is inscribed and endorsed (in French) and signed by "H. Harris", also as "Henri". In view of the fact that the book lists in its trade directory, a "Harris, J. attorney and notary" as well as a "Harris" who was an innkeeper, it cannot be certain that this is Henry Harris, although it is likely to be in view of the fact that "Harris, H, watchmaker" is listed in High Street (p. 84).

[109] Research by Carol P. Nicholson; letter to Alex Jacob, 7th January 1972.

[110] Williams, 1847.

[111] Letter from Arthur Barnett, JHSE, to Alex Jacob, 29th December, 1953.

[112] Duschinsky (1921, p. 141). Or, more likely, during a Royal tour of the south-west in 1844.

moved to London where they lived in Islington. Esther died there on 1st August 1871 and Henry on 25th September 1872.[113]

Morris Hart Harris, who had married Rebecca Jacob (daughter of Jacob Jacob and Sarah Kate Simons of Falmouth) in 1844, traded as a "bead merchant" in Bury Square, St. Mary Axe, EC (in 1861) and later (in 1871) in Camden Town.[114] Samuel Harris lived and traded in Houndsditch as "wholesale and export warehouse for jewellery, cutlery, combs & brushes; importer of beads, bugles & foreign fancy goods."[115] Samuel Harris became the Houndsditch representative of the Council of London, and on 28th October 1856 he was granted the Freedom of the City of London.[116]

Abraham Aaron & Son: surgeons, Lemon St. (Pg. 1830)

Israel Harris: watch & clockmaker, jeweller, 9 St. Nicholas St. (Pg. 1844)

Berenger & Schwerer: watchmakers and jewellers, Church Lane. (Sl. 1852/3; Br. 1849 & 1856.)

T. Solomon: plumber, glazier, carver, gilder, decorator, etc. 19 King Street (Kelly 1873). It is not certain that he was Jewish.

Jones Mandoffsky, who may have been Jewish, opened a bazaar in Truro in 1834.

His brother, Moses Jones Mandoffsky, had a similar establishment in Plymouth.[117]

From Bernard Susser's research (August 1994: Letter to Godfrey Simmons)

13th November 1770: Two Jews arrested in Truro on suspicion of being involved in the Chelsea murders; also a Jew at Falmouth on suspicion of being Coshay, one of the gang.[118]

---

[113] cf. Nicholson, ibid; death certificates, and 1871 census.
[114] Research by Michael Gandy; Letter to Godfrey Simmons, January 30th 1999.
[115] Gandy, ibid.
[116] PRO Kew, Ref. 9095SO; Arthur Barnett, ibid.
[117] IR 51.6; Stamp Office 1831. Letter from Betty Naggar to Keith Pearce, November 1998.
[118] Rumney, *Economic & Social Development of the Jews in England*, unpublished Ph.D. thesis, London, 1933, p. 78.

30th December 1770: Sir John Fielding wrote to Truro & Falmouth that although the arrested Jews probably took part in some of the robberies, no evidence could be produced and they should be sent back to Holland.[119]

16th September 1826: (*Royal Cornwall Gazette*) Advertisment that Dr. Aaron effects cures and could be contacted at Tippett's opposite Pearce's Hotel, Truro, where he sells a *Balm of Gilead*. [Susser comments that he thinks that Aaron was from Liverpool]

6th March 1829: (*West Briton*). Advertisement that the partnership of Lyon Levy & Harman Semmons of the Borough of Truro, Jewellers & Hardwaremen, has been dissolved by mutual consent. All debts should be paid to Mr. Lyon Levy.

Towns with Minor Jewish Settlement

In these towns there is rarely evidence of more than two or three Jewish families resident at any one time, more often there was only one, but it should be borne in mind that there may have been several, or even many more. In spite of their small numbers, these isolated and scattered families represent an important factor in the development of provincial Jewish life, as they provided a kind of cross-country hostelry, always ready to welcome a Jewish hawker . . . or simply to help a poor Jew on his way to the next Jewish community, where he would find food, shelter, the offer of a job, and financial help.[120]

Susser's admonition that these isolated pockets of Jewish residence should not be overlooked is important, and an illustration of his from Somerset has particular resonance: "A Jewish pedlar, down on his luck, making his way to Bridgwater in 1821, was asked if he had friends there. 'No, but there are Jews there and they will help me'."[121]

Redruth

Only five or six Jewish familes are known to have lived in Redruth from the 1760s to the 1860s. One of the earliest to settle in the town was the family of Moses and Sarah Jacob, from Falmouth.

---

[119] ibid., p. 83.
[120] Susser, 1993, p. 47.
[121] Susser, 1993, p. 280.

Moses Jacob (1733–1807)

Although his birthplace is not known, Moses ben Jacob was most likely a son of one of the earliest settlers in Falmouth. He married Sarah Moses, a daughter of Alexander Moses (Zender Falmouth).[122] Zender's strict religious observance meant that he would have been very selective in his approval of a prospective son-in-law, and it would seem that Moses Jacob was indeed a man of meticulous orthodoxy. Sarah Moses shared this inclination, and was said to lead the prayers in the synagogue in Zender's absence. By all accounts she was a formidable woman with a forceful personality. Sarah and Moses Jacob had a total of fifteen children, three of whom died in infancy. Three of the others were deaf mutes, a congenital tendency which affected, in varying degrees, some members of the family in succeeding generations.[123]

By 1766 Moses and Sarah had moved to Redruth, a growing industrial and mining town. Moses Jacob set up business in Cross Street where he remained for the rest of his life. His landlord was Captain Richard Paynter, a mine manager, and from this connection, Moses Jacob became one of the first people to deal in mineralogical specimens. When Paynter died in 1787 the property passed to his daughter, Ann, who was the wife of William Murdoch, the local manager of the firm of Boulton and Watt. Murdoch was responsible for the installation of pumping-engines in the mines as well as watching the financial interest of his employers. Moses remained Ann Murdoch's tenant, as did a Simon Levy, who lived in a house which another of Paynter's daughters (Sally) had inherited.[124]

Moses Jacob was known primarily as a clockmaker,[125] and his business must have prospered because by 1769 he was able to employ a James Dawson as a watch and clockmaker. Dawson had led a colourful and interesting life. In an examination sworn on oath before the magistrate Joshua Howell in Redruth on 4th May 1769, he recounted how he had been born in Dieppe in Normandy some 40 years previously, where he had learned his trade as a clock and watchmaker from his father. From the age of 19 he had served in the French army for some years, before travelling and plying his trade across Europe, living, amongst other places, in Vienna, Berlin, Cologne, and Amsterdam,

---

[122] Generally regarded as the founder of the Falmouth Jewish community and who died in 1791.
[123] For their twelve children, see Fal. 2:9 in chapter 5.
[124] Mitchell (1985 edition, p. 54).
[125] H. Miles Brown (1970, p. 82).

never spending more than a year or two in any town, or indeed any country. He eventually travelled from Rotterdam to Harwich, coming to London around 1758, subsequently living in Wales and Ireland before arriving in Plymouth where ". . . he wrought upward of one year with one Abraham Joseph at the wages of eighteen pound a year, with meat, drink, washing and shaving twice a week . . . ".[126] From Plymouth he had come to Redruth, and worked in Moses Jacob's business for the rest of his career, settling at last into domestic life, and marrying Grace. Working for Moses Jacob seems to have had its attractions, one of which was his contract of employment which paid him sixteen shillings a week for a five-day week, together with paid Jewish holidays, when of course, the business was closed.[127] The Jacob/Dawson agreement is an example of one of the earliest "holidays with pay" contracts, and Dawson's value to the business must have been considerable for Moses to consider such generous terms of employment.

Although maintaining his loyalty to Orthodox Judaism, Moses Jacob integrated with ease into the host community. The earliest record of his social activities is to be found in masonic records. The first masonic lodge in Redruth was the Druid's Lodge, and his name is mentioned in the first list of members, Midsummer Quarter 1777, where he is described as having been initiated previous to 1777. Certainly freemasonry was one of the few activites where men of different religions, countries and backgrounds could mix socially without the problems which would have been encountered in the everyday world. An example of both the liberality of the members of the Druid's Lodge and the character of Moses Jacob was at a Lodge meeting on 6th May 1779 when a French gentleman, M. Martial Raillon, presumably a paroled prisoner-of-war, was proposed for membership. Moses Jacob seconded the proposition which was "unanimously accepted".

Upon his death in 1807, Moses Jacob's will, signed in cursive Hebrew, left all the tools of his trade to his son, Levy Jacob, and the business to his wife Sarah, who continued to carry it on (with Levy and Dawson) until her death in 1831. An eight-day grandfather clock of Moses Jacob (c.1780) still exists, with a dial depicting a rocking ship, and there is another clock with King Neptune riding the waves in the arch.[128] There are at least two references to Moses Jacob in contemporary documents. Between 1782 and 1784, a "Mr. Cornish", a tinsmith and leading Quaker in Redruth, kept an account-book of his various dealings, amongst which is listed "Jacob Moses, Clockmaker,

[126] Mitchell, 1985, pp. 48–9.
[127] Susser, ibid. pp. 94–5 and 293.
[128] Mitchell (1985), p. 48; Brown, ibid. p. 82.

Moses Jacob of Redruth – Fal 2:9. [courtesy: David Sonin and the *Jewish Chronicle*].

Clock by Moses Jacob. [courtesy: Godfrey Simmons's archive]

Redruth". In 1804, the cash-ledger of a Mr. Alfred Jenkin records: "Paid for mineral specimens, Moses Jacob, to pd Isaac the Jew[129] . . . for 8 specimens of Wh Fanny Tin 16/- . . ."[130]

On 8th May 1903, the *Jewish Chronicle* published the obituary of Alexander Jacob (b. 1841), a descendant of Moses Jacob. It mentioned that he had been a founder-member of the Hampstead synagogue and noted that he had originally come from Falmouth, where his father "Moss J Jacob"[131] was for many years the warden and "main support of the congregation". It also mentioned that the Falmouth cemetery contained the graves of four generations of the Jacob family.

On 15th May 1903, the *Jewish Chronicle* published a letter from Alexander Jacob's brother, Samuel Jacob:[132]

> The Jacob Family of Falmouth,
>
> SIR, referring to the obituary of my brother in your issue of the 8th, the following details may be of interest to your readers. Prior to the last of us brothers leaving Falmouth in 1880, there were, living and dead, six generations of the family there; all in turn supported the congregation and many were the old tales told of their ancestors. The first was that of an old lady, an 18th century dame, who laid *Tephillin*, acted as parnass in the absence of her lord and perhaps master (our ancestor, Moses Jacob) fasted on Mondays and Thursdays a half-day in memory of Moses going and returning after receiving the Tablets of the Law, superintended the horsing and packing of the animals and departure of her spouse, who was accompanied by a pony and a boy leading a pack-horse. The husband was a very little man who rode a very big horse.
>
> Regularly every Monday this procession went forth, returning every Friday for the Sabbath. (At this stage Moses Jacob acted as his own journeyman.[133]) He was most orthodox, his mid-day prayers never omitted and said on horseback. He had taught the animal to stand perfectly still during the *Amidah* and even to step backwards (as ritual demands) when the proper time arrived for doing so.[134] This may be said to have been a truly Jewish beast.
>
> This ancestor settled his son (Levy) in Redruth as a clock-maker, who in turn placed his son . . . in Camborne as a draper.

---

[129] This would be the Isaac Joseph mentioned by Roth in chapter 4.

[130] Mitchell, ibid. pp. 52 and 69.

[131] Jacob Jacob ben Moses, 1812–60.

[132] Published simultaneously in *Jewish World*, 15th May 1903.

[133] A *Journeyman* was not a travelling salesman (as the term might imply) but a former apprentice who had served his time and had become qualified and employed as a skilled craftsman.

[134] Tradition has it that on one occasion the horse did so as required, only to deposit Moses Jacob in a ditch!

Such was his [Moses Jacob's] integrity that people would wait on Saturday night for the appearance of the Three Stars, the sign of the finish of the Sabbath, to do business with him. (There were) . . . 12 brothers and sisters . . . one married a Reverend Mr. Simmons, a Londoner (appointed to Penzance by Dr. Hirschell, the then Chief Rabbi). His daughter married a Mr. Rintel of Bury Street, London, EC, a great Mohel . . . who was appointed to Falmouth (as rabbi) . . . and remained there for seventeen years. . . . Such is the short account of our family who resided in Cornwall for about a century and a half . . .

Simon Levy: occupation unknown, c.1787, as above.

Joseph Joseph: watch & clockmaker, and jeweller, Fore St. (Pg. 1823/4 & 1830/44; Br. 1823) . . . and mineralogist (Wi. 1847).
"To be seen at the house of Mr. Joseph, Redruth, a most Perfect Block of what is termed *Jews' House* Tin, which was lately found in that neighbourhood, the age of which is variously stated to be from 1600 to 2000 years." (1844)
"Sale of Mineral Specimens and Shells by J. Joseph, Redruth." (1846).[135] Joseph Joseph moved to Plymouth in 1849.

Isaac Joseph: tin-man & mineralogical specimens. (Roth, ibid. c.1820s; 1804, above)

Emanuel Cohen (1766–1849): watch & clockmaker and jeweller. (pg. 1830/44).
Cohen, it was said, could be seen waiting on Fridays (the Sabbath eve) for sunset so that he could close his shop, and again on Saturdays to re-open it. He subscribed five shillings to starving Jews in Tiberias in 1849. The *West Briton*, after his death, carried a notice on 22nd June 1849 that his business was to be disposed of. He was affiliated as a member of the Penzance congregation. An eight-day grandfather clock (c.1820) and a silver pear-case watch (hallmark 1821) still exist as examples of his work.[136]

Berenger and Schwerer: watch & clockmakers and jewellers, Fore St. & West End.
(Pg. 1844; Sl. 1852/3; Br. 1844; Kelly 1856.)

Frederick Lazarus: hawker. Penryn St. (birth certificate of his daughter, Annie, 1862)

---

[135] Mitchell, ibid. pp. 124 and 129, quoting from the *West Briton*.
[136] Brown, ibid. p. 82; Mitchell, ibid. p. 48.

Camborne

Moss J. Jacob, and Amelia Jacob (later wife of Henry Joseph of Penzance) were born in Camborne in 1813 and 1812. (Susser, ibid p.48)

Jacob Jacob: draper. (Roth, ibid)

Hannah Harris: cabinet makers. (Sl. 1852/3).

St. Agnes

Isaac Jacob, a travelling Jew, had deposited his box of Chapman's Wares as a security for indemnifying the Parish of St. Agnes in respect of an illegitimate child of which he was reputed to be the father. He had failed to return as required and unless he did so (by October 18th 1770) in response to the published notice, his box would be opened and the contents appraised and sold towards maintenance of the child (*Sherborne Mercury*, 24th September 1770).

West Cornwall

Hayle

Joanna (a non-Jew), wife of Henry Moses, was born in Hayle in 1812. (Susser, ibid p. 48).

Samuel Jacob: occupation unknown. (Roth, ibid c 1820s, gives Jacobs)

Lazarus Lazarus: hardwareman. (Pg. 1844)

St. Ives

Gabriel Rosenthal: "miscellaneous". (Pg. 1830)

Scilly

Samuel Jacob: occupation unknown. (Roth, ibid c.1820s. This is the same as above)

Central and North Cornwall

St. Austell

Barnet Levy: silversmith, 1758–1775. (Susser, ibid p. 48). Later at Falmouth.

Samuel Solomon: tailor. (Un. 1799)

Philip Samuel: jeweller. (Israel Solomon's *Records of My Family*)

J. Joseph: watch & clockmaker. (Br. 1820)

Samuel Harris: tin-man & brazier. (Pg. 1830)?

John Jacob: tailor. (Wi. 1847)?

William Jacob: boot & shoemaker. (Wi. 1847)? } It is not certain that they were Jewish

Bodmin

Martha, wife of Henry Woolf, was born in Bodmin in 1829. (Susser, ibid p.48).

Jonson & Abraham: watchmakers & silversmiths, Fore St. (Br. 1844) Sale upon moving to Falmouth (West Briton, 6th September 1844; Pg. 1844).

George Solomon: grocer & tea dealer, St. Leonard's St. (Wi. 1847)?

Liskeard

Edel, wife of Joseph Joseph, was born in Liskeard in 1771. (Susser, ibid p. 48).

Nathan Harris: apprenticed to a gunsmith, 1762. (Susser, ibid pp. 94 and 292–3). It is not certain that he was Jewish.

Webb & Abraham: watch & clockmakers. (Pg. 1823)

Joseph Beer: groceries & sundries, Dean St. (Pg. 1830) It is not certain that he was Jewish.

Launceston

Solomon Levy: general shopkeeper, Southgate. (Pg. 1830)

Callington

Betsy, wife of Abraham Abrahams, was born in Callington in 1799. (Susser, ibid p. 48).

Henry Silberman: stationer & bookseller, Higher St. (Wi. 1847).

Lostwithiel

Aaron Abrahams: watchmaker. (Br. 1821) Moved to Plymouth.

Morwenstow

Aaron Harris: watchmaker. (Br. c. 1830) It is not certain that he was Jewish.

Itinerant

Mordecai Jacobs: umbrella maker, in Cornwall c.1753–73. (Susser, ibid pp. 49 & 162).

Unidentified

Susser, (ibid p. 51) gives one family at each of Cawsand (1815), Stratton (1821) and Saltash (1831).

Freemasonry

The importance of freemasonry to Jews, especially when they were faced with various legal disabilities and a struggle to gain acceptance and advancement in Gentile society, cannot be underestimated. Through its charitable activities and its opportunities for social contact beyond the confines of Jewish congregational life, masonry enabled Jews to establish themselves on a firm basis. Some members of the affluent and influential Cornish Gentile families, such as the Bassett family of Tehidy, near Redruth and the Branwell and Borlase families of Penzance were masons and especially supportive of the Jewish congregations. As we have seen, freemasons, such as the High Anglican Sir Frances Bassett (Lord de Dunstanville), a Whig in politics who owned land at Penryn and Falmouth, gave the Falmouth Jewish community a plot for its cemetery at Ponsharden. The Methodist Branwells helped build both synagogues in Penzance.[137]

Early masonic records are not readily accessible, although it has been possible to gain some information. These records are not referenced here and neither are masonic members' handbooks, but

---

[137] It should be noted, however, that Jews comprised only a small proportion of the total membership of masonry. In view of the links between Jews and shipping in both Penzance and Falmouth, it is of interest that mariners were well-represented in masonic lodges. (Information in this section is from Godfrey and John Simmons.)

J.G. Osborne's invaluable *History of Freemasonry in West Cornwall, 1765–1828*[138] contains various references to masons who were Jews, and it is from this book that most of the information in this section has been drawn in some chronological sequence. Osborne also contributed a series of articles under the general title "Jewish Names" to the *Freemasons' Magazine* of 1866. These appeared in eleven issues of the journal from 29th September to 8th December 1866. The first article is titled "A History of the Craft in Cornwall" and subsequent ones as "A History of Freemasonry in Cornwall".

They are based entirely on the minute book of the Falmouth Love and Honour (later No. 75) Lodge, starting with 12th June 1751 and ending with 24th June 1771.[139]

> 12th June 1751. Alexander Moses, founder member of the Lodge, and Master Mason. (Osb. FM, p. 247)
>
> 24th June 1751. Alexander Moses, Warden. (Osb. FM, p. 265)
>
> 13th August 1761. Alexander Moses, Senior Warden. (Osb. FM, p. 361)
>
> 11th February 1762: reference to "Brother Polack", likely Isaac, (Osb. FM, p. 362) and 11th August 1763: reference to "Brother Benjamin", likely Wolf, (Osb. FM, p. 382).
>
> 27th December, 1764. Alexander Moses, Junior Warden. (Osb. FM, p. 401)[140]
>
> 12th July 1769. "Jacobs" of Redruth. "Visiting".
>
> 24th June 1771. M. Jacob of Redruth Lodge, present at Masonic procession.

St. Ives. *Ship Lodge No. 240.*

Brother Cohen (possibly father of Emanuel Cohen of Redruth) presented three candles to the Lodge (March 3rd 1767). (Osb. pp. 6/7)

Visitant, brother Isaac Benjamin (March 3rd 1772). (Osb. p. 13)

Redruth. *The Druid's Lodge of Love and Liberality.* First list of members, Midsummer quarter, 1777.

June 17th 1777: Moses Jacob present; initiated previous to 1777.

---

[138] Referenced here as Osb.

[139] References to these articles from the *Freemasons' Magazine* are given as Osb. FM.

[140] On 8th June, 12th July and 28th December 1769, a "Josiah Hart" is mentioned as Secretary (p. 421). It is not known that he was Jewish. He does not appear on Colyer-Fergusson's family tree of the Harts of Penzance, referred to earlier.

May 6th 1779: Moses Jacob seconds proposal for the membership of a "French gentleman". (Osborne, pp. 53–57)

Falmouth. Worshipful Master, Aaron Delisser, 1784.

Redruth. *Druid's Lodge.*

February 13th 1789. Visit by members of the Falmouth Lodge of Love and Honour, Wolf Benjamin, Senior Warden, and Jacob Wolfe. (Osb. p. 61)

May Ist 1798: Lemon Hart, age 30, Merchant, Penzance. Initiated. (Osb. p. 73)

August 2nd 1799: Lemon Hart of Penzance present. (Osb. p. 82)

April 5th 1803: Jacob Hart, age 24, Merchant, Penzance. Initiated. (Osb. p. 107)

July 10th 1805: Lemon Hart proposed to the Royal Arch. (Osb. p. 135)

September 17th 1805: Lemon Hart exalted to the Royal Arch. (Osb. p. 136)

August 13th 1806: Lemon Wolfe, age 24, Merchant, Penzance. Initiated. (Osb. p. 137)

November Ist 1808: Four candidates from Penzance, including Moses Isaacs, "Gentleman". (Osb. p. 90)

October 10th 1809: Moses Isaac (sic.), age 30, Gent., Penzance. Initiated. (Osb. p. 169)

August 2nd 1813: Levi Jacobs, age 24, Jeweller, Falmouth. Initiated. (Osb. p. 197)

August 27th 1817: Lemon Woolf, as one of the members, confirms the rules of the Chapter. (Osb. p. 165)

August 15th 1821: Druid's Royal Arch, meeting at Foss's (late Pearce's) Hotel, Redruth. Brother Lemon Woolf, Merchant, age 38, was proposed by Richard Pearce. Lemon Woolf paid his annual fees of 12/-. (Osb. p. 147)

August 16th 1826: Lemon Woolf acting as "Junior Scribe". (Osb. p. 154/5)

Provincial Grand Lodge of Cornwall (1865)

Truro

Phoenix Lodge, 1854. Henry Harris. (331)

Fortitude Lodge, 1864. E.B. Solomon. (131)

Penzance

Mount Sinai Lodge, 1865. Jos. . . .Levin. (121)

Falmouth Lodge Records

Love and Honour Lodge, May 10th 1892. Nathan Vos re-admitted as a member of the Lodge. He is described as a ships' chandler, and he attended meetings irregularly until his death in November 1913. Curiously, there are no records between 1854 (the earliest date when he could have been previously admitted at the minimum age of 21) and 1892 of his either joining or leaving the Lodge.[141]

The Josephs of Cornwall

In 1938, William Schonfield read a paper to the Jewish Historical Society of England on the Josephs of Cornwall,[142] prepared from information compiled in a "lengthy written communication" from Barnet Lyon Joseph to his son, Lionel Barnet Joseph, in which B.L. Joseph recounted ". . . a sketch of his own career, together with what he knew of his immediate and remoter ancestry." Like the Hart family, the Josephs were some of the earliest Jewish settlers in Cornwall in the eighteenth century.[143]

---

[141] Letter from R. John Hall, Almoner and Archivist of the Lodge, to Eric Dawkins, February 1st 1999.

[142] The editors are grateful to Jack W.L. Schofield (William Schonfield's grandson) for the information that he is unaware of any subsequent publication of this paper, and for his approval to incorporate its contents into this book: Letter to Keith Pearce, 8th December 1998. The basic details of some of Schonfield's material has been extracted in outline, not always verbatim, and with some commentary.

[143] The complexity of the inter-relationships through marriage of the Cornish Jewish families has been mentioned previously, and the editors have decided not to attempt any detailed genealogical study or to include comprehensive family trees but to refer readers to the expert treatment of these matters in the work of Anthony P. Joseph, ibid.

The Josephs of Cornwall

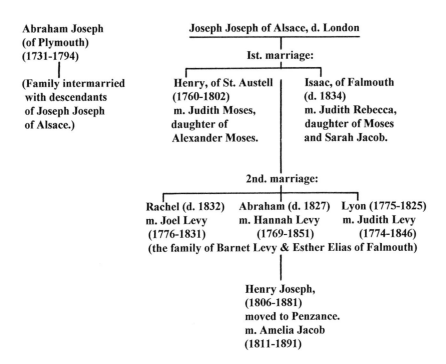

**Abraham Joseph
(of Plymouth)
(1731-1794)**

Joseph Joseph of Alsace, d. London

Ist. marriage:

(Family intermarried
with descendants
of Joseph Joseph
of Alsace.)

**Henry, of St. Austell
(1760-1802)
m. Judith Moses,
daughter of
Alexander Moses.**

**Isaac, of Falmouth
(d. 1834)
m. Judith Rebecca,
daughter of Moses
and Sarah Jacob.**

2nd. marriage:

**Rachel (d. 1832)
m. Joel Levy
(1776-1831)**

**Abraham (d. 1827)
m. Hannah Levy
(1769-1851)**

**Lyon (1775-1825)
m. Judith Levy
(1774-1846)**

(the family of Barnet Levy & Esther Elias of Falmouth)

**Henry Joseph,
(1806-1881)
moved to Penzance.
m. Amelia Jacob
(1811-1891)**

Josephs of Penzance:

Joseph Joseph (1761-1845)

**Abraham Joseph (1799-1868)
m. Eliza Woolf (d. 1850),
daughter of Lemon Woolf
    of Penzance.**

Source: Schonfield, Anthony P. Joseph & Godfrey Simmons.

In Plymouth, Abraham Joseph (1731–1794), for whom James Dawson had worked, founded a large family which intermarried with the descendants of Joseph Joseph of Mulhausen, Alsace. In the early part of the eighteenth century, Joseph Joseph had come to London, where he died. Joseph Joseph's two sons by his first marriage, Harry (Henry) and Isaac, had settled in Cornwall: Henry (1760–1802) in St. Austell and Isaac (d.1834) in Falmouth. Henry (Fal. 2:4) married Judith Moses (Fal. 4:5; 1768–1843), a daughter of Alexander and Phoebe Moses of Falmouth, and Isaac (Fal. 2:5) married their grandaughter, Judith Rebecca (Fal. 3:7; 1768–1849), a daughter of Moses and Sarah Jacob of Redruth.

Joseph Joseph had married a second time and from this marriage there was a daughter, Rachel (d. 1832), and two sons Abraham (d.1827) and Lyon (1775–1825). Rachel, Abraham and Lyon all married into the family of Barnet Levy[144] and Esther Levy (née Elias) who came from London to live in Falmouth. Rachel Joseph married Joel Levy (1776–1831), Abraham married Hannah Levy (Pz. 1:2; 1769–1851), and Lyon married Judith Levy (1774–1846). Abraham and Hannah Levy's son, Henry (1806–1881) who has been mentioned previously in this chapter, moved to Penzance and established a branch of the Joseph family there. He became a successful businessman in the town and an influential member of the Hebrew congregation.

Lyon and Judith Joseph had nine children, Esther dying young and Joseph in infancy. The others became widely dispersed: Arabella married Solomon Levy of Exeter, Kate (Kitty) married Moses Cohen of London, Hannah ("Nanny") married Moses Levin of London and Henry married Maria, daughter of Abraham Samuel of London. Benedict (d. 1851) married Jane Feuchtwanger of New York, a native of Hamburg, and Frederick was drowned in a bathing accident in the Schkikl (sic.)[145] River in America. Barnet (1801–1880) married Betsy (1801–1889), a daughter of Nathan Jacob of Dartmouth, an immigrant from Bohemia. Barnet Joseph moved to Bristol where he became the president of the Bristol Hebrew Congregation at the age of 24. He left Bristol to live in Liverpool in 1835 where he became a founder of the Hope Place Synagogue and the Hebrew Schools.[146]

Lyon Joseph had a colourful and eventful life. He started out as a pedlar in buckles for shoes and other items of clothing, and also in

---

[144] Also known as Issachar Baer, Bernard Beer, or Jewell.

[145] This is Schonfield's spelling. This is the River Schuylkill which runs south-eastwards from the Blue Mountains of Appalachia in Pennsylvania, down to Philadelphia, where it joins the River Delaware.

[146] Samuel (1997, pp. 103–4).

cutlery, jewellery, watches and small silver items. He eventually became a shopkeeper and a shipper. Napoleon Bonaparte had gained control of much of Spain and Portugal and did much to restrict and damage British trade to those countries. Lyon Joseph, together with other Falmouth merchants, took advantage of the British Government's eagerness to promote and encourage free trade by despatching commodities by the packet boats to parts of the Iberian Peninsula not occupied by the French, and in so doing he became a wealthy man. Eventually the Government reversed this policy and ordered that such trade should cease or be declared contraband. Lyon Joseph continued, however, and as a result his goods were seized and he is said to have made a loss of some twenty thousand pounds, a considerable fortune at that time.

He also suffered losses in other directions and became involved in a number of bad speculations. He had come to be the owner of a ship, the *Perseverance*, which he had sent with its cargo to Gibraltar but the captain ran into Lisbon instead, appropriated some of the goods and absconded. Lyon Joseph was informed and went to Lisbon in time to save the ship itself with part of its original cargo. He was soon to suffer another commercial mishap, however, through some relatives of his named Solomon who came to Falmouth and who were sent by Lyon Joseph to Gibraltar, where they appeared to be trading successfully. Lyon consigned considerable quantities of goods to their care but they proved dishonest and disappeared, leaving the goods to be seized by creditors. After a long and expensive litigation, Lyon recovered only £700 out of their total value of £8000.

Another of Lyon's unfortunate commercial ventures was the result of a connection with a Moses Abecasis who lived in Malta and who became so strongly recommended that Lyon sent him on consignment "a merchandise of considerable value". Abecasis sold it all and with the proceeds purchased a cargo of Zante currants which turned out to be water-logged and rotten. To save duty, and being valueless, they were destroyed. Even though Lyon Joseph went to Malta to try to recover his original property, after three years he had received nothing. He also lost some £3000 in value from commodities sent to a Victor Levy of Cadiz. A ship carrying uninsured goods to the value of £1500 was wrecked off Cork, the partially salvaged cargo was seized by the Government under a law of "Droits of Admiralty" and all that Lyon recovered from that episode was a mere £60.

In 1810 he entered into a partnership with Alexander Cohen, Baruch de Phineas Tolendano, and Maurice and Stephen Hart of London to trade between London and Gibraltar, but a dispute led to the partnership being dissolved. All of these various financial losses so reduced his means that it badly affected his health. He retired to Bath, a broken man, where he is said to have lived in impoverished circumstances, dying there at the age of only 51. During his residence in Falmouth, Lyon Joseph had been elected *Rosh Hakahal* (Head of the Community), a title he retained until he left. It was principally through his efforts that the Falmouth synagogue and adjoining property were built. He is buried in the the old Jewish Cemetery on Plymouth Hoe (Row: A 13).[147]

Conclusion

This extensive chapter has attempted to show the considerable range of trades and occupations practised by Jews in Cornish towns in the eighteenth and nineteenth centuries: from the familiar and traditional, such as shopkeepers, jewellers and watch and clockmakers to such ventures as involvement and investment in mining and shipping. From Cornwall, many of these familes migrated to the developing towns and cities of the United Kingdom where their story can still be told and where the memory of their Cornish origins is still preserved, in many cases as proudly as the Continental origins of their forebears. More extensive still is the history of emigration from Cornwall where Jews, together with their Christian neighbours, travelled to the Americas, South Africa and Australasia. Many settled in those places for life and founded new communties and congregations.

The story of this particular diaspora would require another book to do it justice.

The role of masonry in Cornish life, especially in the nineteenth century, has been emphasised by writers on Cornish history such as Sharron Schwartz who has visited Cornish settlements in the United States and has drawn attention to the fact that the majority of Cornish burials in public cemeteries are still to be found in the sections reserved for freemasons, of which the following may serve as an example:

> Carn Marth miner, Joseph Kemp, buried at the Glenwood Cemetery in Park City, Utah, has Masonic insignia on his headstone.[148]

Likewise, Philip Payton, who has written extensively of Cornish emigration, says of the mining frontier towns of North America:

---

[147] Susser (1972, p. 8).
[148] Sharron Schwartz and Roger Parker (1998, p. 152).

> . . . Masonic Lodges often behaved as surrogate Cornish associ-
> ations or trade union branches, providing solidarity and security
> in an otherwise volatile environment . . . furthering the interests
> of the Cornish wherever possible. . . . The continuance of the
> Masonic tradition abroad . . . would also have strengthened the
> kin network. . . . Significantly, one of the first buildings erected in
> the overwhelmingly Cornish town of Gold Hill . . . in Nevada,
> was the Masonic Lodge . . .[149]

For Jews, as a cultural and religious minority amongst these Cornish
pioneers, the masonic community of which many were members would
have been of special importance in assisting their adaptation to an
unfamiliar country and an uncertain future.

And so, even as the Jewish congregations in Cornwall were drawing
towards their close, they were at the same time bestowing new life
upon Jewish communities abroad. The loss of the relatively short-lived
Jewish communities in Cornwall must inevitably be a matter of regret,
but theirs was of a transitional nature and their purpose, perhaps, was
to give to their descendants the memory and confidence that Jewish
life could indeed be lived out in the circumstances of tolerance and
security which Cornwall had given them.

Main Documentary Sources

Directories:

Bailey's Western and Midland Directory, 1783. (abbreviated Ba 1783)
Bailey's Universal Directory, 1791. (Ba 1791)
Universal British Directory of Devon and Cornwall, 1799 (Vol. 4). (Un 1799)
Holden's Directory, 1811. (Ho 1811)
The Falmouth Guide, 1815. (Fa 1815)
Pigot's Directories: of 1823, 1824,1830 and 1844. (Pg etc.)
Williams's Commercial Directory of Cornwall, 1847. (Wi 1874)
Slater's Royal National and Commercial Directory of Cornwall, 1852–3. (Sl
  1852/3)
Charles Coulson's Directory of Penzance, 1864. (Co 1864)
Warn's Directory, 1864. (Wa 1864)
Postal Directories, 1862 & 1873.(Po. 1862/1873)
Kelly's Directories, 1889 & 1902. (K. 1889/1902)

---

[149] Philip Payton (1999, pp. 37–8).

Publications:

Penzance, Past and Present G.B. Millet (lecture, 1878), Beare & Sons, 1880. (Mil)

History of Freemasonry in West Cornwall, 1765–1828 J.G. Osborne, Frederick Rodda, Penzance, 1901 (Os)

(Old masonic members-handbooks, for individual Lodges, published annually and available only privately, can sometimes be found in second-hand bookshops, but they are not referenced here. Some Jewish names are to be found in them)

Cornish Clocks and Clockmakers H. Miles Brown, David & Charles, 1970. (Br)

(The dates given as Br. in brackets refer to those given by Brown to the subject's work and activities, not the date of publication; ditto Jackson, below)

Annals of an Ancient Cornish Town (Redruth) Frank Mitchell, Dyllanson Truran, Trewolsta, Trewergie Redruth, 1985 (Mit)

Jackson's Silver & Gold Marks of England, Scotland & Wales Edit 1. Pickford, Antique Collectors Club. 3rd. edition, 1994 (Ja)

Census lists, Aliens lists (Lipman) and newspaper references are given individually. Various travel guides to Cornwall, to be found in most public libraries, also make occasional reference to and carry advertisements for Jewish businesses in Cornish towns. So, the *Guide to Falmouth* (1815) is referenced as (Fal).

Precise page references to directories are not given but names can be traced by reference to the individual towns or professions.

Information from the book/archive/correspondence of Bernard Susser: (Su).

Records of My Family
1887–5647[1]

Israel Solomon

[original styling retained]

My grandmother, Esther, was a native of London and her maiden name was Elias. (Edit 1) Her father was a German by birth and nick-named "Fine Schneider"; and, being a tailor of repute he employed many work people. Esther married early in life an Alsacian by birth named Bernard Beer who, on arriving in London, was seeking the house in which lived a townsman of Bernard Beer. The house was in the same street in which Esther resided, but Bernard was ignorant of the number of the house his friend resided in; so he knocked at hazard at the door of Elias, trusting that the inhabitant could give him the information. Esther answered the knock, and seeing the stranger was a Jew, said to him in German, "What do you want?" He told her the reason for troubling her. The name and residence were familiar to Esther and she stepped into the street and pointed out the house, but her delicate and kind way quite captivated Bernard who formed within himself the hope that fortune would be favourable so that he might become her husband. He inquired of his friend the name of the family, etc., of his charmer, and very naturally it became the dream of his existence. He was by trade a soap boiler and wished to obtain employment at the London manufacturers, but the Shabas prevented his obtaining any employment unless he sacrificed his religious scruples, which he could not do, and was obliged against his wishes to become a pedlar of small wares for a sustenance. He struggled on until he arrived at Falmouth; there he was hospitably received by Zender Falmouth whose real name was Henry Moses; but in those days any Jew settling down within a town and having a certain respectability amongst Jews had the name of the town attached to his first name. Zender kept a stock of buckles, small cutlery, jewellery and watches to supply to hawkers, and gave credit to young

---

[1] Published privately in New York (1887). Reprinted here in slightly abridged form.

men on certain conditions and, where it was necessary, advanced money to obtain the hawker's license. The conditions were to return every Friday early enough to form one of the Minyan, and on Sunday morning square up the accounts by paying over what money he had and receive fresh goods on credit. But when the hawker's license was procured, Zender insisted that his name should be quite a Jewish name and, instead of the name Bernard Beer, his name was inscribed Barnet Levy and the family ever after became Levy instead of Beer.

Bernard prospered and lost no time in turning towards the magnet of attraction. He went to London, called on Elias the tailor and told him his errand and hopes. Elias himself had no objections if Barnet's references were respectable, etc. Barnet then referred to Zender Falmouth and, as by a strange coincidence, Zender was uncle to Elias' wife, a favourable answer was received from Zender, and Esther became engaged.

Barnet returned to Falmouth, took a house and shop, furnished the house, and returned to London and was married. After the marriage, the time soon arrived in those days to enter the house and commence its duties, but in those days the distance from London to Falmouth was beyond three hundred miles by the mail coach. Fare was very heavy and the cost of postchaise not to be thought of for people of moderate means. The next great travelling conveyance was Russel's wagon, an immense vehicle covered by canvas with six heavy horses, a driver and a guard, heavily armed with blunderbusses, and who rode on a stout pony either at its head or followed behind the wagon. It took from three to four days and nearly as many nights before the wagon from London reached Falmouth. In the front of the wagon, space was kept before the packages and boxes for passengers, and their seats were straw and hay on which men, women and children were placed. Such a conveyance could not suit Esther so she rode behind her husband on what is called a pack-saddle horse, riding all the way, stopping when the day was drawing to night at any inn on the road in the village or town frequented by Jews; and at that time, down to 1830, inns where Jewish travellers rested were to be found in all the roads and towns of England. The landlord then, especially to gain their custom, kept a cupboard or closet containing cooking utensils entirely for their use so that they might eat Kosher. The landlord kept the cupboard locked and guarded the key on his own person. When a Jew used the utensils he saw to the cleaning of them and, before putting them away, he wrote with chalk within the bottom of the utensil his name, day of the month and year, with the portion of the law read on the Sabbath of that week all in Hebrew. Some of these hotels were in the centre of populated districts, and the pedlars going round the district would congregate of a Friday evening at these hotels and stay over Saturday, and on Sunday they trudged again on their laborious rounds. They generally formed a club, and one of the number who was licensed by the rabbi to slaughter animals, was paid by the club for one day's loss of profit from his business to get to the hotel on Friday early enough to kill animals or poultry, purchase fish, etc., and either cook or superintend it that it should be quite kosher by the time the brotherhood came there, and ushered in the Sabbath gladly singing hymns. After a copious but frugal repast, some Hebrew literature or tales of the past and present were related by one or the other with all the happy freedom allowed to speech in dear old England; although those happy lovers of English soil were not allowed the perfect equality now enjoyed by their children.

Esther died early in life leaving three sons and five daughters. (Edit 2) The eldest son died unmarried. One son Joel married Rachel Joseph, sister of Lyon and Abraham Joseph. These married two sisters, one Hannah and the other Judith, both daughters of Esther. The third daughter, Sheba, remained with her father and the other daughters until after Hannah and Judith married. Then Barnet Levy, the father, who had been sick for a long time, died. The fourth sister Sarah was a baby when her mother died, and Abraham the third son was a little boy, so that the management of the family and the trade in the shop devolved on the fifth and eldest daughter, my mother. Hannah and Judith before their marriage were dressmakers. Sheba, hearing about so many people becoming rich in London, left to search for gold, but after spending nearly all her means, took service in a Jewish family and some time after married Elias, the brother of her mother who was much younger than his sister. (Edit 3) The father of Elias gave them, for that time, a liberal education for respectable middle class society. But the education of Elias gave him foolish pride and he would not become a tailor to follow the trade. He became a bookkeeper, letter writer, etc., and afterwards a trader in a species of drygoods. He failed in it and afterwards came with his wife to Falmouth. Having no children, he was supported by the other members of the family.

Elias was a well-instructed Englishman and very free in speech on political subjects. I remember him; his dress was then ample, the coat in Louis XIV fashion, waistcoat the same, breeches with buckles fastening at the knee, long woollen stockings with shoes, and heavy, large white metal buckles. His hair, with a long quantity behind the neck, tied with a large black ribbon in a knot , and white necktie, very ample, folding around the throat and half covering up the chin. We all trembled when he cursed the despotism of Lord Castlereagh's Ministry and the crime of the Cato Street conspiracy; a plot gotten up by the secret police under the Government, and I believe my memory says it was in 1823 or 1824 that Castlereagh commited suicide with a knife he purchased from a Jew boy in the city.

Abraham, the third son of Esther, married and lived and died in Plymouth. (Edit 4) About the year 1828 he purchased the freehold house in which he lived, but being a Jew, although English born and the second generation English, he could not become possessor of any freehold in England. The house was bought for him by a neighbour and leased to him on a peppercorn rent for 999 years. Abraham left a large family of sons and daughters, and all, I believe, married and rich. Joel Levy was very unfortunate in losing his wife and eldest son within one week. This unsettled his mind and some months afterwards he died, leaving one son and two daughters. The son and eldest daughter came to America and died, leaving no issue to regret their loss; but one sister became the wife of Professor Isaacs of Manchester and recently lived there, a widow with one or more unmarried daughters.

Sarah, the youngest daughter of Esther, lived with my mother who married Solomon Solomon, my father. (Edit 5) Sarah never married but helped with the housekeeping and, with my parents, brought up my brother and myself, and only parted from us after the death of our mother Betsy Solomon (née Levy, the eldest daughter of Esther). My mother died and was buried in Bristol and over her remains a very thick tombstone reposes, but so surrounded with iron guards that the epitaph was not at all readable. My mother visited London at the time the old London bridge was being taken down and the new bridge nearly finished. I went with her to see the two and while regarding the structure she repeated what occurred to her mother who, when young, went with a group of young girls to see the bleeding heads on poles on the entrance to London Bridge and on the top of Temple Bar. These were the heads of the leaders of the last great Scotch rebellion, and the penalty for not going to see this barbarous exhibition was to be called by the neighbours, Jacobite. (The execution took place about 1746)

My grandmother, Bella Solomon, was a Dutch woman by birth and her maiden name was Wolf (sic). She was married in Penzance, Cornwall, where a brother and sister resided. Her sister was married to Eleazer Hart, father of Lemon Hart, at one time the largest spirits merchant in London and for many years contractor to the English government for supplying the British Royal navy with rum. (Edit 6) The tombstone over my grandfather Israel Solomon's remains I could not discover as many tombstones were injured by the atmosphere and the letters nearly effaced. My grandfather, Israel Solomon, was a German by birth and he was born in Ehrenbreitstein on the Rhine. His family name was Behrends, but he stood in the same position as my grandfather Barnet Levy to Zender Falmouth and altered his name to Solomon. The family of Israel and Bella Solomon consisted of three sons and three daughters. (Edit 7) Two sons and two daughters were married; one son and one daughter never married; this son died early and the single daughter, named Leah, died very old in years. The second daughter ran away from home and married a soldier and went to India. From there she returned a childless widow, and her brothers allowed her a small income but she was not to reside in Falmouth. I only saw her once when she came to Falmouth and knew nothing further respecting her. The other daughter, Judith, married a German named Harriss. (Edit 8) They had one son who married a grand-daughter of Zender Falmouth. He, Henry Harriss, was a noted silversmith and lived in Truro, from whence he retired from business and lived in London. (Edit 9) He had two sons and two daughters married, and lived in London. One, Samuel Harriss, was a bead merchant. Joseph Levy, general merchant, married a daughter, and other portions of the family are still resident in London. One son married a great-great-granddaughter of Zender Falmouth, and a daughter married one of the Franklins from Manchester, both of whom died early and left one son and one daughter, I believe, now very wealthy and related to the banker Samuel Montague.

My father was the son of Israel and Bella Solomon. (Edit 10) He died suddenly in Lisbon in January 1819, twenty-one days after his arrival from Falmouth. I was with my father, and his death occurred on Friday. We had just taken a suite of rooms or a flat in a tenement house, unfurnished, and an acquaintance from Cornwall, named Phillip Samuel, a Polish gentleman, was invited by my father to sup with us. After supper, I prevailed on him to stop for the night and to accompany us the next day to the synagogue. Some time after, I was in bed and was awakened by the groans of my dying father. I called Mr Samuel and I left him with my father and rushed away at midnight, at which hour at Lisbon, the streets are filled with thousands of dogs who lived on offal and garbage thrown every night from the windows of every house. I rushed through the terrible night to the apartments of Madame Julia Delivant, an old London friend, who had taken up her residence in Lisbon. How I reached her house is quite a mystery, what with the frightful yells and attacks of the dogs, and covered as I was with the refuse thrown from the houses. After awakening the inmates and procuring a doctor, who declared life was extinct, the family of Mr Schemeya Cohen was aroused and the domestics, of whom the cook was named Benrimo, watched and remained all night with me. My father was about 55 years of age when he died. Mr Phillip Samuel remained with me and never left until I had finished, with his aid, all the commercial affairs of my father that required attention. This lasted more than one year and then I returned to my mother's house at Falmouth.

Mr Samuel was a native of Warsaw and his life was full of romance. He was the son of the secretary of the great synagogue there and highly educated in Hebrew. Marriages in Poland in those days were at an early age, and his marriage was not a happy one. He had one daughter, who married, but her name I have forgotten. His trade was that of a silk merchant. He purchased from importers at Dantzig. Travelling in those days was done by caravan, and the Jewish trader took with him ten men so as to say prayers three times a day. These religious observances became opposed to the activity required for commercial pursuit and quicker means of transport came into vogue. He was then living in Vilna. When he found it necessary to make a journey to Dantzig in the winter, he left early in the morning in a sledge, arriving the same evening at Dantzig. For this breach of an old custom of travelling, the rabbis, so-called, who formed the travelling party of ten excommunicated Phillip, and in spite of the cherem he burst asunder these superstitious trammels, not any more to be observed in any country or city. He laughed at the edict and continued on longer journeys without a retinue of followers. He traded with Russia, and having a good customer in Moscow, it was requisite for him to visit that city to settle up accounts. The Moscow merchant invited him to his house when in that city. The merchant was at that time in advance of the general prejudices against foreigners and Jews in particular. He told Phillip in confidence that his wife and servants would have the sleeping apartment, bedding and every chair on which he had sat scrubbed, washed, and purified with the sprinkling of holy water to protect their Slavonic holiness from pollution that a Jew might leave behind him.

One winter, in travelling with a train of wagons laden with silk and other merchandise and crossing a frozen river, the ice gave way and the wagons sank into the river. He escaped with his life with just sufficient money to rush away from Russian dominion because bankruptcy would have followed his loss, and for bankruptcy in Russia imprisonment follows. He arrived at last in England; but the life of the ordinary Polish emigrant, supported by peddling, was disgusting to the educated Phillip. Visiting at the house of the chief rabbi, Herschell, the rabbi got him the place as reader of prayers in the synagogue at Penzance in Cornwall. (Edit 11) For this he was not fitted. Attached to which office was then the slaughtering of cattle and poultry kosher, and as about this time the trade of collecting gold for Government requirement to pay troops and war supply in the Continental with the first Napoleon was profitable, he became an agent for buying gold for my uncle, Lyon Joseph of Falmouth. Phillip trusted some money to a fellow Polander to purchase gold and the poor fellow, who was named Valentine, was enticed by a landlord at Plymouth Dock and murdered. The murderer was discovered and hanged. After the gold business was ended, he and a fellow-countryman settled down in St Austell, Cornwall as jewellers. I there for the first time met Phillip Samuel whilst changing horses and the passengers of the mail coach on which I was riding were taking refreshments, and we called at his shop and residence. I may relate here that Highgate, then a village out of London, was the place whither we were going because Hurwitz, the best schoolmaster in England, had a school there and the best Jewish families in England sent their sons to be educated. Highgate at that time was three hundred miles from Falmouth: the journey took two days and nights; now it can be done in eight hours.

Disappointment in business matters seemed to follow Phillip. My uncle Lyon Joseph advised him to go to Portugal where my uncle, as well as my father, had commercial relations; and from there he bore letters of recommendation to Schemaya Cohen, the richest resident of Lisbon. Phillip was a handsome gentleman, wearing a black beard. But in those days, no one but Jews in European dress wore beards. On board the ship on which he was the passenger, he felt so impressed with the prejudice that his beard would arouse amongst the Portuguese rabble that before he left the vessel, he shaved his beard. This he afterwards regretted because he considered that at that time so many private Jewish families of the best mercantile class resided in Lisbon, and descended from the old Jewish families who became outward Christians, observing outward ceremonies to save fortune and family from the cruel butchers of the Holy Inquisition; but in the privacy of family worship they always remained Jews until the opportunity arrived to dispose of their possessions and property, and emigrate to Holland, Germany and other countries. Phillip became acquainted with some of these secret Jewish families and was always received by them as a friend. I remember one Saturday evening two gentlemen came to Mr Cohen's house to ask the date of Kippur and they bowed low to the Ark; one knelt and wept like a child.

I left in the year 1820 for Falmouth. My poor friend Phillip continued his commercial pursuits and had received from a French house a consignment of gold watches. He was always charitable and a young poor orphan was recommended to him as an aid in his commercial affairs. He took the lad into his home and confidence, and one day on returning to his home, he found the young lad in apparent trouble. He said that he had left the house for a short time and in his absence it was entered and the stock of gold watches stolen. Poor Phillip was bewildered and went to the police, accompanied by the lad, who told his story. Some weeks afterwards, Mr Samuel was advised to call personally at all the jewellers to see if any clue could be got, and he requested the young lad to go with him. At one house the lad said: "Don't go in, I have already been there." But Samuel went in and insisted on the youth entering with him. As soon as the jeweller espied the youth and heard Samuel's question, he said that he had bought of that lad a gold watch; and when such proved to be one of the stolen articles the lad was given into the hands of the police and put in prison. He was converted to Christianity and was set free by the intercession of his god-father, an influential resident of Lisbon. The thief met my friend in the open street and insulted him. The sudden meeting of the culprit killed poor Samuel, for he went home and died a few hours after from a broken heart. Poor Samuel was well versed in Jewish literature, and seeing so many educated Jews of Morocco and Arabia at our house, and talking with us, discussing over their books, I could have readily learned much from these sources. They would have gladly taught me Hebrew to converse and read with them in the Hebrew books. But, like the majority of young people, light reading I preferred, and when reaching middle age I bitterly regretted losing that enormous fund of knowledge I could have easily gained.

My uncle, Simon Solomon, son of Bella and Israel Solomon, was by trade a painter and possessed artistic qualities which could not expand at that time in the town of Falmouth. (Edit 12) His life-like panel paintings of fish, and also the painting for a large round table the subject of which was from the history of Joseph and his brethren, and his transparencies when national illuminations took place, were the admiration of the inhabitants of Falmouth. He was married to Kitty Solomon, granddaughter of Zender Falmouth. Simon Solomon was a sickly man and died and was buried in Falmouth.

Kitty Solomon, my uncle's wife, after his death resided in Penzance where she died and was buried in the same cemetery where a nephew of our grandmother Bella was buried. (Edit 13) His name was Jacobs. He went to London and assisted an elder brother (Edit 14) in the business of their uncle, Lemon Hart, and took that name. In the course of time, these brothers became partners in the house, adding the wine trade; and Jacob, the younger brother (see Edit 14), became intimately acquainted with the young Lord Palmerston, the intimacy arising from Jacob supplying the Clubs with wine. A quarrel arising between the uncle and his brother, he retired from commercial pursuits, and through the friendship of Lord Palmerston obtained the place of English Minister at one of the small German states, and after some years returned to England and took apartments in Mivart's aristocratic hotel in London;

but Jacob did not inform any one of his relations of his arrival, except his brother. He had two sisters and one half-sister named Magnus; his mother having married a second time. His two sisters were married, and one, living in London, married a manufacturer of combs. The other sister was married to a man named Simons, a native of the town of Truro and also a grandson of Zender Falmouth. (Edit 15) This man and his family were in very poor circumstances, living in Plymouth. His sister, the comb-maker's wife, hearing that her brother Jacob was in town and staying at Mivart's Hotel, went to see him and sent up word by the waiter without giving her name, that a lady wished to speak to him. She was ushered into his apartments, accosting him with "Brother Jacob" but he insulted her and called her an imposter, and the waiter was ordered to turn her out of the hotel. Some months elapsed and Jacob was taken seriously ill and a medical man was called, who, seeing his dangerous condition, told his patient to prepare against accidents and advised him to settle his worldly affairs. Jacob then requested his doctor to send for a solicitor. The doctor hastily procured a solicitor, and Jacob requested him to remain while he dictated his instructions for a will, and he commenced by leaving money to various charities. At last the doctor said to Jacob: "Everyone has some relations, and probably poor ones, to whom charity was first to be given and you should leave them some of your wealth." The right chord to his heart was struck and he said: "Doctor, you are right. The solicitor must commence a new will; I have two sisters;" one of whom he had insulted so grossly, and he desired each to receive after his death twenty thousand pounds. He added that he was a Jew and wished his remains to be buried in the cemetery at Penzance with the remains of his forefathers; but as to his poor half-sister Magnus, he never mentioned her name or left her any of his money.

My wife's maiden name was Caroline Mayer. (Edit 16) She was a French woman by birth and was born in Paris where I married her. Three children were born to us, one son died in infancy, and the second son was attacked with scarlet fever in his third year which rendered him deaf and dumb and otherwise afflicted him. He is now, and has been for about twenty-six years, in a great government institute and a private boarder to the governors of the institution, Messrs L' Abitte Freres. My son is now 40 years of age, a fine man, but quite incapable of doing anything useful. My wife's relatives are all dead, excepting a niece, the daughter and only child of her eldest sister. This niece was married to an Israelite named Shamreck. Shamreck's sister was married to the brother of a rising speculator who is now one of the noted millionaires in Paris, and he married his only daughter to the Prince Polignac. They were married by the Archbishop of Paris who made a witty play on words in his address to the young couple, complimenting the bridegroom as a descendant of "Sang pure" and the bride of "cent per cent", which in French pronunciation is "Sang pour sang". Since that marriage my wife's niece and family ceased all correspondence.

The father and mother of my wife were natives of Nancy, Lorraine, and they were married in the year of the Terrorists in France when all ceremonies were forbidden by the then Government under severe penalties. The marriage ceremony was in the square yard of a house into which no windows looked, and it was inhabited by Jews who carefully guarded all entrances into the yard. My wife's father's occupation was a retailer of dry goods. At that time, the circulating medium was mainly paper, denominated assignats, coins having virtually ceased to circulate. These assignats soon depreciated. The government had an auction sale in the different towns of France of all the property that had been confiscated from the church and the nobility that had emigrated, payment to be made in assignats, at part the value. My father-in-law did not follow the advice of friends to purchase at these terms, as he believed the government would in time redeem the paper in coin; but such currency depreciated more and more until it finally became worthless. My wife remembered having seen in her younger days a whole room at her father's residence papered with these assignats as a memento of "former riches". My wife's uncle, Leon Mayer, was an excellent portrait artist, and in consequence, on very intimate terms with the rich and noble families in Paris, and amongst them the family of Prince Ghika, which formerly was the reigning family of Romania, and I became acquainted with the Princess Victoria Ghika from seeing her in my brother-in-law's studio.

In the house in Paris where my wife's family lived, their neighbours were the family of the Halevys – at that time supplying groceries to Israelitish customers. One of this family became the great musical composer and another a poet. (Edit 17) Their intimacy was kept up with my mother-in-law until after her death, when it ceased. When Napoleon was overthrown, Princess Ghika emigrated to London and was a constant visitor at my house. When Mr Peixotto was appointed American Consul at Romania, my brother gave him a letter to me and requested me to introduce him to the Princess because members of her family still were prominent nobles. I introduced him to the Princess and asked her to give Mr Peixotto a letter. She did so, and wrote also to her brother in Bucharest with whom Mr Peixotto was on friendly terms whilst he resided there.

My daughter married Henry Abenheim, a native of Stuttgart. His father was a pensioner of the Court, having for fifty years filled the position of Leader of the Opera and Maitre de Chappelle to the Court. Henry's mother was of the Auerbach family, an aunt of the noted Author Auerbach. My daughter's children are four: Bessy, born January 7th 1871; Barnet, February 13th 1875; Lina, September 23rd 1878; Rivka, February 19th 1881.

My mother died in the early part of 1832 at Bristol, to which city we came from Falmouth, and in Bristol I carried on a retail silver and jewellery trade, combined with pawnbroking. My brother Barnet was there apprenticed to the cabinet and upholstery business. After the death of my mother, we broke up our residence and business in Bristol with the intention of emigrating to Australia, but by the advice of our cousin Benedict Joseph, we determined to go to New York and in that year, 1832, our business transactions in England were almost completed so that my brother and the late Benedict Joseph went down to Liverpool to secure three berths on a clipper ship sailing to New York, leaving me in London to close up all business left unfinished. Upon their arrival in Liverpool, the government had issued an order that all passenger ships must have a doctor on board, and on this account the price would be increased five pounds for each passenger. To save the ten pounds it would have cost them had they waited for me, they started for America without me. When I arrived in Liverpool with the intention of following them, my cousin Barnet Joseph advised me to go to Paris and become agent or commissioner for purchasing French manufactured articles to send to England. His arguments being strengthened by a friend of mine, one Behrends, I followed his advice, and on the saving of ten pounds passage money all my future depended, until I abandoned England forever in June 1881.

My brother Barnet arrived in New York after a nine week trip. The cholera was then raging which cause prevented him from getting any position in his trade. (Edit 18) After travelling over a portion of the United States, he returned to New York and was induced to open a cigar store in which he continued for about one year, when, through the advice of a friend, he renewed his own trade in the year 1834, occupying a store on Broadway between Grand and Canal streets. The location was considered then far up-town. He succeeded in business, and in the year 1835 he married Julia, a daughter of John I. Hart of New York. My brother's family consisted of four sons and five daughters, all of whom married and are now living happily in New York; excepting however the youngest who died in 1879, leaving a daughter to emulate her virtues. My brother remained in active business for nearly fifty years, retiring in 1878, since which time the firm he established has been continued by B.L. Solomon's sons.

Israel Solomon was born in Falmouth, England, August 28th 1803, and Barnet L. Solomon on June 14th 1806. We remember very well the celebration of George III's jubilee after his reign of fifty years, and this year (1887) we hope to read about the ceremonies attending Queen Victoria's jubilee after reigning a similar period.

> Esther Levy, died aged about 40 years.
> Barnet Levy, died aged about 60 years.
> Bella Solomon, died aged about 90 years.
> Israel Solomon, died aged about 78 years.
> My mother Betsy lived to be 75 years old, my father died in his 56th year.

My brother Barnet and myself were the only children of our parents Solomon and Betsy (née Levy) Solomon. My wife died September 8th 1873 and was buried in the Jewish Cemetery at Ham, London. My brother's wife died May 28th 1880 and was buried in Salem Fields Cemetery near Brooklyn, New York.

When I first went to Paris to live, my firm was Joseph and Solomon and subsequently for many years the name remained without the conjunction Joseph Solomon. After returning to England, retaining my business connection with France, and having an agency for Delicourt's famous paper-hangings, I added the optical business and became known to photographers throughout the world by the magnesium lamp I patented and manufactured. All legal documents I sign thus: Joseph Israel Solomon.

Editorial Notes

Edit 1. This refers to his maternal grandmother, Esther Elias, who died c.1780. She married Barnet Levy (1731–91). See the Falmouth cemetery (1:11 and 1:4). Their daughter Elizabeth (Betsy) was the writer's mother (see Fal. 1:4 and Edit 5).

Edit 2. See Fal. 1:4.

Edit 3. See Fal. 3:8.

Edit 4. See Fal. 1:4.

Edit 5. Solomon Solomon (1764–1819) married Betsy Levy (1757–1832: see Fal. 1:4). He was the son of Israel Solomon, nee Behrends, (d. 1802) from Germany and Bella Woolf (1726–1816) from Holland, the writer's paternal grandparents: see Fal. 2:1 and 3:2. Solomon Solomon died in Lisbon and Betsy Levy died in Bristol.

Edit 6. See chapter 7.

Edit 7. See Fal. 2:1.

Edit 8. This is Samuel Harris (Fal. 3:12). "Harriss" is Solomon's spelling.

Edit 9. Henry Harris: see Fal.3:12.

Edit 10. See Edit 5. above.

Edit 11. See chapter 6.

Edit 12. See Fal. 3:3.

Edit 13. This is not correct. Kitty Jacob may have lived in Penzance at some time, but she is not buried in the cemetery there, but in Falmouth (5:4) where Bella Woolf is buried. Jacob James Hart (or Jacobs) is buried in Penzance (5:3).

Edit 14. Israel Solomon has confused the identities of the two Jacobs brothers. It was the elder brother, Jacob James Jacobs (1784–1846) who entered into a partnership with his uncle Lemon Hart, commencing 1st January 1807, and then went to London to establish the business there. If the younger Jacobs brother subsequently joined the London business, then this would have been Frederick Jacobs (1790–1853) who had married his first cousin, Lemon Hart's daughter Rebecca (as her second husband).

Edit 15. Jacob "Hart's" sisters were Letitia, who married a Glickenstein (the manufacturer of combs) and Rose who married Isaac Simons, a son of Samuel Simons of Truro (Fal. 4:4) and Rosa Moses (Fal. 4:2) and brother to Sarah Kate Simons (Fal. 5:2). The "other sister" (of Jacob James "Hart") referred to was a daughter of Elias Magnus, the second husband of Rebecca Jacobs (formerly Hart). Ref. Jacob Hart's death (p. 287; see also p. 145).

Edit 16. She died in 1873.

Edit 17. This was Jacques Francois Halevy (Elias Levy: 1799–1862) composer of operas, the most famous being *La Juive*. The "poet" brother was the dramatist and librettist of comic operettas, Leon (1802–1883).

Edit 18. See the section on Falmouth in chapter 7, part 2.

The Disappearing Heritage: the Synagogues and their Ritual Artefacts

Evelyn Friedlander and Helen Fry

There are still visible traces of Cornish Jewish worship in the eighteenth and nineteenth centuries in the form of two purpose-built synagogues. Even though the shells of these buildings today provide a picture for posterity, nothing now remains of their original interiors.[1] They testify to an age now past and to an often forgotten era of Jewish life in Cornwall. It is possible, however, to reconstruct something of that life. Knowledge about both the synagogues and their form of worship has come down to us through lease documents, newspaper articles, a few photographs, descriptions by scholars who visited 30–40 years ago, and the few ritual objects which have survived.

By 1766 sufficient Jewish families lived in Falmouth to warrant the establishment of the first synagogue in Hamblyn's Court near the harbour, on the site of the much later gasworks.[2] The building used may previously have been a bakery. With the further growth in numbers, a permanent building was erected on Smithick (or Parram) Hill, then known as Fish Street Hill, in a prominent position overlooking the harbour. It opened in circa 1806–8.[3] In James Trathan's guide to Falmouth,[4] the following appears: "The Jews' Synagogue. Fish Street Hill. Was built in the year 1808. The Jews first had a Synagogue in Falmouth in 1766. They meet for the celebration of their religious rites, at the usual times. Mr Lyon Joseph is the president; and Mr Samuel Harris, steward." The *Falmouth and Penryn Directory* of 1864 describes it as: "an excellent and convenient building for the performance of their ancient religious worship."[5] That such a visible site was

---

[1] With the exception of a retaining pillar in Falmouth synagogue.
[2] This was subsequently known as Dunstan's Court.
[3] The original conveyance documents have not been sighted to confirm the precise date. The *Falmouth and Penryn Directory & Guide* of 1864 dates the synagogue to 1806, whereas *The History and Description of the Town & Harbour of Falmouth*, 1828, p. 86 dates it to 1808.
[4] Described as "A View of Falmouth in July 1815"; cf. pp. 46 & 47.
[5] *Falmouth and Penryn Directory & Guide*, 1864, p. 41.

acceptable as a non-Christian place of worship, indicates the import-ance and self-confidence of the Jewish community, as well as suggesting a considerable degree of religious tolerance in the town.[6] The elevated location was particularly useful as it enabled the local Jews to keep an eye on ships entering and leaving the bay.

The original building, which is unexpectedly large for a relatively small community, still exists, although the adjoining cottages were pulled down in the 1950s.[7] In its architectural style, the synagogue has great affinity with nineteenth-century non-conformist chapels. It has the same simplicity of form and employs arched windows. Because of its historical significance, the National Monuments Record in Swindon has recorded the building and describes it thus:

> Red brick with blue headers and granite quoins to road-frontage end, otherwise rendered; round arches to principal elevations; asbestos slate hipped roof. Rectangular plan. Road front has 2 original large hornless saches with spoked fanlight heads and small panes; central oculus over . . . 3 similar original saches to right-hand return. Two later windows high up to left-hand return; porch at far left. Interior not inspected.[8]

The exterior has changed little over the years. A wide door has been added in the front, east side of the building, just below one of the arched windows. This could not have been part of the original construction as it would have meant entering immediately adjacent to the Ark, which was not the usual practice. It was probably added during the period when the synagogue served as a furniture ware-house, in order to gain direct access from the road. Originally access had been through the rear of the building.[9] Two windows have been added to the side wall since its original construction.[10] As late as 1970, pipe marks on the outside wall could be seen leading to the stone surround of the *mikveh* in the undergrowth, and the stone steps which led down to it, but the area has since been covered over with tarmac.[11] The synagogue had a seating capacity of 80.[12]

---

[6] The prominent location is unusual in the south-west. In Penzance, Exeter and Plymouth the synagogue exteriors are modest, with access through an alley.

[7] The original cottages can be seen in a photograph in Alex Jacob's archive.

[8] National Monuments, ref: SW8032NE.

[9] cf. letter dated 31st August 1958 from Edward Jamilly to Alex Jacob. The original letter is in Alex Jacob's archive.

[10] ibid.

[11] An Ordnance survey map of Falmouth for 1880 shows a well close to the site of the *mikveh*.

[12] Ordnance survey map, op. cit.

The former Falmouth synagogue in October 1998. [courtesy: Helen Fry]

As to the interior, no comprehensive description and no photographs or paintings of it have been found which could convey any idea of its design and furnishings. The only reference which has been found amongst a wealth of research material comes in a letter from the architect Edward Jamilly to Alex Jacob in 1958: "It would appear that there was a gallery at the rear on timber columns. There is a remnant of panelling on the ground floor very similar to the little wooden pilasters above the men's seating in Plymouth synagogue. . . . At least one big suspension hook in the ceiling remains as evidence of the candelabra mentioned in your paper."[13]

In April 1881, the *Cornubian* newspaper reported the demise of the Jewish congregation: "All of these families have now totally disappeared. The last representatives of the Jewish residents was Mr. Samuel Jacob who left some few months since for London. Mr. Jacob, before he left, thoroughly repaired the synagogue and placed it on a lasting holding from the lord of the manor. The synagogue is now closed and deserted."[14] The Chief Rabbi ordered its sale in 1892, after it had again fallen into a deplorable state, but it is unclear whether it was in fact sold, or even saleable, and the circumstances which led to its eventual re-use are unclear.

Today, Falmouth synagogue's perfectly preserved exterior houses an artist's studio and is in private ownership. It can be seen by the casual visitor who may walk from the town centre up towards Smithick Hill. It retains its listed status,[15] but whether that will afford any long-term protection remains to be seen.

The first purpose-built synagogue in Penzance was constructed in 1768. It was leased to the congregation under contract to a member of the Branwell family. The Branwells also lent funds for the synagogue and were involved in its construction.[16] They similarly leased and helped to build the second synagogue on the same site in 1807–8.[17] It is this building which is still visible today. Access to it was gained through a narrow alley off New Street. It was significantly smaller

---

[13] Op. cit. This description comes from a period when most of the original synagogue interior had been dismantled.

[14] *The Cornubian*, 15th April 1881, p. 5.

[15] Letter from Carrick District Council to the Board of Deputies of British Jews, 25th May 1979.

[16] Fuller details of the leases and conveyances are outlined in part 2 of chapter 4 of this book. This information has not, therefore, been repeated here.

[17] The dating of the building of synagogue to 1807-8 is supported by the recent dating of its Decalogue to 1807. The Decalogue, now in the Jewish Museum in London, was recently assessed for possible renovation work and it was dated to 1807 by a restorer.

than the synagogue in Falmouth and seated about 20. The *Cornishman* of August 1889 describes it as follows: "We have said 'the modest little synagogue,' and few would suspect that the narrow doorway just below the carriage entrance to the Star Hotel leads to so large a place of worship – large for its usual congregation, small when compared with other places of worship. . . . Nor do the plain swing-doors, reached by a step and a turn in the pavement approach, bespeak the large and well-lit room built and used for so many years as a synagogue."[18] Susser, writing in 1964, says this about the synagogue exterior:

> . . . was built in the back yard of a private house and shared its alleyway entrance – a somewhat mean approach for its late date. Roughly rectangular, it is quite lofty for the size of the building. The walls are of thick, stone rubble, the upper part hung with slates and covered by a low-pitched, slated roof. First impressions are of a sound and solid, if unexciting structure.[19]

Commenting on its size, he writes: "The synagogue was only about 24 feet square and 20 feet high, yet, by a miracle of orderly planning, completely fitted in every detail".[20]

As to the interior, an article in the *Cornishman* of August 1889 provides a fascinating and detailed description:

> Two spacious windows admit abundance of eastern light. . . . Between these windows the space from floor to wall-plate is occupied by the modern substitute for the ark or the chest of the Book-of-the-Law . . . before its closed doors hangs the veil, in this case of damask. Above the ark is an inscription. A wooden screen, topped by pillars, and two gates of the same material and pattern surround it. The gates are approached by two steps. Between the sanctuary, with its eight-branched lamp on the right and the entrance doors, is another raised and railed-in platform, reached midway on either side by a step.[21] Inside this space at its west end is a plain, uncushioned bench. Its east end, which faces the ark and the windows, has a sloping desk. . . . The four corners of the rails are marked by tall candlesticks with massive candles. Three sides of the room are wainscoted and around them are plain benches – on the north and the south side double rows of them. At intervals in these benches are what sailors would call 'lockers'

---

18 This article has a full description of the bar mitzvah of Harry Bischofswerder which took place in the synagogue.

19 *The Cornishman*, July 16, 1964. The architect Edward Jamilly provided Susser with much of the information contained in this description.

20 *The Cornishman*, op. cit.

21 This would have been the *bimah*.

The former Penzance synagogue in 1999. [courtesy: Frank Dabba Smith]

The interior c.1970s [courtesy: David Giddings]

297

and they are locked and covered spaces for books. . . . All this
floor-space is devoted to the male portion of the congregation.
Females sit in two galleries at the west end and the south side of
the synagogue.[22]

The synagogue was not sold in 1913 as Cecil Roth has implied and
as subsequently assumed. Owing to the decline of the community, it
had already been sold to the Plymouth Brethren seven years earlier in
1906. Two photographs have been found which give some indication
as to the appearance of the interior from the period of its use by the
Brethren. Neither photograph provides an overall view of the synagogue; however, they do show part of the Ark and the balustrades of
the ladies' gallery. Despite the fact that some fixtures remained in the
building, there is no direct evidence that the Plymouth Brethren
permitted, or that the few remaining Jews like Morris Bischofswerder,
felt it appropriate to continue to use the building for Jewish worship.
This was more likely to have taken place in a modified form in a
private house.

The ritual silver and other artefacts and the various Sifre Torah
(Scrolls of the Law) were removed before the sale, but the empty Ark,
the Decalogue panel (containing the opening words of each of the Ten
Commandments) and some panels inscribed with scriptural quotations
were left in situ until the early 1980s when the "Upper Room Fellowship", as it was then known, moved to other premises.[23] Although
the interior had been thought to have been given listed status,[24] and
had remained intact throughout the period when the building was
used for Christian worship, it was effectively stripped and gutted at
this point: the Ark was dismantled and scrapped, but a local couple
who had been members of the Fellowship (one of whom had Jewish
ancestry) were alerted and intervened in time to save the Decalogue.

Susser provides a description of the interior when he visited it in the
1960s. He describes it thus:

> The interior has been partially dismantled but the carcass of a
> wooden Ark – deprived of its railed dais – still stands between a
> pair of tall sash windows with semicircular heads set about six
> feet apart in the east wall. Bench seats, each with a locker

---

[22] The editors are grateful to Elizabeth Brock for drawing this article to their
attention from her research.

[23] This information has been taken from Godfrey Simmons' archive.

[24] No listing for Penzance synagogue was found by the National Monuments Record
at Swindon. cf. letter from Nigel Wilkins of the National Monuments Record to
Keith Pearce, dated 10th October 1997, ref: B/5313/97. No other documentary
evidence has so far come to light about any local listing.

The two decalogue tablets of the Torah from the Penzance synagogue, now in the Jewish Museum, London. [courtesy: Jewish Museum, photograph by Keith Pearce] *Below:* Hebrew inscription on panel from the synagogue. [courtesy: Jean and Tony Gillman, photograph by Frank Dabba Smith]

underneath to store prayer books, ran along the north and south walls but some have been removed. The walls were panelled to a height of five feet and plastered above. A gallery extends along the north and west walls over the entrance: its front is plain panelled to half height with a carved lattice above. In the centre of the ceiling, from an ornamental panel, about six feet in diameter, hung an elaborate candelabrum over the reading desk: both objects have now disappeared.[25]

The building was eventually purchased by the Devenish brewery and incorporated into the adjoining public house, the Star Inn. Now nothing remains of the synagogue's interior to identify its original use. When visited in the mid-1990s, the upper part (formerly the women's gallery) housed an enclosed children's playroom, painted in garish primary colours, while the lower body of the building has become the pub's chilled beer cellar.[26] What remains of the exterior, visible only from the rear, is in dire need of repair and renovation.

Sadly, the discussion of the artefacts of the two communities is almost entirely one of loss. Falmouth has yielded some happy surprises but nothing whatsoever remains of the ritual objects from Penzance. One can only surmise that when the community ceased to function, they were transferred to another synagogue, but since transactions of that nature within the United Synagogue are never recorded, their whereabouts are now lost. One can only hope that at some point in the future, someone will look at an inscription and recognise it as having come from Penzance, but this is probably too optimistic a thought.

It is known that Penzance possessed ritual objects and textiles as they were listed in the minute books of the congregation. In 1810, Lemon Hart presented the congregation with a Torah scroll that had formerly belonged to Mr. Lazarus Solomon (deceased)[27] along with a silver hand for reading, six brass candlesticks, two large chandeliers and a curtain of red satin with a white border.[28] In 1883, the minute book has a list of property belonging to the congregation. It lists four silver pointers, a silver goblet and a silver spice-box but no mention is made of any *rimmonim* or shields to decorate the Torah scrolls, of which there seem to have been four. The same source lists numerous textiles:

---

[25] *The Cornishman*, 16th July 1964.

[26] From the interior, the original arched windows have been boarded over and are now only visible externally from the rear of the building.

[27] Lazarus Solomon (of Goodmans Field, London) was Lemon Hart's father-in-law.

[28] Minute book, 19th October 1810. These items were donated for permanent use by the congregation rather than on loan.

2 Desk coverings, one brocaded silk curtain and one silk Dressing (sic) in addition to those on the *Sefarim* (scrolls). A Worked silk curtain given by Mr Selig Senr., 2 White dresses for Sefer & W curtain given by Mr H. Joseph. White desk covering given by Mr Woolf. Dyed silk curtain not made. 2 Damask coverings for Reading Desk by Mr H. Joseph. Brocaded silk & velvet curtain by Do. White silk Drapery for Sefer by H. Joseph. 1 Striped corded silk for Do. by H. Joseph.

The foregoing entries in the minute book were made by Henry Joseph. He further lists:

. . . for Burials. Pr Trussels (trestles), Cleansing Board, hand rail for carrying the dead. 2 Black Cloths 2 Cloaks a silk Damask covering for Almemer (pulpit) lent for use by Mr B.H. Joseph. White Curtain & White covering for Almemer presented by friends from Penzance in Birmingham.[29]

An additional entry reads:

1883/5643 May. 3 Handsome Mantles for the 3 Scrolls of the Law presented by Mr & Mrs Barnett H. Joseph Birmingham to commemorate the Bar mitzvah of their son Selim.

Everything has vanished without a trace. The minute books themselves came into the hands of Cecil Roth and are now in the collection that bears his name in the Brotherton Library at the University of Leeds. Known as Pinkas (regulations, minutes and accounts), Dr. Roth lent the book covering 1807 to 1829 to the exhibition of Anglo-Jewish Art and History which was held at the Victoria and Albert Museum in 1956 to commemorate the tercentenary of the Resettlement of the Jews in the British Isles.

As already noted, after the Plymouth Brethren vacated the synagogue, all of the interior was ripped out. According to local sources, the furnishings were piled in the road so that today the only relics we have are the Decalogue which once surmounted the Ark and the Hebrew inscription beneath which reads in translation, "He opens unto us the Gates of Mercy". The inscription survives in the living-room of a private house in the Penzance area.[30] The Decalogue is now in store in the Jewish Museum, in such a state of disrepair that it will probably not even be possible to restore it.

---

[29] Minute books, 1883, op. cit. Copy from Godfrey Simmons's archive.
[30] The editors are grateful to Jean and Tony Gillman for information and access to the panel.

The fate of the Judaica from Falmouth has been a trifle happier although sadly no minute books survive. Several Torah scrolls have been located in the Library of the Royal Institution of Cornwall in Truro,[31] and there is every reason to assume that they are complete in number. They were donated to the library by Samuel Jacob in the early part of the twentieth century.[32] A pair of rimmonim of Dutch origin and dating from the late seventeenth century, were taken from Falmouth to the Hampstead Synagogue in London and have subsequently been on a long-term loan to the Jewish Museum. One of the rimmonim is engraved: "These bells formerly the property of the Falmouth Synagogue were acquired for the Hampstead Synagogue by Alexander Jacob".[33]

Two Torah pointers from the Falmouth synagogue have also survived and are in the Jewish Museum's collection. One has an Exeter assay mark and dates from 1815. The maker's mark is S.H. (Simon Harris) and the translation of the Hebrew inscription reads: "Israel b. Naphtali Hirsch, Truro, 5596 (1836)". It has a spirally fluted shaft and octagonal handle divided by a basket work knop with a similar finial.[34] The second is probably English, dating from the early nineteenth century and unmarked. It has a plain cylindrical shaft and the lower part of its square section has a compressed knop and finial. It has a chain, and its Hebrew inscription records the names of four donors or owners, all of Falmouth and so recorded (in translation): "Abraham b. Joseph, Jehuda b. Joseph, Isaac b. Joseph and Meir b. Isaac".[35]

The wooden, painted Decalogue from the Falmouth Synagogue is on permanent display at the Jewish Museum.[36] Dating from the early nineteenth century, it is painted in a dull green and has a double arcaded top supported by three circular turned columns. The Ten Commandments are written in gold and shaded Hebrew lettering. It had been found quite by chance in a dealer's shop in Falmouth in the 1930s by Mr H. Danglowitz who later gave it to the museum.[37] It is of

---

[31] Letter from Angela Broome of the Royal Institution of Cornwall to Helen Fry, dated 25th March 1998. A number of other Jewish items were also donated to the RIC by Alfred de Pass, including a scroll of the Book of Esther, a Prayer Book dated 1752 (Printed in Florence), and a Pentateuch (printed in Hamburg 1663–64).

[32] Letter from Angela Broome of the Royal Institution of Cornwall to Evelyn Friedlander, dated 22nd March 1999.

[33] Barnett, ed. (1974, catalogue no. 104, p. 26).

[34] ibid. catalogue no. 169, p. 35.

[35] ibid. catalogue no. 170, p. 35.

[36] ibid.

[37] *Jewish Chronicle*, 19th July 1935.

Torah scroll from Falmouth synagogue. [courtesy: the Royal Institution of Cornwall, photograph by Frank Dabba Smith]

The Falmouth synagogue rimmonim (torah scroll adornments).

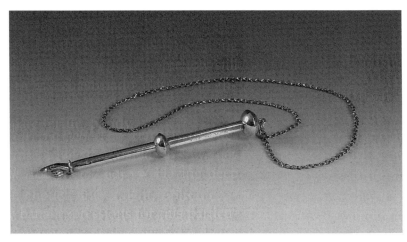

Early nineteenth-century torah pointer from Falmouth synagogue. [both pictures courtesy: Jewish Museum, London, photographs by Ian Lilliecrapp]

a very similar style to that of Penzance, except that it is in significantly better condition.

The two Cornish communities really ceased to function at around the turn of the century and, in some ways, that their buildings and a few artefacts have survived at all is actually rather remarkable. Their fate can be seen as one which foreshadowed that of many communities today. As communities across the country close down, the buildings are sold off, and their artefacts are disposed of and dispersed. An awareness of "physical history" is a very recent one, and has come far too late to rescue so much of the heritage which has already been lost. Even the listing of buildings does not prevent them from being at risk, and it is hard to make a declining community understand the importance and value to history of its holdings, especially when commercial factors play a part.

Unless the local community can take over and ensure a continuity of interest and upkeep, which is most unlikely, the synagogues of smaller provincial communities will go on disappearing. It is a dilemma, and perhaps all one can do is initially to try and raise local awareness of the importance to local history, and should that fail, as it probably will, to at least ensure that the building is properly recorded, surveyed and photographed. This is now happening,[38] but it has of course come far too late for Penzance and Falmouth.

---

[38] The Survey of Jewish Monuments, under the leadership of Sharman Kadish, is systematically recording all of the Jewish-built heritage in the UK and Ireland.

Conclusion

The Jews who lived in Cornwall in the eighteenth and nineteenth centuries may be lost as communities but diligent private research by numerous people over sixty years has been incorporated into this book with a determination that these "Lost Jews" should not be entirely forgotten. It is to be hoped that this book will serve to raise awareness of the colour and richness of the life of these obscure communities where Jews lived without persecution or fear and where they contributed so much to the county which became their home.

We trust that the book will fill a gap in both Anglo-Jewish and Cornish history, and that it will help to serve a heritage which can only be saved through diligence and great care. This project has been a genuinely co-operative enterprise between Jews and non-Jews, differing greatly in their backgrounds and beliefs, but drawn together in a common purpose. Perhaps a co-operative model of this kind between amateur historians and professional academics could lead to similar projects to research and record important areas of provincial Anglo-Jewish history and local history, at present under-represented as a matter of public record.

For the future, there may be those who, after reading this book, will recognise that they have in their possession further information which could contribute to this subject. The editors hope that a second, revised edition of this book will be forthcoming from such material. We therefore invite individuals who have contributed so much to this book, and others, to continue sending us any additional materials which they think may be of help in extending our knowledge of these communities. Our project has reached publication but not completion. Research into the Jews of Cornwall will go on.

Any information sent to the publishers will be forwarded to the editors.

Godfrey Simmons, Keith Pearce and Helen Fry, May 1999.

Persons mentioned in the Records of the Minutes, Penzance from 1808–1829 and 1843–1892

Compiled by Godfrey Simmons

The following provides a list of the names occurring in the Penzance minute books from 1808–1829 and 1843–1892. This does not imply the presence of each individual at a meeting, but that their names came up for discussion. For example, although the Chief Rabbi Dr. Adler and Sir Moses Montefiore are mentioned in the minutes, they did not visit Penzance.

1808: Joseph Branwell, Lemon Hart, Hyman Woolf, Henry Ralph, Lemon Woolf, . . . Magnus, . . . Levy, L. Jacobs, Sam Joseph, Mr. Johnson (Plymouth), Henry Bottrel, . . . Brewer, Thos. Nichols, Peter Roberts, Jno. Wallis, Peter Richards, . . . Bolitho & Sons, Joseph Tonkin, Robt. Edwards, Richd. Coulson, F . . . Michael (Swansea).

1809: Mr. Woolf, Mr. Ralph, Mr. Magnus, L. Jacobs, H. Woolf, H. Ralph, E. Hornblower, Lemon Hart, Thos. Broad.

1810: Lemon Hart, H. Woolf, H. Ralph, E. Magnus, L. Woolf, L. Jacobs, Moses Isaac, Lazarus Solomon (deceased), I. Jacobs (Camborne).

1811: Lemon Hart, Jacob Hart (London), Saml. Jacobs (Scilly), H. Woolf, Mr. Ralph, Elias Magnus, L. Woolf, L. Hart, L. Jacobs, J. Jacobs, A. Symons, J. Cohen, . . . Alexander, Jacob Hart, Lemon Jacobs, Isaac Joseph (Redruth), Sam Jacobs, . . . Selig, Mr. Margues ??, Mr. Simmons.

1812: H. R . . ., E. Magnus, Lemon Woolf, Samuel Jacob, Lemon Jacobs (London), M. Hart, Jacob Hart (London), Jacob Jacobs (Camborne), Isaac Joseph (Redruth), . . . Jacobs (Exeter), Aaron Selig, . . . Simmons, H. Woolf.

1813: H. Woolf, E. Magnus, L. Woolf, Samuel Jacobs (Hayle), Aaron Selig, Jacob Jacobs (Camborne), Isaac Joseph (Redruth), Jacob Hart (London), B.A. Simmons.

1814: H. Woolf, L. Woolf, S. Jacobs, A. Selig, B.A. Simmons, I. Jacobs (Camborne), I. Joseph (Redruth), . . . Magnus, (Rabbi) Mortera.

---

[1] Appendices 1–3 are from Godfrey Simmons' archive.

1815: H. Woolf, L. Woolf, A. Selig, S. Jacobs (Hayle), B.A. Simmons, I. Jacobs (Camborne), I. Joseph (Redruth), Israel Levy (Truro), . . . Mortera, . . . Branwell, . . . Symons, Hyman Woolf, Joseph Barrow (Jamaica), Lemon Hart, A. Selig, B.A. Simmons, Samuel Jacob (Hayle), I. Jacob (Camborne), Isaac Joseph (Redruth), Israel Levy (Truro), . . . Foxwell, . . . Harvey, Hyman Selig.

1816: Hyman Woolf, L. Woolf, A. Selig, B. Van Oven??, B.A. Simmons, Samuel Jacob, Harvey, Branwell, Jacob, Magnus, Bryan, Williams.

1817: H. Woolf, E. Magnus, L. Woolf, A. Selig, B.A. Simmons, Samuel Jacob, Jacob Moses, Mr. Edmonds, Joseph Wallis, Solomon Ezekiel.

1818: Hyman Woolf, L. Woolf, E. Magnus, A. Selig, B.A. Simmons, I. Jacob, Solomon Ezekiel, Mrs Branwell, John Wallis.

1819: I.B. Sutherland, Harvey, Moses Levi, Levi Jacob, Ellis Magnus, H. Woolf, Lemon Woolf, B.A. Simmons, Solomon Ezekiel, Samuel, Jacob, Isaac Symons, Mr. Wallis, William Eva.

1820: Isaac Symons, H. Woolf, L. Woolf, A. Selig, B.A. Simmons, Samuel Jacobs, Solomon Ezekiel, Levi Jacob, Cohen, Wallis, Foxhall, Cohen (Redruth), Mrs. I. Joseph.

1821: L. Woolf, A. Selig, B.A. Symons (sr), Samuel Jacob, Isaac Symons, Levy Jacob, A.S. Solomon, Alex Symons, E. Cohen (Redruth), I. Levy (Truro), Simmons (Truro), Eva, Godfrey, Foxhall (Foxell), Lyon Levi (Truro), Hyman (Truro), Mrs. Joseph (Redruth), Mordi? Symon, Henry Levin, John Mortara.

1822: Lemon Woolf, B.A. Symons, Samuel Jacob, Isaac Symons, Levi Jacob, A. Symons, Symons (Truro), Eva, Foxhole.

1823: L. Woolf, B.A. Simmons, Samuel Jacob, Isaac Symons, Levi Jacob, Alex Symons, Eva, Foxhole, Mary Borlase, Jenny . . ., Henry Levin.

1824: Samuel Jacobs, Alexander Symons, Lemon Woolf, B.A. Simmons, A. Selig, Levi Jacob, H. Lavin, Eva, Tho. Thomas, Alice . . ., William Small, John Ellis, William Eddy, Samuel John, Eva.

1825: Lemon Woolf, Samuel Jacobs, B.A. Symons, Henry Lavin (Levin), Sophia Jacobs, Aaron Selig, Abraham Davidson, Isaac Davidson, Harry Levi, Eva, I. Dobb, John Messina, Solomon Johnson, Hart Symonds, Solomon Ezekiel, Isaac Pollack, Hart Symmonds.

1826: Lemon Woolf, Samuel Jacobs, B.A. Simmons, Henry Lavin, John Messina, Solomon Ezekiel, Sophia Jacobs, A.B. Davidson, Isaac Davidson, Solomon Johnson, Harry Levy, Hart Symons, Eva, Mary Kenefic, Abraham Joseph, Bodilly, Henry Levin, Aaron Selig.

1827: Lemon Woolf, A. Selig, Samuel Jacob, B.A. Simmons, Henry Lavin, John Messina, Sophia Jacob, Harry Levi, B. Selig, H. Joseph, Mr. Joseph, Nicholls, Thomas Mason, Mary Kenefic, Ellis, Solomon Johnson, Mr. Batten.

1828: Lemon Woolf, Aaron Selig, Samuel Jacob, Abraham Joseph, B.A. Simmons, Henry Levin, Henry Levi, H. Lavin, Sophia Jacob, B. Selig, Eva, Mary Kenefic, W. Ansell, L. Moyle, Joseph Joseph, M. Marcus?, M. Myar?, Isaac Lazarus, Lemon Hart, Amongst recorded donations "up to 22nd June 1828": Marcus, W. Meyer, Isaac Lazarus, . . . Lep? Lazarus, Mr. Rosenthal.

1829: Lemon Woolf, Moses Woolf, Aaron Selig, Samuel Jacob, H. Lavin, Abraham Joseph, Harry Levy, Sophia Jacob, Joseph Joseph, Rabbi My—his?, Makir?, B.A. Simmons, Nicholls, Henry Lavin, Rosethal, P. Simon?

31 March 1843 (5604): A meeting of the Select Committee: L. Woolf, H. Joseph, H. Levin, M.H. Harris, M.B. Simmons.

3rd August 1843: A vestry meeting and read at a public meeting of the members of the Congregation. Signatories of the revised rules of the Congregation: Lemon Woolf, Henry Joseph, Henry Levin, Benjamin Aaron Selig, Moses B. Simmons, L. Hyman, Moses Woolf, Morris H. Harris, Alexander Levin, Simon Harris, Samuel Oppenheim, Solomon Teacher.

1843: Henry Harris, Morris H. Harris, Henry Joseph, Hyman Lazarus, Henry Levin, Samuel Oppenheim, Moses B. Simmons, Lemon Woolf, Moses Woolf.

1844. . . . Ezekiel, Morris H. Harris, Samuel Harris, Simon Harris, Henry Joseph, Alexander Levin, Henry Levin, Samuel Oppenheim, Benjamin Aaron Selig, Moses B. Simmons, Lemon Woolf, Moses Woolf.

1845: Dr. Barham of Exeter (see ch.5), Morris H. Harris, Henry Joseph, Hyman Lazarus, Alexander Levin, Henry Levin, Samuel Oppenheim, Benjamin A. Selig, Barnett A. Simmons, Moses B. Simmons, Lemon Woolf, Moses Woolf.

1846: Morris H. Harris, S. Harris, Frederic Hart, Jacob Hart, . . . Hyman, Henry Joseph, Hyman Levin, Samuel Oppenheim, Joseph Rintel, Benjamin A. Selig, Barnett A. Simmons, Solomon Teacher, Lemon Woolf.

1847: Morris H. Harris, Samuel Harris, Simon Harris, . . . Hyman, Miss Jacob (of Falmouth), Henry Joseph, Henry Levin, Samuel Oppenheim, Benjamin A. Selig, Barnett A, Simmons, Mrs. B.A. Simmons, Moses B. Simmons, Solomon Teacher, Lemon Woolf.

1848: S. Ezekiel, Henry Harris, Morris H. Harris, Henry Joseph, Mrs. H. Joseph, Alex. Levin, Henry Levin, Israel Oppenheim, Samuel Oppenheim, E.W.W. Pendarves MP, Joseph Rintel, Mrs. J. Rintel, Benjamin A. Selig, Barnett A. Simmons, Moses B. Simmons, . . . Somers, Solomon Teacher, Mrs. L. Woolf, Moses Woolf.

1849: Morris H. Harris, Henry Joseph, Mrs. H. Joseph, Alex. Levin, Henry Levin, Sir Moses Montefiore, Sampson Samuel (Sec. to M.M.), Samuel Oppenheim, Benjamin A. Selig, Moses B. Simmons.

1850: Morris H. Harris, Henry Joseph, Samuel Oppenheim, Benjamin A. Selig, Moses B. Simmons, Solomon Teacher.

1851: Henry Joseph, David Levin, Samuel Oppenheim, Barnett A. Simmons, Solomon Teacher.

1852: George Foot (beadle), . . . (Rabbi) Herman of Falmouth, David Levin, Benjamin A. Selig, Barnett A. Simmons, Solomon Teacher.

1853: Dr. Adler (Chief Rabbi), . . . Colenso, . . . Cohen, Miss Jacobs, Henry Joseph, Mrs. H. Joseph, Miss Joseph, Henry Levin, Israel Levin, Mrs. Levin, Miss Levin, Sir Moses Montefiore, Samuel Oppenheim, Mrs. Oppenheim, . . . Scrann, Benjamin A. Selig, Mrs. Selig, Lionel and Morris (Selig?), Barnett A. Simmons, Mrs. Simmons, Samuel Solomon (London), Solomon Teacher, Mrs. Teacher.

1854: Solomon Cohen, Henry Joseph, Henry Levin, Israel Levin, Samuel Oppenheim, Benjamin A. Selig, Barnett Asher Simmons, Solomon Teacher.

1855: Henry Joseph, Henry Levin, Israel Levin, Samuel Oppenheim.

1856: Joseph Barnett, Dr. Adler, . . . Hyman, Henry Joseph, Barnett A. Simmons, . . . Staalhagens, Mrs Teacher, Teacher (infant).

1857: Henry Joseph.

1858: Henry Joseph

1859: Dr. Adler, Hyman Greenborough, Henry Levin, Israel Levin, Henry Joseph, Samuel Oppenheim, Barnett A. Simmons.

1860: Hyman Greenbourgh, Henry Levin.

1861: Henry Joseph, Henry Levin, A. Lupp(s)hutz.

1862: Henry Joseph.

1863: Barnett H. Joseph, Henry Joseph, Henry Levin, Israel Oppenheim, Mr. Spiro.

1864: Samuel Jacob (Falmouth), Barnet H. Joseph, Henry Joseph, Henry Levin, Israel Oppenheim, Mr. Spiro.

1865: H. Levin, Henry Joseph, Mr. Spiro, Samuel Oppenheim, Israel Levin, Israel Oppenheim, Mrs. George Goodman (Newbridge, Wales).

1866: Henry Joseph, I. Levin, I. Oppenheim, B.H. Joseph.

1867: Israel Oppenheim, Mr. Rittenberg, H. Joseph.

1868: H. Levin, H. Joseph, I. Oppenheim.

1869: H. Levin, Israel Levin, Henry Joseph, S. Oppenheim, Harris Beirnstein (Dowlais S. Wales), Levy, Mr. Gorfunkle (Liverpool).

1870: Mr. Freeman (Aberdare), Henry Joseph, Mr. Oppenheim.

1871: H. Levin, H. Joseph, I. Oppenheim.

1872: H. Joseph, I. Oppenheim.

1873: H. Joseph.

1874: Mr. (Rabbi) Bischofswerder, Mr. Levin snr., Henry Joseph, Israel Levin, Israel Oppenheim.

1875: Henry Levin, Henry Joseph, Mr. Bischofswerder, Dr. Harvey, I. Oppenheim, Alderman I.B. Coulson, Councillor Marwell, Mr. Cornish, Mr. Mounder, Sir Moses Montefiore, Mr. Emanuel.

1876: Henry Levin, Henry Joseph, Israel Levin, Samuel Jacob (Falmouth), Israel Oppenheim.

1877: H. Joseph, Samuel Jacob (Falmouth).

1878: H. Joseph, Israel Levin, Israel Oppenheim.

1880: Henry Joseph, I. Levin, Mr. Oppenheim, Mr. B.H. Joseph.

1881: Mr. J. Joseph, Mr. I. Oppenheim, Mr. I. Levin, Mr. David Bischofswerder, Israel Levin.

1882: Israel Levin, Barnett Joseph, Joseph Joseph, David Bischofswerder, Morris Bischofswerder, George Bischofswerder, Henry Joseph (deceased), A. Pooley, A. Cohen M.P.

1885: B.H. Joseph (Birmingham), Mrs. Joseph (Birmingham), I. Oppenheim, I. Levin, David Bischofswerder, Morris Bischofswerder.

1886: I. Oppenheim, D. Bischofswerder, M. Bischofswerder, I.H. Levin, B.H. Joseph, I. Rubinstein.

1887: I. Levin, David Bischofswerder, Israel Oppenheim, Morris Bischofswerder, I.A. Rubinstein, Dr. Adler, B.H. Joseph, J. Joseph, Alexander Levin, Miss I. Jacobs?, Mr. Wallis, George Bischofswerder, Rev. Michael Lancrom (sic).

1888: David Bischofswerder, I. Oppenheim, G. Bischofswerder, M. Bischofswerder, Rev. M. Lancrom (sic).

1889: D. Bischofswerder, I. Oppenheim, M. Bischofswerder, B.H. Joseph.

1890: D. Bischofswerder, I. Oppenheim, M. Bischofswerder, J. Joseph, Harry Bischofswerder.

1891: D. Bischofswerder, I. Oppenheim, J. Joseph, B.H. Joseph.

1892: David Bischofswerder, Morris Bischofswerder, Harry Bischofswerder, B.H. Joseph, Israel Oppenheim.

Note: the names have been recorded as faithfully as possible. However, because of handwriting and spelling idiosyncracies by the original authors, there is the possibility of error in the transcription. The names of Jacob and Jacobs are obvious examples.

List of circumcisions performed by Rabbi B.A. Simmons (1821–1846)

The list is entered in the back of a calf-bound book in Godfrey Simmons's archive containing the order of service for brit (circumcision). The following circumcisions were performed by Rabbi B.A. Simmons in Cornwall:

1 Mazzel Tob! The circumcision in the congregation of Falmouth of the child Isaac son of Joseph on Monday, Erev Pesach, 5581.

2 . . . place of Truro . . . Moses son of Napthali on Friday, 17 Ellul, 5581. Sondek: Samuel Harris.

3 . . . Penzance . . . Haim son of Asher Isaac on Wednesday, 3 Tishri, 5582

4 . . . Penzance . . . Tseve son of Samuel on Saturday, 13 Tammuz, 5582. Sondek: L. Jacob

5 . . . Truro . . . Israel son of Napthali on Saturday, 4 Adar 5583. Sondek: L. Jacob

6 . . . Truro . . . Simeon son of Napthali on Thursday, last day of Pesach, 5583. Sondek: L. Levy

7 . . . Falmouth . . . Abraham son of Moses on Thursday, Rosh Chodesh Ellul, 5583. Sondek: Mr. Larance

8 . . . Truro . . . Samuel son of Napthali on Tuesday, 11 Adar 5585. Sondek: Jacob Jacob

9 . . . Truro . . . Simeon son of Napthali on Sunday, 11 Tammuz

10 . . . Penzance . . . my son, Asher son of Abraham Issacher on Friday, 2 Ellul 5586. Sondek: Dr Meune

11 . . . Penzance . . . my son, Judah son of Abraham Issacher on Monday, 8 Ellul 5588. Sondek: Abraham Joseph

12 . . . Penzance . . . Israel son of Tseve on Saturday, 16 Adar Shine, 5589. Sondek: L. Woolf

13 . . . Penzance . . . Abraham son of Abraham Issacher on Saturday, 2 Adar, 5590. Sondek: L. Woolf

14   . . . Penzance . . . Simeon, my son, son of Abraham Issacher on Monday, 17 Shebat Feby. 1st, 5596. Sondek: M.B. Simmons

15   Mazzel Tob! Born on the 1st day of Rosh Chodesh Tammuz. Penzance . . . Israel son of Samuel Hoffenheim on Wednesday, 3rd Tammuz, 5603. Sondek: Alex. Levin

16   . . . Thursday, 2nd Tammuz, June 16th, 5607, . . . Penzance . . . my grandson Abraham son of Moses, on Thursday 9th Tammuz, 5607. Sondek: Moses Giddin: M. Woolf

APPENDIX 3

Rabbi B.A. Simmons' Family Birth Register

(From the original in Godfrey Simmons's archive)

B.A. Simmons made a register of the births of his children. In itself this was not unusual because it was common practice not only amongst Jews but also in Christian families. The register is of significance because it is typical, and when combined with further information (such as that from marriage certificates) provides a familiar picture of inter-marriage between the Penzance and Falmouth congregations, and marriages contracted with families in South Wales, London and Newcastle. It also shows what must have been a characteristic pattern of mobility, migration and emigration. The children moved from Penzance to live in other centres of Jewish population, emigrating from Cornwall to Australia and South Africa, as well as New Zealand, America and Canada. This was common during the nineteenth century and helped to establish Jewish communities in those countries.

B.A. Simmons. Born London January 1784; died 18th November 1860, aged 77 years. Buried in the Penzance Jewish cemetery.

Flora Simmons (née Jacob), daughter of Moses Jacob, originally of Falmouth. Wife of Rabbi B. A. Simmons. Born at Redruth, 13th January 1790. Died 2nd December 1874, aged 84, at 28, Victoria Street, Merthyr Tydfil, South Wales. Buried at the Jewish Cemetery, Merthyr Tydfil.

The children of Barnet Asher and Flora Simmons:

1. Fanny Simmons, born 23rd August 1814. Married Rabbi Benedict Joseph Rintel, (originally of Hamburg, Germany), minister of Falmouth, on 6th June 1838. They moved to London.

2. Phoebe Simmons, born 4th December 1815. Married Joseph Heilbron of Falmouth, on 5th August 1846.

3. Moses Barnett Simmons, born 15th May 1817. Married Rose Aaron (Mitchell) of Falmouth, on 10th June 1846. Later moved to Bury Street, London E.C.

4. Catherine (Kate) Simmons, born 13th January 1819. Married Hyman Feinburg of Newport, South Wales, on 12th June 1850.

5. Sarah Simmons, born 5th April 1821. Married Rabbi Harris Isaacs at Newport on 20th June 1855. Died 24th December 1892, at Summer Hill Terrace, Birmingham, aged 72. Buried at Witton Cemetery, Birmingham.

6. Pessia Simmons, born circa 1824. Died as a victim of the cholera epidemic in the autumn of 1832, and was buried in the Penzance Jewish cemetery on a Sabbath (14 Heshvan 5593). For some reason B.A. Simmons did not include her in his register of births.

7. Amelia Simmons, born 3rd October 1825. Married Isaac Davidson in London, later emigrating to Australia.

8. Arthur B. Simmons, born 21st September 1826. Also emigrated to Australia.

9. Levy Barnett Simmons, born 11th August 1828. Married Phoebe Levy, Houndsditch, London.

10. Abraham Barnett Simmons, born 26th February 1831, died in Ballarat, Australia in 1908. Married Leah Holman of Melbourne, Australia.

11. Simon Barnett Simmons, born 26th January 1836. Married Rachel Joseph of Portsea.

APPENDIX 4

Penzance Census 1851

Census date: 30 March 1851[2]

(Ho 107/1918) 9 Leskinick Terrace, Penzance[3]

Pe5/1 Jacob, Samuel	hd	m	73	Jew jeweller (deaf)	Redruth
Pe5/2 Jacob, Sally	wf	m	68		Truro
Pe5/3 Jacob, Bettesy	da	u	26	dressmakr (deaf & dumb)	Penzance

(Ho 107/1918) 16 Leskinick Terrace, Penzance

Pe5/4 Simons, Barnet A.	hd	m	67	Jew Minister	Middx. London
Pe5/5 Simons, Flora	wf	m	61		Redruth
Pe5/6 Simons, Kitty	lg	wd	79	annuitant	Redruth
(Read, Grace sv 28)					

(Ho 107/1918) 35 Leskinick Terrace, Penzance

Pe5/7 Teacher, Solomon	hd	m	39	jeweller	Bavaria
Pe5/8 Teacher, Maria	wf	m	36		Penzance
Pe5/9 Teacher, Annah	da		1		Penzance
(Caday, Jane sv 16)					

(Ho 107/1918) North Street, East Side, Penzance

Pe5/10 Ezekiel, Solomon	hd	m	69	tin plate worker	Newton Abbot
Pe5/11 Ezekiel, Hannah	wf	m	75		Redruth

(Ho 107/1918) Market Place, Penzance

Pe5/12 Joseph, Henry	hd	m	44	pawnbrk & outfitter	Falmouth
Pe5/13 Joseph, Amelia	wf	m	39	pawnbroker's wife	Cambourne
Pe5/14 Joseph, Hannah	mo	wd	80	widow of pawnbrkr	Falmouth
Pe5/15 Joseph, Selina	da		15	scholar	Penzance
Pe5/16 Joseph, Rose	da		13	scholar	Penzance
Pe5/17 Joseph, Lionel	so		11	scholar	Penzance
Pe5/18 Joseph, Morris	so		9	scholar	Penzance
Pe5/19 Joseph, Esther	da		8	scholar	Penzance
Pe5/20 Joseph, Jos	so		5	scholar	Penzance
Pe5/21 Joseph, Kate	da		3	scholar at home	Penzance
Pe5/22 Joseph, Betsey	da		2	scholar at home	Penzance

[1] From: *The Decennial Census* by Bernard Susser, privately published, 1995. Reproduced here by kind permission of Mrs Susser and Hanna Yaffe.

[2] Susser's analysis of the 1851 census returns would appear not to be complete. For example, the families of Samuel Oppenheim and Henry Levin are not included even though they lived in the town at this time.

[3] The spelling today is *Leskinnick*.

316

Pe5/23 Simmons, Sarah   28   domestic asst   Penzance
                                      'servant' superimposed
Pe5/24 Simmons, Simon   15   shop assistant   Penzance
    (Birch, Elizabeth 17 child's maid; Uren, Nanny, house maid)

(HO 107/1918) Temperance Hotel, Princess Street, Penzance
Pe5/25 Marks, Joseph   lo   m   47   com trav   Portsea

(HO 107/1918) North Street, Penzance
Pe5/26 Selig, Benjn Aaron hd m   37   watchmaker   Penzance
Pe5/27 Selig, Catherine   wf   m   31   Penzance
Pe5/28 Selig, Aaron   so   1   Penzance
Pe5/29 Selig, Lemon   so   4 months   Penzance
Pe/30 Jacobs, Phoebe   sl   u   23   pawnbroker's asst   Penzance
    (Hall, Jane 21 house servant)

Falmouth Census 1851

Census date: 30 March 1851

(HO 107/1911) 51 Killigrew Street, Falmouth
F5/1 Herman, Samuel   hd   m   49   Rabbi of Heb Cong   Poland, Russia, Konin
F5/2 Herman, Frances   wf   m   51   Neustadt
F5/3 Herman, Abraham   so   u   23   bookbinder   Poland, Russia, Konin
F5/4 Herman, Rose   da   u   20   Poland, Russia, Konin
F5/5 Herman, Phoebe   da   u   10   scholar   Poland, Russia, Babiak
F5/6 Silverstone, Simeon   vs   u   25   stationery trav   Poland, Austria, Cracow

(HO 107/1911) 146 Porham Street, Falmouth
F5/7 Davidson, Grace   hd   u   56   Milliner   Kent, Sheerness

(HO 107/1911) 209 Fish Strand, Falmouth
F5/8 Simmons, Solomon   lg   m   73   pedlar   Truro

(HO 107/1911) Market Street, Falmouth
F5/9 Jacob, Moss J.   hd   m   38   pawnbroker/tailor   Cambourne
                                 * 3 men 5 women
F5/10 Jacob, Francis   wf   m   39   Portsmouth
F5/11 Jacob, Hannah   da   11   scholar   Falmouth
F5/12 Jacob, Michael   so   10   scholar   Falmouth
F5/13 Jacob, Alexander   so   9   scholar   Falmouth
F5/14 Jacob, Laurance   so   7   scholar   Falmouth

F5/15 Jacob, Sarah K.	da		1	scholar	Falmouth
F5/16 Joseph, Moses			25	shop assistant	Devonport
(Kelly, Constance		u	26	house servant	Penzance
Perry, Rosina		u	18	childs maid	Givennafe
Crocher, Elizabeth		u	35	house servant	Hendron)

(HO 107/1911) Market Strand, Falmouth

F5/17 Aarons, Morris		u	34	traveller	London
F5/18 De Costa, A. G.		m	33	traveller	London

(HO 107/1911) Porhan Lane, Falmouth

F5/19 Moses, Henry	hd	m	47	hawker	Falmouth
F5/20 Moses, Joannah	wf	m	39		Hayle
F5/21 Moses, Phillip	so		9	scholar	Falmouth
F5/22 Moses, Elizabeth	da		7	scholar	Falmouth
F/5 23 Moses, John	so		5	scholar	Falmouth
F5/24 Moses, Thomas	so		3	scholar	Falmouth
F5/25 Moses, Joseph	so		1	scholar	Falmouth

(Martin, Eliza sv 15 servant Cornwall)
(The Moses family share their house with a mason)

(HO 197/1911) 14 Killigrew Street, Falmouth

F5/26 Cohen, Rose	hd	m	47	pedlar's wife	Falmouth
F5/27 Cohen, Hannah	da		14	milliner's apprt	Penzance
F5/28 Cohen, Sarah	da		13	scholar	Penzance
F5/29 Cohen, Phoebe	da		12	scholar	Falmouth
F5/30 Cohen, Josiah	so		10	scholar	Plymouth

APPENDIX 5

CONDOLENCE

A LETTER

FOR CONDOLE VID

LE REV. MONSIEUR LE GRICE

Cure of Sancta Maria, dan Penzance

BECAUSE OF DE

J E W L E T T E R

FROM

RABBI HART SIMONDS
****

BY J.J. ROUSEAU

Maitre de Dance, a present malade a Penzance

****

Penzance:

Printed and Sold by G. Glanvill,
Stationer, Bookbinder, &c.
Greenmarket

1824.

Price One Penny.

Eh, monsieur, I have de grand plaisir of condole vid you, because of dat rascallion of a Jew, who vas write a book for you as Cure of Penzance. Ah, mauvais, mauvais, de Jew Monsiuer Simonds, he write you in Hebrew! O de great brigand to address mon Praeter in de language of etranger. Monsieur, he be one grand bigot among de Juifs of dis country. He say in dis book of his, dat "you so bad as de Jews." O de negre! suppose he on my plantation at Guadeloupe, ah, I flog, flog, flog, vid de slave vip, till he cry peccavi. Monsieur, I have de great concern for you, though I belong not to dis country.

Ven I come to Penzance, for to teach de dance of my nation, de people say, Mr. Francois go to de Cure, for he be one Frenchman, and I ask you name – de people say "Le" – Ho! den, my heart leap about in my body, and I sing vive Henri quatre vid joy; for I say sans doute, Monsieur Cure be mon countryman. – Eh bien Monsieur, tene I vas going for certain to you Tuilleries, ven de rogue of de Jew book have met me in you market pour cabbage dan Penzance. Parbleu I cry, vat is dat! Monsieur Praeter of de Palais Royal, a Treive? "le demand," I cried to de bookman, – "le demand you insolence for print de Jew book." he bow, "Monsieur voulez vous have de Rabbi letter." I nod my head, and say, restee tranquil une petite moment, Mr. bookman. I read "that Mr. Le G. himself has broken the command, and that his works are not perfect." O de rogue, I cry, O de Jew, he be boco boco villian, for abuse vid de great assurance, of Marat himself, mon countryman. I have difficile pour comprehend, but I read again. "Now allow me to ask you, Sir, what good deeds do you perform." Ah, rascal of de Jew, pour ask such question – I wou'd send him a horse, Monsieur, to run away vid him. Transport de brigand to Patagonia for his calumby. I read again "if each day bring forth leaping and dancing, so that he at last forgets his latter days, his dependence is only on a rotten foundation." I jump up on de counter of de bookman vid de great furor, and cry, Rogue Jew! rogue Jew! vat he libel mon grand profession – he tell de Cure mon brave countryman, suppose he dance, he have une rotten foundation pour dance on. – O monsieur bookman vere have you de Bastile vere de house of Monsieur le grand Inquisitor. – I vill go in petit moment vid de book, and Mr. Jew vill have de dungeon of de Inquisition, for his mauvais Jew tricks.

Eh bien, say de bookman, ve have no Bastile, no Inquisition dan Penzance. O miserable! miserable! pour mon cher ami et countryman in de jardin of de Tuillere a Treive, de rogue jew print de book and no grand prison, mauvais Angletterre!

I read vonce more de Jew book, and I come to de part of de "drunkeness, revellings, and such like," and den he say to Monsieur, pray how can you boast of righteousness?" I have such great anger dat I strike de board vid my boulogne kane – I tear de Jew book and give de bits to de vind – I take une grand jump from de bookshop, and ven I come on my foot again, I have to lose de balance, ou de centre of gravity, dat I fall forward, and nock down une poor voman, and de table de cabbage vid house for to keep vay de rain; so by dis great accidens, I have de great bruise all over my body, dat I have been lay two days in de bed at Monsieur James house, de duc de Cumberland, in de North Street: so you see Monsieur, mon bon countryman, I have my dancing spoil, and cannot come to you jardin of delight; but de Docteur de Physic, of Rue de Chapelle, say to me, to day, you have stop de Jew book and de printer sell no more. – O dis give me such grand plaiser dat I almost dance de carmagnole in mon bed. You will now rest tranquil Monsieur in you jardin de plant, and ven you sortee pour le promenade to le grand ville de Penzance, voulez vous do me great honeur to entre mon maison de public. and demand dat Monsieur James, as une grand maitre de ceremone, conduct you to mon chambre, ven I vill have de great honeur pour receive you visit, and display de bocoup vound I have get in defence of mon bon countryman Monsieur le Cure of Penzance, dan le province le Cornvalle, dan le empire of grand Britaigne. As une prince of my profession, receive Monseigneur, de assurance of mon distinguish consideration.

> Jean Jaques Rousseau,
> Citizen dan le Paris,
> et member le legion de honeur, late
> Capitaine de Cuirassair de grand
> army of le Empereur Napo-
> leon, le grand, et Citizen of
> Hayti, a present le
> Voyageur dans
> Penzance.

March 15th, 1824.

G. Glanvill, Printer, Penzance

BIBLIOGRAPHY

Helen Fry

Unpublished
Archives of Allied Domecq
Archives of the Board of Deputies of British Jews
Archives of the Chief Rabbinate, The Metropolitan Library, London
County Record Office, Truro
Archive and personal papers of Eric Dawkins
Archive and personal papers of H.C. Faulkner
Archive and personal papers of Alex Jacob
Merchant Shipping Registers, Penzance 1786–1823, County Record Office, Truro
Archive and personal papers of Tony Pawlyn
Public Record Office, Kew
Cecil Roth Collection, Brotherton Library, the University of Leeds
Royal Institution of Cornwall Library, Truro
Archive and personal papers of Godfrey Simmons
Archive of Bernard Susser, The Metropolitan Library, London

Primary Sources

The Cornishman
The Cornish Advertiser
The Cornish Echo
The Cornish Telegraph
The Cornubian
The Daily Telegraph
The Dorset Sherborne Mercury
Falmouth Packet
The Jewish Chronicle
Jewish World
Journals and Account Books of William Borlase (Courtney Library, RIC Truro)
Royal Cornwall Gazette
The Times
West Briton
Western Flying Post
Western Morning News

322

Secondary Sources

Journals

Israel Abrahams, "Joachim Gause: A Mining Incident in the Reign of Queen Elizabeth", in *The Transactions of the Jewish Historical Society of England (TJHSE)*, vol 4, 1889

J. Bannister, "Jews in Cornwall", in *The Journal of The Royal Institution of Cornwall (JRIC)*, vol II, 1867

G.T. Clark, *Report on the Sanitary Condition of Penzance*, HMSO, 1849

J.S. Courtney, "Chronological Memoranda", in the *7th Annual Report to the Royal Polytechnic Society of Cornwall*, 1839, Courtney Library, RIC, Truro

Alfred Dunitz, "The Rise and Decline of Jewish Communities in Georgian England", in *Le'ela*, September 1993

Anthony P. Joseph, "Genealogy and Jewish History", *TJHSE*, vol 34, 1994–6

Anthony P. Joseph, "Jewry of the South-West and some of its Australian Connections", in *TJHSE*, vol 24, 1970–73, pub. 1975

Norman Nail, "The Cornish Curator and the Cosmopolitan Collector", in *JRIC* (New Series II), vol 1, pt. 3, 1993

R. Morton Nance, "When was Cornish last Spoken Traditionally?", in *JRIC*, vol 7, 1973

Francis Rodd, on the finding of a "Jews House", in the *Annual Report of the Royal Institution of Cornwall*, 1850 (Courtney Library, RIC, Truro)

Cecil Roth, "Jew's Houses", in *Antiquity*, vol XXV, June 1951

John Rowe and C.T. Andrews, "Cholera in Cornwall," in *The Journal of the RIC*, vol 7, part 2, 1974

William Schonfield, "The Josephs of Cornwall" (1938: unpublished)

Bernard Susser, "When Jews Worshipped in Penzance", in *The Cornishman*, 16th July 1964

C. Thomas, "Cornish Volunteers in the Eighteenth Century", in *Devon and Cornwall Notes and Queries*, vol. XXVIII, 1959

Books

Juliet Barker, *The Brontës* (London: Phoenix, 1995)

R.M. Barton, ed., *Life in Cornwall in Mid/Late/at End of the Nineteenth Century* (Truro: D. Bradford Barton, vols 1971, 1972 & 1974)

William Borlase, *Natural History of Cornwall (1758)* (London: E and W Books Ltd, 1970)

Mrs. Bray, *The Borders of the Tamar and the Tavy* (London, 1838)

H. Miles Brown, *Cornish Clocks and Clockmakers* (Newton Abbot: David and Charles, 2nd. Edition, 1970); ref. 1769 and 1790/1

William Camden, *Britannia* (London: Edmund Gibson, 1695 ed)

Richard Carew, *Survey of Cornwall (1602)* ed. F.E. Halliday (London: Andrew Melrose, 1953)

Bibliotheca Cornubiensis (Boase & Courtney) Vols i (1874) & ii (1878)

Collectanea Cornubiensa (Boase: 1890). (Courtney Library, RIC Truro)

H.R. Coulthard, *The story of an Ancient Parish – Breage with Germoe* (Camborne Printing & Stationery Co, Ltd, 1913)

J.S. Courtney, *Guide to Penzance* (London: E. Rowe, Longman, Brown, Green, 1845)

Tony Deane and Tony Shaw, *The Folklore of Cornwall* (London: Batsford, 1975)

N. Denholm-Young, *Richard of Cornwall* (Oxford: Blackwell, 1947)

H.L. Douch, *Old Cornish Inns* (Truro: D. Bradford Barton, 1966, 1st ed)

D.C. Duschinsky, *The Rabbinate of the Great Synagogue, London, 1756–1842* (London, 1921)

Richard Edmonds, *The Land's End District* (London: J. Russel Smith, 1862)

Eilert Ekwall, *The Concise Oxford Dictionary of English Place-names* (Oxford, 1960)

Peter Berresford Ellis, *The Cornish Language and its Literature* (London, 1974)

Susan E. Gay & Mrs. Howard Fox, *The Register of Baptisms, Marriages and Burials of the Parish of Falmouth 1663–1812* (Exeter: Devon and Cornwall Record Society, 1914)

C.S. Gilbert, *Survey of Cornwall* (Plymouth Dock: J. Congdon, 1817, vol I)

D. Gilbert, *The Parochial History of Cornwall* (London: J.B. Nicholls and son, 1838)

Geoffrey L. Green, *The Royal Navy and Anglo-Jewry, 1740–1820* (London: 1989)

G.V. le Grice, *Pamphlets Published in 1824*, no 24, Morrab Library, Penzance.

J. Hatcher, *English Tin Production and Trade before 1550* (Oxford: Clarendon Press, 1973)

Henry Hawkins, "The Jews in Cornwall", in *Through West Cornwall with a Camera* (London: Thomas Mitchell, circa 1897)

Charles Henderson, *Essays in Cornish History* (Oxford: Clarendon Press, 1935)

History of the Jewish Wars (Whiston's Josephus: London, 1811)

History of the Worthies of England (London: F.C. and J. Rivington, 1811)

R. Hunt, *British Mining* (London: Crosby Lockwood, 1884)

Robert Hunt, *Popular Romances of the West of England* (London: 1871)

A.R. Hyamson, *A History of the Jews of England* (London: Chatto and Windus, 1908)

A.K. Hamilton Jenkin, *The Cornish Miner* (London, 1927)

Sharman Kadish (ed.), *Building Jerusalem: Jewish Architecture in Britain* (London: Vallentine Mitchell, 1996)

Richard Larn, *Cornish Shipwrecks, the Isles of Scilly* (Newton Abbot: David & Charles, 1971)

G.R. Lewis, *The Stannaries* (Truro: D. Bradford Barton Ltd, 1908, reprinted 1965)

G.R. Lewis and G. Randall, *The Stannaries* (Cambridge: The Riverside Press, 1908)

G.R. Lewis, *The Victoria County History of Cornwall* (London: James Street, 1906)

V.D. Lipman (ed.), *Three Centuries of Anglo-Jewish History* (London, 1961)

David S. Lysons, *Magno Britannia* (London: Caddell and Davies, 1814, vol. III)

Frank Mitchell, *Annals of an Ancient Cornish Town; Dyllanson Truran, Trewolsta Trewergie, Redruth* (1946, 2nd ed. 2nd imp. 1985)

Friedrich Max Müller, 'Are there Jews in Cornwall?', *Chips from a German Workshop* (London, 1867)

Betty Naggar, *Jewish Pedlars and Hawkers 1740–1940* (Porphyrogenitus, 1992)

Venetia Newall, *The Encyclopedia of Witchcraft and Magic* (London, 1974)

C.T. Onions, ed., *Oxford Dictionary of English Etymology* (Oxford: Clarendon, 1966)

J.G. Osborne, *History of Freemasonry in West Cornwall* (Penzance: Rodda, 1901)

O.J. Padel, *Cornish Place Names* (Penzance: A. Hodge, 1988)

O.J. Padel, *Cornish Place Names Elements* (Nottingham: English Place Name Society, 1985)

Philip Payton, *The Cornish Overseas* (Alexander Associates: Fowey, 1999)

R.D. Penhallurick, *Tin in Antiquity* (London: Institute of Metals, 1986)

J. Picciotto, *Sketches of Anglo-Jewish History* (London, 1875)

R. Polwhele, *History of Cornwall* (London: Caddell and Davies; Law and Whitaker, 1808, vol III)

Peter Pool, *The Branwells of Penzance* (Penzance: Penlee House Museum, 1990)

Peter Pool, *History of Penzance* (Penzance: Penzance Town Corporation, 1974)

H.G. Richardson, *The English Jewry Under the Angevin Kings* (London: Methuen, 1960)

Cecil Roth, *A History of the Jews in England* (Oxford: Clarendon Press, 1964)

Cecil Roth, *The Rise of Provincial Jewry* (London, 1950)

Cecil Roth, *History of the Great Synagogue* (London, 1950)

Alfred Rubens, *A History of Jewish Costume* (London, 1973)

V. Russell, *West Penwith Survey* (Truro: Cornwall Archaeological Society, 1971)

Judith Samuel, *Jews in Bristol: The History of the Jewish Community in Bristol from the Middle Ages to the Present Day* (Bristol: Redcliffe Press 1997)

David Samuelson et al, *Bertie, the Life and Times of G.B. Samuelson* (currently in preparation for publication)

Saundry, *One and All Almanac* (Penzance: 1933 & 1935; Courtney Library, RIC)

Sharron Schwartz and Roger Parker, *Lanner: a Cornish Mining Parish* (Tiverton: Halsgrove 1998)

Israel Solomon, *Records of My Family* (New York: Stettiner, Lombert and Co, 1887)

John Stow, *A General Chronicle of England* (London: 1631)

Bernard Susser, *The Decennial Census* (Privately published, 1995)

Bernard Susser, *The Jews of South-West England* (Exeter: The University of Exeter Press, 1993)

Bernard Susser, *An Account of the Old Jewish Cemetery on Plymouth Hoe* (Privately published, 1972)

Charles Swainson, *The Folklore and Provincial Names of British Birds* (London, 1885)

Thomas, *History of Mount's Bay* (Penzance: J. Thomas, 1820; Courtney Library, RIC)

R. Thomas, *History and Description of the Town & Harbour of Falmouth* (Falmouth, 1828)

James Trathen, *The Ancient and Modern History of Falmouth* (Falmouth, 1815)

E.S. Tregoning, *History of Falmouth and its Vicinity* (Falmouth, 1865)

Joseph Wright, ed., *The English Dialect Dictionary* (London, 1902)

Note: For copies of Anthony P. Joseph's (1975) article referred to in this bibliography, containing detailed genealogies of the Jews of Cornwall, enquiries should be addressed to The Jewish Historical Society of England, 33 Seymour Place, London W1H 5AP.

GLOSSARY

Archa	Official storage-box for Jewish deeds
Ashkenazim	Jews originating from central and eastern Europe
Arban kanfot	A prayer shawl worn under outer clothing
Bimah	Reading desk in the synagogue
Bar mitzvah	A boy's entry into adulthood at thirteen years
Chazan	A cantor
Dayan	A judge in matters of Jewish law
Gabbai	Treasurer
Kosher	Food prepared according to Jewish law
Marranos	Jews who had converted to Catholicism during the Inquisition but who continued secretly to practise their Judaism. Mainly in Spain and Portugal
Mikveh	A bath for ritual immersion
Mohel	Performs ritual circumcision
Parnas	President
Sedrah	The prescribed weekly reading from the Torah
Sephardim	Jews originating from the Mediterranean coastal regions, including North Africa, often of Spanish or Portuguese descent
Sefer (pl Sifre) Torah	Parchment Scroll of the Torah
Shochet	Ritual slaughterer
Takkanot, or Tikkunim	Congregational regulations
Talmud	The written traditions of Jewish oral law, used especially in study of Rabbinic teachings
Tallit	A fringed prayer shawl
Tefillin	Prayer boxes, attached to the forehead and left forearm
Torah, or Pentateuch	The first five books of the Hebrew Bible

LIST OF ILLUSTRATIONS

Advertisement for T Solomon, general contractor, Truro 1873   12
Advertisement for S. Jacob, jeweller, Falmouth 1875   12
Lanlivery-Bodwen figurine   27
Falmouth High Street, c.1904   60
Falmouth Church Street, c.1910   60
Maps of Falmouth and Penryn   62
Map of Penzance   74
The Jewish Cemetery, Falmouth   106
Alexander Moses headstone   107
Barnet Levy headstone   107
Hart Elias headstone   118
Lewis Falkson headstone   118
Portrait of Sarah Kate Simons of Falmouth   125
Portrait of Jacob Jacob of Falmouth   126
The Jewish Cemetery, Penzance   134
Elizabeth and Samuel Oppenheim headstones   137
Hannah and Aaron Selig headstones   140
Jacob James Hart headstone   146
Joseph Rintel, Rabbi of Falmouth   163
– birth certificate, Hamburg   164
– travel pass   165
– naturalisation papers   166
Rabbi B.A. Simmons, letter of introduction from Lemon Hart   172
– reports from Chief Rabbis Hirsch and Adler   177
– presentation gift on leaving Penzance in 1854   180
– portrait   182
– headstone   183
Flora Simmons headstone   183
– portrait   183
Rachel and Isaac Bischofswerder, c.1880   187
Amy Bischofswerder, grandchild, with friend   188
Rabbi Michael and Esther Leinkram, c.1910   192
Family tree: Moses, Levy, Jacob & Solomon of Falmouth   206
Great Condurrow Mine, Camborne   209
Swan Poole Mine, Falmouth: Jacob family interest   209
Alexander Jacob with Cornish miners, c.1859   210
Falmouth: High Street fire, 1862 and Market Street fire, 1870   219
Family tree: Hart family (with some Woolf & Jacob connections)   231

Lemon Hart portrait 232

   – headstone in Brady Street Jewish Cemetery, London 232

Oppenheim's advertising board, Penzance c.1890 239

Levin's upholstery store c.1880 239

Henry Levin receipt, 1852 240

Oppenheim advertisements 241–243

Israel Levin, jeweller's shop, Penzance 247

Market Jew Street, c.1890, with Oppenheim's store 247

Israel Levin advertisement, 1878 248

Rabbi Isaac Bischofswerder and family 248

Moses Jacob of Redruth headstone 264

Clock by Moses Jacob 264

Family tree: Josephs of Cornwall 273

Former Falmouth synagogue in 1998 294

Former Penzance synagogue in 1999 297

   – the interior 297

   – two decalogue tablets of the Torah 299

   – Hebrew inscription on panel 299

Falmouth synagogue: torah scroll 303

   – rimmonim (torah scroll adornments) 304

   – early nineteenth-century torah pointer 304

INDEX

Keith Pearce

Dates and locations have been given in order to help the reader distinguish between individuals with similar or identical names. Those buried in the two Jewish cemeteries are also indicated by the referencing used in chapter five. Where known the original family surname of women is given as well as their married surname. Page references are not given for all of the names found in the appendices, which contain some names not listed in the index. Page numbers may refer either to the main text or to its footnotes. Names are not referenced in footnotes on every occasion that they appear. Whilst care has been taken to identify dates accurately, certainty is not always possible, and there may be occasional discrepancies between sources. Hopefully, readers will find that this index also serves as a general, if not definitive, genealogical guide

Aaron, "of Cornwall" (arrested Uxbridge 1244) 39

Aaron of Lincoln (d. 1186) 31

Aaron, Rabbi (of Penzance, c. 1808/9: may be identical with Selig, below) 75, 169

Aaron, "*praedictus Judeus*" (see Deudone & Simon de Dena) 39

Aaron, Abraham (of Falmouth, c. 1846: may be same as below) 213, 252

Aaron, Abraham (of Truro, c. 1830) 213, 252, 260, 261

Aaron, Rose (or Rosa; Simmons, of Falmouth; married M.B. Simmons 1846) 252, 314

Aaron of York (13th. cent. CE) 31

Aarons, Morris (b. 1817, of London; Falmouth 1851) 318

Abecasis, Moses (of Malta, c. early 1800s) 275

Abelson, Abel (ref. Penzance, c. 1869–70) 254

Abenheim, Henry (of Stuttgart, c. 1870) 288–9

Abenheim, Barnet (b. 1875) 289

Abenheim, Bessy (b. 1871) 289

Abenheim, Lina (b. 1878) 289

Abenheim, Rivka (b. 1881) 289

Abraham of Berkhamsted (c. 1250–65) 14, 15, 31, 37, 38

Abraham of Felmingham (12th. cent. CE) 32

Abraham the Tinner (c. 1342–58) 32, 38, 39

Abraham, Isabella (Lemon, of Penryn; b. 1840) 215

Abraham, John G. (of Penryn, b. 1859) 215

Abraham (Jonson &; St. Austell, c. 1844; later in Falmouth) 268

Abraham, Joseph (of Penryn, b. 1837) 215

Abraham, Sarah (of Falmouth, c. 1815–30) 213

Abraham (Webb &; Liskeard, c. 1823) 268

Abraham, William M. (of Falmouth, b. 1860) 215

Abrahams, Aaron (Lostwithiel, c. 1821; later in Plymouth) 269

Abrahams, Betsy (b. Callington, 1799; wife of Abraham Abrahams) 268

Abrahams, Gabriel "George" (of Falmouth, b. Germany 1763, d. 1831) 198, 204, 212

Abrahams, Israel (1889) 39

Abrahams, Jane Lovely (Symons, m. 1819) 212

Abrahams, Sam (of Falmouth, c. 1889) 215, 220, 221

Abrahams, L.J. (of London, c. 1798) 170

Adler, Dr. Nathan Marcus (1803–90), Chief Rabbi from 1842. 59, 68, 82, 167, 178

Agar, Mrs. (Truro, c. 1840) 155

St. Agnes 267

A.H.H. (infant, Fal. 3:1; d. 1846/7) 114

Alexander, son of Samuel, of Truro (ref. Plymouth, c. 1815–22) 258

Alexander, son of Zvi (Fal. 1:7; d. 1804) 110

Altstadter (Hart), Abraham (d. circa 1710–1720) 222, 231

Altstadter (Hart), Asher (d. before 1682) 222, 231

Altstadter (Hart), Asher (d. circa 1745–1752) 94, 169, 222, 231

Amelia (ship) 233

Amos, Samuel (of Evesham, m. Louise Hart 1832) 235

Amsterdam 65

Anglicization 200, 201

Ansell, Mr. (of London, 1828) 78

Archae 30

Arthur, King (c. 6th. cent. CE) 17

Arundell Family 33

Asher, "the unmarried" (Penzance 1808) 88

Asser, Emanuel (Falmouth 1861; b. 1806) 216

Attall Sarazin 22

Athelstan, King (925–940) 22

St. Austell 54, 66, 76, 170, 218, 267, 268, 285

Banfield, Richard (St. Ives, c. 1805) 233

Barbados 65

Barham, Rev. Thomas Foster (1766–1844, of Exeter) 131

Barham, Thomas Foster (son, 1794–1869) 81, 93, 131, 132
Bar Kochba Rising (135 CE) 36
Barnes, Levy (Falmouth, c. 1799) 211
Barnet, Joseph (of St. Ives: Pz. 8:2; d. 1856) 80, 97, 133, 153, 246
Baroness (ship) 208
Barons' Wars (1264: reign of Henry III) 31
Barrow, Joseph (of Jamaica, 1815) 78
Basley, William (of Padstow, c. 1790) 226, 227
Bassett Estate/Family of Tehidy 102, 269
Bassett, Sir Francis of Tehidy (1757–1835: Lord de Dunstanville, from 1796) 55, 68, 71, 102
Bassett, Susan (of Falmouth; ref. David & Mary Hart, in London, 1861) 234
Bath 57, 276
Batten, Mayor J. Jnr. (Penzance, c. 1790) 226
Beadle (Penzance) 75
Beer, Barnard or Bernard (Barnet(t) Levy or Jewell) 52, 54, 55, 64, 71, 103, 109–111, 135, 205, 207, 211, 267, 274, 279–282
Beer, Joseph (Liskeard, c. 1830) 268
Behrends, Israel (Israel Solomon, Aaron Levi Segal ; from Erhenbreitstein, c. 1727–1802; Fal. 2:1) 111, 206, 282, 283
Behrends, Israel (Israel Solomon, b. 1803; d. New York; ref. Ch. 8) 51, 52, 70, 110, 170, 205, 206, 207, 279–291
Beirnstein, Aaron Harris Mark (of Dowlais; m. Penzance 1869, b. 1848) 80, 185, 254
Beirnstein, Abraham (of S. Wales, c. 1869: father of above) 254
Beirnstein, Esther (daughter of Henry Joseph of Penzance: see Pz. 6:5; m. 1869, b. 1843) 150, 185, 254, 316
Belerion 18, 19
Belfast 193
Belgravia St. (Penzance) 186
Bengal, Famine Relief Fund (ref. Penzance 1874) 81, 93
Benjamin, Deborah Giteleh (Fal. 1:1; d. 1794) 58, 108
Benjamin, Isaac (ref. visiting St. Ives, 1772) 270
Benjamin of Tudela (12th cent. CE) 34
Benjamin, Wolf (Isaac Menasseh, Fal. 1:2; d. 1790) 58, 103, 108, 270, 271
Benjamin, Zipporah (later Levy; of Plymouth (1784–1861): see Fal. 1:4) 109
Berenger (& Schwerer: various dates and locations) 214, 249, 260, 266
Bickford, R. Scott (Penryn/Budock, c. 1770) 102
Bing, I.I. (of London, c. 1798) 170
Birch, Elizabeth (see Pz. 6:5; b. 1834; Penzance 1851) 150, 317
Birmingham 61, 194
Bischofswerder, Amy (photo) 188
Bischofswerder, Augusta (b. 1862) 185
Bischofswerder, David (b. 1854; see Pz. 6:3 & 7:4) 84, 85, 94, 185, 193, 249, 254
Bischofswerder, David Harry (infant, d. 1881) 193
Bischofswerder, Emma (Hawke, m. 1892; b. 1865) 98, 191, 193, 254
Bischofswerder, George (ref. Penzance marriage 1892) 254

Bischofswerder, H. 254
Bischofswerder, Harry (b. circa 1876; bar mitzvah 1889) 98, 193
Bischofswerder, Harry (Henry: b. 1885) 193
Bischofswerder, Harry (b. 1892) 193
Bischofswerder, Harry (c. 1887–91; later in Birmingham) 193, 194, 204
Bischofswerder, Helena (see: Pz. 6:3 & 7:4) 193
Bischofswerder, Henrietta (Yette Pearlson; b. circa 1850–5 ; m. 1876) 185, 189, 254
Bischofswerder, Isaac (Pz. 8:3; 1822–1899; Rabbi of Penzance from 1860s to 1886) 84, 94, 133, 153, 158, 184–189, 193, 194, 249, 254
Bischofswerder, Julia (Yittel Joseph: Pz. 7:6; 1851–1911; m. 1884) 99, 150, 152, 189, 193, 194, 254
Bischofswerder, Marcus (b. 1852/3) 185, 189, 193, 254 (or brother below)
Bischofswerder, Marks (Mark(c)us: b. 1858) 98, 185, 191, 193, 254 (marriage of)
Bischofswerder, Michael (b. 1899) 189
Bischofswerder, Millie (Malka, infant: Pz. 6:3; d. 1880) 149, 193
Bischofswerder, Morris (Moses, b. 1856; m. 1884) 85, 90, 99, 185, 189, 193, 194, 249, 254, 298
Bischofswerder, Rachel (Rahle Weile, daughter of Mann: Pz. 7:3; 1831–1886) 151, 185
Bischofswerder, Saby (b. 1860) 185
Bischofswerder, Sarah (b. 1864) 185, 189, 193
Bischofswerder, Sarah Cicilia (Tsilla or Zilla; child: Pz. 7:4; d. 1891) 151, 152, 193
Black Death (1348–1351) 33
Board of Deputies of British Jews 100, 104, 156
Bodener, William (of Mousehole, d. 1789) 40
Bodmin 66, 268
Bodmin Manumissions 21
Bodwen figurine 27, 28
Bolitho Family (of Penzance) 91, 255, 256
Borlase, Mary (d. 1822) 131, 132
Borlase, Samuel (Penzance, c. 1781) 238
Borlase, Walter (c. 1810) 131
Borlase, William Rev. (c. 1756–1772) 19, 26, 94, 95, 223
von Bosch, Max (ref. Falmouth 1913) 104
Boulton and Watt (ref. Murdoch, Redruth) 262
Bradley, Francis (St. Michael's Mount, Marazion: c. 1781) 238
Brady Street Jewish Cemetery (London) 236
Branwell Family (of Penzance) 68, 89–90, 131, 175, 255, 256, 269, 295
Branwell, Anne (Carne: 1743–1809, Maria's mother) 255
Branwell, Benjamin Carne (1775–1818) 255, 256
Branwell, Joseph (b. 1748:) 89, 91, 233
Branwell, Joseph (1789–1857) 89
Branwell, Maria (Bronte: 1783–1821) 256
Branwell, Richard (1744–1812: uncle of Maria) 255
Branwell, Richard (1771–1815: cousin to Maria) 255
Branwell Sutherland (c. 1768) 89
Branwell, Temperance (Matthews, c. 1807–18) 90
Branwell, Thomas (1746–1808: Maria's father) 225, 244, 255, 256
Branwell, Thomas (b. 1801; grandson of above) 255
Breslau 216

Brighton 236
Bristo, Johanna (Moses, née Richards, b. c. 1811: of Budock, formerly of Hayle) 199, 215, 217, 267, 318
Bristol 61, 73, 274
British Columbia 61, 220
Brontë family and sisters 256
Brontë, Patrick (1777–1861) 256
Bryant, William (St. Ives, c. 1805) 233
Budock (Parish) 199
Burgh, Hubert de (d. 1243; regent 1219–32) 29

Caday, Jane (b. 1835; Penzance, c. 1851) 246, 316
Cadiz 275
California 61, 220
Callington 268
Camden, William (1551–1623: *Britannia*: 1586) 25, 42, 43
Camelford 216
Carew, Richard (1555–1620: *Survey*: 1602) 22, 26, 33, 42, 43, 48
Carne, Anne (Branwell, 1743–1809) 255
Camborne 54, 267
Cawsand 269
Cemeteries: Falmouth: 55, 63, 101–129, 269. Penzance: 78, 92, 97, 130–154, 218 Truro: 155–157
Chaluz 25
Chard, Alderman A.W. JP. (ref. Falmouth 1913) 104
Charitable donations 81, 93, 266
Chiwidden 44, 45
Cholera epidemics 45, 150–151, 218–220
Chrysostom, St. John (c.350–407) 21
Cock, Emily (Lazarus, m. 1861) 203, 253
Cock, Thomas (father of above) 253
Cohen, Alexander (of London, c. 1810) 275
Cohen, Betsy (ref. 1791 baptism, Falmouth) 59, 198
Cohen, Emanuel (Redruth, 1766–1849) 77, 266
Cohen, Emanuel (father ? of above) 270
Cohen, Hannah (Falmouth; b. 1837, Penzance) 214, 318
Cohen, Josiah (Falmouth; b. 1841, Plymouth) 214, 318
Cohen, Kate (or Kitty Joseph, daughter of Lyon & Judith Joseph) 274
Cohen, Moses (ref. 1791 baptism, Falmouth) 59, 198
Cohen, Moses (of London, m. Kate Joseph of Falmouth) 274
Cohen, Phoebe (b. 1839, Falmouth) 214, 318
Cohen, Rose (b. 1804, Falmouth) 198, 199, 214, 215, 318
Cohen, Sarah (Falmouth; b. 1838, Penzance) 214, 318
Cohen, Schemeya (of Lisbon, c. 1819) 283, 285
Cohen, Solomon (Rabbi of Penzance 1854–1857) 83, 179, 195
Cohen, William (b. 1783; ref. 1791 baptism, Falmouth) 59, 198
Colenso, Mr. (Penzance, 1848) 81
Colenso, William (ref. J. Thomas' *History of Mount's Bay*, 1820 & 1831) 89
Colyer-Fergusson, Sir Thomas (genealogist: 1866–1951) 73, 222, 225, 231, 234, 270
Comitissa (13th. cent CE) 31

Congregational: Minister (Foxell, of Penzance) 131. Cemetery (Falmouth) 101, 102
Constantine, Emperor (306–337 CE) 21
Conversion (& marriage) 198–203
Conveyances (& minute books, Penzance) 88–94
Coombe v. Woolf 238
Corbett, Captain William (of sloop *Mary*, 1790) 226
Corin, James 65
Cork 226, 275
Cornish, Mayor Jas. (James, Falmouth c. 1830) 161
Cornish, Henry (Penzance 1860: may be same as below) 179, 180
Cornish, Mr. (Penzance, 1875) 93
Cornish, Mr. (Redruth, c. 1782–4) 263
Costa, A. (ref. Falmouth 1913) 104
de Costa, A.G. b. 1818, of London; Falmouth 1851) 318
Coulson, Alderman (Penzance 1875) 93
Coulson's *Directory* (1864) 245
Coulthard (1913) 48
Courtney, J.S. (*Guide to Penzance*, etc. 1839–1845) 90
Cracow (as Krakow) 191, 317
Crocher, Elizabeth (b. 1816; Falmouth 1851) 318
Crusade, Third (1189–1192) 25

Dale, John (Penzance, c. 1781) 244.
Dandy & New Dandy (ships) 208
Daniel, Michael (Penzance 1847) 249
Daniel, Nicholas (Penzance 1844) 249
Daniell Family (of Truro) 224
Danglowitz, H. (c. 1930s, Falmouth) 302
Dan(t)zig 75, 170, 284
David, Henry (as Henry Levin, Penzance) 73
Davidson, Abraham (of Falmouth, b. 1801) 213
Davidson, Amelia (Simmons; wife of Isaac, below) 315
Davidson, Arabella (of Falmouth, b. 1836) 213
Davidson Brothers (Penzance, c. 1825) 73
Davidson, Eliza (of Falmouth, b. 1832) 213
Davidson, Grace (b. 1795; Falmouth 1851) 214, 317
Davidson, Henry (of Falmouth, b. 1834) 213
Davidson, Isaac (of Falmouth, b. 1830; m. his first cousin, Amelia Simmons) 213, 315
Davidson, Isaac (of London; m. Phoebe Joseph: see Fal. 2:5) 112, 116
Davidson, Phoebe (Joseph, wife of above; see Fal. 2:5 & 3:6) 112, 116
Davidson, Rosetta (of Falmouth, b. 1806) 213
Dawson, Grace (Cornish wife of below) 263
Dawson, James (b. Dieppe, c. 1729; in Redruth from c. 1759) 262, 263, 274
Delisser, Aaron (or Delissa; Falmouth 1784) 271
Delivant, Julia (of London, then Lisbon. c. 1819) 283
Decline of Falmouth Community: 218–221
Deudone, son of Samuel 39
Diodorus Siculus (c. 1st. cents. BCE/CE) 18, 19
Donnall, Robert Sawle (trial of: Launceston Assizes, 1817) 212
Downing, Elizabeth (murder of: Launceston Assizes, 1817) 212
Druids 18
Dunitz, Alfred 100, 218

Edil, daughter of Asher (Woolf, Pz. 5:6; d. 1847) 147

Edmonds, Richard (1862) 19

Edmonton Federation Cemetery 193

Edmund, Earl of Cornwall (1272–1299/1300; son of Richard Plantagenet) 14, 29, 32

Edrisi (Arab geographer: 12th cent. CE) 34

Edward I (1272–1307: Expulsion of 1290) 13, 32

Edward, the Black Prince (1330–76; Duke of Cornwall c. 1337) 32

Edwards, Mr. (ref. Truro, c. 1840) 155

Ehrenbreitstein 282

Elias, Elias (Hart Elias; Jacob Elijah ben Naphtali: Fal. 3:8; d. 1835) 54, 110, 116, 281

Elias, Esther (Levy: Fal. 1:11; c. 1730–1780) 52, 109, 111, 207, 274, 279–282

Elias, Garson (itinerant pedlar, Falmouth; c. 1844) 213

Elias, Gershan (Fal. 2:12; 1784–1868) 114

Elias, Shevya (Levy: Pz. 6:4; 1766–1850) 54, 110, 149, 281

Eliezer son of Isaac (Pz. 6:2; d. 1844) 148

Elizabeth I (Charter of 1595) 42

Ellis, Christ.r (Penzance, c. 1781) 244

Emanuel, Levy (Truro, c. 1748–63) 257

Emanuel, Lewis (of London, ref. Falmouth 1889) 103, 104

Emden, Jacob (of Bristol) 73

Eva, Barbara & William (of Gwinear, c. 1818–1837) 89, 90

Exeter 23, 30, 31, 38, 51, 63, 86, 142, 200, 274, 302

Ezekiel, Benjamin (of Plymouth, b. 1849) 217

Ezekiel, Bernard (of Falmouth, b. 1815; later in Plymouth) 217

Ezekiel, Elizabeth (of Plymouth, b. 1843) 217

Ezekiel, Ezekiel Abraham (of Exeter, 1757–1806; father of Solomon, below) 79, 142

Ezekiel, Hannah (Jacob, Pz. 3:2; 1775–1864; wife of Solomon, below) 113, 142, 143, 249, 316

Ezekiel, John (b. Redruth 1840) 217

Ezekiel, Moses (of Plymouth, b. 1845) 217

Ezekiel, Priscilla (of Bath, b. 1827) 217

Ezekiel, Solomon (Isaac: Pz. 2:3; 1786–1867) 79, 82, 96, 113, 142, 174, 203, 212, 249, 253, 316

Ezra, Ben, of Penzance 48

Falk, Barnet (Barnes Falck: Falmouth, c. 1799–1815) 216

Falkson, Esther (daughter of Samuel, Fal. 3:13; b. Truro 1791, d. 1863) 119, 197, 214

Falkson, Lewis (Fal. 4:9; b. London 1787, d. 1852) 119, 121, 122, 214

Falmouth Docks Co. 208–211

Feinburg, Catherine (Simmons, of Penzance, b. 1819; wife of below, m. 1850) 252, 314

Feinburg, Hyman (or Fineberg; also as Hyam Fienberg, of Newport, c. 1850) 252, 314

Feinburg, Moses (of Newport, c. 1850; father of above) 252

Feival, Rabbi (Philip Samuel, of Penzance; c. 1808) 75, 96, 170, 268, 283–286

Fennell, Jane (Branwell: 1753–1829) 256

Fennell, Rev. John (c. 1811) 256

Feuchtwanger, Jane (of New York, from Hamburg; m. Benedict Joseph) 274

Fires (Falmouth) 220

Fisher (& Abrahams: Falmouth, c. 1889) 215

Flora (ship) 233

Fortitude (Masonic Lodge, Truro 1864) 272

Fowey 32, 57, 216

Foxell, Rev. John (Penzance c. 1810) 131

Franco, Abraham (ref. Plymouth 1829) 200

Franks, E. (ref. Falmouth 1913) 104

Freedman, Abraham (also as Friedman and Freidman, of Aberdare; b. 1842, m. Penzance 1870) 80, 185, 254

Freedman, Kate (Joseph; daughter of Henry Joseph of Penzance; see Pz. 6:5; b. 1847, m. Abraham 1870) 150, 185, 254, 317

Freedman, Samuel (of Aberdare, c. 1870) 254

Freemasonry 58, 68, 104, 122, 124, 128, 216, 223, 255, 269–272, 276

Fuller, Thomas (1811) 20

Gaunze, Joachim (Ganz, Gaunse: c. 1586) 33, 39

St. Germans 218

Ghika, Prince, & Princess Victoria (of Paris, later London) 282

Gibraltar 57, 208, 274

Gibson (1772 edition of Camden's Britannia) 43

Gilbert, C.S. (Survey: 1817) 26

Gisors 25

St. Gluvias Church 160

Godfrey (Penzance, 1821) 77

Glickenstein (husband of Letitia Jacobs) 287, 291

Gold Rush (1859) 61, 220

Goldman, C.S. MP. (ref. Falmouth 1913) 104

Gomasero, (& Losado: ref. Falmouth 1680) 65

Gompertz, Florence (Wattier, m. 1818) 200

Gompertz, Isaac (m. 1818; buried Exeter) 200

Goodman, Amelia (Jacob, b. 1822; daughter of Samuel Jacob of Penzance; m. 1850) 252

Goodman, Charles (of Newbridge, Glamorganshire, b. 1827, m. 1850) 104, 252

Goodman, Ephraim George (of Merthyr Tydfil, b. 1827, m. 1853) 253

Goodman, George (of Newbridge, Glamorganshire, c. 1850) 252

Goodman, George (of Pontypridd, Glamorganshire, m. 1865, b. 1828) 184, 253

Goodman, Mrs. George (of New Bridge, S. Wales; ref. Penzance 1864 & Falmouth 1889) 84, 104

Goodman, Harris (of S. Wales, c. 1853) 253

Goodman, Phoebe (Jacob, m. 1853, b. 1829; daughter of Samuel Jacob of Penzance) 253

Goodman, Rose (Joseph, m. 1865, b. 1838; daughter of Henry Joseph of Penzance) 150, 184, 253, 316

Goodman, Ruth (Falmouth, c. 1852) 253

Gorfunkle, Mr. (of Liverpool; ref. Penzance 1869) 84

Gough (1789 edition of Camden's Britannia) 43

Greenberg (burgh), Hyman (Samuel Hillman: Pz. 2:2; 1837–1861; Rabbi of Penzance 1859–1861) 83, 84, 141, 158, 181–184

Greenberg, "Rabbi" Simeon (father of above, Penzance c. 1861: see Pz. 2:2) 141, 184

le Grice, Rev. Valentine (of Penzance, c. 1824) 174, 175

Halevy, Jacques Francois (Elias Levy, French composer: 1799–1862) 288, 291

Halevy, Leon (1802–1883) 288, 291

Halford (Hyam) Family 95

Hall, Jane (b. 1830; Penzance 1851) 317

Hals, William (1703) 26

Halse, James (St. Ives, c. 1805) 233

Ha–Melitz 190

Hamburg 30, 162, 274

Hampton, Arthur (Penzance, c. 1802) 233

Hancock, Edmund (c. 1859) 208

Handley, J.T. (Penzance c. 1875) 186–189

Hanseatic League (13th. to 15th. cents. CE) 14, 30

Hardwicke, Lord (Marriage Act of 1754) 201, 202

Harris, Aaron (Morwenstow, c. 1830) 269

Harris, Arabella (of Truro, b. from 1820s) 259

Harris, Esther (Jacob, of Redruth: 1784–1871; m. Henry Harris in 1819; d. London) 113, 259

Harris Family of Truro 204, 259, 260

Harris, Hannah (Camborne, c. 1852) 267

Harris, Henry (1787–1872; of Truro from 1823; d. London) 80, 82, 113, 117, 212, 213, 259f, 272, 283

Harris, Israel (Truro, c. 1844) 260

Harris, Jacob (son of above; b. from c. 1820s) 259

Harris, Judith (Solomon/Segal: Fal. 4:7; 1764–1839; wife of Samuel, mother of Henry) 111, 112, 259, 283

Harris, Morris Hart (Penzance, 1844–50, then Truro & London; son of Henry, b. from 1820s) 80, 84, 123, 217, 246, 259

Harris, Nathan (Liskeard, c. 1762) 268

Harris, Phoebe (of Truro, daughter of Henry; b. from 1820s) 259

Harris, Rebecca (Jacob; daughter of Jacob Jacob & Sarah Kate Simons of Falmouth; m. Morris Hart Harris in 1844; see Fal. 5:2) 123, 213, 217, 260

Harris, Samuel (son of Naphtali, Fal. 3:12; d. 1824; father of Henry) 111, 117, 212, 259, 292

Harris, Samuel (Penzance, c. 1843) 80

Harris, Samuel (St. Austell, c. 1830) 268

Harris, Samuel (of Truro; son of Henry; b. from 1820s) 259, 260, 283

Harris, Simon (Exeter) 302

Harris, Simon (of Henry and Esther, d. infant) 259

Harris, Simon (as above, 2nd son) 259

Hart Family Tree 231

Hart, Abraham (Altstadter: d. circa 1710–1720) 169, 222, 231

Hart, Abraham (Solomon Lazarus: d. 1784) 73, 94, 169, 222, 223, 231, 235, 238

Hart, Anna (b. 1750) 223, 231

Hart, Asher (Altstadter: d. before 1682) 222, 231

Hart, Asher (Altstadter: d. circa 1745–1752) 94, 169, 222, 231

Hart, Charles (b. 1846) 234

Hart, David (1799–1868) 231, 234

Hart, Eddle (Woolf: Pz. 5:5) 225

Hart, Edel (b. 1747) 223, 231

Hart, Eleazar (Lazarus, or Kazanes Heart: 1739–1803) 73, 217, 223–231, 282

Hart, Frederick (nephew of Lemon Hart; b. Jacobs 1790–1853. Colyer-Fergusson's date of death is uncertain) 231, 235, 291

Hart, Harriet (McTernan: 1796–1879) 235

Hart, Jacob James (nephew of Lemon Hart; b. Jacobs: Pz. 5:3. 1784–1846) 70, 81, 145–147, 234–236, 286, 287, 291

Hart, John I. (of New York, c. 1835) 289

Hart, Josiah (Redruth 1769) 270

Hart, Julia (of New York, c. 1835; m. Barnett Solomon) 289

Hart, Leah (1770–1840; sister of Lemon Hart) 231

Hart, Lemel (b. 1755) 223, 231

Hart, Lemon (Asher Lemael ben Eliezer, 1768–1845: buried in London) 57, 68, 72, 78, 87–89, 91, 95, 131, 169, 171, 173, 179, 204, 229–236, 255, 271, 282, 286. 300

Hart, Letitia (Michael, of Swansea, d. 1803: first wife of Lemon Hart) 77. 230, 231

Hart, Letitia (niece of Lemon Hart) 291 (Edit. 15)

Hart, Louise (m. Samuel Amos 1832) 235

Hart, Madel (b. 1743) 223, 231

Hart, Mary (Solomon, of London, 1758–1852: second wife of Lemon Hart; m. 1804) 230, 231

Hart, Mary (Pidwell, m. 1831; wife of David Hart) 234

Hart, Maurice (of London, c. 1810) 275

Hart, Mord(e)chai (b. 1736) 223, 231

Hart, Rebecca (Woolf, wife of Eleazar Hart) 217, 231

Hart, Rebecca (m. 1. Lazarus (Isaac) Jacobs; 2. Magnus: 1766–1841. Sister of Lemon Hart) 231, 235

Hart, Rebecca (1798–1874: m. 1. Walter Levi; 2. her first cousin Frederick Jacobs. Daughter of Lemon Hart) 231, 234, 235

Hart, Rose (Michael: 1824–1863) 235

Hart, Stephen (of London, c. 1810) 275

Harvey (carpenter, Penzance 1815) 92

Harvey, Dr. (of Penzance, 1875) 185

Hawaii 61, 220

Hawke, Emma Boramlagh (m. Markis Bischofswerder, Penzance 1892; b. 1865) 98, 191, 193, 254

Hawke, Thomas (father of Emma) 193

ben Hayyim, Rabbi "Mowsha" (see Moses Hyman, Falmouth) 53, 67, 120, 161

Hayle 267 (& ref. Johanna Bristo)

Hayne, Samuel (ref. Falmouth, 1685) 65

Hebrew Society for the Promotion of Religious Knowledge (Penzance) 249

Heilbron, Isaac (of Falmouth, c. 1846; father of below) 213, 252

Heilbron, Joseph (Jonas, of Falmouth; m. 1846) 213, 252, 314

Heilbron, Phoebe (Simmons of Penzance, b. 1815; m. 1846, wife of above) 245, 252, 314

Helston 218

Henderson, Charles (1935) 22

Henry I (1100–1135) 23

Henry II (1154–1189) 32

Henry, Emperor VI (1191–1197) 25

Henry III (1216–1272) 13, 14, 28, 29, 30, 31, 38

Herman, Abraham David (b. 1828; Rabbi of Falmouth c. 1852) 167, 317
Herman, Frances (b. 1800, wife of Samuel) 317
Herman, Phoebe (b. 1841) 317
Herman, Rose (b. 1831) 317
Herman, Samuel (b. 1802; Rabbi of Falmouth c. 1851) 167, 317
Herodotus (5th. cent. BCE) 18
Hill, Richard (Penzance, c. 1781) 244
Hillman, Rabbi Samuel (Hyman Greenberg: of Penzance) 83, 84, 141, 158, 181–184
Hiram, King of Tyre (c. 940 BCE) 18
Hirsch, Israel ben Naphtali (Truro, c. 1836) 258, 302
Hirsch, (Rabbi of Penzance, c. 1810–11) 75, 169
Hirschell, Chief Rabbi Solomon (1762–1842) 76, 82, 171, 176, 266, 284
Holman, Leah (Simmons; of Melbourne) 315
Howell, Joshua J.P. (Redruth, c. 1769) 262
Hull 189
Hutson, M. (Penzance, c. 1790) 227
Hyman, Harriet Elizabeth (of Falmouth, b. 1811; ref. 1830) 160, 161, 198
Hyman, Rabbi Moses ("Mowsha" ben Hayyim, Fal.4:3; b. 1765, d. 1830) 53, 67, 120, 161
Hyman, Sally (of Falmouth, c. 1830) 162
Hymans, Mr. (of Truro, c. 1820s) 77

Ingoldsby Legends (1837) 58, 108
Isaac of Felmingham (12th. cent. CE) 32
Isaac of London (12th. cent CE) 31
Isaac of Norwich (c. 1233) 15
Isaac, Abraham (of Falmouth, b. 1828) 213
Isaac, Amelia (of Falmouth, b. 1829) 213
Isaac, Betza (of Falmouth, b. 1821) 213
Isaac, Frederick W. (of Falmouth, b. 1860) 215
Isaac, Harriet (of Falmouth, b. 1826) 213
Isaac, Isaac (of Falmouth, b. 1786) 213
Isaac, Isaac (shell dealer) 214
Isaac, Judith (of Falmouth, b. 1796) 213
Isaac, Lazarus (of Falmouth, b. 1816) 213, 214
Isaac, Meir ben (of Falmouth, c. early 19th. cent.) 302
Isaac, Moses (Rabbi of Penzance, c. 1810; may be identical with Moses Levi) 75, 169
Isaac, Sarah (of Falmouth, b. 1832) 213
Isaac, Susan G. (of Falmouth, b. 1837) 215
Isaac, William (of Falmouth; b. Truro 1830) 215
Isaacs, Rabbi Harris (Newport) 315
Isaacs, Moses (Penzance, c. 1808–9) 271
Isaacs, Sarah (Simmons) 150, 315, 317
Ishaya ben Moses (Fal. 3:4; 1809–1827) 115
Israel son of Moses (child: Pz. 6:8) 151
St. Ives 65, 80, 246, 267

Jackson Bros. (Totnes, c. 1800) 95
Jacob, son of Reuven (Fal. 1:9; d. 1880/1) 110
Jacob, Alexander (of Falmouth, 1841–1903) 61, 210, 214, 220, 265, 318
Jacob, Alexander (infant, see Fal. 5:2) 123
Jacob, Amelia (Mirele, unmarried; Pz. 3:1; 1794–1864) 113, 142, 213
Jacob, Amelia (Goodman, m. 1850; b. 1822: daughter of Samuel Jacob of Penzance) 252

Jacob, Amelia (Joseph, Pz. 6:6; 1812–1891) 123, 150, 267, 316
Jacob, Betsy (b. 1767; unmarried daughter of Moses Jacob: see 2:9) 113
Jacob, Betsy (Moses, Fal. 3:9; d. 1838) 109, 116
Jacob, Betsy (unmarried daughter of J. & K. Jacob, Fal. 5:1; 1822–1838) 122, 123
Jacob, Betsy (Joseph, daughter of Nathan Jacob of Dartmouth; m. Barnet Lyon Joseph) 274
Jacob, Betsey (see Pz.1:9; b. 1825) 139, 316
Jacob, Catherine (Selig, m. 1847, b. 1820; daughter of Samuel Jacob of Falmouth) 141, 245, 252, 317
Jacob, Eleanor (b. 1850) 217
Jacob, Esther (b. 1810, Camborne; unmarried, see Fal. 5:2) 123
Jacob, Esther (Harris, see Fal. 2:9 & 3:12: 1784–1871) 113
Jacob family of Falmouth (investment-book) 58, 204, 207–211
Jacob, Flora or Bluma (Simmons 1790–1814: see Pz. 1:8; d. Merthyr Tydfil) 53, 57, 113, 176, 181, 183, 206, 246, 314, 316
Jacob, Frances (of Portsmouth; b. 1812) 214, 317
Jacob, Hannah (Henne Ezekiel, Pz. 3:2; 1775–1864) 113, 142, 143, 249, 316
Jacob, Hannah (Anne or Annie, of Falmouth; b. 1840) 214, 317
Jacob, Henry (infant, see Fal. 5:2) 123
Jacob, I. (Penzance, c. 1838) 251
Jacob, Isaac (see Fal. 5:2) 123
Jacob, Isaac (St. Agnes, itinerant: c. 1770) 267
Jacob, Issachar (refer to Ba(e)rnard Beer & Barnet Levy; ref. Fal. 1:4, & see Pz. 6:4)
Jacob, John (St. Austell, c. 1847; not as below) 268
Jacob, (John) Jacob (President of Falmouth Congregation, Fal. 5:3; b. Redruth 1774, d. 1853; m. to Sarah Kate, below) 53, 59, 99, 113, 123, 124, 126, 206, 212, 213, 217, 260, 267
Jacob, Judith Rebecca (Joseph, Fal. 3:7; 1768–1849) 112, 113, 116, 273, 274
Jacob, Kitty (see Sarah Kate/Killa Simons, below)
Jacob, Kitty (Killa Solomon/Segal, b. c. 1772; Fal. 5:4; d. 1854) 54, 57, 111, 113, 124–127, 212
Jacob, Lawrence (of Falmouth, b. 1844) 214, 318
Jacob, Levi(y) (b. 1788; m. S. Mordecai, below: see Fal. 2:9; Levy Jacob was a son of Moses Jacob of Redruth) 113, 263
Jacob, Michael (of Falmouth, b. 1841; possible ref. Pz. Marriages No. 13) 214, 254, 318
Jacob, S. (b. Mordecai: see Fal. 2:9) 113
Jacob, Moses (of Redruth: Fal. 2:9; 1733–1807) 53, 54, 55, 109, 113, 176, 204, 206, 207, 213, 237, 246, 262–265, 270, 271, 274
Jacob, "Moss" Jacob (son of Jacob Jacob, Fal. 5:5; 1813–1860: President of Falmouth Congregation (1853–1860) 53, 59, 123, 127, 214, 265, 267, 317
Jacob, Moses Jacob (of Falmouth, c. 1854–73; also known as "Moss") 215, 220
Jacob, Moses Levi (of Falmouth, b. 1819; later in Birmingham) 217
Jacob, Moses Samuel ("Mosam", Fal. 4:10; 1815–1858) 122, 214
Jacob, Nathan (of Dartmouth, d. 1831) 274
Jacob, Phoebe (infant, see Fal. 5:2) 123

Jacob, Phoebe (Goodman, m. 1853, b. 1829;
daughter of Samuel Jacob of Penzance) 253
Jacob, Rebecca (Harris, see Fal. 5:2; b. 1825; m.
Morris Hart Harris in 1844) 213, 213, 217, 260
Jacob, Rebecca (Woolf, see Fal. 2:9 & Pz. 1:1;
1781–1853) 113, 206, 237
Jacob, Rose (b. 1770: see Fal. 2:9) 113
Jacob, Samuel (of Penzance, son of Moses Jacob: Pz.
2:1; 1777–1860, also in Hayle and on Scilly, as
Jacobs) 113, 139, 141, 246, 252, 253, 267, 316
Jacob, Samuel (of Falmouth; b. 1838) 12, 61, 80, 99,
103, 104, 168, 214, 215, 220, 302
Jacob, Sara (of Falmouth; b. 1850) 214, 318
Jacob, Sarah (Sally Levy of Truro; Pz. 1:9;
1784–1868) 117, 139, 246, 258, 316
Jacob, Sarah (Moses, daughter of Alexander Moses,
& wife of Moses Jacob of Redruth:
Fal. 4:1; 1748–1831) 53, 54, 63, 109, 119, 159, 207,
213, 262–265, 274
Jacob, Sarah Kate or "Kitty" (Killa Simons; Fal. 5:2,
1777–1846; m. to Jacob Jacob, above) 113, 122,
125, 206, 213, 217, 260
Jacob, Sarah (of Portsmouth, b. 1825) 217
Jacob, Simon (infant, see Fal. 5:2) 123
Jacob, Sophia (Lazarus, see Fal. 5:2) 123
Jacob, Sophia (of Penzance, c. 1830) 244
Jacob, William (St. Austell, c. 1847; ref. John above)
268
Jacobs, Abraham (of London: c. 1798) 170
Jacobs, Betsy (Levy: of Barnstaple, c. 1800) 95
Jacobs, Rev. D. (ref. Falmouth 1913) 104
Jacobs, Frederick (Hart: 1790–1853; first cousin, and
second husband of Lemon Hart's daughter
Rebecca; Frederick's mother was Lemon Hart's
sister Rebecca) 231, 235, 291
Jacobs, Isaac (of Totnes, c. 1800) 95
Jacob(s), Jacob (of Camborne, c. 1820s) 77
Jacobs, Jacob James (Hart, Pz. 5:3; 1784–1846; elder
brother of Frederick; a nephew of Lemon Hart)
70, 81, 145–147, 231, 234–236, 286, 287, 291
Jacobs, Joseph L. (of Plymouth; ref. Falmouth 1913)
104
Jacobs, Lazarus (Isaac: first husband of Rebecca,
sister of Lemon Hart) 231, 235
Jacobs, Levi (of Penzance, c. 1809–1823) 73, 244,
271
Jacobs, Mordecai (itinerant, c. 1753–73) 269
Jacobs, Phoebe (b. 1828; Penzance 1851) 245, 317
Jacobs, Rebecca (later Magnus; formerly Hart, of
Penzance: 1766–1841; sister of Lemon Hart) 231,
235
Jacobs, Rebecca (formerly Hart & Levi; 1798–1874;
daughter of Lemon Hart) 231, 234, 235
Jacobs, Samuel (of Hayle; of Penzance; of Scilly, c.
1820s; likely the same person) 77, 78
Jacobs, Solomon (of Penzance, c. 1803) 244
Jamaica 78, 224–226, 256
Jamilly, Edward 295, 296
Jenkins, Alfred (Redruth, c. 1804) 265
Jerome, Saint (c. 345–420) 20
Jerusalem, Fall of (70 CE) 13, 36, 41
Jeu, John & Sir Roger (14th. cent. CE) 32
Jewish Disabilities, Removal of (ref. Penzance 1848)
81, 82, 93

Jew Beetle 16
Jew's Bowels 16
Jew Crow 17
Jew's Ear 16
Jew's Eye 16
Jew's Fish 16
Jews' Houses 16, 19, 20, 28, 34, 35, 36, 37, 38, 44
Jews' Leavings 16
Jews' Offcasts 16
Jews' Tin 16, 266
Jews' Whidn or Works 16
"To Jew" (verb) 16. (ref. also Susser 1993, p. 292:
connotation "to cheat")
Joan, sister to Henry III (dowry of 1221) 30
John, King (1199–1216; Charter of 1201) 23, 26, 28,
39
Johns, Henry (of Mylor; ref. David & Mary Hart, in
London, 1861) 234
Johnson, Solomon (of Penzance, 1825) 73
Joseph of Arimathea 16, 20
Joseph, Abraham (1799–1868; Rabbi of Penzance in
1817: third son of Joseph Joseph of Penzance,
1761–1845) 75, 80, 173, 238, 273
Joseph, Abraham (child: Pz. 4:1; d. 1839) 143
Joseph, Abraham (of Falmouth: 3:5; 1768–1827; son
of Joseph Joseph of Alsace by his second marriage.
Abraham Joseph married Hannah Levy: Pz. 1:2)
54, 110, 115, 135, 121, 238, 273, 274, 281
Joseph, Abraham ben (Falmouth, c. early 19th cent.)
302
Joseph, Abraham (of Plymouth: see Pz. 6:7;
1731–1794) 150, 263, 273, 274
Joseph, Alexander (infant: Fal. 2:6) 112
Joseph, Amelia (Jacob, Pz. 6:6; 1811–1891) 123,
150, 267, 316
Joseph, Anthony P. (genealogist, of Birmingham) 67,
68, 101, 197, 231, 272
Joseph, Arabella (Levy, 1806–1897: daughter of
Lyon & Judith Joseph) 274
Joseph, BH (Barnett Henry, of Penzance, later
Birmingham) 85, 90, 254, 301
Joseph, Barnet Lyon (1801–80: son of Lyon & Judith
Joseph) 101, 103, 213, 272, 274
Joseph, Bella (m. Rabbi Meyer Stadhagen of
Plymouth: see Fal. 2:5) 112
Joseph, Benedict (d. 1851, America; son of Lyon &
Judith Joseph) 274, & 289 (ref. 1832)
Joseph, Betsey (Bessie or Beila: Pz. 7:5; 1848–1900)
133, 150, 152, 317
Joseph, Betsy (Jacob, daughter of Nathan Jacob of
Dartmouth; m. Barnet Lyon Joseph) 274
Joseph, Edel (b. Liskeard, 1771) 268
Joseph, Eliza (Woolf, of Penzance: 1808–1850) 238
Joseph, Elra (Hendele Levy: Pz. 1:2; see Hannah
Joseph, below)
Joseph, Esther (of Falmouth, d. young; daughter of
Lyon & Judith Joseph) 274
Joseph, Esther (Beirnstein: see Pz. 6:5; b. 1843, m.
1869 in Penzance) 150, 185, 254, 316
Joseph, Fanny (Solomon) 112
Joseph, Frederick (son of Lyon & Judith Joseph; d.
America) 274
Joseph, Hannah (Levy, Pz. 1:2; 1769–1851) 110,
135, 274, 281, 316

Joseph, Hannah ("Nanny", daughter of Lyon & Judith Joseph; m. Moses Levin of London) 136, 274

Joseph, Henry (Elimeleh ben Joseph, or Zvi ben Abraham: of Penzance, Pz. 6:5; b. Falmouth 1806, d. Penzance 1881; grandson of Joseph Joseph of Alsace, by his second marriage; son of Abraham Joseph of Falmouth) 80, 82, 84, 88, 90, 132, 149, 150, 184, 185, 189, 213, 237, 238, 245, 251–254, 273, 274, 301, 316

Joseph, Henry (Zvi ben Joseph, of St. Austell: Fal. 2:4; 1760–1803; son of Joseph Joseph of Alsace, by his first marriage) 53, 54, 64, 109, 112, 238, 273, 274

Joseph, Henry (see Fal. 2:5; d. Brazil) 112

Joseph, Henry (of Falmouth; son of Lyon & Judith Joseph; m. Maria Samuel of London) 274

Joseph, Isaac (of Falmouth; son of Joseph Joseph of Alsace, by his first marriage) 53, 54, 273, 274

Joseph, Isaac (Isaac the Jew, of Redruth; c. 1804) 77, 266

Joseph, Isaac ben (Falmouth, c. early 19th cent.) 302

Joseph, Jane (Feuchtwanger, of New York; m. Benedict Joseph) 274

Joseph, Jehudah ben (Falmouth, c. early 19th cent.) 302

Joseph, Jos (see Pz. 6:5; b. 1846) 150, 317

Joseph, Joseph (of Mulhausen, Alsace; dates uncertain; d. London) 238, 273, 274

Joseph, Joseph (Fal. 1:5: infant son of Lyon & Judith Joseph) 274

Joseph, Joseph (see Fal. 2:5: a son of Moses Isaac Joseph) 112, 213

Joseph, J. (St. Austell, c. 1820; may be same as below) 268

Joseph, Joseph (Redruth, c. 1823–1849; then to Plymouth) 266

Joseph, Joseph (infant: Fal. 2:8; but see 6:1; d. 1790) 110, 112, 127

Joseph, Joseph (of Penzance, 1761–1845) 238, 244, 273

Joseph, Josephus (of Falmouth, 1827–1916; brother of Lionel, below) 61, 220

Joseph, Judith (Levy, of Falmouth, 1774–1846; wife of Lyon Joseph) 54, 110, 207, 274, 281

Joseph, Judith (Moses, Fal. 4:5; 1768–1843) 212, 274

Joseph, Julia (Bischofswerder, m. 1884; Pz.7:6; 1851–1911) 99, 150, 152, 189, 193, 194, 254

Joseph, Judith Rebecca (Jacob, Fal. 3:7; 1768–1849) 112, 113, 116, 273, 274

Joseph, Kate (Kitty Cohen: daughter of Lyon & Judith Joseph; m. Moses Cohen of London) 274

Joseph, Kate (Freedman: see Pz. 6:5; b.1848, m. 1870) 150, 185, 254, 317

Joseph, Lionel (son of Henry Joseph of Penzance; see Pz. 6:5; b. 1840) 150, 316

Joseph, Lionel (of Falmouth, c. 1859; brother of Josephus, above) 61, 220

Joseph, Lyon (of Falmouth; buried Plymouth. 1775–1825; son of Joseph Joseph of Alsace, by his second marriage; Lyon's wife was Judith Levy: 1774–1846) 53, 54, 56, 57, 76, 99, 170, 207, 212, 273, 274, 281, 285, 292

Joseph, Lyon J. (of Falmouth, b. 1827; later in Birmingham) 212, 217

Joseph, Maria (daughter of Abraham Samuel of London; wife of Henry Joseph, son of Lyon & Judith Joseph) 274

Joseph, Morris (see Pz. 6:5; b. 1842) 150, 316

Joseph, Moses (b. Devonport 1826; Falmouth 1851) 214, 318

Joseph, Moses Isaac (Fal. 2:5; d. 1830) 112

Joseph, Philip (Uri, infant: Fal. 2:7; but see 6:1; d. 1790) 112, 127

Joseph, Phoebe (Feigele 1806–1830; m. Isaac Davidson of London: Fal. 3:6) 112, 115

Joseph, Rachel (Levy, d. 1832: see Fal. 1:4; daughter of Joseph Joseph of Alsace, by his second marriage) 54, 109, 273, 274, 281

Joseph, Rachel (Simmons; of Portsea) 315

Joseph, Ray (Hyman: ref. Falmouth 1889) 104

Joseph, Rose (see Fal. 2:5; em. Australia) 112

Joseph, Rose (Goodman, m. 1865, b. 1838; daughter of Henry Joseph of Penzance: see Pz. 6:5) 150, 184, 253, 316

Joseph, Ruth (of Plymouth: Pz. 6:7; 1812–1832) 150, 151

Joseph, Samuel (infant: Pz. 4:2; d. 1844) 143

Joseph, Selina or Sarah (Pz. 4:3 & ref. 6:5; 1835–1872) 143, 150, 316

Joseph, Solomon (see Fal. 2:5; d. London) 112

Josephs of Cornwall 272–276

Josephus, Flavius (c. 37–100 CE) 21

Jubilee Hall (Penzance 1887) 193

Judah son of Moses (Pz. 4:4; d. 1824) 144

Judah son of Naphtali (Pz. 8:1) 152, 153

Julyan, John (Penzance, c. 1786–1801) 228, 229

St. Just-in-Roseland 20

Kalman, Thérèse (Rintel) 162

Kelly, Constance (b. 1825; Penzance 1851) 318

Kemp, Joseph (Carn Marth, later Park City, Utah) 276

Killigrew, Sir Peter (Falmouth c. 1680) 65

Kistler, George (Penzance 1856–73) 249

Kistler, Matthew (Penzance 1844) 249

Kistler, Mathias (Penzance 1873) 249

Kistler, Michael Daniel (Penzance 1847) 249

Knockers 15, 16, 22

Konin 167, 317

Krakow (Cracow) 191, 317

Laemle ben Solomon Aharon Ha-Levi (Penzance, c. 1808) 88

Lancrour (sic) see Leinkram, Rabbi Michael 85, 94, 96, 98, 159, 190–193, 254

Landjew 19, 20

Lanlivery 28

de Lange, Rabbi Dr.Nicholas 28, 100, 101, 103, 130, 173

Launceston 57, 212, 268

Laurence, Alex (ref. Falmouth 1889) 104

Lawrence, Joseph (of Falmouth, c. 1861) 167

Lawrence, Judith (Moses, Fal. 4:5; d. 1843) 109, 120

Lawrence, Lazarus (Moses Eliezer, Fal. 4:6; d. 1841) 67, 109, 120, 121, 212

Lawry, W. (Falmouth, 1830) 162

Lazarus Family (of Falmouth) 103

Lazarus, Annie (b. 1862, Redruth) 253

Lazarus, Eliza (of Falmouth, b. 1815; later in Exeter) 217

Lazarus, Emily (Cock, of Penzance, later Redruth; m. 1862, b. 1839) 203, 253

Lazarus, Frederick (b. 1837, m. Penzance 1862; later in Redruth) 203, 253, 266

Lazarus, Hyman (Penzance, c. 1843–5) 80

Lazarus, Isaac (of Exeter, b. 1817) 217

Lazarus, Isaac (ref. Pz. Minute-Books 1828) 253

Lazarus, Jonas (d. before 1862: father of Frederick) 253

Lazarus, Julia (of Exeter, b. 1847) 217

Lazarus, Lazarus (Hayle, c. 1844) 267

Lazarus, Lewis (of Exeter, b. 1845) 217

Lazarus, Solomon (see Abraham Hart, d. 1784)

Lazarus, Sophia (Jacob, see Fal. 5:2) 123

Lean, Thomas (of Marazion, c. 1901) 90

Leb Hanau (Penzance, c.1809, d. 1817) 77

Leib, Judah (ref. below) 75, 173

Leib, Moses ben Judah (Jacob Moses; Rabbi of Penzance 1817–1818) 75, 173

Leinkram, Caroline (Crozy: b. 1898, Belfast) 193

Leinkram, Esther (Riesenfeld, of London; m. 1887) 191, 192

Leinkram, Gertrude (b. 1904, Belfast) 193

Leinkram, Maurice (b. Penzance 1892) 191

Leinkram, Michael (Mikael ben Schloma, from Poland, 1852/4–1923; Rabbi of Penzance 1887–c. 1896: Ref. also , incorrectly, as Lancrour and Lankion:) 85, 94, 96, 98, 159, 190–193, 254

Leinkram, Sarah (Sadie, b. 1896) 191

Leinkram, Solomon (Solly Barnett; father of Michael) 191

Leinkram, Solomon (Solly or Samuel, Blazelle Bear: b. circa 1894; son of Michael) 191

Leland (c. 1538) 42

Lemon Family (of Truro) 224

Lemon, Alice H. (of Scotland: Falmouth, c. 1861) 215

Lemon, George (husband of above) 215

Lemon, Isabella (Abraham, b. 1840) 215

Leskinnick, Penzance 130, 131, 132

Lescudjack, Penzance 131

Letter of Condolence (Penzance 1824) 174, 175, 319–320 (full text of)

Levi, Abraham (of Falmouth, circa 1790) 203, 217

Levi, Ann (Paskoe, of Falmouth; c. 1825) 217

Levi, Benjamin (Falmouth, c. 1852) 253

Levi, Israel (Truro 1820s) 258

Levi, Jacob (Falmouth 1811, later in Truro; likely same as Jacob John Levy, below) 212

Levi, Jacob (probably of Falmouth; father of Walter, below) 235

Levi, Moses (Rabbi of Penzance, c. 1810; may be identical with Moses Isaac) 75, 169

Levi, Rebecca (of Falmouth, c. 1790) 217

Levi, Rebecca (formerly Hart, later Jacobs; 1798–1874; daughter of Lemon Hart) 231, 234, 235

Levi, Thomas (of Falmouth, b. circa 1790) 198, 217

Levi, Walter (probably of Falmouth, d. 1828; first husband of Rebecca, daughter of Lemon Hart) 235

Levin, Alexander (of Penzance, 1828–91; later of Birmingham) 80, 246

Levin, David (Pz. 5:7; 1833–1873) 136, 147, 148, 252

Levin, Hannah (Joseph, of Falmouth; daughter of Lyon & Judith Joseph; m. Moses Levin of London) 136, 274

Levin, Henry (or Lavin: Moses Hayim ben Abraham, or Zvi son of Yekutiel; Pz.1:5; 1798–1877) 73, 81, 84, 90, 135, 136, 158, 159, 244, 252, 254

Levin, Henry (Levy, of Truro; c. 1823/4; see Fal. 3:11) 251, 258

Levin, Hyman (Hayyim: Pz. 5:8; 1830–1844) 136, 148

Levin, Israel (Pz. 1:3; 1829–1887) 85, 90, 135, 249, 254

Levin, Jos . . . (ref. Penzance 1865) 272

Levin, Julia (Yuta, Pz. 1:4; 1792–1879) 135, 136

Levin, Moses (of London: see Pz. 1:5) 136, 274

Levy(i) Family (of Truro) 258, 259

Levy, Abraham (see Fal. 1:4: c. 1841; a son of Barnet Levy; he moved to Plymouth, and was the father of Markis Levy, who married Lemon Woolf's daughter Bella in 1841) 109, 251, 181

Levy, Anna (b. Truro, c. 1813–22) 199, 258

Levy, Arabella (Joseph, daughter of Lyon & Judith Joseph; m. Solomon Levy of Exeter) 274

Levy, Barnet (Ba(e)rnard Beer, or Jewell; Behr son of Joel: Fal. 1:4; b. circa 1731, d. 1791 See also Pz. 6:4, where he is Issachar Jacob) 52, 54, 64, 71, 103, 109–111, 135, 205, 206, 207, 211, 267, 274, 279–282

Levy, Bella (Woolf , daughter of Lemon Woolf of Penzance; m. Abraham Levy 1841) 251

Levy, Ben, of Truro 48

Levy, Betsy (Elizabeth Solomon, see Fal. 1:4. d. Bristol) 65, 110, 282

Levy, Betsey (see Pz. 1:9) 139

Levy, Catherine (Pz. 7:2; d. 1864) 97, 132, 133, 151

Levy, Charles (of Truro, c. 1813–1856) 199, 258

Levy, Elias (Jacques Francois Halevy, French composer:1799–1862) 288, 291

Levy, Elizabeth (Levi, of Truro, c. 1813–22) 199, 258

Levy, Elizabeth (daughter of above, b. Truro c. 1813–22) 199, 258

Levy, Elizabeth (Beila Oppenheim, Pz. 1:6; 1798–1879; m. 1839) 117, 136, 137, 251

Levy, Elra (Hannah/Hendele Levy, or Elra Joseph, below)

Levy, Esther (Elias, Fal. 1:11; wife of Barnet Levy of Falmouth) 52, 55, 103, 109, 111, 206, 207, 274, 279–282

Levy, Hannah (Hendele or Elra Joseph, Pz. 1:2; 1769–1851) 54, 65, 110, 135, 273, 274. 281, 316

Levy, Hannah (Henne Moses, Pz. 5:1; d. 1841) 54, 109, 144, 145

Levy, Henry (Levin, of Truro; c. 1823/4; see Fal. 3:11) 117

Levy, Henry (b. Truro, after 1822, to c. 1853; son of Jacob & Elizabeth Levy) 258
Levy, Henry (of Penzance, c. 1830) 244
Levy, Israel (Israel ben Ezekiel Aryeh of Truro, Fal. 3:11; d. 1823/4) 54, 64, 109, 117, 145, 206
Levy, Jacob (John Levi, of Truro; c. 1813–47) 155, 198, 199, 258
Levy, Jacob (John, son of above, b. Truro, c. 1813–22) 199, 258
Levy, Joel (see Fal. 1:4; 1776–1831) 109, 206, 273, 274, 281, 282
Levy, Jonas (ref. Penzance, c. 1869) 254
Levy, Joseph 283
Levy, Judith (1774–1846, see Fal. 1:4. wife of Lyon Joseph) 54, 65, 110, 206, 207, 273, 274, 281
Levy, Judith (see Fal. 3:11) 117
Levy, Kitty (Truro, c. 1845) 259
Levy, Levy (son of Issachar, Fal. 1:6; d. 1791) 64, 109, 110
Levy, Lyon (d. circa 1809: see Fal. 1:2) 58, 108
Levy, Lyon (Truro 1829) 261
Levy, Markis (of Plymouth, c. 1841) 251
Levy, Menachem (of Exeter: see Pz. 6:1) 148
Levy, Phoebe (Simmons; Houndsditch, London) 315
Levy, Rachel (Joseph, above; d. 1832; see Fal. 1:4.) 54, 109, 273, 274, 281
Levy, Sarah (Sally Jacob, Pz. 1:9; b. Truro, 1783; d. 1868) 113, 117, 139, 246, 258, 316
Levy, Sally (see Fal. 1:4) 110
Levy, Shevya (Elias: Pz. 6:4; 1766–1850) 54, 110, 149, 281
Levy, "spinsters" [Falmouth 1792] 65: presumably three daughters of Barnet Levy [see Fal. 1:4: later married as Betsy [Solomon], Hannah [Joseph] & Judith [Joseph] above
Levy, Simon (Redruth, c. 1787) 262, 266
Levy, Solomon (Phineas/Pinchas, son of Menachem, above: Pz. 6:1; 1785–1841) 148
Levy, Solomon (of Exeter; possibly same as above; m. Arabella Joseph) 274
Levy, Solomon (Launceston, c. 1830) 268
Levy, Zipporah (Benjamin, of Plymouth 1784–1861; see Fal. 1:4) 109
Levy, Victor (of Cadiz, c. early 1800s) 275
. . . son of Libche (Truro, c. 1796) 258
Liber Rubeus (The Red Book: 1197) 24, 25, 37
Liepman, R. (Truro, c. 1820s) 77, 96
Lindo, David Abarbanel 58
Lipman, H. (Penzance 1830) 96
Lipman, Nathan (Rabbi of Falmouth 1871–1875) 53, 68, 168
Little Bera (Rabbi B.A. Simmons) 176
Lisbon 56, 76, 96, 170, 275, 283, 285, 286
Liskeard 218, 268
Liverpool 261, 274, 289
Looe 20
Lopes Family of Plymouth 224
Lopes, Charlotte (Yeats: m. 1795) 200
Lopes, Manasseh (m. 1795) 200
Losado, (& Gomasero: 1685) 65
Lostwithiel 269
Lousada Family (c. 1800) 200
Love, Thomas (Penzance, c. 1787) 225

Love & Honour (Masonic Lodge, Falmouth) 104, 223, 270
Love & Liberality (Druid's Masonic Lodge, Redruth) 255, 263, 270, 271
Lubeck 30
Ludgvan, near Penzance 131
Lupschutz, RA (Rabbi of Penzance 1861–1862) 84, 184

Magnus (half-sister of Jacob James Hart) 287
Magnus, Elias (of Penzance, c. 1808–19) 73, 78, 89ff. 231
Magnus, Rebecca (formerly Hart, then Jacobs: 1766–1841; sister of Lemon Hart) 231, 235
Malta 275
Mandoffsky, Jones & Moses (Truro & Plymouth, c. 1834) 260
Mapwell, Councillor (Penzance 1875) 93
Market Jew (& Cornish variants) 13, 17, 40, 41, 43, 44, 45
Marazion (& Cornish variants) 13, 16, 17, 19, 40, 41, 42, 43
Margoliouth, Moses (1818–1881) 70, 72
Marks, Charlotte (b. 1852) 168
Marks, Jebbeth (b. 1831; wife of Morrice) 168
Marks, Joseph (of Portsea, b. 1804; in Penzance 1851) 317
Marks, Lena (b. 1860) 168
Marks, Morrice (or Marks/Markus Morris, b. 1827, Prussia: Rabbi of Falmouth from 1860) 167, 168
Marks, Willy (b. 1856) 168
Marks, Samuel (of Falmouth, c. 1864) 215
Marranos 76, 170
Marriage (& conversion) 198–203
Marriages: Falmouth 217; Penzance 98, 251–255
Martin, Eliza (Falmouth c. 1851) 199, 318
Mary (ship) 226
Mary's St., Church (Penzance) 174
Mathews, John (Penzance, c. 1802–5) 233
Mawnan 174
Mayer, Caroline (Solomon; b. Paris, d. 1873) 287, 291
Mayer, Leon (portrait artist) 288
McFarland, John (of Plymouth, c. 1802) 233
McTernan, James (m. Harriet Hart 1830) 235
Menheniot 19
Merthyr Tydfil 179, 253, 254, 314
Messina, Dr. John (ref. Penzance, 1825) 79, 80, 96
Methodism 68, 255
Meyers, Bessy (of Exeter, b. 1833) 217
Meyers, Isaiah (of Exeter, b. 1838) 217
Meyers, Israel (of Bavaria, b. 1791; later in Exeter) 216
Meyers, Jacob (of Exeter, b. 1845) 217
Meyers, Meyer (of Exeter, b. 1836) 217
Meyers, Rebecca (of Exeter, b. 1843) 217
Meyers, Tobiah (b. Falmouth 1791; later in Plymouth) 216
Michael, F. (Frederick David, of Swansea: 1780–1870) 77, 230
Michael, Jacob (of Swansea, d. 1882) 235
Michael, Letitia (Hart: of Swansea; d. 1803) 177, 230, 231
Michael, Rose (Hart) 235

Michel, Abraham (of London, c. 1798) 170
Millett, George Bown (Penzance, 1878) 245, 250
Mines 20, 194, 209, 211
Mining 13–48, 61, 194, 211, 224
Minute books (Penzance) 86–94 (& numerous
    footnote references)
Montefiore, Sir Moses (1784–1862) 58, 81
Moore, William (ref. Truro, c. 1812) 150
Mordecai, S. (married Levy Jacob, b. 1788 above)
    55, 113
Mortara, Elhanan Joseph (Rabbi of Penzance
    1813–1814, formerly of Verona) 76, 173
Mortara, Rabbi Hayyim Solomon Levi (Rabbi of
    Verona, and father of above) 76, 173
Morwenstow 269
Morris, Marks Rabbi (of Falmouth, from 1860: see
    Morrice Marks) 167, 168
Moscow 75, 284
Moses, Alexander (Henry): Zender Falmouth (Fal.
    1:3; 1715–1791) 50–53, 55, 56, 63, 67, 99, 102,
    108, 112, 159, 199, 205–207, 211, 262, 270, 274,
    279ff
Moses, Rabbi (of Penzance, c. 1808) 75, 169
Moses, Betsy (Jacob, Fal. 3:9; d. 1838) 109
Moses, Elizabeth Ann (of Falmouth, baptism 1844)
    215, 216, 318
Moses, Hannah (Henne Levy: Pz. 5:1; d. 1841) 109,
    144, 145
Moses, Henry (see Alexander Moses of Falmouth,
    above)
Moses, Henry (of Falmouth, b. 1804) 198, 199, 203,
    217, 318
Moses, Jacob (Moses ben Judah Leib: Rabbi of
    Penzance 1817–1818) 75, 173
Moses, Johanna (Bristo, née Richards of Hayle; b.
    1812) 199, 215, 217, 267, 318
Moses, John Alexander (of Falmouth, b. 1849) 216,
    318
Moses, Joseph (of Falmouth, b. 1853) 216, 318
Moses, Judith (Yetele Joseph, later Lawrence, Fal.
    4:5; 1768–1843) 54, 109, 120, 274
Moses of Mevagissey 48
Moses, Moses (of Le Havre: see Fal.1:3ii) 53, 54, 59,
    109
Moses of Penryn (1759) 102
Moses, Philip, "Phill" (Uri Shraga, Fal. 2:2; d. 1831)
    55, 109, 111, 112, 199
Moses, Phillip (of Falmouth, b. 1842) 215, 318
Moses, Phoebe (Feigele, Fal. 2:3; d. 1804) 50, 64,
    108, 112, 205, 206, 274
Moses, Richard (of Falmouth, b. 1857) 216
Moses, Rosa (Simons, Fal. 4:2; 1756–1838) 109
Moses, Sarah (wife of Moses Jacob: Fal. 4:1;
    1748–1831) 53, 55, 99, 109, 119, 159, 207, 213,
    274
Moses, Thomas Henry (of Budock) 215, 318
Moses, Thomas King (of Falmouth, b. 1851) 215,
    216, 318
Moses, William Adolphus (of Falmouth, b. 1855)
    216
Mounder, Mr. (Penzance 1875) 93
Mount Sinai (Masonic Lodge, Penzance) 272
Mousehole (near Penzance) 19, 40, 43
Müller, Friedrich Max 13, 17, 26, 39, 40, 42–45

Murdoch, Ann (Paynter; Redruth, c. 1787) 262
Murdoch, William (Redruth, c. 1787) 262
Myers, J. (ref. Penzance marriage 1892) 254

Nance, R. Morton 39, 40
Nancy & Betsy (ship) 225
Nancy (Lorraine) 288
Nathan, Mr. (of Falmouth c. 1896) 104
Neot, Saint 17
Neptune (ship) 244
Newlyn (near Penzance) 68, 186, 218
New Year Dinners (Penzance c. 1892) 193, 194
New York 186, 274, 289
Nicholls, Joseph (Penzance, c. 1802) 233
Ninnis, William (St. Ives, c. 1805) 233
Norden, John (1728) 22, 43
Northern Empire (ship) 208
Noy, John (Penzance, c. 1817) 237
Noy, William 253

Oppenheim Family of Penzance 97, 204, 242
Oppenheim, Annie (Salanson, b. Penzance 1868; d.
    1948) 245
Oppenheim, Elizabeth (Beila Levy, Pz. 1:6;
    1798–1879; m. 1839) 117, 136, 137, 251
Oppenheim, Israel (of Penzance, c. 1850–70; only
    son of Samuel and Elizabeth) 82, 84, 85, 90, 239,
    241, 243, 245
Oppenheim, Mathilda (Joseph, 1841–1931;
    daughter of B.L. Joseph of Falmouth, and wife of
    Israel, above) 245
Oppenheim, Nathan (of Penzance) 251
Oppenheim, Samuel (ben Nathan; Pz. 1:7;
    1800–1869) 80, 81, 136–138, 245, 251
Orler, Samuel (last known Rabbi of Falmouth
    1875–80) 168
van Oven, Isaac (Falmouth, c. 1771–85; b. 1730)
    257

Packet Boats 61, 218
Palmer, Mary (Falmouth, c. 1841) 214
Palmerston, Lord (c. 1811) 81, 147, 236, 286
Paris 287
Paskoe, Ann (Levi, of Falmouth; c. 1825) 217
de Pass, Alfred Aaron (1861–1952) 63, 104, 105, 302
de Pass, Daniel (ref. c. 1947) 104
de Pass, Elias (ref. S. Africa, c. 1846) 104
Paul (village near Mousehole) 218, 234
St. Paul 20
Paynter, Ann (Murdoch; Redruth, c. 1787; daughter
    of below) 262
Paynter, Captain Richard (Redruth, d. 1787) 262
Paynter, Sally (Redruth, c. 1787; daughter of above)
    262
Pearce, Richard (Redruth, c. 1821) 271
Pearlson, Abraham (father of below, c. 1876) 254
Pearlson, Elias Rabbi (of Newcastle; b. 1853, m.
    Penzance 1876) 189, 254
Pearlson, Gustav (son of Elias and Henrietta) 189
Pearlson, Henrietta (Bischofswerder; b. 1855, m.
    1876) 185, 189, 254
Peixotto, Mr. 288
Pendarves, E.W.W., M.P. (ref. Penzance, 1848) 82,
    93

Penryn 54, 159, 160, 211
Pentreath, Dolly (of Mousehole, late 18th cent.) 40
Penwerris 102
Perry, Rosina b. 1838; Falmouth 1851) 318
Perseverance (ship) 275
Pfaff, Joseph (Falmouth, c. 1864) 216
Phillimore parish 160
Phoenicians 16, 18, 19
Phoenix (Masonic Lodge, Truro 1854) 272
Pidwell, Joseph (Falmouth, c, 1864) 234
Pidwell, Mary (Hart: m. David Hart 1831) 234
Piran, Saint (Perran) 44
Plymouth 51, 57, 61, 70, 86, 105, 186, 200, 276
Plymouth Brethren 90, 298
Polack, Frances (Penryn, c. 1799) 211
Polack, Isaac ("Jewish Priest" of Falmouth, c.
    1760–76) 71, 159–161, 198, 217, 270
Polack, Mary (Stoughton; m. 1760) 159, 217
Polglase, Mary Ann (Budock, c. 1840) 199
Polwhele (1808) 22, 26
Ponsharden 102
Pool, P.A.S. (Peter, Cornish historian) 130–132, 218,
    255
Price, John (Penzance, c. 1781) 238
Price, Sir Rose (Penzance, c. 1820) 79, 97, 174, 224,
    249
Pytheas of Massilia (4th/3rd. cents. BCE) 18

Quakers 201, 202, 263

Rabbis of Cornwall 158–195; of Falmouth 168; of
    Penzance 194, 195
Railways 61, 207, 220
Raillon, Monsieur Martial (Redruth, c. 1779) 263
Ralph, Abraham (of Barnstaple, d. 1805) 95
Ralph, Betsy (Devon, c. 1800) 95
Ralph, Catherine (Devon, c. 1800) 95
Ralph, Henry (Penzance, c. 1809; Plymouth by
    1814) 73, 89ff. 95, 244
Ralph, Miriam (Devon, c. 1800) 95
Ralph, Rosie (Devon, c. 1800) 95
Ralph, Samuel (buried Plymouth, 1867) 200
Read, Grace (b. 1823; Penzance 1851) 246, 316
Redruth 54, 133, 218, 261–266
Richard I (1189–1199) 23, 24
Richard Plantagenet, King of the Romans, Count of
    Poitou, Earl of Cornwall (1225/7–1272: son of
    King John, & brother to Henry III) 13, 28, 29,
    30–32, 37, 38, 42, 47
Richard Strongbow (Richard de Clare, Earl of
    Pembroke, d. 1176) 24
Richards, John (of Hayle; ref. Budock, c. 1840)
    199
Richards, William (Penzance, c. 1802) 233
Riesenfeld, Esther (Leinkram, m. 1887) 191, 192
Riesenfeld, Moses (Morris, of London; c. 1887) 191
Rintel or Rintely, Benedict Jacob (c. 1809) 53, 162,
    251
Rintel, Fanny (Simmons, b. 1814; m. 1838) 53, 162,
    167, 251, 314
Rintel, Joseph Benedict (b. 1809, Hamburg; Rabbi
    of Falmouth 1832–1849) 53, 59, 80, 162–167,
    179, 251, 266, 314
Rintel, Thérèse (Kalman: c. 1809) 162

Rittenberg, M. (Rabbi of Penzance 1866–c. 1868)
    94, 184, 254
Robert, Count of Mortain (d. 1091: half-brother of
    William I) 13, 42
Robinson (ship-owner, c. 1850s–1860s) 208
Rodd, Francis (1850) 35
Rogers, Brian (1680) 65
Rogers, Canon John (Rector of Mawnan; ref. c.
    1810–41) 131, 132, 174
Rollins, John (ref. Truro, c. 1840) 156
Rosenstein, Rabbi V. (of London, 1887) 191
Rosenthal, Gabriel (St. Ives, c. 1830) 267
Rosevean, Penzance 130, 179
Rouen 23
Row, Mark (Penzance, c. 1817) 237
Rowe, Richard (1835) 132
Royal Navy 235, 236
Rubinstein, Isaac Aryeh (Rabbi of Penzance
    1886–1887) 85, 94, 184, 189, 190, 254
Russia & Poland, poor of (ref. Penzance 1869) 81
Russell, Samuel (Falmouth 1792) 65
Rutland 31

"Saavil", Rabbi (Samuel Ha-Levi, Fal. 2:11;
    1741–1814) 53, 113, 114, 161
Salanson, Annie (Oppenheim) 245
Salzman, Adolf (Avner ben Hayyim Israel,
    1889–1964; Pz. 8:4) 99, 133, 153
Sampson, John (Penzance, c. 1769) 95
Samuel, Abraham (of London) 274
Samuel, Edgar 37, 65
Samuel, Maria (Joseph) 274
Samuel, Rabbi Phil(l)ip (of Penzance; c. 1808; also
    St. Austell; eventually Lisbon) 75, 96, 170, 268,
    283–286
Saracens 22
Saundry (Almanacs) 89, 90
Saxons 21, 22
SS Schiller, Wreck of (Scillies, 1875) 186–189
ben Schloma, Mikael (Rabbi Michael Leinkram:
    Penzance, c. 1887–96) 85, 94, 96, 98, 159,
    190–193, 254
Schram, Abraham (b. 1851 in Plymouth) 216
Schram, Angelina (b. 1843 in Truro) 216
Schram, Anna (b. 1816, Gwennap) 216
Schram, Henrietta (b. 1845 in Truro) 216
Schram, Jacob (b. 1842 in Falmouth) 216
Schram, Marianna (b. 1849 in Plymouth) 216
Schram, Nathaniel (b. 1804 the Hague; in Falmouth
    1841) 216
Schwerer, Jacob (various dates and locations; see
    Berenger & S.) 214
Scilly, Isles of 78, 186, 225, 267
Segal, Israel (Solomon, Aaron Levi, & see Behrends;
    Fal. 2:1; b. circa. 1727, d. 1802) 111, 206, 282,
    283
Segal, Israel (Solomon/Behrends; b. c. 1803, d. New
    York) 51, 52, 70, 110, 170, 205, 206, 207,
    279–291
Segal, Kitty (Solomon, née Jacob, Fal. 5:4; d. 1854)
    54, 57, 111, 113, 124, 127, 212, 286
Segal, Leah (Solomon, Fal. 1:10; 4:8; d. 1842) 111,
    283
Segal, Jacob (see Pz. 5:4) 147

Segal, Moses (Solomon, Fal. 1:8; d. 1798/9) 110

Segal, Simon (Solomon, Fal. 3:3; d. 1825) 54, 57, 111, 114, 115, 286

Segal, Solomon (Zalman, Pz. 5:4; d. 1823) 95, 147

Selig, Rabbi (of Penzance, c. 1809; may be identical with "R. Aaron", above and with Aaron Selig: 1782–1841) 75

Selig, Aaron (son of Phineas, Pz. 1:11; 1782–1841) 75, 78, 90, 139–141, 169, 245, 246, 252

Selig, Aaron (grandson of above: see Pz. 1:11; b. 1850) 245, 317

Selig, Benjamin Aaron (see Pz. 1:11; b. 1814) 82, 84, 90, 141, 245, 246, 251–253, 317

Selig, Catherine (Jacob, of Falmouth; see Pz. 1:11; b. 1820, m. 1847) 141, 245, 252, 317

Selig, Hannah (Hindele, daughter of Hayyim, Pz. 1:10; 1779–1847) 139–141, 246

Selig, Hyman (Rabbi of Penzance 1815–1816) 173

Selig, Lemon (grandson to Aaron: see Pz. 1:11; b. 1850) 245, 317

Selig, Maria (Teacher, b. 1815; see Pz. 7:1) 151, 246, 252, 316

Semmons, Harman (Hyman Simmons?: Truro 1829) 261

Sennen 189

Shamreck (m. Israel Solomon's niece) 287

Ship (Masonic Lodge, St. Ives) 270

Shortman, Samuel (Penzance 1823) 249

Silberman, Henry (Callington, c. 1847) 268

Silverstone, Simeon (b. 1826; Falmouth 1851) 214, 317

Simon de Dena 39

Simonds, Hart Rabbi (or Symons: of Penzance from 1818) 75, 79, 174, 175, 319, 320

Simons, Isaac (see Fal. 4:2) 117, 120

Simons, Kitty (Sarah Kate, below: Fal. 5:2, & see Fal. 4:2)

Simons, Kitty (of Redruth; c. 1851 Penzance) 246, 316

Simons, Phoebe (Feigele, infant: Fal. 3:10; d. 1824) 117

Simons, Rosa (Moses, Fal. 4:2; 1756–1838) 54, 109, 119

Simons, Sarah Kate (Jacob; Kitty or Killa, Fal. 5:2; 1777–1846) 113, 123, 125, 213, 217, 260

Simons, Samuel (of Truro; Fal. 4:4; 1740–1832) 54, 109, 120

Simons, Solomon (b. Truro 1778) 258

Simmons, Abraham Barnett (1831–1908; d. Australia) 315

Simmons, Amelia (Davidson; b. 1825; em. Australia) 315

Simmons, Arthur B. (b. 1826; em. Australia) 315

Simmons, Rabbi Barnett Asher (Abraham Issachar, Pz. 1:8; 1784–1860; Rabbi of Penzance, intermittently, 1811–1859) 53, 57, 68, 82, 92, 93, 113, 138, 158, 162, 169, 170–173, 175–183, 246, 251–253, 266, 312–315, 316

Simmons, Catherine (Kate Feinburg or Fineberg; b. 1819) 252, 314

Simmons, Fanny (Rintel; b. 1814; m. 1838) 53, 162, 167, 251, 314

Simmons, Flora (Bluma Jacob; b. Redruth 1790; wife of Rabbi B.A. Simmons; d. Merthyr Tydfil 1874) 53, 57, 113, 176, 181, 183, 246, 314, 316

Simmons, Godfrey (archive of, and as author: ix, 68, 84–94, 100–278, 307–315, & numerous footnote references)

Simmons, Leah (Holman, of Melbourne; wife of A.B. Simmons) 315

Simmons, Levy Barnett (b. 1828) 315

Simmons, Moses (M.B. of Penzance, c. 1844–7; b. 1817; later in London) 82, 167, 245, 252, 314

Simmons, Mr. (of Truro, c. 1820s) 77

Simmons, Phoebe (Heilbron; of Penzance, c. 1844; b. 1815) 245, 252, 314

Simmons, Phoebe (Levy; of Houndsditch, London) 315

Simmons, Pessia (Pz. 5:2; d. 1832) 145, 176, 315

Simmons, Rachel (Joseph, of Portsea) 315

Simmons, Rose (Rosa Aaron, of Falmouth; m. 1846) 252, 314

Simmons, Sarah (Isaacs; see Pz. 6:5; 1821–1892) 150, 315, 317

Simmons, Simon Barnett (see Pz. 6:5; b. 1836) 150, 252, 315, 317

Simmons, Solomon (of Truro, b. 1778; Falmouth 1851) 214, 317

Sithney 131

Slavinsky, Rev. I. (ref. Falmouth 1913) 104

Sleeman, Henry (Penzance 1833) 249

Slowman, Benjamin (son of Mary Solomon, Lemon Hart's second wife) 230

Smyrna Schools (ref. Penzance 1852) 81

Society for Promoting Christianity amongst the Jews 162, 174, 249

Solomon, Abraham (see Simon Solomon, below)

Solomon, Amelia (Woolf of Penzance, later Newcastle; m. 1841) 251

Solomon, Barnet (d. 1806) 206, 289, 290

Solomon, Bella (Woolf, Fal. 3:2; 1726–1816) 111, 114, 206, 282, 283

Solomon, Betsy (Levy) 110, 282

Solomon, Caroline (Mayer) 287, 291

Solomon, Duke of Cornwall (4th cent. CE) 21

Solomon, George (Bodmin, c. 1847) 268

Solomon, E.B. (Truro, 1864) 272

Solomon, Isaac (of Newcastle, c. 1842) 251

Solomon, Israel (Aaron Levi Segal: Fal. 2:1; & see Behrends; b. Ehrenbreitstein, c. 1727, d. 1802) 111, 206, 282, 283

Solomon, Israel (Behrends, b. 1803; d. New York) 51, 52, 70, 110, 170, 205, 207, 279–291 (*Records of my Family*)

Solomon, Josiah (Penzance, c. 1842; of Newcastle) 252

Solomon, Judith or Yetele (Harris: Fal. 4:7; 1764–1839) 111, 121, 259, 283

Solomon, Julia (Hart, of New York; m. Barnet Solomon 1835) 289

Solomon, King (c. 950 BCE) 18

Solomon, Kitty (Killa Jacob, Fal. 5:4; d. 1854) 54, 57, 111, 113, 124, 127, 212, 286

Solomon, Lazarus (of London, father of Mary Solomon, second wife of Lemon Hart) 78, 230, 300

Solomon, Leah (Segal: Fal. 1:10; 4:8; d. 1842) 111, 121, 283

Solomon, Mary (Hart, of London; m. Lemon Hart 1804) 230–231

Solomon, Moses (Segal: Fal. 1:8; d. 1798/9)

Solomon, Phillip (of Newcastle, c. 1841) 251

Solomon, Samuel (St. Austell, c. 1799) 268

Solomon, Samuel (of London, ref. Penzance 1853) 83

Solomon, Simon (Abraham Simeon Segal, Fal. 3:3; d. 1825) 54, 57, 111, 114, 115, 286

Solomon, Solomon (see Fal. 1:4., 1764–1819, d. Lisbon) 110, 111, 206, 282

Solomon, Solomon (see Fal. 2:5; unmarried, d. London) 112

Solomon, Solomon (of Penzance, c. 1769–1781) 95, 238, 244

Solomon, T. (of Truro, from c. 1822–1873) 260

Solomon, Thomas (of Penzance, d. 1793) 244, 256

Speake, Jennifer 100, 101, 103, 130

Speculation (ship) 89, 233

Spero (or Spiro), Marcus (Rabbi of Penzance 1863–1866) 84, 93, 94, 184, 249

Spry, Sir Samuel (ref. Truro, c. 1840) 156

Stannaries (Pre-Norman/Angevin date not known; received protection under John's Charter from 1201) 15, 23, 24, 25, 32, 37

Star Hotel, Penzance 90

Stadthagen, Rev. Myer (Plymouth 1829–62) 112, 246

Statutum de Judeismo (Winchester: 1275) 32

Stone, John (Penzance, c. 1787) 225

Stoughton, Mary (Polack, c. 1760) 159, 198, 217

Stow, John (1631) 23

Stratton 269

Susser, Bernard (numerous footnote references)

Sydney (ship) 208

Symons, Eliza (of Falmouth, b. 1824) 213

Symons, Francis (Falmouth 1792) 65

Symons, Frederick (of Falmouth, b. 1828) 213

Symons, Hanna (of Falmouth, b. 1823) 213

Symons, Harriet (of Falmouth, b. 1838) 213

Symons (or Simonds), Hart (Rabbi of Penzance from 1818) 75, 79, 174, 175, 319, 320

Symons, Isaac (of Falmouth, b. 1796) 213

Symons, Jane Lovely (Abrahams) 212

Symons, Julia (of Falmouth, b. 1825) 213

Symons, Rebecca (of Falmouth, b. 1840) 213

Symons, Rosetta (of Falmouth, b. 1800) 213

Symons, Sarah (of Falmouth, b. 1835) 213

Symons, Solomon (of Falmouth, b. 1827) 213, 258

Symons, Walter (of Falmouth, b. 1829) 213

Symons, Walter (ref. Falmouth 1889) 104

Synagogue, The (Jacob family boat, Falmouth) 58

Synagogues: Falmouth 56, 63, 67, 70, 71, 103, 207, 220, 276, 292–295, 302–305; Penzance 72, 78, 89, 90, 95, 99, 251–254, 269, 295–301; Other 63, 89, 167, 171, 191, 265, 302

Syria, poor of (ref. Penzance 1861) 81

Tarragona 34

Tarshish 18

Teacher, Annah (b. circa 1850) 246, 316

Teacher, David (b. 1854) 246

Teacher, Maria (Selig, b. 1815; wife of below) 151, 246, 252, 316

Teacher, Markus (father of below; c. 1846) 252

Teacher, Solomon (of St. Ives: Pz. 7:1; 1811–1856) 80, 96, 97, 132, 151, 246, 252, 316

Teacher, Solomon (b. 1856; son of above) 246

Teacher, Solomon (son of David, above) 246

Telegraph Service 61, 220

Terkelsen, Barend (ref. Penzance, c. 1781) 244

Thomas, J. (*History of Mount's Bay*, 1820 & 1832) 89

Thomas, Richard (1814 *Survey of Penwerris*) 102

Tikkunim (of Penzance) 86–88

Tiberias, distressed Jews of (ref. Penzance, 1848) 81

Titus (79–81 CE) 21

Tolendano, Baruch de Phineas (c. 1810) 275

Tonkin, John Easton (Penzance 1861) 253

Tonkin, Thomas (cited Gilbert 1817) 22

Treassowe in Ludgvan 131

Trebartha 35

Tredavoe (near Newlyn, Penzance) 68

Trengwainton 224, 249

Trestrail, James (Truro; deceased, c. 1812) 156

Trojans 18

Truro 54, 61, 257–261, 271

Trythall, John 253

Turner, Dr. (ref. Falmouth cemetery, 1759) 102

Turner, Edmund (mortgage document Truro) 156

Twyne, John & Thomas (*De Rebus Albionicis*, 1590) 18

Uren, Gertrude Kate "Daisy" (c. 1903) 188

Uren, Nanny (see Pz. 6:5) 150, 317

Vancouver 61, 220

Vandsburg, (Bromburg) Prussia (Bydgoszcz, Poland) 185

Val(l)entine, Isaiah Falk (*shochet* from Plymouth; murdered Fowey 1811) 57, 216

Val(l)entine, Martin (d. Camelford 1844) 216

Verona 76

Victoria, Queen (1837–1901) 69, 259

Vilna 75, 170

Voice of Jacob, The 167.

Volunteers (Fuzileers, Pioneers & Rangers) 233, 234

Vos, Frederick N. (of Falmouth, b. 1868) 215

Vos, Henry (of Falmouth, b. 1870) 215

Vos, J.B. (a son of Nathan and Mary; ref. funeral 1913) 104

Vos, Mary Ann (of Falmouth, 1841–1914) 215, 221

Vos, Meir 128

Vos, Nathan (Fal. 6:2, formerly of Holland: 1833–1913) 61, 104, 127, 128, 215, 221, 272

Vos, Rosalie (of Falmouth, b. 1873) 215

Wallis, Jno. (Penzance 1808) 91

Wallis, Mr. (Penzance 1887) 94

Warsaw 75, 96, 170, 284

Wattier, Florence (Gompertz) 200

Weile, Berthe (daughter of Solomon & Rachel; adopted by Isaac Bischofswerder) 185

Weile, Rahle (Rachel, wife of Isaac Bischofswerder, 1831–1886: Pz. 7:3) 151, 185

Weile, Solomon 185

Weinheim 222

Wellington (New Zealand) 141

West India Dock 236

West Indies 50, 224, 225

Wheal Helena Mine (near Marazion, c. 1891–95) 194

White Book of Cornwall 32

William of Malmesbury (mediaeval chronicler) 23

William I (the Conqueror: 1066–1087) 13

William II (Rufus: 1087– 1100) 23

William the Marshal (Earl of Pembroke, regent: 1216–1219) 29

William IV (1830–1837) 259

William of Worcester (c. 1478) 42

William of Wrotham (Charter: *Liber Rubeus*, c. 1197) 24, 25, 28, 37

Wills: Alexander Moses (d. 1791) 63, 64. Barnet Levy (d. 1791) 64, 65. Moses Jacob (d. 1807) 263. Lemon Hart (d. 1845) 230. Jacob James Hart (d. 1846) 287

Windsor 200

Woolcock, William (Scilly, c. 1787) 225

Woolf, Amelia (Solomon; b. Penzance, m. 1842) 251

Woolf, Bella (Beila Solomon: Fal. 3:2; 1726–1816) 111, 114, 206, 282

Woolf, Bella (Levy; daughter of Lemon Woolf of Penzance; b. 1812, m. 1841) 251

Woolf, Benjamin (Wolf(e)) 206, 211, 224

Woolf, Eddle (see Pz. 5:5) 147, 231

(Woolf) Edil (daughter of Asher, Pz. 5:6; d. 1847) 147

Woolf, Eliza (Joseph, of Penzance: 1808–1850) 238, 273

Woolf, Henry 268

Woolf, Hyman (Hayim ben Benjamin, c. 1808: see Pz. 5:5) 73, 76, 78, 80, 87, 88, 89ff, 147, 171, 173, 224, 231, 237

Woolf, Jacob (Wolfe, sic of Falmouth, c. 1789) 271

Woolf, Lemon (Asher Laemel ben Hayim: Pz. 1:1; 1783–1848) 73, 79, 80, 88, 89, 113, 132–135, 231, 236–238, 244, 251, 255, 271

Woolf, Martha (b. Bodmin 1829; later wife of Henry Woolf, above) 268

Woolf, Moses (Penzance, c. 1843) 80, 90

Woolf, Rebecca (of Falmouth; m. Eleazar Hart 1763) 217, 224

Woolf, Rebecca (Jacob of Redruth 1781–1853; m. Lemon Woolf of Penzance) 113, 206, 237

Wyatt, William (Fowey, c. 1811) 57, 216

Ximenes, Moses (c. 1802) 200

Yeats, Charlotte (Lopes, m. 1795) 200

Yiddish 75

Youngman, Barnard (d. near St. Austell, 1845) 66

Zalman, Solomon (son of Jacob Segal: Pz. 5:4; d. 1823) 95, 147

Zeffertt, Herman 100, 173

Zender Falmouth (see Alexander Moses)